After Eden

ALSO BY JOHN CHARLES CHASTEEN

Born in Blood and Fire:
A Concise History of Latin America

Born in Blood and Fire:
Latin American Voices

After Eden

A Short History of the World

John Charles Chasteen

W. W. NORTON & COMPANY

Celebrating a Century of Independent Publishing

For my brother Tom

Scientist, true-blue democrat
Lifelong intellectual companion

CONTENTS

Part II

Modern World.

Size of country name indicates relative population size, showing all counties awith 100 million inhabitants or more in 2023. The countries labeled on the map totaled approximately two thirds of world population.

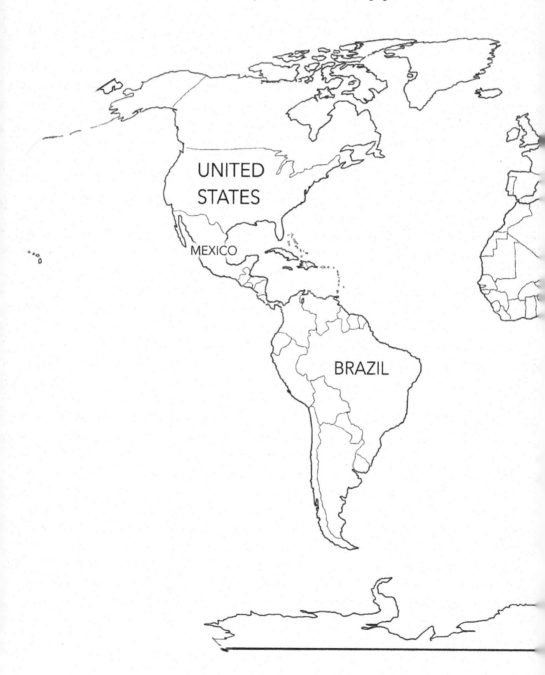

© David Wallace—USA TODAY NETWORK

An Epiphany

Any sudden revelation of a life-changing truth can be an epiphany, even if it doesn't happen on the official date of Epiphany, January 6. Watching the rioting crowds of misguided partisans invade their nation's capitol on January 6, 2021, many Americans experienced a dark epiphany. It *can* happen here. Our proud democratic traditions can be lost if we refuse to honor them. It is already happening.

Why?

The immediate cause lies in a deliberate choice of political tactics. Proximate causes lie in changing demographic and economic realities. This book is about the ultimate cause. Democratic traditions are among the most recent and fragile of human creations. Democratic self-governance depends on the strength of our collective self. It depends on our shared commitment to each other. Today, we are challenged to act like one nation.

There is a timeless tension between our commitment to each other, our need for one another, and our ability to get along. *Homo sapiens* exhibits a disturbing penchant toward conflict. This history of humanity traces the roots of endemic conflict reaching back to the earliest civilizations. But it starts with a time *before* civilization, when human beings the world over lived mostly in peaceful, cooperative small groups. Life wasn't easy in our ancestral hunter-gatherer groups, but chronic violence was much less common. Divisive conflict is therefore *not necessarily* basic to human nature. We can definitely do better than this.

And yet, world history often does seem one long chronicle of conflict. It's tribe against tribe, religion against religion, nation against nation, city against country, rich against poor, even men against women. The list is incomplete, but you get my drift.

Our divisive conflicts can stem, apparently, from almost anything, or from almost nothing. Within societies, many social and political interactions become *habitually* conflictive. Low-grade violence then becomes a routine mode of interaction, baked into the social structure. "Polarizing" political leaders encourage it intentionally, for their own purposes. Many societies have a dominant group that needs, periodically, to enforce its claims of ethnic or racial superiority using violence. Claims of male superiority find an outlet in quotidian domestic abuse.

Conflict is also routine *between* societies. Writ large, world history becomes a parade of wars and empires. Militarism ranks among the world's most enduring political phenomena. The world's largest political units have, with few exceptions, always rested on might, rather than right. Idealistic justifications for their self-serving power are rarely absent, though. Kingdoms, nations, and other large-scale political institutions have always employed ideological talking points to complement their basic reliance on brute force. Historically, kings (and queens) have often justified misrule and conquest in religious terms. Ideological justifications have replaced religions ones only recently and partially. When it comes to war, it seems, everyone has gods on their side. Religious and ideological justifications are rarely the actual reasons for violence, however. More often, they are used as salvos in a parallel political propaganda war.

Consider political trends at the dawn of the new millennium. Nationalist demagogues have upstaged more thoughtful ideologies in country after country, harnessing explosive ethnic or racial resentments, not least in the United States. Magical thinking and atavistic impulses run rampant in a digital world of space travel, gene editing, and globalization. Our ability to cooperate dwindles even as we confront the challenges of rapid climate change, mass extinction, and destruction of the natural environment.

To confront these challenges, we need a new global awareness of our shared humanity. It's a big challenge. Human beings evolved, over hundreds of thousands of years, mostly in hunter-gatherer groups of only a few dozen individuals. In human groups that small, everyone is "us." There is no "them." Sadly, such groups hardly exist anymore, and their way of life is no option in a world of eight billion people. But considering their place at the beginning of human history provides a valuable perspective. Once upon a time, humans lived with much less interpersonal violence, without harsh patriarchal domination of women, and without systemic social inequities in general. Life wasn't easy, but social exploitation and inequity figured much less than in later, civilized societies. That is the "Eden" of this book's title. Our penchant for regular, organized interpersonal violence, the real worm in this apple, started *after* Eden, when we settled down, and our populations grew much larger.

Part of our problem seems to lie in numbers themselves. *Homo sapiens* is emphatically not a herd animal. Herd people together, and the result typically isn't pretty. Primate species normally live in socially bonded groups of a specific size. Primate bonding involves constant interactions—snuggling, sniffing, grooming, food sharing—among creatures who relate to each other as individuals. Compressed into larger groups with whom they are unable to bond, creatures like us can get a bit unhinged. We often don't care much for strangers and have difficulty making common cause with them. Like sharing in kindergarten, civic cooperation seems *not* to be instinctive. Xenophobia and race prejudice are the deplorably common grown-up version of children's struggles to share and get along. Like sharing in kindergarten, however, respect for all people *can* be nurtured and learned—given opportunity, determination, resources, and good teachers.

A greater part of our problem is five thousand years of practice at endless feuding and systemic social inequality. As long as civilization has existed anywhere, virtually all complex human societies have had poor laboring families at the bottom, composing the great bulk of the population, and a tiny minority of rich and well-armed families at the top. Those at the top boast superior bloodlines or test scores or divine favor. The justifications vary historically, but the basic situation is similar. The biggest change has come in the last two hundred years, during which ruling families have shared more wealth with a middle tier, while the poor laborers still compose the vast majority and enjoy the fewest benefits. This recent sharing had not advanced very far, globally, before the trend was reversed in the last generation, trending back toward greater concentration of wealth at the top.

In order to prosper in the twenty-first century, we desperately need a new sense of our shared human story. People who share a history can reimagine themselves as one people because, in fact, they are. The good news is that all people alive today really do share a history. And parts of our shared history are inspiring, too. Our ancient religious and ethical teachers, our modern political ideologies, have tried to unite us around worthy collective goals and values, but with mixed success. Clearly, we have the capacity to work together cooperatively to solve the global problems of the twenty-first century, if we will just do it. But *will* we? Our overall record to date is, frankly, not encouraging.

Fifty centuries of querulous self-aggrandizement will be hard to overcome. On the other hand, tackling our current global crisis can give us the opportunity to build trust as we try to advance our common cause.

Perhaps we have something to learn from our ancestors' experience. For greater self-understanding as we face our common future, let's consider our common past. In the beginning, all *Homo sapiens* were hunter-gatherers, or, as they are now more often called, foragers. There was no other way to live. Human evolution in foraging groups is the topic of Chapter One.

First, though, let's go back to the very beginning, to start with a real bang.

After Eden

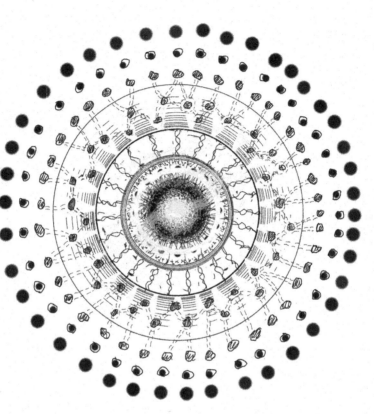

In the Beginning

In the beginning was the Big Bang.

Big Bang cosmology explains the actual observations of modern physics. It posits a precise moment at which the universe exploded into being. Theoretically, that explosive expansion can be described with split-second precision, drawing on the data collected by astronomers who have learned to measure movement of distant galaxies. This cosmology also fits the findings of experimental physics, all those subatomic particles the existence of which was still unknown when I was born in the 1950s. Here's the gist of this modern creation story.

Thirteen billion years ago something unimaginably dense and hot—and infinitesimally tiny, perhaps smaller than an atom—expanded into something infinitely huge, and began to cool.

Gradually energy congealed into the building blocks of matter, the subatomic particles called quarks, and from quarks, into protons and neutrons that would eventually constitute the nuclei of atoms. All this in the first one hundredth of a second. A few seconds later, there were electrons. Then, maybe three hundred thousand years after that, the light-filled universe cooled further, and its energy further congealed in the formation of the simplest atoms. The most basic and plentiful atoms were hydrogen (with one proton and one electron) followed by helium (with two protons and two electrons).

An astrophysicist could provide a more detailed and precise account, obviously, but this quick-and-dirty description is good enough to suit our purpose here. And anyway, a physicist would be in no better position than a historian to say what, if anything, *preceded* the Big Bang, the most interesting question of all. Despite the rather full picture of the early universe that emerges from modern scientific accounts, absolutely *all* our evidence relates to the unfolding of that process. None of the evidence, precisely zero, zip, zilch—*nothing* relates to what, if anything, may have preceded the Big Bang.

We simply have no clue. Did anything exist pre-bang? We can only speculate. Perhaps time is cyclical at the largest level, with no beginning and no end. Perhaps the universe eventually reboots, collapsing into itself, and then expanding again with another bang, the way that the Hindu deity Shiva reportedly dances to destroy the universe, only to restart it over and over. Perhaps there was nothing at all, pre-bang. Bottom line: the universe as we know it began thirteen billion years ago. That's thirteen thousand times a million years.

No more than a billion years had passed, post-bang, before hydrogen and helium atoms, attracted to one another by gravitational force, began to collapse into massive objects called stars. In the cores of stars, high temperatures began the atomic reaction called fusion, whereby two hydrogen atoms fuse to create a helium atom, releasing energy in the process. Stars began to shine. Countless stars were distributed through the universe in great whirls called galaxies, that themselves configure countless clusters, still expanding outward, an unimaginable enormity in which the presence of our own star, the sun, dwindles away to comparative nothingness.

Stars made matter more complex by creating larger atoms. Elements six to twenty-six on the periodic table, carbon to iron, were created inside stars. The rest of the elements were created in the spectacular blasts called *supernovas* that often end the lives of larger stars. Either way, successive generations of stars provided the familiar elements of our planet.

Our sun is a rather large star of middling brightness. It is about 4.6 billion years old, so it has existed for about a third of the life of the universe. Astronomers calculate that our sun probably has another four to five billion years before it burns out, which is good. At least we don't have to worry about that for a while! Earth and the other planets were formed at the same time as the sun, as part of the same process. First, gravity shaped a great cloud of space dust into a rotating disk. Gravity took the center of the cloud and fashioned the sun, and of the particles of matter that composed the disk's rotating edge, it fashioned an infinity of planetesimals. Over more than four billion years, these consolidated themselves into the planets, moons, and asteroids of our familiar solar system. The process of consolidation involved repeated, cataclysmic collisions and impacts.

Once this "Hadean" stage of frequent asteroid impacts had ended, Earth became remarkably suited, little by little, to organisms that require liquid water—because, amazingly, most of Earth maintains year-round temperatures in the narrow range between the freezing and boiling points of water. Earth is one of the inner, rocky planets of our solar system, planets that are made primarily of silicon and oxygen, iron and magnesium. Of these, Mercury and Venus are hellishly hot, and only chilly Mars seems even remotely hospitable to life as it has evolved on Earth. The outer planets are eternally frozen gas giants, Jupiter being almost big enough to be a small star itself. Recently scientists are investigating the possibility of life inside the liquid-centered moons of these frozen gas giants. Nowhere else in our solar system, however, is fit for human habitation. Nowhere outside our solar system is close enough to consider. When it comes to human history, the planet Earth is all we've got and all we're likely to have, ever.

And get this: Earth isn't flat, and it isn't solid, either. Okay, so you knew it isn't flat, because by now we are very familiar with the way that Earth looks from space—that blue, watery-looking globe hanging in the limitless void. But did you realize that it isn't solid either? Earth has a solid crust which is only about seven kilometers thick over most of the planet's surface where it is covered by oceans. The continents, on the other hand, are several times thicker. Still, Earth's crust is analogous in thickness, given the bulk of the planet, to the shell of an egg. Underneath is a slurry of molten and solid rock and iron—iron especially, at Earth's core. The rock slurry flows within the mantle, rising in some places, sinking in others, sometimes erupting to the surface in volcanos. Very gradually, these flows of Earth's mantle move the eggshell crust that floats on its surface. The result is continental drift. The oceans and continents have reconfigured themselves constantly over the last few billion years. The world's climate has been utterly transformed many times in the process.

Growing in those oceans and on those continents, beginning possibly four billion years ago, were various forms of life. The impressive antiquity of life on Earth is attested by abundant fossil evidence, especially by fossils called stromatolites, created by teeming colonies of single-celled organisms. The four-billion-year age of stromatolites amounts to *four thousand million* years, most of the history of the planet. Not *too* shabby for the local life forms of an insignificant speck in the infinite void, even if the life we are talking about was something more akin to pond scum than people during three thousand million of those years. People have more in common with pond scum than you may imagine.

Terrestrial life forms give many signs of common descent. They are mostly composed of the same things as Earth—hydrogen, nitrogen, oxygen—with the special addition of carbon. Carbon, hydrogen, nitrogen, and oxygen are the basic component elements of amino acids, the complex molecules that compose proteins. Human beings share a lot of DNA, as it turns out, with much simpler organisms, such as fruit flies or yeast. In fact, all living things are believed to have a common ancestor that lived about one thousand six hundred million years ago. Back then, this ancestor would have to be a one-celled organism of some sort. The human family has no reason to be embarrassed about these humble beginnings.

Most life has always been single-celled, as are modern bacteria, too tiny to be seen by a human eye. As single-celled organisms we developed a complex internal structure, became capable of purposeful locomotion, and learned to capture the energy of the sun through photosynthesis. As single-celled organisms, we innovated, reproducing ourselves periodically using DNA. Gradually, it seems, single-celled organisms even teamed up to form larger, multi-celled organisms. Here is another amazing fact of the history of life on Earth that was unknown when I went to school in the middle of the twentieth century. Our modern human bodies still harbor an enormous number of single-celled organisms possessing their own DNA, blurring the line between us and life around us. These life forms within us are essential to our health. If we succeeded in eliminating them, we too would die. After decades of desperately spraying disinfectants, it turns out that we are partially composed of germs ourselves.

Five hundred million years ago, in the so-called "Cambrian explosion" of life forms, more complex living things proliferated, swam, slithered, and eventually swarmed over Earth. Dinosaurs had their long time in the sun, ending probably with an asteroid impact—a random but effective reminder of the Hadean stage—about sixty-six million years ago. The cooler resulting climate favored warm-blooded primates, who tended to share the four-limbed, five-digit body plan (with tail) favored by so many land vertebrates, a basic layout clearly indicative of their shared descent. Seven million years ago, some of those four-limbed primates started to walk upright habitually on two feet.

They evolved into people, and our story begins in earnest.

Part I

CHAPTER ONE

Eden

A common Middle Eastern myth, shared by Muslims, Christians, and Jews, describes a paradise called Eden, a natural landscape that provided food in abundance, simply for the taking. Our modern creation story begins similarly, with the Paleolithic period—the time before human beings produced food by planting crops or raising livestock, living instead from what the landscape provided. *Paleo + lithic* is Latin for Old Stone Age. Until about twelve thousand years ago, all people hunted animals and gathered wild plants for food across a seasonally changing landscape. There was no other way to live.

Paleolithic life was really no paradise, even if it suited human beings, in some ways, more than the life we lead now. It wasn't a past golden age, but rather a formative period for our species, lasting many thousands of generations. This is deep time, evolutionary time. The human body and brain evolved entirely within the Paleolithic period. Only very small changes in our bodies and brains have occurred since. We descend from prehistoric populations, and we carry their genetic legacy in our bodies, whether we know about it or not.

One look at the hand stencils that Paleolithic people left on cave walls, among humanity's earliest art, suggests how closely related we are to them in spirit. These stencils, often located quite deep in the caves, go back thirty-five thousand years. They have been found in all the world's major sites of cave painting, from South America to Europe, from North Africa to Indonesia. Some of the stencils are obviously of children's hands, but most are of men's or women's hands. Because varying ratios of finger length distinguish men and women, we can hypothesize women's hands appear somewhat more often. All in all, one can hardly imagine a better candidate for humanity's first self-portrait. High-five your distant ancestors!

It's easier, though, to comprehend the significance of formative origins than to find evidence of human life in prehistoric times. For prehistoric times we lack the written sources upon which historians normally depend. Evidence about prehistoric life is gathered not by historians but by paleoanthropologists. Until quite recently, when human genome studies became a source of information, these scientists dug most of their evidence out of the ground. Before microbiology, our evidence was basically stones and bones. Even with the genome, our evidence of remote prehistory is dauntingly fragmentary—an exercise in connecting the dots if there ever was one.

Scattered dots of evidence connected by logical inferences. That's how one must approach prehistory. The question of evidence is so crucial that any description of *what* we believe must include some discussion of *why* we think so. Most of what we "know" about Paleolithic life is actually a web of probabilities, a logical surmise based on scrutiny of limited evidence. Imagination is therefore one of the paleontologist's most essential tools. To imagine the lives of human beings so distant in time, we must first focus on seemingly trivial detail. The most important evidence about paleo people regards food. The first thing to understand about any life form, after all, is what it eats.

Stones and Bones

First, let's consider the evidence. By dint of arduous and prolonged study, scientists have been able to find rare glimpses of our evolving ancestors, all of whom apparently lived in Africa before populating the rest of the world. The glimpses come in the form of stone tools and fossilized bones.

The bones show how human bodies evolved from our distant ancestors. Our ancestors changed, during the enormously long period covered by this chapter, from upright apes—called australopithecines—to anatomically modern people. What distinguishes our australopithecine ancestors' bones are the arched feet, narrow pelvis, and somewhat s-shaped spine—all adaptations for walking. Bipedal walking is the most basic human trait. The ancient Chinese character for *human being* represents two legs striding. Even before we were really people—not yet very smart, our brains still only one-third of modern size—we were already bipeds. To look at the fossilized Laetoli footprints discovered by paleontologist Mary Leaky in Ethiopia's Olduvai gorge is to recognize that they were left by someone eerily like us. There they were, one feels, walking side by side through recently fallen volcanic ash, more than three million years ago, leaving footprints like our own, two of our quite distant ancestors, an adult and a child, apparently holding hands.

Upright walking helped our ancestors find food in the open savanna environments that were expanding in Africa during a period of general environmental cooling. Ours was no longer the fruit-based diet of forest-dwelling, tree-climbing chimpanzees and gorillas. As australopithecines, we had developed powerful jaws and chewing muscles and broad, flat teeth, enabling us to chew hard, fibrous foods such as seeds, nuts, roots, tubers, and bulbs—the basic foods of a savanna environment. Savannas are usually a more food-rich environment for *Homo sapiens* than are forests. Forest plants put more energy into not-very-nutritious stems and leaves, while plants in savanna environments put more energy into highly edible forms of nutrition storage, i.e., seeds, nuts, roots, tubers, and bulbs. Very few of the world's principal food crops started as forest plants.

Savannas could support much larger populations, but only if those populations were quite mobile. Unlike forest tree-climbers, creatures of the open plains need to master distances. The crucial human trait of walking on two legs seemingly emerged in pursuit of a savanna diet that did not, at first, feature meat.

Something else about our bipedal australopithecine predecessors of three million years ago: Enough bones have been found to say that they were notably *dimorphic*, which means the males were much larger than the females. As a general rule, high dimorphism in animal populations is associated with mating scenarios in which one dominant male subordinates others to establish privileged access to several breeding females. The australopithecines were not people, not truly "us." Fast forward a few million years to about 150,000-200,000 years ago. *Now* the hominid bones look almost like ours. Their owners were fully people, and some (though not all) were *Homo sapiens*, exactly like us. And, while less so than australopithecines, our near ancestors were still dimorphic.

Specifically, we're now talking about the people called Neanderthals and those formerly called Cro-Magnons.* Cro-Magnon people, we now believe, were *Homo sapiens*, whereas Neanderthals were archaic humans, people not quite identical to modern ones. All humans had undergone a big change in diet as compared with australopithecines. Human teeth now included more sharp incisors for slicing and tearing flesh. This can only mean that meat had become more important in our diet. Another change, our reduced dimorphism, indicates that human reproduction was now less driven by male conflict over females. In other words, humans were moving away from the gorilla model, in which larger males monopolize females and do precious little childcare. Instead, we were moving more toward the cooperative partnership visible among many nesting birds, in which mother and father are of similar size and work together in partnership to raise their brood. Gradually, the remaining archaic humans were replaced by anatomically modern humans with a slightly different skull shape.

---

* Both names come from the places in France where their bones were first discovered.

Enough bones for now. Let's talk stones.

Hominids began making and using stone tools two million years ago. Think about that for a moment. We've been using stone stools (also, walking on two feet, which leaves hands free for tools) since before we were fully human. Later, species of hominids seemed to have learned tool making from earlier hominids, without needing to reinvent stone-tool making from scratch. No doubt all of them made many tools of wood, as well, but those have totally vanished, while stone lasts forever, or close enough.

The most ancient tools, basically round stones intentionally broken to produce an edge, are termed "Oldowan" because they were found in the same Olduvai Gorge that held australopithecine remains. Oldowan tools had spread as far as Java by 1.8 million years ago and to northern China by 1.6 million years ago. The later, more refined "Acheulian" tools involved carefully chipping around the edges of an already sharp stone to improve the edge. These tools could be used to dig, to scrape, to pound, and to grind plant food, but some were clearly used for scraping meat off bones. We've found bones with scrape marks to prove it.

Archaic humans later refined the two-million-year-old stone-tool tradition. The result was the "Mousterian" technique found at Neanderthal sites. Neanderthals used a so-called prepared-core chipping method to strike off sharp-edged stone flakes of a determined size and shape. The result, some time 150,000 to 200,000 years ago, was stone-tipped spears like those carried by Neanderthal cartoon characters. This stone tool was unambiguously a stabbing weapon, and it seems to have been used especially for hunting big game. It was still crude, however. The delicacy required for arrowheads came only in with the "Aurignacian" technique, toward the end of the last Ice Age (a mere twelve thousand years ago), and is associated with *Homo sapiens*. In addition, the Aurignacian technique includes more implements of bone, including fishhooks.

In sum, stones and bones together provide some basic facts upon which to erect our understanding of human prehistory. The facts are few, though, and require elaboration. First, the bones tell us that for millions of years our upright ape predecessors were mobile, bipedal foragers with an omnivorous diet of mostly plants. Hands that had first evolved for tree climbing eventually fashioned tools for foraging on the savannah.

Stone-tool-making technique was passed on, changing very slowly, over hundreds of thousands of years. Bones indicate that, over this vast span of time, human gender was evolving toward an equal partnership between male and female. Second, both stones and bones tell us that, over time, our ancestors ate more meat, becoming more and more a predator species. These basic facts are the dots, so to speak, that we must connect in a meaningful way to imagine prehistoric life.

Such an imaginative reconstruction must depend, for its basic premises, on our understanding of foraging—the life of people who live from hunting and gathering wild food, without agriculture or domesticated animals. And our idea of foraging must come primarily from studying more recent foragers, who are either still alive today or who lived in the not-so-distant past. Many Native Americans, aboriginal Australians, non-Bantu people of southern Africa, and other groups live or have lived within recent times as mobile hunter-gatherers, without crops or domesticated animals. Foragers' lives have certainly changed over the millennia in ways we cannot know. Still, their recent ways of living provide our best model of prehistoric foraging. Facing questions such as when a favorite food will ripen, what game to hunt, or where to move camp, modern foragers encounter the same challenges that prehistoric foragers did. If stones and bones amount to scattered dots of historical evidence, the study of modern foragers supplies the logic that we need to connect the dots.

The Foraging Life

Living foragers have long stood for prehistoric people in European thought. The seventeenth-century English philosopher Thomas Hobbes was thinking of foragers when he posited a primitive state of nature, when life was supposedly "nasty, brutish, and short." For Hobbes, everything good about human society was a product of post-forager civilization. He discerned an upward direction in human history. The eighteenth-century French philosopher Jean Jacques Rousseau, on the contrary, believed that foragers represented "the noble savage." Primitive people were corrupted, rather than improved, by civilization, according to Rousseau. Anthropologists have been studying foragers for generations and have described hundreds of groups in ethnographic detail. They have also incorporated the reports of early European explorers concerning people whose foraging ended centuries ago. The modern anthropological study of foragers crystalized at a Man the Hunter conference in 1966. The anthropologists at the conference combined their observations to produce a new general understanding of the character of these small, mobile societies.

The normal size of a foraging band, about twenty-five to thirty individuals, is amazingly consistent around the world. Foraging bands are typically bound together, in part, by ties of kinship. Imagine three to five somehow-related nuclear families, including grown children and a few elders. Perhaps three of the husbands are brothers with wives from other bands. Perhaps one of those wives has her brother and mother with her.

Foraging bands do not just wander around hoping to find food. Rather, they move cyclically across a landscape whose locations and life rhythms they know intimately. Their composition and organization may vary seasonally as they exploit different natural resources. Many bands will gather at a particular time of year with other members (possibly all the members) of their tribe, a group numbering perhaps in the thousands. These large gatherings are made possible by some particularly abundant, temporary food source. Such gatherings are exciting social events, a good time to find a spouse. (Monogamous marriage is basic to foraging. Polygamy exists in few foraging societies and is never the norm.) After a few weeks, it's time to find more food and the group divides, once more, into foraging bands.

Defined only partially by family ties, bands are loose and variable. They have no social distinctions based on wealth because they have no wealth. Their composition varies from year to year. Bands may disappear or be totally reconstituted, at intervals, as people go separate ways. My grown daughter and her family may come with my band this year, or maybe they'll go with her husband's band.

As a rule, foragers cannot feed themselves in one place year round. Therefore, they *must* be mobile, and that puts sharp limits on food storage and on accumulation of material wealth. Several times a year, at least, foragers carry everything they have to a new, possibly distant camp. Paleolithic foragers had no large domesticated animals to help carry loads or supply meat on the hoof. Foragers were the world's first jacks of all trades. The nuclear families of an interrelated band forage together and share food as well as childcare and other chores. Reciprocity is key. Today I share my windfall with you, tomorrow you share yours with me. Surplus food has to be eaten anyway, because it cannot be stored.

In addition, modern foragers—whether in Australia, Siberia, South Africa, or Amazonia—tend to prize their autonomy. Decisions affecting the whole band are made in discussions that involve all the adult members, both men and women. Leadership seeks consensus above all. It arises from individual qualities, such as experience, persuasiveness, or force of character. It is mostly informal, never hereditary. Among foragers no one is born owning, and no one, owing. No social classes or castes divide a foraging band. There is no room in a foraging band for anybody but *us*. Anyone we let into our band becomes one of us.

Overall, the Man the Hunter conference established a highly positive view of the foraging life. Ironically, given its title, the conference downplayed hunting. It was attended mostly by university faculty and graduate students eager to embrace the idea that foragers lived simple but satisfying, and amazingly egalitarian, lives. As 1960s critics of capitalist consumerism, they liked the idea that foragers can find contentment by desiring little. And they welcomed the news that hunter gatherers often eat more plant food than meat. Indeed, the term *hunter-gatherer* lost favor at the time, among anthropologists, to be replaced by *forager*. Some aspects of this picture faded as anthropologists did more and more ethnographic studies of groups around the world. As it turns out, the foraging life involves sometimes going hungry, the rate of infant and child mortality is high, and violent rivalry between alpha males is not rare.

Stern, comprehensive male dominance—patriarchy—is more or less unknown among foragers, and yet, foragers are all about gender roles. They normally consider hunting "male," gathering "female." Signs of male dominance are clear in many groups. Men often have more ritual importance and are more likely than women to speak at meetings. Men may eat different, and if so, better food than women do. The tilt toward male dominance is slight, much less than in agricultural societies, but it disappears only if one prefers to avert one's eyes. As a general rule, foraging women have more personal autonomy and exercise more influence over men than is typical among farmers or herders.

Hunting turns out to be basic to foraging societies after all. Ethnographic data indicate that meat and fish consumption varies, the low range being around one-third of the diet among tropical foragers. Some groups in high latitude, particularly arctic, environments, on the other hand, eat *mostly* flesh. In addition, meat is often a preferred food, even when foragers' diet is substantially plant-based. Modern foragers may complain of hunger when out of meat, even though plant food is available. Moreover, hunting is almost invariably a prestigious activity. Hunting often involves cooperation among many hunters to drive and entrap game. Storytelling events about the hunt and distribution of meat by successful hunters are socially important among most foragers. The prestige of the hunt accrues almost entirely to males. Women certainly do hunt, but women's hunting tends to be much less central to their activities. Women may spot small game and hunt it while out gathering, for example, but they almost never hunt big game in cooperative groups.

Paleolithic foragers were no doubt unlike modern ones in many ways. Early hominids probably scavenged the carcasses killed by large carnivores on the African savanna, learning only gradually, over thousands of years, to hunt for themselves. Notably, the earliest primitive tools associated with meat eating were not used to kill or butcher animals, but rather to break open leg bones or the skull so to get at the marrow or brains left behind by another predator. When our ancestors became predators, their game was most often large animals, herded cooperatively to their deaths (off a cliff, say) by many human hunters working together. The bones of thousands of hunted horses, a major prehistoric European game animal, have been dated to four hundred thousand years ago. Toward the end of the ice ages, archaic humans hunted mammoths cooperatively on the Russian steppe. The climate allowed them to store frozen meat in pits, and they built shelters for themselves, in the absence of trees, using the enormous bones of mammoths. These Neanderthal mammoth hunters, with their stone-tipped spears, were still not anatomically modern, however, much less behaviorally modern. In their Ice Age environment, surrounded by now long-extinct megafauna and not possessing the bow, there is little chance that they lived exactly like today's foragers.

As the Ice Age ended and modern people replaced archaic ones, circa fifty thousand to ten thousand years ago, things changed. The invention of bows and arrows was one sign. The

bow-and-arrow was a far better hunting tool than a spear, but lightweight, elegantly tapered arrowheads required expert stonework. The modern humans who populated Australia (over fifty thousand years ago) did not yet possess bows and arrows, whereas those who colonized the Americas (no less than twelve thousand years ago) did. Bows and arrows went along with the general trend of late Paleolithic hunting, toward a greater variety of smaller game, requiring new methods. The late Paleolithic tool kit also eventually included fishhooks, as we have seen, and awls that could be used to stitch leather clothing. Eventually there's evidence of nets. By the end of the Paleolithic, the technology of prehistoric people was beginning to look a lot like what today's foragers use. Their hunting practice was no doubt similar, too.

One takeaway message here is that it won't do to downplay the importance of hunting in world history. Several million years of evolution made humans into an apex predator, capable of hunting megafauna to extinction, as apparently happened when they first arrived in Australia and then, a bit later, in the Americas. A capacity for aggressive violence necessarily accompanies predation of large prey. Obviously, man the hunter had to be man the killer, too.

In sum, we know pretty well how prehistoric people got food. And the ethnographic data establishes that, as foragers, the great majority of prehistoric humans must have lived in small, mobile, relatively egalitarian bands, structured by kinship, friendship, and gender. Exceptions to this general rule will be considered in due time. Meanwhile, let's look at how advances in paleobiology are revealing previously unknown dimensions of human prehistory.

Family Ties and the Birth of Human Cultures

If paleo people lacked social hierarchies, they did not lack family ties. Foragers make much of kinship, often devising extremely intricate systems to guide marriage choice. Gender structures their lives pervasively, as does the fundamental partnership between men and women. Almost certainly, the same was true for prehistoric people. After considering how a life form gets food, the next most basic question is how it reproduces.

Again, the starting point, when considering our species, is mobility. Over millions of years, bipedal hominoids evolved narrow hips to swing their legs directly forward and backward and walk like people, rather than rocking from side to side like chimpanzees or gorillas. As a species, our closest relatives are forest-dwelling apes adapted for climbing. They can stand and walk only a little. Hominids' narrow hips made walking efficient, allowing them to cover a lot of ground, a crucial adaptation to the mobile foraging life.

Another crucial hominid evolution, a physical adaptation traceable through the painstaking analysis of fossilized skull fragments, was toward a larger brain. In biological terms, intelligence is a general characteristic of non-specialist omnivores. A larger brain allowed our ancestors to hunt and gather a wide variety of foods, partly by creating those stone tools. In addition, and even more importantly, larger hominid brains probably reflected an increasingly complex interpersonal life and a growing web of family ties.

Long before the emergence of modern humans—several million years before the present—the brainy bipeds' new adaptations began to interfere with each other. At birth, expanding infant brains had a harder and harder time passing through narrowing maternal hips. This bottleneck in the birth canal made labor more difficult and more dangerous for humans than for most other mammals. It seems a design flaw, but of course, design was not involved. An intelligent designer would have gone back to the drawing board and rerouted the birth canal. Instead, the solution that evolved quite unplanned over countless millennia was to give birth early, so to speak, before those expanding little brains, with their painfully large protective skulls, got too big to pass harmlessly through narrowing maternal hips.

But the solution to one problem created another. Those undeveloped newborn brains would require a long time to complete their maturation outside the womb—not months but years, and not just two or three years, either. During perhaps a quarter to a third of the human life span, which was then shorter, young humans could not feed or take care of themselves. Newborn children meant *both* new mouths to feed *and* fewer full-time foragers among the adults to do the feeding because helpless and vulnerable young needed a lot of attention from adults. The extraordinarily long childhood of humankind had a large impact on the social evolution of our species.

Childcare is demanding for modern foragers. Infant and child mortality among them is high because of accidents and disease.

Losing children is grievous because so much—affection, resources, plans, dreams—has been invested in them. Some animals have scores of young and care for them little or not at all. Some have few and care for them closely. As a species, we take the latter approach. In the language of the twenty-first century, long human childhoods, even prehistoric ones, required a long-term parenting commitment—yet another challenge for foragers on the move.

The solution to *this* problem, in evolutionary terms, or at least part of the solution, was a stable parental partnership. Humans are not purely monogamous, of course, but they do tend to be so, over-all. Neither chimpanzees nor gorillas show any tendency to mate monogamously the way humans do. Nor does the father help feed the young in any case. And that brings us back to those dutiful song-bird fathers who even sometimes warm the eggs temporarily so that the female can get some exercise and food. Once hatched, the raven-ous chicks cannot feed themselves at all and, the parents have to fly back and forth all day, foraging and stuffing worms into those gaping little maws.

Because we are mammals, women's side of a parenting partner-ship has generally involved breast feeding. Modern hunter-gatherers often breast feed for years because doing so provides not only safe and portable nourishment for their young but also suppresses the mother's fertility, allowing her to regulate the time between pregnan-cies. Childcare constitutes an encumbrance to food gathering, not to mention hunting.

Inevitably, women with several small children spend more time with them in camp, processing what has been hunted or gathered. By four hundred thousand years ago, as we can tell by signs of habitual campfires, "processing" already included cooking. Cooking makes everything easier to eat and digest. It both unlocks nourishment and widens the range of possible foods. Cooking defined meals. Meals defined where, when, and with whom people ate. Around the world, the hearth and the sharing of meals came to symbolize home and family and provided a powerful form of social bonding. Cooking thus constituted an enormous step in human development, and it was generally the work of women. Meanwhile, the father's side of this ancient partnership involved a commitment to provide enough food.

This gendered division of labor has structured most human societies, whether we like it or not. The idea of male-female difference and complementarity is basic to the ethnography of all foraging societies, every aspect of which seems governed by gender-specific rules. Men and women have contrasting responsibilities, privileges, and tasks. Even when working together on the same task, men and women do complementary aspects of it. Unquestionably, these ancient patterns lie at the root of traditional gender stereotypes that persist today. Their antiquity does not make them desirable or inevitable. Prehistoric foragers never grew food, but that doesn't make it a bad thing to do. Nor are human sacrifice or infanticide or cannibalism recommendable because they are ancient practices. We do need to recognize, though, that long human childhoods shaped prehistoric families, and one result was a gendered division of labor.

The long human childhood also seems to have made us a collaborative species *within our bonded group*. Among humans, other individuals beyond the parents often help care for the young in various ways. This pattern, which behavioral scientists call "cooperative breeding," has evolved independently in a small number of birds and mammals, and it correlates strongly with long childhoods. For example, of 261 species of songbirds (whose breeding habits are easily observed) 34 species often breed cooperatively, and the cooperative breeders feed chicks, on average, *twice as long* as the mating pairs who get no such cooperation. The mating pairs sometimes take advantage of the help by starting a second nest while the first is still occupied. Lions and elephants are cooperative breeders. So are modern foragers.

Among people, cooperative breeding implies the frequent participation of grandmothers, aunts, sisters, and older daughters in raising children, while the father's performance varies. Here is another adaptive behavior that, while variously expressed, appears in diverse cultures around the world. Cooperative breeding must have intensified personal interactions within prehistoric bands and knit them more tightly together. And the way that human groups are knit together matters enormously.

For millions of years, foraging bands of hominids were knit together mostly by ties of family and personal friendship. Then, possibly fifty thousand years ago, *Homo sapiens* began a new sort of knitting together. We can detect this in "symbolic behavior" such as body adornment and funerary practices, both of which indicate ritual behavior. This was the birth of humanity's diverse cultures. Culture is the Swiss Army knife of human adaptations, the key to our species' ability to survive anywhere on a changing Earth, and the beginning of our eventual career of world domination. A small evolutionary change in our brains may have gotten the ball rolling in the late Paleolithic period.

Some evidence comes from skulls. Archaic humans like Neanderthals had skulls that contained brains the size of ours, or even larger, although the shape was a little different. The bone structure of the modern human face differs from that of our archaic predecessors, so that the upper and lower jaws protrude less. The different shape of *Homo sapiens'* skulls suggests new brain development. The change probably helps explain why *Homo sapiens* spread over the entire habitable surface of the globe even as archaic humans gradually became extinct.

Here's the story.

Modern humans evolved in Africa one or two hundred thousand years ago and began to disperse around the world. Finds of their bones can be dated to around sixty thousand years ago in Asia and to around forty thousand years ago in Europe. Modern humans were not the first to migrate out of Africa, however. Archaic humans, especially *Homo erectus*, had done so more than a million years earlier, becoming well established throughout southern Asia. The people we call Neanderthals first migrated mostly to Europe. When modern and archaic humans encountered each other, they seem to have competed for food. We brainy *Homo sapiens* apparently helped drive our archaic cousins to extinction. Although now classed as different species of human being, the archaic and modern people were enough alike that they could procreate successfully together under some circumstances. There is just enough Neanderthal presence in the modern European genome to confirm it.

Modern humans had capabilities that archaic ones did not have. We've already considered *Homo sapiens'* superior stone tools, beginning about fifty thousand years ago in the late Paleolithic period. Other characteristics of the late Paleolithic include evidence of fishing, burial rites, colored beads, cave painting, basket weaving, simple clothes making, and long-distance trade. The number of occupied sites seems to proliferate, suggesting population growth, and regional styles of artifacts appear, indicating more frequent innovation. Paleontologists take special note of rock carving, cave painting, and the use of ochre, a body paint that survives in burial sites long after the painted bodies have turned to dust. They also observe how humans began to bury their dead with tools and food. *Homo sapiens* took all this to a higher level than had any archaic humans. So the archeological evidence suggests that anatomically modern people became behaviorally modern by creating fully developed cultural systems, which cannot exist without fully developed human language, the most fundamental symbolic behavior of all. And this cascade of innovations coincided with changes in brain shape.

Back to bones.

Modern facial bone structure, when contrasted with archaic skulls, provides substantiation for the idea that only *Homo sapiens* could ever talk the way modern humans do. When modern human jaws got shorter, the tongue, too, shortened, and the voice box dropped lower in the throat. The resulting configuration sometimes creates problems when un-chewed food slips into a space behind the tongue, which could not happen so easily in archaic humans. Thus, the current model of human being can choke on dinner with disconcerting ease. This apparent defect was retained because it brought with it a corresponding, more powerful benefit. The lowered voice box and shorter tongue could, together, generate many more distinctive consonants and vowels, the nuts and bolts of speech. The contours of modern human skulls (when compared with Neanderthal people) indicate larger brain areas involved in speech, memory, and cognitive skills. In sum, stones and bones coincide to indicate the emergence of complex language and diverse human cultures about fifty thousand years ago.

Homo sapiens is a cultural animal above all else. Culture, in a nutshell, is a world of *shared* practices, understandings, and attitudes. Language is the prime medium of that sharing. Acquisition of a mother tongue became a central feature of the long human childhood. Language is above all about social bonding. Typically, modern foragers—like other people—spend much of their time schmoozing, kidding, arguing, complaining, teaching, scolding, gossiping, whispering secrets, and storytelling. Occasionally someone explains a skill or plans a hunt, but this is less vital than bonding. Language is *the* main form of human interaction, basic to our social identities, essential to group cohesion. That is true among the several dozen people who interact constantly face-to-face in a foraging band. And it's even more true of any larger group, all the way up to modern nations. The larger a human group, the more its members lack direct personal and family connections, the more their relationship relies on shared values, customs, and myths encoded in language. People tend to identify with those who "speak their language," literally and figuratively.

Historically, a shared culture came to define all human groups. Without human language, human culture as we know it could hardly exist. For tens of thousands of years before the invention of writing, and even after, humans committed to memory enormous masses of cultural knowledge and social memory embodied in language. In fairly recent times, it was still frequent for people to memorize the Bible or the Quran verbatim. The meter and rhyme of poetry in languages around the world was invented to make content more memorable. In a word, language made cultural learning *cumulative*, and the long human childhood became the chief setting for its transmission across time, as each generation acquired cultural knowledge at its parents' knee.

The advent of fully developed human language explains a quickening accumulation of cultural innovation in the late Paleolithic. And that probably explains how modern people out-competed archaic ones. Culturally evolved adaptations have many advantages over physically evolved ones. Cultural adaptations make physical ones unnecessary, as stone tools replace fangs and claws, clothes replace fur, and so on.

Moreover, compared to the evolution of physical adaptation, cultural ones can happen in the blink of an eye. Cultural adaptations permitted *Homo sapiens* to colonize Earth from polar environments to the tropics.

Actual Foragers

A foraging life is, above all, a collective adaptation to a particular natural landscape. Foragers must live where the land offers them food. Overall, they must live spread out, at very low population densities, gathering seasonally to socialize in situations of abundant food or forced inactivity. Let's look at a few specific examples of foragers who have been studied by anthropologists in modern times. To imagine how modern foragers relate to prehistoric ones, remember that modern ones have had their own history. The life ways of modern foragers have responded to their own internal dynamics and, more recently, to outside intrusion, over hundreds and thousands of years. Very often, they have been driven into desolate, arid territories by agricultural peoples who regard them as vermin. Modern foragers are not "primitive" people and certainly not changeless living fossils. They are *Homo sapiens*, just like the rest, facing a given environment with a given technology. They live a foraging life on the same terms as prehistoric foragers lived. In them, we can see a repertoire of strategies, a range of possibilities, and a set of limits that govern the foraging life, whenever and wherever people live it.

We'll use the "ethnographic present" tense to describe their lives as observed by anthropologists in the recent past. Many have now abandoned the foraging life.

Take, for example, the Shoshone people of the Great Basin in the western United States. Modern Shoshones have a spectrum of social adaptations, depending on the setting in which they live. We'll describe the simplest sort of Shoshone band. They live in a challenging desert environment with mountains over twelve thousand feet high, progressively wetter as one ascends them, creating five distinct climate zones with distinctive vegetation. Shoshone people take advantage of the differences to forage seasonally at specific altitudes on the mountainside. Their diet is quite varied. The higher elevations offer an important staple, pine nuts, as well as the opportunity to hunt elk, deer, and mountain sheep. Low elevations offer nuts, fruits, roots, and tubers, as well as an occasional bison and many kinds of smaller game, such as jack rabbits, and also fish in the larger rivers. Plants foods constitute perhaps 80 percent of their diet, however.

To get this food, the Shoshone families spread out and "live off the land" during most of the year. They make their own dwellings and their own tools, which are simple and portable: digging sticks, baskets, bows and arrows. Families cooperate for some tasks that require many hands, as when the women harvest wild grain together or the men hunt a large animal. All the members of several bands collectively hunt rabbits by driving them into long nets. Much less frequently, they hunt antelope in a similar fashion, guided by an "antelope shaman" who helps direct the fleeing animals into a corral rather than a net.

In the fall, Shoshones gather in the pine nut groves of the mountains for the harvest. Men and women work together during the pine nut harvest, the men knocking the cones out of the trees to be collected and processed for storage by the women. When the snows

come, Shoshone families settle into winter camps of five to ten families, eating their stored rations and hunting. In the spring, the bands
disperse to spend the summer foraging for themselves separately. In
the fall, they will once again join forces for the pine nut harvest,
and then settle mostly into the same winter camps as snow covers
the mountains.

Individual families will decide for themselves, however, where to
spend the winter, just as they decide where to go in the summer.
Even in a winter camp of perhaps fifty people, Shoshone families
recognize no group leader aside from the temporary organizers of
cooperative hunts. In the winter, they are voluntarily cooperating,
pooling resources, and living together, for now. Large cooperative
hunting ventures do require command and coordination, but participation there, too, is voluntary. Voluntary cooperation is the only
kind of social organization that foragers know about. The largest
Shoshone gatherings (perhaps fifteen bands together) are occasions
for feasting and dancing, ceremonial activities that define Shoshone
cultural identity. These are the occasions in which people normally
look for a spouse.

Any foraging band must have a larger group within which to
intermarry. That larger group cannot be defined by kinship. The
whole point is to create a powerful affinity among potentially marriage partners who are *not* kin. Intermarriage within a closed kinship
group will eventually destroy that group. Therefore, the affinity of
the larger group must be cultural—a result of shared beliefs, values, expectations, and language. Such groups can be called tribes,
although that is not a frequent anthropological term. We should
notice that the people we are describing here have no chief and never
go "on the war path."

Shoshone groups lay claim to resources like pine groves, but they
rarely fight over them, and generally they are not very territorial.
Individual conflicts certainly occur, as do individual acts of violence.
But resource competition seems limited by the preference of Shoshone families to spread out and feed themselves most of the time.

They have learned to live, and live well, where no one else knows how. What they have, and what they like, is lots of space.

Also rich in space are the !Kung people of the Kalahari Desert in southern Africa. (The exclamation mark represents a tongue-click sound for which there is no letter in any alphabet.) The Kalahari is high, flat, and sandy, but the climate is less extreme than that of Shoshone country. Still, water is the bottleneck for all forms of life in the Kalahari. !Kung technology, which is quite minimal, includes, in addition to the digging stick and bow-and-arrow also used by the Shoshone, a canteen fashioned from an ostrich egg. The !Kung divide their year into five seasons to guide their foraging. Like the Shoshone, the !Kung are broad-spectrum foragers whose diet is seasonally varied and consists mostly of plants. One well-studied group of them could identify a hundred species of edible plants in their environment, including thirty kinds of fruit and forty kinds of root, tuber, or bulb. They especially prize the fruit of the mongongo tree, and its nut, which is available year-round. They also hunt large-hoofed animals, such as wildebeest.

Each !Kung family forages for itself. The !Kung require little social organization or leadership beyond the level of the monogamous family. Membership is flexible, and individual families may join any of several camps in which they have relations. Age and gender define family structure. Women are the principal gatherers. They do most of the cooking and all the childcare. Men hunt, gather, and make tools. Women and men tend to do their jobs individually. The exception is hunting of large animals, but since there are no herds in the Kalahari Desert, there are no large cooperative hunts such as those practiced by the Shoshone. Two to four men are enough to stalk a single wildebeest, butcher it, and carry the meat back to camp. As with almost all hunters, sharing the kill is socially important. It builds the prestige of the hunter to distribute highly valued food. In the absence of any means to preserve and store meat, routine sharing ensures that none will be wasted. And even the best hunters sometimes come home empty-handed. By sharing their kills, successful hunters build good will. Share and share alike is good policy, and it's standard practice among foragers, who have much perishable food.

Summer rains allow !Kung bands to disperse over the landscape to forage in small camps of related nuclear families, each a circle of half a dozen grass huts. Each band makes a tour of mongongo groves, and they stay at each for only a few days, eating first what is near at hand, then what is further away, and finally moving camp. Winter droughts force several camps to cluster around a limited number of year-round water sources. This is the time for !Kung socializing, ceremonies, and exchange. Like the Shoshone winter camp, the !Kung winter congregations have no leader. Asked who their headmen might be, !Kung men joke that each is a headman over himself.

Foragers like the Shoshone and the !Kung are able to provide for themselves with a minimum of social organization. Foragers are the world's true self-reliant "rugged individualists," living off the land, with only occasional help from those whom they, in turn, occasionally help, without anything like a government. Given an opportunity to come out of their wilderness home and settle down, foragers are reluctant to leave the foraging life. Living the way that people evolved to live clearly suits them fine.

Presumably this was all the more so among prehistoric foragers who lived in more abundant environments. Why, then, did prehistoric foragers finally settle down and become farmers?

Curtain Raiser

The first part of the answer is that no individual foraging band ever suddenly settled down and survived. To make foragers stop moving is, basically, like stopping birds from migrating. To destroy their ancestral way of life is to destroy them as a group. The advent of fully sedentary agriculture was a gradual, variable process that advanced—and, in places, went back and forth—over thousands of years.

Homo sapiens' journey out of Africa throughout Asia to Europe,

Australia, and finally the Americas occurred as Ice Age glaciers gripped the land. Then the climate warmed, and the glaciers receded about twelve thousand years ago. Northern expanses of frozen tundra contracted, and mid-latitude forests expanded. The warmer and more hospitable climates of what is called the Holocene Epoch have lasted down to our own times. During the Holocene, people began to domesticate plants and animals. Gone forever was the day when all humans were foragers. Nonetheless, foragers still inhabited most of the world, especially in Australia and the Americas, across northern Asia and southern Africa, until only a few centuries ago. What finally made them settle down was being massacred and enslaved by farmers and herders, so-called pioneers, who wanted the "unused" land for themselves.

By the time the glaciers retreated, all surviving humans were *Homo sapiens*, archaic humans like Neanderthals having become extinct well before the thaw. *Homo sapiens* had evolved a distinctive profile as a species. At least partly, we had become a carnivorous and predator species. Humans are uniquely endowed, among animals, with the ability to run long distances and the ability to throw projectiles accurately, and both these distinctive abilities probably arose as physical adaptations for hunting. On the other hand, our adaptations for hunting are more cultural than physical. Ancient human cultures celebrated hunting, although plant foods gathered by women were often a larger part of the diet. *Homo sapiens* had evolved to live at very low population densities, a common trait of predator species.

Predation certainly did not make us unique among animal species, but our language and our cultural adaptations did. The cultural behavior of human beings is much more adaptive than any instinctive behavior could be. That, more than anything else, sets us apart from all other animal species. Furthermore, *Homo sapiens* had another unique quality as the only species that walks easily on two feet. To be born with hands free and an innate propensity to speak, like the mythical Adam and Eve, was to inherit the world. The cultural animal had become the apex predator of any environment that it entered, and it entered them all. Man the hunter drove some creatures to extinction, but more importantly, woman the gatherer began to make other living things part of the family.

Finally, we can say that if male aggressiveness and sporadic violent competition do seem to be general aspects of human nature, group violence, social inequality and subordination are generally *not*—at least not when we live in the social conditions under which we evolved as a species. Those conditions changed as the domestication of plants and animals ended the Paleolithic period and began the *Neolithic* period, our next stop.

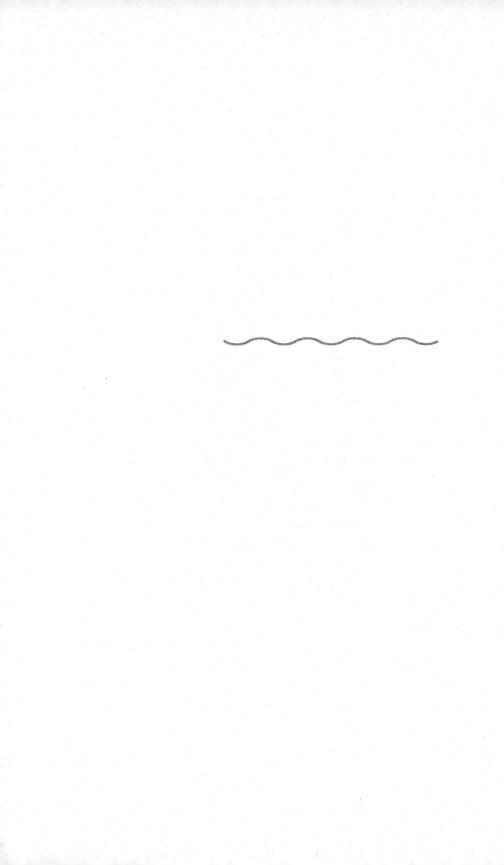

CHAPTER TWO

Dominion

Around 10,000 BCE the Ice Age (or, more properly, "last glacial maximum") ended after a frigid hundred thousand years. The entire period of modern humans' evolution and expansion around the globe had occurred during a protracted sequence of glaciations and intermittent thaws. Foraging *Homo sapiens* had become the world's most widespread apex predator, occupying all the continents except for Antarctica.

There was still plenty of ice around, however, when the so-called ice man died in the Italian Alps about 5,300 years ago. We have no idea what his real name was, or even what language he might have spoken. The ice preserved his body until 1991, when he turned up in a snow melt because of recent global warming. He was all there, down to the contents of his stomach, which showed that his diet included cultivated wheat. The invention of agriculture was a defining aspect of his world, as was his elaborate material culture, including baskets, leggings, shoes, a wood-framed backpack, and a stitched fur coat. He had an unhealed gash in his hand, apparently made while defending himself against an attacker's copper-bladed ax or flint-bladed knife, not unlike those he himself carried. He also carried a powerful six-foot bow, as well as a quiver of arrows not unlike the one that, in the end, hit him in the back, severing an artery and killing him. His wounds and weapons were another defining aspect of the late Neolithic period.

The previous chapter's rapid overview of the Paleolithic world encompassed hundreds of thousands, occasionally millions, of years. Those vast expanses of time had shaped *Homo sapiens* as a species, physically and mentally. The big Paleolithic story was evolution. Now we leave evolutionary time behind, however. During the mere ten thousand years of Neolithic time, human bodies changed little. The Neolithic millennia shaped us culturally and socially rather than physically.

The big Neolithic story is the domestication of plants and animals, the so-called Agricultural Revolution. Agriculture may not sound like much of a story, but the Agricultural Revolution changed almost everything. Picture two *Homo sapiens* standing in their dwelling places, one in 10,000 BCE, one today. Naked, with a haircut, the *Homo sapiens* of 10,000 BCE will look pretty much exactly the same as the *Homo sapiens* of today—presuming that you're imagining this correctly. Except for the two naked *Homo sapiens*, though, pretty much *everything* else in the two pictures would have to be different. One *Homo sapiens* sleeps under a bush, the other in a high-rise apartment building. The ten-thousand-year Agricultural Revolution was the single biggest cause of the difference. By domesticating plants and animals, we harnessed other living things to serve our purposes, and, through selective breeding, even reshaped them to serve us better. In so doing, we took a decisive step toward material abundance and world domination. The ancient Hebrews thanked their creator God for giving people dominion over other living things. Modern people can credit the Agricultural Revolution.

Now let's step away from the metaphor of revolution, however. While revolutionary in the sense of hugely transformative, the domestication of plants and animals was neither rapid nor organized. On the contrary, domestication was a diffuse and gradual process, whose accidental character is essential to understanding it. Ten thousand years may be an evolutionary blink of the eye, but it is a long, long time in human terms. No one who lived during this "revolution" experienced rapid change because of it, or even knew that it was happening.

Neolithic time ended before the invention of writing. Neolithic life has therefore normally been studied by anthropologists rather than historians. It lacks personal names, precise dates, colorful characters, and outrageous anecdotes. Thrilling yarns have occasionally survived from the Neolithic world only as myths and legends. The Neolithic story matters not because of its entertainment value but because of how it shaped us. It made *Homo sapiens* the world's dominant species, but also brought war, patriarchy, and all kinds of social exploitation and systematic brutality. To tell the Neolithic story, however, we cannot use a traditional historical narrative. Instead, we must interpret a variable process that began in maybe twenty places and proceeded simultaneously but unevenly over ten thousand years. One element of the timing is crystal clear. The process began as a response to climate change—more specifically, global warming.

The geographic spread of *Homo sapiens* was predictable as the climate warmed after 10,000 BCE. Thriving edible plants supported more population, but oversized groups are impossible for foragers to maintain, as we have seen. When foraging populations grew, they became centrifugal, spreading out more or less automatically. And, in locating new hunting grounds, the apex predator *Homo sapiens* suffered the same lack of constraints as the gorilla in the joke: "Where does an eight-hundred-pound gorilla sleep? Anywhere he likes." Bad-ass *Homo sapiens* could live anywhere they could find enough food.

By sampling mitochondrial DNA in current global populations, it is possible to trace the Paleolithic migration of *Homo sapiens* out of Africa along the shores of the Indian Ocean, as far as Indonesia and Australia. Mitochondrial DNA is not organized in the familiar double helix that recombines in every generation, so that children inherit half from their mothers and half from their fathers. Instead, mitochondrial DNA is inherited fundamentally unchanged across many generations, and it is inherited only from one's mother. Its stability makes it a convenient tracer of historical migrations. That's how we know that all living women descend from a "mitochondrial Eve," a single female ancestor who lived more than 100,000 years ago in east Africa. By the time our migrating ancestors arrived in what is now Malaysia—on their way (although they didn't know it yet) to Australia—a wide stretch of open ocean confronted them.

Although the evidence has largely disappeared under the waves, we now suspect that some Neolithic people became competent sailors. Archaic humans had never made it to either Australia or the Americas, but *Homo sapiens* apparently had no trouble. The original occupation of Australia by *Homo sapiens* occurred before fifty thousand years ago, when it necessitated a significant open-ocean crossing. Late Paleolithic glacial periods lowered sea levels (locking much of the planet's water in ice) and uncovered a land bridge between Asia and North America. Now, however, there is persuasive evidence that *Homo sapiens* peopled the Americas partly by sea, using boats or rafts. Archeologists have excavated an extremely ancient settlement of early maritime-oriented migrants who lived very far south on the Pacific Coast of Chile, almost at the southern tip of South America. Their coastal Monte Verde archeological site is now the oldest confirmed place of human habitation in the Americas. The Monte Verde encampment of twenty to thirty individuals, like so many early human encampments, stood on the banks of a stream, which eventually flooded and became a bog. By limiting oxygen, bogs preserve organic matter, allowing archeologists to determine that the occupiers of this encampment used half a dozen kinds of seaweed. Unquestionably, the people encamped at Monte Verde lived on intimate terms with the sea.

A look at Oceania, the last part of the habitable Earth to be colonized by *Homo sapiens*, shows us that some Neolithic sailors could cross thousands of miles of open ocean. These sailors, the forerunners of the Polynesians, settled the archipelagos of the South Pacific, starting from continental Southeast Asia and China. As often happens with prehistoric people, we cannot know what they called themselves. Our only actual evidence of them is their pottery, recently excavated on islands where they settled. Their Lapita pottery styles were spread from New Guinea across a thousand miles east into the open Pacific Ocean, as far as the island of Fiji. The seafaring that made that possible was done on double-hulled canoes, or large-hulled single canoes with outriggers.

That gets us ahead of our story, though.

One final bit of terminology—the dating system used in deep historical time—requires a bit of explanation. Neolithic time begins, as we've said, around 10,000 BCE (previously written BC). The old term BC (before Christ) established a countdown to the birth of Jesus of Nazareth. A hundred years before Jesus's birth was 100 BC, followed by 99 BC, then 98 BC, and so on. After the birth of Jesus, the years counted back up, now labeled AD (*anno domini*, Latin for the year of Our Lord). Thus, the one-hundredth year after Jesus's birth was 100 AD, followed by 101 AD, then 102 AD. Now world historians apply terminology more appropriate for the world as a whole, using CE (Common Era), instead of AD, and BCE (Before the Common Era), instead of BC. Counting down (and then back up) is cumbersome but cannot be avoided.

Domestication

Thanks to the warming climate after 10,000 BCE, more and more people began to organize food production rather than simply hunt and gather what already existed. The domestication of plants and animals occurred as the warming climate encouraged plant growth. How can we envision the process? You might assume that people chose to become farmers because farming offered a better life. That would be wrong.

For starters, foragers could not choose a farming life until one existed. The basic techniques of planting, cultivating, watering, harvesting, preservation, and storage had to be invented individually before they could be assembled into a fully functional, permanently

sustainable system of agriculture. Plants and animals had to be modified over centuries by selective breeding to create domestic species.
These days, anthropologists posit a gradual, variable, sometimes
reversible process of *intensification.*

Many Neolithic people—foragers all, at first—were beginning to
plant things as a supplement to their traditional hunting and gathering. Their foraging was becoming more complex, able to feed more
mouths. Mobile foragers took advantage of opportunities like seasonal flooding to scatter seeds in the rich and well-watered sediment,
returning later to harvest the result. Their hunting became more
ambitious and diverse. It now included fishing. Aquatic resources
created some exceptions to the normal rule that non-agricultural
populations were always small. Ancient Japanese foragers apparently
thrived in large numbers by gathering seafood. They made the first
known baskets, seemingly to cover with clay, thereby making pots
to boil shellfish. Neolithic foragers had not yet been displaced from
food-rich environments, as later occurred everywhere. The warmer
climate made their foraging more productive. They encouraged the
growth of nut-bearing trees, creating natural orchards. Using fire in
grasslands and building dykes in wetlands, they began to modify
landscapes. Hunters might avoid killing their prey's young, so that
their food animals could reproduce themselves. Herds of wild animals like bison and reindeer could be guided using barriers and fire.
People learned to collect and plant seeds millennia before they began
to rely on cultivation as their principal food source. Agriculture was
not so much a choice as an unplanned final result of this diffuse,
ongoing intensification. It is the process, rather than the end point,
that characterizes the Neolithic life overall.

Moreover, fully sedentary farming, when it appeared, did *not*
offer a better life than foraging. Aside from the violence that we will
explore in the second part of this chapter, early farming was simply
less healthy than foraging. The skeletons of early farmers suggest
poorer nutrition as a result of a less varied diet, one overly dependent on a few staple crops. Moreover, we can detect greater ravages

of communicable disease among farmers as compared to foraging communities, principally because large, sedentary communities had sewage disposal issues. Domestic animals, a crucial part of the new way of life, were principal vectors of disease. Most diseases afflicting agricultural populations came from their domestic animals. Finally, farmers' days included more backbreaking, repetitive labor than did foragers' days.

Farming *was* indisputably "better" in one way, however. Farmers could feed more people. A lot more. Foragers, after all, can feed only themselves. Depending on the terrain, game, and vegetation, many square miles of land are needed to feed each member of a foraging band, whereas a single intensively worked rice paddy the size of a football field can feed hundreds of people. If foraging defines one end of our spectrum of intensiveness, rice paddies (or, today, hydroponic gardening) define the opposite end. As productive activities gradually intensified in Neolithic societies, their populations rose, they moved less, and they depended less on hunting and gathering wild food. Population concentrations in the hundreds or thousands simply cannot be fed by foraging under ordinary conditions. Once a large population depended fully on agriculture, it had passed a point of no return. The foraging life was no longer an option. Wild plants and game are depleted too quickly by hundreds and thousands of hungry mouths. Once out of Eden, there was no going back.

Domestication began in over a dozen world regions. The environmental conditions of those regions, their particular endowment of wild flora and fauna, were chief determinants of the process. Areas around the world had distinctive repertoires of domesticated plants and animals, which varied according to the wild species available for domestication. The nutritious seeds of grasses became a common staple food. Grains, we call them: corn, wheat, barley, millet, oats, and rice. The protein-rich seeds of vine-growing pulses (beans, peas, lentils, peanuts, and many others) were also basic. Like grains, the seeds of pulses can easily be dried, stored, and eaten or planted later. Eaten together, grains and pulses can rival meat as a source of high-quality protein. In tropical forest environments, root crops like yams were more important than grains and pulses, however. Monsoon-soaked areas of Southeast Asia produced a tradition of cultivation not dependent on the plow. Plants from that region (such as plantains, sugar cane, taro, and rice) are propagated from cuttings in moist ground, or, in the case of rice, transplanted as seedlings into a flooded field. The resulting distribution of world food resources was therefore uneven. Domesticated plants and animals were largely shared along Asia's long, climatically similar east-west lines of latitude—giving the Old World a large, shared repertoire of domesticates.

New World people had a full repertoire of domesticated plants, but these were less easily shared because the Americas' long north-south lines of longitude *crossed* many climate zones. As for domesticated animals, Old World cattle, donkeys, horses, pigs, sheep, goats, chickens, or geese had few counterparts in the New World. So Eurasians were in luck. To ride on a horse or carry loads on a donkey, to deploy the strength of an ox or an elephant, to possess a herd of sheep for wool, milk, and meat—these possibilities multiplied human potential marvelously. But Americans and Australians had only dogs, the hunting human's best friend, the one animal domesticated in Paleolithic times.

Meanwhile, across North Africa and much of Asia, some people became herders.

Keeping a few animals, such as pigs or chickens, was advantageous for farmers, too, but herding sheep, cattle, or goats was something different. Herd animals instinctively stick together and follow a leader. (Animals without this instinct cannot be herded, period. Try to herd cats.) A numerous herd can be managed by a single herder, especially with the help of dogs. Herd animals can subsist by grazing in steep, arid country unsuitable to farming. Moreover, they can quickly destroy a farmer's crops, so that herding and farming famously don't go together. A large herd must eat a lot, and it eats by foraging, so herders must move with the cycle of the seasons. This seasonal movement of herds is called transhumance.

Neolithic herders typically lived in tents and made no permanent settlements. Herders were rich, nonetheless, compared to foragers. Their food resources "on the hoof" were self-storing, whereas food preservation and storage posed a difficult problem for farmers. Herders' wealth on the hoof was also self-transporting, even a little too mobile, as it could easily wander off or be stolen. Wealth on the hoof tempted herders to become raiders, preying on each other's herds. In this, herders imitated the competitive, combative style of the rams and bulls and stallions that sired their herds. They also learned to change the behavior of unruly male animals by castrating them, making them easier to control.

Farming and herding were complex technologies by which we *Homo sapiens* gained dominion over other species. Sometimes we took over other species completely, modifying their form unrecognizably through centuries of selective breeding to suit our needs and preferences. The contrast between Chihuahuas and Great Danes, both descendants of wild wolves, testifies to this transformative power. Many modern horses and cattle and sheep and dogs and cats are designer versions that depend completely on *Homo sapiens*. Likewise, many domesticated plants have lost the ability to reproduce in the wild. Their continued existence now depends on human beings. Learning to bend other Earthlings to our will and make them serve us was our biggest power grab ever as a species.

Yet, from 10,000 BCE to 4000 BCE, human populations remained small. People still rarely dominated the landscape, and almost everyone still hunted or gathered most of their food. Most human populations still migrated seasonally. People who lived exclusively from farming or herding were still comparatively few. Yet Neolithic people were beginning to coordinate their activities across wider areas. Megaliths and mounds that still dot the landscape indicate scattered Neolithic populations in communication, capable of meaningful cooperation although not yet living in large groups. Between 9500 and 8000 BCE, many megalithic structures were erected in the eastern Mediterranean region, notably those of Gobekli Tepe in southern

Anatolia. Gobekli Tepe is an early outlier, however. The main period of megalithic constructions started around 5000 BCE, when many megaliths appeared in western Europe. Stonehenge (circa 2500 BCE) is the best known and one of the most recent. As far as we can tell, these megaliths marked, not settlements, but rather meeting places with a ritual significance. Building these structures would have required the voluntary convergence and coordinated labors of people from a wide area. Megaliths therefore indicate widening social connections as well as burgeoning populations. In the Americas, beginning around 3500 BCE, carefully designed mound structures in the Mississippi basin reveal a similar process under way in the New World. Like Old World megaliths, the earliest Mississippi basin mound complexes were not agricultural settlements but instead indicate the convergence of scattered populations for ritual purposes.

Back in southern Anatolia, not so far from the Gobekli Tepe megaliths, stood the stunning proto-agricultural village of Catalhoyuk. Beginning around 7400 BCE, Catalhoyuk was populated over 1500 years and probably looked bit like a Native American pueblo. Catalhoyuk houses were entered through the roof. They pressed together without intervening alleys, without central organization, without public buildings, having simply accumulated like a coral reef. The inhabitants of Catalhoyuk kept sheep and goats, and ate grains and pulses, which they no doubt cultivated in a neighboring seasonal wetland. They also hunted large, fierce bullish aurochs and adorned the interiors of their dwellings with the skulls. A nearby migration route may have renewed wild game more quickly than would otherwise be the case. Catalhoyuk exuded permanence. Each house kept the remains of previous generations, their bones ritually adorned, incorporated into the masonry.

Catalhoyuk is one of a kind, so far, in the archeological record. It stands, or stood, in the oldest area of human settlement (roughly, on the pathway by which *Homo sapiens* originally migrated out of Africa), also the world's most intense region of domestication. Its extreme earliness alone makes it atypical, but it cannot have been unique. It shows us that a fully formed agricultural way of life existed in a few places fully nine thousand years ago. It shows us that fully sedentary agriculture itself did not—as is sometimes asserted—automatically generate social conflict and war, kingship, and governance. Significant evidence of warfare was absent from Catalhoyuk.

Man the Warrior

After 4000 BCE, archeological evidence of warfare starts to become routine at agricultural sites. Note, however, that this is not because farmers became warriors. Rather, farmers became the warriors' target. The fruits of agricultural society offered rich prizes, an accumulation of food, drink, clothing, and all manner of useful things there for the taking, as long as the takers were well armed and skilled in violence. Not among the farmers, at first, but rather among their neighbors, qualities associated with man the hunter were transferred to a new personal ideal: man the warrior. The results are still with us today.

Because farming societies emerged first in the Old World, war-oriented societies did as well. Late Neolithic farming societies were village societies. Neolithic farmers normally lived in villages of a few hundred inhabitants each, large enough for protection and resources, small enough to watch their crops nearby. Oxen were a chief resource that Old World villagers shared after the invention of the plow, which came rather late. The first plows were technically uncomplicated, little more than an ox harnessed to a digging stick. The ox, a castrated bull, was the key. Steadily farmed soils decline in fertility unless they are given a rest. By engaging the weight and muscle power of a team of oxen—a Neolithic tractor—plowmen could eventually cultivate enough ground to let some of it lie fallow each year, restoring its fertility. Moreover, the animals' manure contributed fertilizer. Plows and manure made agriculture fully sustainable in a permanent location. Plowing worked better in large, squarish fields, so it literally shaped the Old World agricultural landscape. The advantages of plowing were so great that it spread right across mid-latitude Eurasia, along with a basic kit of technologies, such as wheeled vehicles, food crops, and domesticated animals—all in Neolithic times. New World farmers did without ox or plow and, for the most part, manure, but still produced brilliant results, as we will see in a moment.

Sedentary farmers produced food aplenty, but how to preserve and store it? What do you do with hundreds of pounds of perishable food and no refrigerator? The advantage of grains and pulses came partly from the relative facility of drying and storing them in pots. Because pots are both heavy and fragile, foragers on the move had never invented them. To preserve many perishable foods, Neolithic people learned to sun- or freeze-dry them, and they also harnessed the power of other living things in a thousand ways. Over centuries, people learned to encourage the growth of microorganisms to preserve stored food. The special flavors (and other properties) of yogurt and pickles and beer and a hundred other fermented foods were a result of this process. Gradually, Neolithic people learned to do many other things with animal products. Wool could be woven into clothing, milk could be made into cheese (preservation again), and the muscle power of large quadrupeds could provide traction. Neolithic farmers learned to cultivate fiber crops as well as food crops. Hemp and flax were principal fiber crops. The most amazing fiber was surely silk, which involved harnessing the cocoon-weaving energies of silkworms by feeding them mulberry leaves, and then harvesting their cocoons to make thread.

The main early farming societies of the Old World had herder neighbors. From the Sahara to Mongolia, a huge swath of arid or semiarid plain runs through the middle of the Old World. From 8000 to 6000 BCE, the Sahara Desert was not as arid as today. Back then, the Sahara supported vast herds of cattle. Continuing to the northeast, across the great deserts of Arabia and Southwest Asia, lies the prairie-like steppe, a broad two-thousand-mile highway connecting the Black Sea with the Pacific Ocean. Unirrigated agriculture is rarely worthwhile in this vast area, but hoofed animals like cattle and sheep can thrive if they move seasonally. Therefore, this was a land of nomadic, horse-riding herders, who play a leading role in our story.

People on the Eurasian steppe people had hunted horses for food since Paleolithic times, and when they domesticated the horse around 4000 BCE, it was for food. About a thousand years later, beginning probably in what later became Ukraine, steppe people had learned to ride, which involved inventing the bridle and bit—although no stirrups yet, for a few thousand more years. Horses made possible the management of large herds of sheep and cattle, and ox-drawn wagons made possible large-scale transhumance across hundreds of miles of steppe.

Archeologists have excavated some of the world's earliest large permanent settlements, which began about 5000 BCE at the western end of the steppe. The people there grew grains and pulses, raised livestock, and operated looms. Over eight centuries, their settlements show little sign of social hierarchy or warfare. By the mid-3000s BCE, however, many signs of hierarchy and war began to appear. Large burial mounds called kurgans tell the tale. Being something like rustic pyramids, kurgans required a lot of manpower to build, and the people buried there clearly belonged to a social elite. Their clothing—even their children's clothing—was sometimes adorned with hundreds and thousands of animal teeth, requiring untold hours of labor. Adult males were buried with stone battle axes, javelins, bows and arrows, horses, and war chariots. Some stone maces (bludgeons for smashing skulls) were shaped like horse heads, indicating the centrality of the horse to a new war-oriented way of life. Bones of sacrificed horses and retainers were often buried around the kurgans to accompany the deceased warlord into the underworld.

At a place called Sintashta in the Ural foothills, archeologists have unearthed the earliest known war chariots, which seem to have been invented on the edge of the steppe. Chariots carried an archer and a driver, pulled by two horses. Chariots were not really a form of transportation, any more than a modern tank is a form or transportation. Chariots were intricate, expensive war machines that required specialized manufacture and a numerous support team to put a single aristocratic warrior on the battlefield. Spoked wheels and horses made war chariots fast. Around 2000 BCE, Sintashta was a walled, military stronghold and a full-blown center of chariot and weapons manufacture including, by that time, copper smelting. Metal working gets us ahead of our Neolithic story, though.

In sum, the first appearance of Neolithic farming communities is closely followed by the advent of warfare, but it was not usually the agriculturalists themselves who became warriors. Instead, war became the vocation of people who lived around farming communities, the way that people who live by the sea are likely to become fishermen. In the Old World, horse-riding herders often specialized in pilfering from farming settlements. In some ways, the herding way of life itself encouraged the development of warfare. Herders had lots of horses, not only mounts, but remounts, and each mounted warrior had to change horses frequently in battle. Their herds were organized by pugnacious stallions, bulls, and rams that modeled rule by dominant male, their dominion to be decided by individual combat. Herders had to subdue their animals physically and, as we have noted, sometimes castrated them to do so. Eventually they castrated their war captives for a similar purpose.

In the New World, by contrast, there were practically no herders. Yet there was no shortage of warriors there, either, after the invention of agriculture. Man the hunter did not require a herding way of life to become man the warrior. The Aztecs offer an excellent example. Aztec knights were nobles who focused on defeating other nobles in individual combat. Their objective was to win personal prestige by capturing enemy knights and offering them for religious sacrifice. The Aztecs were originally hunter-gatherers from the deserts of northern Mexico until they took control of settled farming societies and ruled over them. Then neighboring societies, too, had to warrior-up in self-defense.

Most readers of this book will be roughly familiar with the basic medieval European pattern of a parasitic war-oriented nobility served by an agricultural peasantry. Some version of that pattern eventually existed in much of the post-foraging world. To better imagine its Neolithic beginnings, let's consider the Yanomami people of Amazonia, a simple warrior-led agricultural society until recently. We will describe them using the ethnographic present tense.

The Yanomami are all about war. They were well studied by anthropologists in the mid-twentieth century, and one can hardly imagine a starker contrast with peaceable foragers. The Yanomami inhabit a tropical highland savanna that is much richer in resources than the Shoshones' Great Basin or the !Kungs' Kalahari Desert. Yanomami population densities, too, are much higher. They are semi-sedentary horticulturalists, rather than fully sedentary agriculturalists. Plots of manioc, plantains, and palm fruit provide their chief food. Yanomami garden plots relocate periodically, and so do their villages. Yanomami villages of a hundred people are *shabonos*, fortress-like structures, surrounded by a palisade ten feet high. Within, there are several long collective dwellings, each occupied by a clan of thirty or so people, called a *teri*. A teri is a string of families living side by side, each with its own cooking fire and hammocks slung around it, several levels high.

Yanomami villagers huddle together in these close quarters for security. They regard their shabono, above all, as a safe refuge from enemy marauders. Mutual protection is the first principle of village life. Yanomami villagers regard not only other tribes but also other Yanomami shabonos as rivals locked an endless struggle for territory. Within each shabono, teris compete for fertile garden space nearby. A general sense of scarcity reigns as the nearby garden plots gradually decline in fertility, year by year, eventually necessitating a move for the whole village, a situation fraught with difficulties in a landscape with many competing claims. The Yanomami world is a threatening place.

Each clan has a designated ceremonial leader who arbitrates disputes among families and manages relations between clans. Whatever his other qualities, he must be a successful warrior and war leader. Whereas foragers like the Shoshone or the !Kung shun overly aggressive males, high-strung, alpha-male pugnaciousness is cultivated among the Yanomami by certain individuals termed *waiteri* men. A waiteri man is the sort of guy who occasionally frightens even his own friends and family. Often, he's not the best company, but you do want him with you in high-stakes disputes involving your clan status, not to mention an outright war with another village.

Man the warrior drew on a hunter's skills, of course, but his role was essentially different. Intra-species violence is different from inter-species violence. The hunter kills to eat; the warrior kills to intimidate, to garner the fruits of victory from the cowering survivors. Intraspecies violence is all about imposing dominance. Ask the large-antlered stags and the beach-master walruses.

Rule by Alpha Male

Man the warrior brought us patriarchy and instituted radically unequal societies unlike anything that had gone before among *Homo sapiens*. Like domestication, these changes were gradual, diffuse, and unplanned. They resulted inexorably from the heightened male dominance of war-oriented societies.

Male bipeds seem to have always dominated females physically, to judge by their dimorphism, which, though diminished, remains a characteristic of our species. And yet, because of the long human childhood, as foragers we generally pair off and develop an unusually stable, collaborative, and in most ways, equal and monogamous partnership.

Man the hunter, we could say, was a domestic partner. Man the warrior, on the other hand, was a conquering hero. His wife was not "woman the gatherer," who provided much of the food. Instead, she was a trophy wife, a prize to be won, enjoyed, and flaunted. A successful warrior could garner many such trophies. War-oriented societies are characterized by pervasive celebration of the warrior's virility and heroic deeds. The triumphs and spoils of war loom large. Societies reorganized for war became more testosterone-driven and their gender relations more male-dominated. Boys practiced fighting from an early age in athletic competitions that might, like javelin throwing, involve weapons. They often earned initiation into warrior society through a prescribed ordeal at adolescence. Rather than a complementary life force, femininity became something scorned and feared by warriors, an enervating threat to masculine power.

Woman's new role was to obey and serve the warrior, feed and clothe him, give him heirs, heal his wounds, mourn his death in battle, and send her sons to take his place. Patriarchy, a comprehensive system of male dominance, was the result. Patriarch gradually eclipsed older cultural modes in warrior-led societies.

The earliest agricultural people apparently had retained the more balanced gender relations typical of the foraging life. Before war leaders built their strongholds and walled entire settlements, Neolithic farming villages were probably ruled by councils of elders among whom women apparently played a significant role. At Catalhoyuk, the clay figurine of a seated female elder clearly indicates social status. It makes perfect sense.

Everything indicates that woman the gatherer had been the chief domesticator of plants. Cooking and weaving, her descendants became the chief processors of plant food and fiber. Neolithic settlements had fiber-weaving looms before they had defensive walls. Neolithic figurines disproportionately represent the female form, as Paleolithic figurines also had done. These so-called Venus figurines are hard to interpret conclusively: Earth goddess? Fertility talisman? Most are, in any case, stylized representations, not individual portraits. Some figurines apparently had ritual functions, and some were found buried at the center of early agricultural villages. Prehistoric female figurines generally have no male counterparts. At Catalhoyuk, interior wall paintings of men and boys show them hunting. Significantly, peaceful Earth mothers tend to disappear from the archeological record with the appearance of battle axes, chariots, and the extravagant tombs of war lords. Human representations in warrior-led societies focus instead on the masculine glories of war.

The new "rule by alpha male" made societies less peaceful and egalitarian in all sorts of ways. Men outranked women in every household. Warrior aristocracies outranked non-warriors overall. The ancient tendency to organize society by lineages (once defined by totem animals) became linked to warrior lineages, the beginnings of a titled nobility and inherited patrilineal social prestige. Virtually all post-foraging societies developed lasting stratifications of wealth and power. Some families lived in bigger houses, owned more land, ate better food, wore better clothes—across generations.

Ultimately, warrior overlords would own all the land and control those who farmed it. Land ownership and inheritance across generations became a chief global mechanism of social inequality. Social inequality was "naturalized" by the passage of time. From then on, some would be born owing, and others, born owning—a basic pattern that came to affect all densely populated societies, lasted for thousands of years, and vastly privileged its beneficiaries.

Triumphant war leaders often became kings. Command is an essential function of war. Kingship emerged in virtually all warlike societies, normally gendered male. A ruling queen was rare, likely a stop-gap representative of her father, husband, or son. The king was chief patriarch, reproducing, at a higher level, the patriarchal authority that dominated each of his subjects' families. Kingship thus flowed from and reinforced larger patterns of stratification. Kings normally derived from the self-described "noble" families at the top of the social heap. The king's warrior nobles enforced his decrees, surrounded him on the battlefield, and gloried in the honors and titles—not to mention the rich plunder—that he bestowed upon them. The earliest kings were probably of the first-among-equals variety, men of demonstrated capacity for leadership, chosen by dominant clans from among their own number. Inheritance of the crown became the general rule, though. Like most forms of social domination, kingship ran in families. Kings gradually strengthened their claims to power by revising their family trees, claiming divine sanction, constructing fortresses and palaces, employing artists to commemorate their warlike glories.

All this will sound familiar, no doubt, to most readers of this book. Feudal Europe comes to mind, with its knights, castles, and serfs. Asian readers will envision Japanese samurai or the feuding kingdoms of pre-imperial China. It is a global pattern, strongly exemplified in European history. Scandinavian Vikings of the 900s and 800s CE offer another vivid example of unprovoked attack, rapine, and plunder along these lines. Homer's *Iliad*, the earliest European epic, offers a hugely influential example. Homer's chariot-driving warriors like Achilles, Ajax, and Hector compete above all for individual dominance and personal glory. They are notably egocentric protagonists in royal family dramas about alliances and rivalries. The plot turns on who has killed whom, abducted whom, sworn an oath to avenge whom. The Greek warriors are besieging Troy, after all, because a Trojan prince supposedly abducted someone's queen, although it seems she went along willingly enough. Through priestly intermediaries, Homeric heroes offer sacrifices to gain the favor of divine sponsors who will protect them in battle. In these "heroic societies," political power and conflict is structured by face-to-face competition among members of warrior families. Individual combat between war captains sometimes decided the outcome of a battle by indicating the will of the gods. The *Iliad* was a verse epic—not written or read, at first, but memorized by bards and recited as entertainment at aristocratic gatherings.

The *Iliad* shows us a world of roughly 1000 BCE—Bronze Age, rather than Neolithic. By this time, agricultural settlements in China, Pakistan, Egypt, Mesopotamia, Mesoamerica, and Peru had become the world's first major population centers. All of these would eventually become highly stratified, patriarchal, and war-oriented. In all, *Homo sapiens* began to concentrate population more and more. Farming villages of a few hundred were eclipsed by urban populations in the tens of thousands. Civilization was upon us, and it wasn't pretty.

Let's recap the Neolithic period.

End of Ice Age. Agricultural Revolution. Man the warrior.

In other words, by harnessing and reshaping other living things to suit our needs during the first few thousand years of a warmer climate, we began to multiply human population and accumulate wealth as never before. It did not take long, however—less than a thousand years—for agricultural societies to become stratified and patriarchal, dominated most often by a warrior nobility and a hereditary kingship. That is the point at which most world histories begin—with writing, metallurgy, and cities centered on temples. The first cities of that sort appeared around 3500 BCE, about the same time, and in about the same place, as the first bronze swords. Cities and swords signal a new chapter in our story.

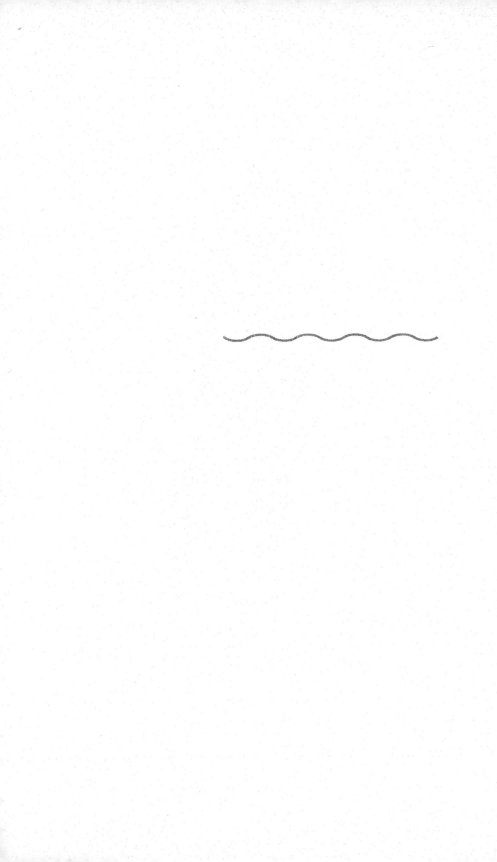

CHAPTER THREE

Babylon

Finally, after around 3500 BCE, we can begin to hear words, know names. Writing has been invented on a flood plain lying between the Tigris and Euphrates Rivers, a place more recently called Iraq. The land between the waters is Mesopotamia. The first Mesopotamian cities began around 3500 BCE, flourished for a thousand years, and then disappeared into high mounds of earth that rise today above the surrounding flatness. The city-builders called this place Sumer.

Their voices exalt Gilgamesh, king of Uruk. They are reciting the world's oldest still-existing poem, written down around 2000 BCE, but drawing on sources many centuries older. The story of Gilgamesh makes explicit many things that we have inferred from archeological evidence. Gilgamesh is a warrior king. He has raised high walls to defend the city of Uruk against constant warfare among rival cities. He intimidates other men by demanding access to their brides on the wedding night. He fights and subdues a "wild man" named Enkidu, who is clearly a forager. Enkidu is attracted to the city of Uruk not only by the insistence of Gilgamesh but also by such urban amenities as wine and prostitutes. Babylon, a later city which stood near today's Baghdad, became a great symbol of urban grandeur and corruption.

If you expected civilization to be "civilized" in the sense of ethically superior, expect to be disappointed. Still, cities were undoubtedly something new under the sun. Dense urban populations had their drawbacks, but they were undoubtedly creative and stimulating. In the Hebrew scriptures that became the Bible's Old Testament, Babylon stands for corruption, but to many people of the ancient world, it stood for grandeur. The city's "hanging gardens" were, chronologically, the first wonder of the world.

Like the Nile River valley in Egypt, the Yellow River valley in China, and the Indus River valley in Pakistan (home, around 2000 BCE, of the sassy ten-centimeter bronze Dancing Girl of Mohenjo Daro), Mesopotamia was a great river valley. In Mesopotamia, two rivers meandered in parallel across a broad plain and converged just before reaching the Persian Gulf. The convergence of the Tigris and Euphrates Rivers was a large, marshy wetland that supported substantial populations even before the beginnings of formal agriculture. The southern Mesopotamian plain offered alluvial soils that could be easily irrigated. Alluvial soils are marvelously easy to plow as well, being loose, level, and unobstructed. In Sumer we find the earliest depictions of plows.

Irrigation and plowing together allowed population densities previously unknown. Eventually, they allowed cities, ruled by kings whose command could mobilize thousands of workers and soldiers. These cities had state religions and official priests and scribes. Their urban ruling classes were surrounded by peasantries. Their craftsmen could cast bronze and, eventually, forge iron.

Sumerian cities were too many to name. One of the first, which is to say, one of the first cities anywhere, was Uruk. Around 3300 BCE, Uruk extended well over four hundred acres. Its population of somewhere between twenty and fifty thousand people lived in a compact complex of temples, workshops, residences, brick manufactories, and colonnaded courtyards. Gradually, during the third and second millennia BCE, cities appeared in the Nile and the Indus River valleys, and then, in the Yellow River valley, too. Each of these civilizations was unique, yet they interacted. If one influenced the whole world more than any other, it was Sumer. All later Eurasian civilizations, even the distant Chinese ones, owed something to Sumerian antecedents.

Early Civilizations

What spark of genius prompted the world's first civilizations? Seemingly, none. Little about them suggests a higher form of human life. Essentially, there occurred a confluence and concentration of earlier innovations. Only the aggregate itself was strictly new. Pottery and basketry, woven and dyed clothing, horses and carts, oxen and plows, beer and bread, oil and wine, kingship and state religion—these came together with synergy in urban life. Urban environments exacerbated social inequality but also unleashed cultural dynamism.

Mesopotamia. The key was intensive, irrigated agriculture. Before cities, Mesopotamia was a parched mudflat that flooded periodically. In its southern reaches, near the Persian Gulf, the Sumerians started plowing. They also learned to control floods and channel water into complex, permanent systems of irrigation. Their dikes and canals transformed the flat landscape. Contrary to common belief, building these public works did not seem to require kingly power or slavery.

Instead, Mesopotamia's early public works drew on traditional patterns of labor obligation owed by all members of the community. Nor did the first Mesopotamian cities, insofar as we can tell, need kingly power to impose social discipline. Routine justice, as in divorce and murder trials, seems to have been meted out by various councils of elders and neighborhood assemblies, involving both men and women. War and warriors were not in evidence, and the earliest Sumerian cities were not originally walled. The city center was occupied by large houses of the gods, which do not seem to have been, or at least, were not principally the scene of sacrificial offerings. Rather, they were principally places of food storage and processing, weaving, and other activities of domestic production, done in the god's name and administered by a scribal bureaucracy.

By about 2900 BCE, however, Mesopotamia's early innocence had dissolved in a welter of temples, kings, war, warriors, and city walls. A cluster of Sumerian cities, each ruled by its own king, competed for dominance over the alluvial plain. By 2000 BCE, when the Epic of Gilgamesh was written down, one king often conquered the others temporarily, the beginnings of empire building on a miniature scale. The Sumerians had invented writing, inscribing their cuneiform script with a sharp wooden stylus on wet clay tablets. They used writing, at first, mostly to inventory their abundant agricultural produce and for various other kinds of record keeping. Their wheeled carts carried produce to the cities. The farming villages on the hillsides around Mesopotamia had been among the world's most prolific centers of original domestication. In addition to wheat for bread and barley for beer, the high-protein pulses garbanzos and lentils are from this part of the world. Wine grapes are, too, as is the historically important fiber crop, flax.

Channeling irrigation waters to evaporate in the desert led, over many centuries, to harmful salinization of Mesopotamian soil. Humankind's first intensively irrigated fields had to be gradually abandoned. Formerly great and glorious cities like Babylon had been built of mud brick and, over thousands of years, they dissolved into enormous piles of dirt. Gradually they were forgotten. European archeologists began to rediscover what we now know about the world's first civilization only in the 1890s.

The rediscovery of ancient Egypt was much easier. In the sphinx and the great pyramids, the ancient Egyptians had built stone monuments that the millennia could not erase. Parallel inscriptions in several languages on the famous Rosetta stone allowed Egyptian hieroglyphic writing to be deciphered in the 1830s. The ancient Egyptians' preparation of royal mummies for a comfortable daily life in eternity had helped archeologists reconstruct Egyptian society from the evidence found in tombs. Neither the earliest nor the most influential early civilization, Egypt's is nonetheless by far the most familiar.

Egypt. Not for nothing has Egypt been called the Gift of the Nile. The Nile River floods annually and, unlike wide and featureless Mesopotamia, the Nile valley is deep and narrow. Instead of trying to control and channel the flood, ancient Egyptian villagers moved seasonally to higher ground and waited for the waters to recede, an extremely ancient pattern, no doubt. The annual flooding renewed the fertility of the deep alluvium along the riverbanks. Allowing the annual floods to soak the soil and recede naturally prevented the buildup of mineral salts that eventually ruined Mesopotamian agriculture. The receding waters annually blurred the property lines between individual fields, so Egyptians learned land surveying by annually reestablishing boundaries. Then, to irrigate during the growing season, the river was always nearby. Ancient Egypt was a strip of land hundreds of miles long but only a few miles wide. There were no large cities like Babylon. Instead, the Egyptians created a complex suburban civilization with the river as its central axis. Everything in Egypt was on one side of the river or the other—fields, villages, temples, palaces, tombs. Transportation downriver happened courtesy of the current itself. Transportation upriver, with sails raised, was courtesy of the prevailing north wind.

Pakistan. The most mysterious early civilization is that of the Indus River valley. Given its size and its duration of a thousand years, it left relatively few cultural artifacts for us to interpret. Among the most common were small clay seals used to indicate the provenance of goods in the marketplace. They provide a good portion of our small Indus writing sample. (Our sample's small size is the main reason that Indus script has never been deciphered.) Yet, in land area, the Indus River civilization that emerged around 2500 BCE far exceeded both Egypt and Mesopotamia in land area, covering much of what is now Pakistan. Indus plowmen, like their Sumerian and Egyptian counterparts, planted wheat. The oxen that pulled its plows, reproduced in clay figurines, belonged to an entirely recognizable breed of Brahman cattle still typical of the Indian subcontinent. Two large

cities have been excavated in the Indus zone, both impressively engineered, standardized in layout and construction, with large public
buildings and sewage systems. We call them Harappa and Mohenjo
Daro, but we have no idea what their inhabitants called them. Like
earliest Uruk, Indus River archeological sites lack evidence of frequent warfare, temples, or royal palaces. The largest construction
appears to be a public bath. Given the perennial power of religious
ideas in India, it is interesting to notice that one Indus figurine shows
a man sitting in the classic lotus posture of meditation.

China. About when people were rediscovering early river-valley civilizations along the Tigris, Euphrates, Nile, and Indus, they rediscovered another one in the valley of China's Yellow River. Here again,
alluvial soils played their crucial role of unleashing the productive
potential of the ox-drawn plow, allowing populations to multiply
beyond what had been possible elsewhere. The alluvial soils of the
Yellow River valley are largely windborne, a gift of the winds that
blow from the steppe. In fact, the China's first civilization—ruled by
the Shang dynasty beginning around 1600 BCE—was stimulated as
much by the proximity of the steppe as by the Yellow River per se.
The herders of the steppe seem to have transmitted basic elements
of the Eurasia's later Neolithic cultural tool kit to China, the horse-
drawn chariot being one example.

Yellow River agriculture drew independently on two major Neolithic farming traditions, the earlier Yangshao (ca. 4000 BCE), which
had domesticated millet, and the Longshan (ca. 3000 BCE), which
included the first areas of rice cultivation. Of these, the later Longshan culture showed defensive town walls and rich tombs that archeologists expect to find on the verge of civilization. Sophisticated
and prosperous, although not really urban before 2000 BCE, China's extensive Neolithic farming cultures had produced ceremonial
objects of glasslike jade, using simple machines to grind, drill, and
polish them, well before the introduction of bronze metallurgy. The
earliest known Chinese city, Erlitou, appeared after 2000 BCE, fol-

lowed a few centuries later area by Shang cities—all obviously built on agricultural wealth. However, compared to Egyptian or Mesopotamian cities, their wealth had a more diffuse and distant origin, drawing on a larger hinterland. The people of the Yellow River grew not flax but hemp for fiber, as did other farmers all over Eurasia, and very early they developed another fiber domesticate, unique in the world, the silkworm. The beginnings of Chinese civilization along the Yellow River lacked monumental public constructions, an enduring trait of China's historical cities. The Shang dynasty did not even establish a permanent capital but rather circulated periodically in the territories it dominated, ruling from a series of temporary capitals.

Peru. Civilization began spontaneously at two places in the Americas as well. The oldest place, which arose more-or-less simultaneously with Sumerian civilization, was in Peru. Norte Chico, we call it, referring to a section of the Pacific coast north of Lima. (We have no idea what its inhabitants called it.) At Norte Chico, fishing in the seafood-rich currents off South America's Pacific coast supported a population density that became urban around 3500 BCE. The Norte Chico civilization drew on a Neolithic cultural kit quite different— and much more limited—than did the civilizations of Eurasia.

Eurasia. The crucial domestic animals of Eurasia (except for dogs) were all absent from the Americas. Plant domesticates abounded, on the other hand. The most important was maize, the grain of Central American origin that spread to South America. Coastal Peru is quite arid, so the grain fields of Norte Chico depended on irrigation. Streams descending from the Andes Mountains could be easily diverted onto the alluvial bottomlands that flank each watercourse. Weaving was an important part of the Neolithic cultural kit in the Andes. The farmers of Norte Chico grew cotton to weave fishing nets as well as clothing. The sea coast orientation of the cities at Norte Chico seems significant, given new ideas about Pacific seafaring in early human history. The cities of Norte Chico crumbled into the coastal desert of Peru about 2000 BCE and were rediscovered by archeologists only quite recently.

Mexico. Olmec civilization, on the east coast of Mexico, was likewise forgotten, despite its signature giant sculpted stone heads, eventually concealed by impenetrable clinging vines of tropical overgrowth. All other traces of the Olmec cities that flourished contemporaneously with China's Shang dynasty have now disappeared. In recent decades, archeologists have identified Olmec cities with pyramid mounds and ceremonial ball courts that eventually became standard throughout this part of America.

Olmec civilization, too, arose in river-borne alluvial soils. Alluvial soils are advantageously fertile, well watered and well drained even without plowing. Instead of plowing large fields, the Olmecs and related peoples planted crops in mixed garden plots that were much less vulnerable to pests and erosion. The American endowment of domesticated plants was extraordinarily rich, with staple foods provided by maize and beans, grown in conjunction. The Olmec cities were abandoned and eventually swallowed by the jungle around 400 BCE, but their maize-centered civilization was inherited by rising agricultural people who will be mentioned later.

IN SUM, large agricultural surpluses concentrated population and allowed the proliferation of specialized arts, trades, and commerce. Various human energies fed off one another. It is as though, by analogy with a nuclear fission reaction, a critical mass of population was reached, and cities appeared. Cities themselves were something qualitatively new, but the future potential of human association was not positively prefigured there. Instead, the first civilizations seem to have been fragile and, once they had disappeared, forgettable. Rather than a cherished discovery or an empowering cultural advance, civilization was the natural by-product of being successful farmers and having a lot of babies. In traditional historiography, however, the first civilizations appear as lights in the darkness. Let's consider the darkness.

Enter the Barbarians

Remember the herders who pioneered warrior culture on the Eurasian steppe? Impelled by drought, they flooded off the steppe and overwhelmed the remaining centers of Eurasian civilization between 1700 and 1200 BCE, imparting a lasting dynamic to world history. But it wasn't just steppe riders. The so-called barbarians were anyone who had remained "uncivilized."

Barbarian was originally a Greek slur for anyone not Greek. (Unable to speak properly, they said only *bar bar*, get it?) Having declined to admire the first civilizations, we will moreover decline to scorn the "barbarians," although we will continue use the word. Strictly speaking, they were anybody who escaped urban taxation. Despite having originated as a slur, the word *barbarian* evokes their presence in world history better than academic euphemisms like "mobile pastoralists." If the barbarians challenged civilization, who could blame them?

And, if civilization trembled, who could blame *it*? As bronze metallurgy was added to the shared Eurasian kit of basic cultural tools around 2000 BCE, the barbarian populations of the steppe were early adopters. Sintashta, the center of chariot manufacture in the Ural foothills, became an important scene of metallurgy as bronze axes, swords, and spear tips gradually replaced polished stone blades and points. The material culture of the steppe predisposed herding people to a warlike existence. The horse gave them speed of attack and escape. Numerous livestock gave them a mobile food source. Archery gave them a devastating weapon.

Steppe barbarians came in various colors. They represent a way of life rather than an ethnic group. Some of the first seem to have been blonde, light-skinned, and blue-eyed. Bronze-age mummies matching this description have been found all over Central Asia, as far as the deserts of northwest China. People of more eastern Asian extraction—like the much later Huns and Mongols—dominated the steppe increasingly over time.

What all herders had in common, though, was a desire for certain things that herders cannot produce. They also shared a remarkable military capacity. Steppe herders learned to ride and, eventually, to shoot arrows from horseback, from a young age. Before the age of mounted warriors, however, came the age of chariots.

Chariots ruled the battlefields of Eurasia for a thousand years. Fighting from a chariot demanded special weapons and constant practice. Steppe people developed a short composite bow (made of animal horn and ligament as well as wood) that was short enough to handle freely in the vehicle's restricted standing space. As barbarians began to test their strength against the world's first civilizations, they encountered steady success.

Ruled by warriors, kept on a permanent war footing, drought-driven steppe barbarians pushed west into Europe, south into the Middle East and India, and east toward China.

There was no stopping them. Their onslaught initiated the ceaseless churn and struggle that would characterize world history over the next three thousand or so years. A repeating pattern emerged: A barbarian king occupies a city. This is a prize that, for the most part, cannot be carried away on horseback. A city is a golden-egg-laying goose—no more goose, no more gold. But these are herders and warriors with no idea how to govern a city. They have to learn from the conquered citizens. Gradually the city absorbs the rude invaders, who eventually become civilized and "soft." Now they are no match, anymore, for their barbarian cousins out on the plains. When the next wave of barbarians looms up, it triumphs, captures the city, and the cycle repeats. This brief telling is a caricature created by ancient historians, but it captures the gist. The actual historical events involve messy accidents like climate change. Historians and climate scientists have found signs of a half century of particularly severe drought across much of Afro-Eurasia from 2200 to 2150 BCE. Inescapably, the long drying trend put pressure on both farmers and herders. As farmers hunkered down and farmed harder, herders began to migrate.

A people known as Hittites began moving south from the steppe in search of greener pastures, eventually filtering into the grassy central highlands of Anatolia. The Hittites were herders who sacrificed horses to sky gods and deployed archer charioteers in war. They ravaged northern Mesopotamia and, in 1595 BCE, sacked great, glorious Babylon, perhaps then the world's largest city. Then the Hittites decided to settle down. Between 1800 and 1200 BCE, a number of Hittite kingdoms emerged in Anatolia, but the copies were always a bit rustic, never as elegant and refined as the Mesopotamian original.

The civilized people of Mesopotamia were shaken by this encounter. Farming harder only accelerated the salinization of irrigated fields. Some cities ceased to exist, and others shrank as harvests declined. Meanwhile, with the Hittites lurking in the north, another wave of climate change expanded the Saharan and Arabian deserts, pushing another wave of displaced barbarian herders into southern Mesopotamia. The beleaguered city dwellers called the newcomers Amorites, "people from the west." Around 2000 BCE, barbarian invaders of various stripes pretty much took over Mesopotamia. They made Babylon their capital city. From now on, Mesopotamian kingdoms would deploy archer charioteers themselves. Meanwhile, new rulers of the world's oldest civilization made sure to endorse the old stories about quasi-divine hero kings. Warrior kings were now all the rage. The old story of Gilgamesh was incised on wet clay tablets at about this point.

In Egypt, the extreme droughts of circa 2150–2050 BCE interrupted the annual flooding of the Nile and, effectively, toppled the Old Kingdom that had ruled Egyptians during a string of dynasties. The problem was not invaders. The power of the Egyptian state seems, rather, to have been undermined internally. Reestablished as the Middle Kingdom, the Egyptian state had been strengthened ideologically by the systematic promotion of a new principal deity closely identified with the pharaoh. In addition, a new prosperity made possible the extension of ancient Egypt's most precious good, the hope for life after death, which, in the Old Kingdom, had been reserved for the pharaoh alone. In the Middle Kingdom, Egyptian warriors, priests, scribes, even merchants would attempt to join the eternal party. Then outside invaders put an end to Egypt's Middle Kingdom. The Hyksos, they were called. They spoke a Semitic language, so they weren't steppe people. But their use of horse chariots and the composite bow tells us they had the playbook. The Hyksos ruled northern Egypt for about a hundred years.

After this short intermission, Egyptian defenders regrouped, became charioteers, and managed to expel the invaders using their own weapon against them. The army of Egypt's newly aggressive New Kingdom began to advance into Palestine and Syria, where Pharaoh Thutmose III led almost a thousand chariots into the 1469 BCE Battle of Megiddo.

Meanwhile, drought-battered Indus River settlements had been shrinking for centuries when steppe barbarians appeared on the scene with their chariots around 1500 BCE. We have no direct evidence of interactions between the Indus River people and these barbarians, who called themselves Aryans. One way or another, though, the cities of the Indus River faded away forever, and the barbarians gradually spread themselves across the north of the Indian subcontinent. Like all steppe barbarians, they were herders who had to learn agriculture from the people they were invading. The invasion created a permanent north-south gradient in Indian culture and demography. In India today, northerners are of lighter complexion, probably reflecting light skin color among the barbarian invaders.

Nazi ideologues of the early twentieth century adopted the term *Aryan* to signify their fantasy of descent from supposedly all-conquering racial heroes of prehistory. Hitler personally reinvented the swastika, an ancient Indian good luck symbol, as the Nazi brand. We cannot blame the historical Aryans for Nazi fantasies, obviously.

The real Aryans were just a typical chariot-driving, horse-sacrificing, sky-god worshipping steppe people. Their complex ritual sacrifices and their priestly use of sacred hallucinogenic drinks were detailed in the Sanskrit recitations called Vedas. The Aryans also brought with them the seeds of the caste system that would become elaborated, over thousands of years, into the most distinctive element of Indian civilization.

As for China, at the eastern end of the steppe, barbarians arrived somewhat later, around 1200 BCE, impelled by yet another wave of climatic drying. In China, they found nothing so imposing as Babylon for them to plunder. Still, the burgeoning walled agricultural towns of the Yellow River valley had just what the newcomers wanted, and they had it wholesale. Shang bronze working was the best in the world. And then there was silk, the most luxurious of textiles. China produced a lot of basic goods that steppe people could easily carry home to the yurt. As a result, the barbarian onslaught had a different character in China, involving war, certainly, but also involving more trade. Above all, it was more protracted than elsewhere. Indeed, the perennial presence of steppe people along the China's northern borders became a central theme of Chinese history, spawning several of its most powerful imperial dynasties

The barbarian challenge therefore energized the Shang dynasty rather than toppling it. Eventually, the inhabitants of Yellow River valley towns showed a strong influence from their rustic, horse-riding neighbors. The influence was strongest at the top. The Shang dynasty's preference for temporary capitals has a whiff of the steppe about it. Moreover, noble warriors of the Yellow River valley soon constructed war chariots of their own. They had larger wheels compared to the standard Eurasian model, allowing them to move over rougher ground, and the wider platform carried three men rather than two. Shang cities eventually deployed thousands of chariots and imported thousands of steppe ponies to pull them.

Shang kings ruled only a small portion of what is today northern China. Yet Shang claims form the seed of the unified Chinese Empire.

Fully a thousand years would pass before emperors of China actually ruled most of the country. And herders from the steppe would remain important political players in Chinese history until modern times. Still, one way or another, despite many ups and downs and periods of fragmentation, and also despite many outside contributions (like tea, rice, and Buddhism), the civilization of the Yellow River was never obliterated and replaced. Rather, its material culture, its script and language, its myths and legends, became the dominant element of all subsequent Chinese civilization. It is this continuity with its beginnings (not the earliness of its first appearance) that makes Chinese civilization particularly ancient.

Cradles of Despotism

Around 1000 BCE, warriors ruled all the so-called cradles of civilization. In many ways, these probably weren't very healthy or attractive places to live. Domestic animals and high population densities made early agricultural populations vulnerable to epidemics, and the first city dwellers were no doubt even more so. Rather than growing, urban populations tended to decline without a steady flow of new arrivals. Politically and socially, rather than being something superior, the first civilizations gradually became caricatures of despotism. In many of them, kings and priests created oppressive institutions of social control, the global beginnings of state power.

Royal power and social stratification became closely tied to state religions. Warrior leadership busily elevated claims to absolute rule by divine right. Not just social inequality, but also out-and-out slavery of various sorts, became normal in early cities, probably affecting a large portion of the population. The pharaoh of Egypt, for example, ruled as a living god on Earth. The entire state was his household, and all the priests, his householders. The most eternal landmarks ever constructed, the Egyptian pyramids, were residences for a royal afterlife. Claims to divinity led to inbreeding in royal families, a problem well documented in the genetic analysis of certain mummified pharaohs. Castrated servants called eunuchs guarded royal harems.

Feuding Mesopotamian kings did not exactly claim to be gods. They imagined a pantheon of rival gods who directed human fortunes. Each city had its patron deity in the pantheon. Sumerian society was structured by the activities of each city's temples, a major part of the urban landscape. The ziggurats, or step pyramids, that gave Mesopotamian cities their skylines for a thousand years, were not tombs like the Egyptian pyramids but rather temples on a high-rise platform. And in one of those temples, at least, Sumerian kings seem to have enacted the joining of spiritual and mundane in ritual coitus with a high priestess. It may have been a pantomime, but the point was clear. Mesopotamian kings were intimate with divine power.

The Shang kings of the Yellow River valley showed their intimacy with divine power differently. In quasi-public ceremonies they queried their deceased royal ancestors about important questions. Would spring bring sufficient rains? Would enemies attack in the fall? And especially, would the empress have a son? Presumably, from their heavenly vantage point, the royal ancestors would know. The question was inscribed on an oracle bone, which was then placed in the fire until it cracked. The answer to the questions could be divined in the shatter marks and official record made of it. The Shang king was called the Son of Heaven.

State power seems to have emerged more slowly in the Americas. Nonetheless, early Olmec society seems to have been stratified and warrior oriented. Those Olmec giant stone heads, one of which brooded over each Olmec city, apparently represented kings. Many religious practices associated the Aztecs and the Mayas originated, in actuality, with the Olmecs. Among these, they construction of stepped pyramids topped, like ziggurats, by temples. And in these temples, Olmec kings seem to have drawn their own blood and burned it in sacrifice to the gods on behalf of their communities.

The strong Aztec and Inca states that existed much later, at the time of the European invasion, had built strong links between royal power and religious ideology.

Cities, writing, standing armies, and theocratic ideology allowed warrior kings to create lasting power structures. Warrior nobles saw their divinely sanctioned superiority over commoners codified by statute and chiseled in stone. Extreme social inequality became a fact of civilized life, automatically assumed, rarely challenged. Once the assumption was in place, the main job of subordination had already been accomplished, the script had been approved, and now it had only to be performed over and over.

Urban spaces were the crucial stages for the enactment of privilege in daily life. In early cities, states commissioned monuments and works of public art, and invested significant wealth in maintaining temples and offering sacrifices to the city's gods. In public spaces like theaters and marketplaces, commoners—not to mention slaves—constantly performed the deference of those accustomed to serve towards their habitual masters. Meanwhile, the ruling classes cultivated contacts, controlled offices and resources, strolled and flirted, frequented the temple, had access to the palace. They inhabited mansions, wore garments and jewelry signifying superior status. Their dominance was given permanence by incessant repetition, as the poor scattered to make way for the rich, bore their sedan chairs through the streets, and served them hand and foot. Armed force, another crucial attribute of state making, was concentrated in cities—barracks, prisons, and fortifications being typically urban. Early states maintained professional military specialists to enforce laws, collect taxes, and imprison or execute offenders.

The intensification of social subordination affected sexuality and gender patterns. Strict patriarchy and formal prostitution were normal attributes of the first civilizations. Throngs of wives and concubines, the conquering warrior's prize, were a standard monarchical perquisite. The dynastic principle of inherited rule made the king's paternity a matter of state. Eunuchs, physically unable to cuckold the king, were considered ideal guards, servants, and companions for the residential inner sanctum of the palace. Cut off from family life, palace eunuchs had less to distract them from institutional loyalties, supposedly, because they had no descendants to favor. Eunuchs became state scribes and bureaucrats across Asia. It was a refinement of dominion that the Americas, short on herder know-how, never developed.

Despite this despotism, cities became productive intercultural meeting places and the scenes of regulated markets that functioned using standard weights and measures, not to mention coins of a specific value. Cities were the site of law courts, the venues of public festivities enabled by state largesse. Specialization in any complex trade was likewise an urban phenomenon. Writing was almost exclusively urban. Only in cities, because of long-distance commercial and administrative connections, could historical people have an awareness of the wider world. Only in cities could they see professional performances, visit a temple, or act as citizens, participating actively in self-governance. The things we regard as high artistic and intellectual achievements were invariably urban. Cities became, and remained ever afterward, a privileged venue of human life.

That was their true spark of genius, a result rather than a cause of urbanization. But when their agricultural base eroded, early civilizations subsided and vanished. The cities of Peru's Norte Chico civilization, those of Mexico's Olmec civilization, and those of Pakistan's Indus River civilization show no signs of having been wiped out in a storm of barbarian violence. Instead, their decline, like that of most other lost civilizations in world history, seems to have occurred simply because they lost the ability to feed their dense populations. Natural climate change and human-made degradation of the landscape are the usual suspects. Contagious diseases no doubt played a frequent role as well. When the urban meeting places were abandoned, the civilizational spark winked out and . . . life went on. How memorable can they have been if they were so soon and so completely forgotten?

Our basic model of premodern societies is almost complete. For-aging bands, clans, villages, kingdoms, civilizations—and shortly, empires. Imperial chronicles tell a story of incessant dynastic wars and family conflicts, privilege and power, rapine and plunder, back-stabbing, treachery, and murder most foul. No topic occupies more pages of world history than dynastic politics, an endlessly recycling fable of good guys and bad guys, distinguished by little more than their particular aristocratic family connections, or lack thereof. Most blow-by-blow imperial histories are just costume drama with little factual basis or actual significance. We will not go too deep into those weeds but instead stick with basic outlines.

Quick, who was the most famous conqueror ever?

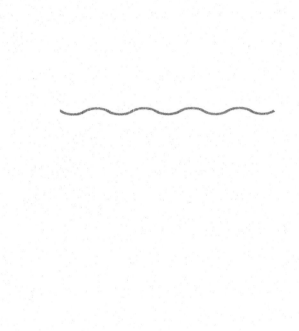

CHAPTER FOUR

Alexander

The conqueror Alexander the Great, depicted here at the decisive Battle of Gaugamela, was like a rock star of the ancient world. His image, defined by the flowing hairstyle visible on circulating coinage, was imitated for hundreds of years after the hero's demise in 323 BCE. Alexander was a paragon of the warrior cult, a champion of Greek civilization, and an empire builder. Empire building is this chapter's central focus. Empires constitute an unavoidable fact of world history. Along with kingdoms, empires have organized our geopolitics for over two thousand years.

What makes an empire imperial? An empire is something beyond a kingdom. A king rules over a country, whereas an emperor rules over many countries. An emperor is a king of kings. Thus, an empire is normally larger and, above all, more multiethnic than a kingdom. Empires project monarchy onto a broader and more complex field. The basic dynastic principles—patriarchy, inheritance, connections to a privileged nobility—are the same. A few women have ruled empires, but they have been a tiny minority. Hatshepsut, the only powerful empress to rule Egypt during its millenarian history, had herself portrayed as male in order not to confuse her subjects, in whose minds command and masculinity went inescapably together.

The world of empires that emerges in this chapter—stratified, warrior-led, focused on cities but predominantly rural, and founded on the productive power of downtrodden agricultural peasantries—

continued as the basic model of civilization until only two hundred years ago. It comprises most of what we usually regard as world history.

Foragers and "uncivilized" farmers and herders still inhabited most of the world, by far. Eventually, all would be sucked into the vortex of world civilization. In the meantime, they stood on the margins of it. This chapter takes us through the Bronze Age and the Iron Age (old-fashioned but still useful terms), from roughly 1500 BCE until the dawn of the Common Era. During those years, world civilization occupied a broad, mid-latitude swath of Eurasia, from the Mediterranean Sea to the East China Sea, as well as small areas in Central and South America. Eurasian civilizations shared much in common but were only dimly aware of each other. When Alexander conquered the "entire known world," it stretched only from Greece to India.

Alexander was not looking for connections, anyway. A true imperialist, he was on a mission to impose his own vision of a better world, one in which everyone would speak Greek. For Alexander, Europe was not an object of interest. His famous adversaries, the Persians, were the imperialists to beat. The Persian Empire, the first really large one in world history, defined the "known world" that Alexander set out to conquer.

City-States and Empire

Now the Mediterranean Sea enters our story.

The eastern Mediterranean Sea drew civilizing influences from nearby Egypt and Mesopotamia. When climate change propelled barbarian herders off the Eurasian steppe, as happened around 2100 BCE and again around 1200 BCE, some of them discovered the shores of the eastern Mediterranean. There they met and mingled with civilized people who had preceded them, and soon enough, they began building cities themselves. Also, over time, they became "sea people" adapted to their new environment, leaving their steppe ways (but not their chariots) behind, to become the world's earliest known routine seafaring traders. Their trading network reached eventually all the way around the Mediterranean and the Black Sea.

Various sea peoples settled the eastern Mediterranean coast from Greece to Palestine and, most especially, they inhabited many islands, large and small. We have one glimpse of what they replaced. At the very beginning of European civilization stand the Minoan people, who built palace settlements in Crete as early as 2000 BCE. Their island life seems to have been relatively secure, and their palaces were not notably fortified. Their graceful art gives prominence, not to warriors or war chariots, but to authoritative women. Then, on the heels of the Minoans came the steppe people, Mycenaean Greeks of Trojan-War fame, who settled the mainland of Greece and subjugated the Minoans, destroying their distinctive culture around 1400 BCE. The most intrepid seafarers of all were the Phoenicians, whose main settlements were Tyre (off the coast of Lebanon) and Carthage, on the African coast near Sicily.

Seaborne trade was the key to Mediterranean life. To avoid the clutches of mainland empires, sea peoples preferred to perch their settlements on islands or remote seacoasts. Their chief routes along the coast of North Africa and southern Europe followed the winds and the tides in a mostly counterclockwise direction around the Mediterranean Sea, with frequent stops to trade. Sea peoples planted wheat and barley in the rocky, thin Mediterranean soils. They built tubby sailing vessels to carry wine, olive oil, timber, and metal ore, always with the wind pushing from behind. They also deployed sleek galleys driven by rank upon rank of oars, the world's first purpose-built warships, their prows armed with rams to perforate the hulls of other warships. Compared with the civilizations of Egypt, Mesopotamia, India, or China, Mediterranean sea peoples worked on a very small scale. They governed themselves without the benefit of a powerful or numerous priesthood. Their characteristic social organization was a single urban center surrounded by a small hinterland—a city-state.

The Greeks were the most numerous, and by far the best known, of these newcomers to Mediterranean shores. Amusingly, they arrived on the scene as barbarians of the sort whom the Greeks later mocked so mercilessly. Today, Greek mythology, philosophy, art, literature, and architecture have virtually defined high civilization in Western popular culture. We often envision the Greeks all by themselves, as players on an empty stage or, at most, busy fighting cinematic throngs of dehumanized Persians. We dote on the cultural achievements of golden-age Athens, a leading city-state, obviously, yet only one among dozens. We identify with Greek thought, Greek sculpture, Greek resistance to Persian invasion. We reenact our celebration of Greek culture periodically at the Olympic Games, which began as an athletic contest among Greek city-states. We run marathons (not me, personally, I confess) without knowing that the race commemorates an Athenian victory over Persia. In the United States, our government and university buildings long imitated Greek temple architecture.

Ancient Greece holds a unique place in the Western imagination. We see it, with some reason, as a wellspring of modernity. Yet we need to imagine the Greeks as actors on a stage crowded with other actors. Around 1000 BCE, the Greeks were typical barbarian invaders, with their steppe-derived language, chariots, and sky gods. The story of the Trojan War, recounted in Homer's *Iliad*, shows their intense focus on patriarchy and the warrior cult. Meanwhile, a significant portion of the Greek population were war captives held in slavery. Greek war galleys were rowed by slaves chained to their benches, doomed to go down with a sinking ship. At the time of the Trojan War, the well-known cultural achievements of golden age Athens still lay a half millennium in the future.

Mediterranean city-states were micro societies when compared with the great empires rising across Afro-Eurasia in the last millennium BCE. Micro societies, even war-oriented ones, were somewhat egalitarian by comparison with empires. They did not lend themselves to the most extreme concentrations of wealth and power. City-states had temples and gods but were not ruled by a priestly or scribal caste. Warrior kings had less need for ideological hocus-pocus to overawe a few thousand subjects. A handful of aristocratic families could govern a minor city-state through appeal to traditional authority, without trumped up claims to divine backing. The Greeks called that arrangement *oligarchy,* rule by a few. It amounted to patriarchy writ large. The head of each aristocratic clan governed his own family and sat on a sort of executive committee of his peers. Sometimes, all the free, high-status males—the citizens—shared power by voting. Given the proportion of subjugated women and slaves in the Greek societies, citizens always comprised a small fraction of the population.

Compared with foragers, the Greeks were hardly egalitarian. And yet they represented something obviously different from the general tendency, observable throughout Eurasia, to create larger and larger political entities, with steeper and steeper social hierarchies, built on the notion that rulers were gods, or godlike, or at the very least, had a direct, ongoing connection to divine authority. Some people in Greek society enjoyed an intellectual and artistic freedom that more theocratic states rarely permitted. This was the rare genius of ancient Greek culture. Ironically, Alexander's attempt to create a Greek-speaking world empire was the beginning of its end. Let's observe how, well before Alexander, this empire building got started.

After 1000 BCE, the Neo-Assyrian Empire, the first notable imperial project in world history, dominated all the kingdoms of Mesopotamia and the eastern shore of the Mediterranean Sea from the Neo-Assyrian capital at Babylon. The Neo-Assyrian god Ashur was officially expansionist, tasking his worshippers with territorial aggression. The god's attitude was tirelessly publicized, as well, by inscriptions and images. The surging ambition of Neo-Assyrian royalty expressed itself in elaborate public architecture and ceremonies. The walls of Neo-Assyrian palaces were carved with images of victories and conquests won by the emperor. In these images, we can witness the imperial war machine in action, rank upon rank of chariots, troops bearing spear and shield, besieging enemy fortifications, taking plunder and enslaving prisoners. War is a glory in Neo-Assyrian ideology, and empire is an end in itself. Or rather, the end lay in the benefits that empire would bring to the conquerors. Ashur's divine plan for the Neo-Assyrian Empire was to extend it, finally, to the whole world.

We must doubt the divine origin of this message. Rather, we should see it as a standard imperial ideology. If divine favor explains and justifies aggressive warfare, and conquest makes you rich, then the gods are obviously on your side. We cannot doubt that powerful men—Assyrian nobles, royalty, warriors, and high priests—espoused this ideology partly because they desired the fruits of empire. The Neo-Assyrian ruling class believed that empire was good because, after all, it had been good for *them*. If Ashur and the other gods told them what they wanted to hear, they had little reason to question it.

Once nobles, royalty, warriors, and high priests were on the same page, the gods supplied ideological confirmation, possibly with a little help from their friends. That is the way that a political ideology always works. It helps unify and mobilize a society around political goals that favor those in power. Assyrian imperialists needed ideological falderal to enthuse the poor devils who would die like flies in expansionist wars.

Imperialist ideologies could motivate expansionist wars, but wars were won by men and weapons. The Neo-Assyrian war machine inaugurated an age of large standing armies, much more numerous than in the past, not recruited for a specific fight, but rather kept on a permanent war footage, training and doing what off-duty soldiers do in any epoch. They carried weapons, not of bronze now, but of iron, and the distinction is significant. Like the other armies discussed later in this chapter, the Neo-Assyrian armies were Iron-Age armies.

People had learned to work bronze first, beginning around 3300 BCE, because bronze starts with copper, which is very soft and easy to refine. But copper is a rather scarce element, and so is tin, which hardens copper to make bronze. Bronze was therefore rare and expensive, normally devoted to the ceremonial and military purposes of warrior nobles. On Bronze-Age battlefields, only warriors of some wealth and status wore bronze armor and carried bronze swords. As recounted in the *Iliad*, bronze-armored princes in bronze-fitted chariots dueled like World War One flying aces, with humble foot soldiers acting as their audience and ground crews.

Iron, in contrast, was metal for the masses, one of the most abundant elements on Earth. Iron was less common than copper or tin above ground but much more abundant beneath it. On the other hand, finding iron, mining it, smelting it, and forging it was a technical challenge. Once iron making had been mastered, however, iron became inexpensive and available for a multitude of uses. Now blacksmiths made farm tools, not just rims for the fancy spoked wheels of war chariots. Blacksmiths now made plowshares as well as swords. Plows with durable blades of forged iron could open their furrows outside alluvial floodplains, vastly expanding arable land resources. The use of iron became notable after 1000 BCE.

Iron-Age armies became larger, as required for empire building. Ranks of infantry with spears and shields displaced chariots, which moved to a supporting role—often a symbolic one. Chariots remained the battlefield conveyance of generals, for example. Moreover, long after they disappeared from the battlefield, chariots continued to compete in brutal public races kept alive by public enthusiasm for the warrior cult. Meanwhile, fighting from horseback was still virtually impossible because stirrups were still not used, and without them, only a rider of the as-if-born-on-horseback variety can swing a heavy sword or skewer enemies with his lance without losing his balance. Therefore, the large standing armies of the Neo-Assyrian and other early empires were composed of massed infantry. Large standing armies had the manpower to raise fortifications and construct siege engines. Battering rams knocked down city gates that tried to shut out the blessings of empire. Siege towers as high as the wall of a besieged city could remove the defenders' advantage of height. Tunnels could undermine city walls and collapse them in places, creating breaches for invaders to gain entry and commence the slaughter.

Finally, the Neo-Assyrian Empire devised new forms of subjugation to keep conquered people in check. Deportations and forced-labor drafts relocated entire populations. Among those affected were the Hebrews, whose imperial relocation is remembered in the Bible as their Babylonian Captivity. The Hebrews' relocation was not a special punishment but rather a general strategy, one later used by empires around the world. (The Inca Empire of South America did the same with conquered groups over two thousand years later.) People uprooted and resettled among unfamiliar neighbors lost the strength that they had possessed on their home ground, becoming dependent on their imperial masters. By swallowing Egypt, the Neo-Assyrian "big fish" managed to engulf the two oldest centers of world civilization.

Then an even bigger fish appeared.

The Persians descended from the Eurasian steppe during the second millennium BCE by approximately the same route as their Aryan cousins. Whereas the Aryans entered India, their Persian cousins went to Iran. Unified by their first great ruler Cyrus during the 500s BCE, the Persians built the first empire that sprawled across several world regions. Starting from the Iranian plateau just south of the Caspian Sea, overlooking Mesopotamia, the Persians took over all Anatolia, then all the territories once ruled by the Neo-Assyrian Empire. Once in control of the entire Middle East, the Persians added the territories of Egypt, modern Afghanistan, and part of Central Asia, as far as the western edge of what is today China. This was the empire that Alexander eventually overthrew and rebranded as his own.

At first, the Persians had the profile of all steppe warriors. The Greek historian Herodotus was obsessed with them. Herodotus said Persian males learned only "to ride a horse, draw a bow, and tell the truth." But like the Greeks and other ex-barbarians, they didn't let rustic beginnings hold them back. The empire of Cyrus and his dynasty fielded the largest armies ever seen. Persian armies deployed both camel and elephant corps. They marched tens of thousands of soldiers across temporary pontoon bridges that could span even the wide and powerful current of the Bosporus that divides Europe from Asia. The Persian Empire also deployed the first regular, full-time navy (crewed by seafaring subject peoples, such as Phoenicians and Greeks).

But more important than their war-making prowess were the more subtle techniques of what might be called Persian soft power. Unlike Neo-Assyrian emperors who wanted to appear terrifying and implacable, Cyrus projected an ethical persona. When adding non-Persians to his empire, Cyrus claimed to be liberating them from their own oppressive kings. Thus, he released the Hebrews, whom the Neo-Assyrians had relocated to Babylon, allowing them to return to Israel. Cyrus died on the battlefield, as befitted a warrior monarch, but not before creating a wide and lasting reputation as a model ruler. It was Cyrus the Great who first famously claimed to be "king of kings."

Persian soft power was aided by religious ideas that set the Persians apart from earlier imperialists. These ideas were attributed to the Persian prophet Zoroaster who had lived (if he was a historical person) possibly five hundred years earlier. Zoroaster resisted the prevailing glorification of war and blood sacrifice. Zoroastrianism presented human life as a contest between good and evil. God favors what is good, so all people should seek the good and shun the bad. An account of their actions will be presented at a final judgment, with consequences for an afterlife. The same general idea is found today in both the Islamic and Christian traditions.

Zoroastrianism was the first major religion to emphasize universal ethical principles. Prior to this, ethics did not figure centrally in religious activities. For example, the shamans of foraging bands had entered the spirit world to restore health, exorcise spirit invaders, and learn about future events. Their spirit work was normally commissioned by the affected parties. The gods who supposedly dwelled in Sumerian temples were asked, above all, to favor their worshippers and smite their worshippers' enemies. The gods were pleased by the attention and loyalty paid to them by worshippers, especially in the form of animal sacrifices. For a helpful sample of amoral deities,

Westerners might call to mind the vain, greedy, squabbling gods and goddess of Mount Olympus, who embody beauty, power, vanity, wisdom, love, life, industry, creativity, war—anything but good vs. evil.

Zoroastrianism was a state religion and an enabling ideology for the Persian imperial project. And yet the goal was ostensibly a universal one, and the Persian emperor ostensibly served it rather than standing above it. Supposedly the emperor was commander in chief of the earthly good guys, specifically endorsed and empowered to organize their triumph over evil. He had to show himself worthy of that awesome responsibility. He had to show, in his own behavior, that he deserved his power. The result was a more persuasive and therefore stronger ideology of rule. Holding monarchs to a higher standard may have improved their performance, too.

The Achaemenid dynasty, founded by Cyrus, lasted for more than six centuries. Cyrus's son, Darius, took up where his father had left off, adding new kingdoms to what was becoming a multicultural patchwork. Darius also inaugurated a formal administrative structure, dividing his empire into provinces, each headed by a *satrap*, or imperial governor. The Persian Empire combined an impulse to systematize with a conservative respect for existing traditions. Egypt was the Fourth Satrapy, Syria the Fifth, and so on. To some degree, each satrapy was allowed to exercise its own local traditions. In imperial statuary, for example, each satrapy might be represented as a figure wearing distinctive regional costume. To foster communication across the largest political unit so far assembled, the Persians built a system of roads, most notably the Royal Road that connected the Persian heartlands with distant Anatolia, 1,600 miles away. Persian roads facilitated the movement of troops and trade, as well as the regularly established system of postal couriers, a sort of pony express. In fact, it was Persian couriers who were deterred by "neither rain, nor snow, nor gloom of night" according to the famous quotation (Herodotus, again), often applied to later postal services. The Persian Empire officially encouraged trade, partly because taxing it provided major revenue for imperial coffers. And nothing facilitated trade like money, the medium by which any product or service could be exchanged for any other. The Persian Empire created the world's first bimetallic currency by issuing gold coins as well as silver.

To administer its comprehensive system of taxation and tribute, the Persian Empire needed a written language that all its bureaucrats could understand. In classic imperial parvenu style, the Persians adopted, not their own language, but Aramaic, as the language of their imperial bureaucracy. Aramaic was a Semitic language, a Middle Eastern lingua franca, spoken by many of the empire's non-Persian subjects. Half a millennium later, Aramaic was the language of Jesus and his disciples. More to the point, however, Aramaic had been the bureaucratic language of the Neo-Assyrians, part of the already two-thousand-year-old scribal tradition of Mesopotamia. Conquest created empires, but as the Persians were learning, communications and organization maintained imperial control.

The Achaemenid dynasty had no close competitors in its heyday. But road building, innovative engineering, philosophical and religious thought, the development of trade and markets—these things were happening also in parts of Eurasia where powerful empires were still absent.

Indian and Chinese Kingdoms

The world's two major population centers, India and China, also practiced sophisticated agriculture, built cities, and engaged in diverse urban trades. The agricultural civilizations of northern India and northern China were each divided into many culturally similar, yet chronically warring, kingdoms. They saw no surge of empire building until the third century BCE. Each, in different ways, was a land apart.

The Indian subcontinent sits on its own tectonic plate, one that has collided with the rest of Asia, forming the gigantic up-thrust pile of the Himalayas. Mountains separate India from the Eurasian steppe almost entirely—with one major exception, the Khyber Pass, a narrow corridor that today connects the far north of Pakistan with Central Asia.

Historically, this door between Central Asia and India has seen a veritable parade of invaders beginning, at least as far as we know, with the Aryans who entered India from the north around 1500 BCE. Anyone arriving from frigid, arid, windswept Central Asia was likely to look at the Punjab region, where the Khyber Pass opens onto fertile, well-watered subtropical plains, as a kind of paradise. Over a couple thousand years, outsiders kept arriving. Just about any conquering horde that happened to be storming up or down the Eurasian steppe might make a detour through the Khyber Pass to warm up, plunder a bit, and leave some children in northern India. The cumulative effect was to create not a melting pot so much as a stew pot, in which constituent elements remained distinct but acquired a common flavor.

The modern Indian caste system has roots in this period. It provided rules to govern social interactions. In that sense, it was an adaptive, cooperative system, a way of allowing potentially conflicting people to live together, preventing scuffles by predetermining, and clarifying, relationships among elements of a diverse population. It is also a system of social control, among the most elaborate human pecking orders ever devised. Many traditional societies have some sort of caste structure. What are castes, exactly?

Castes are social categories defined by birth. Caste status can rarely be altered in an individual's lifetime. Caste is often contrasted with social class. Both are a kind of stratification, but castes are defined by birth, and classes by wealth, which can change. The Indian caste system is based on four social categories, called *varnas*, that are mentioned the Vedas, the oldest Sanskrit scriptures. The highest category is that of Brahmins, who exercised priestly functions, most importantly the fire sacrifices that Aryan sky gods apparently craved. The second highest category was that of Kshatriyas, warrior landowners, the source of practical leadership in this society. Kings were normally Kshatriyas. Then came Vaishyas, who worked the land and practiced trades and commerce. The lowest varna, Shudras, comprised people who served others, doing anything considered dirty work. The Shudra caste was probably invented as way of incorporating non-Aryan menial laborers into the conquering society.

Gradually over many centuries, a new level of complexity was added to the Indian caste system. Each of the varnas was divided into subcategories called *jatis*. Rather than just abstract categories, these were actual groups of people. There were hundreds of jatis organized around particular lineages and trades. Members of a jati followed strict, complex rules regarding diet and interactions with other jatis. Jatis had their own elders at the village level, too. This built-in web of social control meant that kings and law courts governed less. Less power to warriors and bureaucrats meant more power to Brahmins. The rules governing the varnas and jatis were regarded as religious rules. And those most invested in religion were the Brahmins, whose social role was to study, memorize, and apply religious texts. The more seriously people took castes, the more highly they regarded Brahmins. As the titular top caste, Brahmins were both the appointed caretakers and the chief beneficiaries of the system.

The keystone of the caste system was not specifically a part of it. *Samsara*, the Indian idea of cyclical reincarnation, is a common background belief among all the subcontinent's native religions. It is not mentioned in the Vedas, which the Aryans brought with them from the steppe, but only in the Upanishads, religious texts that emerged later in the urban society of northern India. Samsara was probably a commonsense idea already to whoever made that Indus River figurine that appears to be meditating in the lotus position.

Samsara is both sublime recognition of universal spiritual oneness and, unfortunately, a logical reinforcer of the caste system. Samsara involves not only reincarnation but the transmigration of souls throughout the living world, involving animals, people, even gods. One's karma (one's personal score in a cosmic earned merit system) determines whether one's next reincarnation will be desirable or not. Playing the social role specific to one's caste is a chief source of karmic merit. Therefore, for a lowly Shudra, the best way to reincarnate as something better in the next life is to excel, for now, in the role of lowly Shudra. In a famous scene from Hindu mythology, when the warrior Arjuna sees his own family prepared to fight him on a battle-field, he hesitates. Should he fight and possibly kill them? Of course, says his chariot driver (who is none other than the Lord Krishna, incognito), for Arjuna is a Kshatriya. He must play his appointed role as warrior to fulfill his karma.

Such stories of Indian gods and goddesses, like the Greek stories of the Trojan War, were sung in verse from memory, rather than written down. Paradoxically, that is why religion figures so power-fully in Indian history. The Vedas, Upanishads, and other religious texts were passed down in Brahmin families by strict memorization. Meanwhile, the inhabitants of north Indian cities used writing for nonreligious purposes. Unfortunately, they wrote mostly on dried palm leaves, which provided a paper-like surface more practical than a wet-clay cuneiform tablet for most purposes, but which eventu-ally shriveled away to nothing in the hot, humid Indian climate. The details of Iron-Age Indian social and political history have been lost with the shriveled palm leaves. Religious texts, meanwhile, were pre-served by memorization to be written down much later, on more durable media. Today, people's names and specific dates are largely absent from Iron-Age Indian history. Almost all our sources are religious texts.

The opposite is true of Iron-Age Chinese history, which is chock-full of exact dates. Here's why. Although its effective rule was lim-ited, the Bronze-Age Shang dynasty had claimed wide authority over everything "under heaven." That claim was unsuccessful but never went away completely. Instead, it was taken up by a new family, the Zhou, relatively rustic westerners from the edge of the steppe who overthrew the Shang dynasty in 1045 BCE. The newcomer Zhou dynasty revealed typical insecurities in their imitation of Shang ways. They learned to make Shang ceremonial bronzes and to inscribe them with Shang writing. They accepted the Shang idea that an emperor was the Son of Heaven and ruled by divine mandate. The Zhou explained that the Shang had lost that mandate and fallen because they failed to maintain the moral standard required by Heaven. The Zhou would take up the torch, supposedly, and shoulder the Mandate of Heaven. Zhou rulers thus adopted Shang imperial ideology, and they did it using the Shang's own written language to elaborate their position. Thus, names and dates from Shang tradition were copied and recopied over the centuries, using the same script found on the oracle bones.

Thirty-nine members of the Zhou family claimed imperial status between 1045 and 256 BCE, but only the first few Zhou emperors actually exercised power. In practice, Zhou China was nothing like the Persian Empire with its centralized administration and standing army. Instead, Zhou China was more a collection of seven feuding kings, governing regional states, a changing constellation of forces frequently at war with one another. What held this loose structure together was cultural similarity and the Zhou claim to have inherited the Mandate of Heaven, although without the power to enforce it. In 771 BCE, raiding steppe barbarians pushed the Zhou out of their capital on the western frontier, further weakening them.

In the meantime, China showed the new pattern of Iron-Age warfare. Chariots remained present in large numbers. The brunt of battle, however, was born by grungy foot soldiers with iron halberds, poleaxes that could pull drivers and archers out of chariots and hack them apart in the dirt. New Iron-Age tactics called for a throng of infantry to press their shields together into an impenetrable wall, bristling with iron-tipped spears. The Chinese made the carnage of war even less glorious by introducing the crossbow. The crossbow fired an iron bolt, a projectile about halfway between a wooden arrow and a leaden bullet. The crossbow was a modest mechanical wonder that any peasant could learn to handle quickly. It did not require flair or expertise. Just crank it up, load a bolt into it, point it, and pull the trigger. Splat. Crossbows and bolts were mass produced by the hundreds of thousands, putting Chinese Iron-Age warfare ahead of its time. But where was the glamor? Crossbows had a similar killjoy effect when they were adopted in Europe more than a thousand years later.

The men who ruled Iron-Age China were often *not* warriors above all else. The contrast with the West is enormous. To a surprising degree, Chinese rulers were not warriors at all, but office-holding scholars. A bit like Brahmins in Iron-Age India, Chinese scholars composed a pervasive power behind the local throne, a group whose function was to manipulate ideas and process information. We will call these Chinese scholar-bureaucrats "mandarins," a much later Portuguese term, but a famous and useful one. Unlike Brahmins, mandarins did not study religious texts. Mandarins were text-oriented in the extreme, but they weren't at all priests. Instead, they were clerks, scribes, secretaries, administrators, bureaucrats, ministers—employees and allies of the state. All states must have literate functionaries. The unusual thing about mandarins was their social prestige, which was on a par with that of senior scribes in the service of the Egyptian pharaoh. In Iron-Age China, young members of the elite might choose a life of scholarship, something practically unheard-of in a period when, throughout civilized Eurasia, upper-class males preferentially trained to be warriors. The character of literacy in China may partly explain things.

Mandarins were masters of a complex, non-alphabetic, character-based writing system, similar in origin to Mesopotamian cuneiform or Egyptian hieroglyphics. All readers of this book are familiar with alphabetic writing. It comprises consonants and vowels, the constituent sounds of speech. Learn a few dozen letters representing consonants and vowels, and you can write any word alphabetically. In contrast, the continuity of the Chinese literary tradition has preserved an alternative, partly *ideographic*, form of writing. Chinese characters mostly represent things, actions, and ideas (马 horse, 天 heaven, 希望 hope) rather than sounds. To some degree, ideographic characters enable communication between people who speak different languages. If we both recognize 马 as the animal that pulls a chariot, we can both read the word, whether we pronounce it "m⊠" or "horse." So characters facilitated communication across linguistic divides. They also made of calligraphy an art form. The big problem is that an ideographic system requires a distinctive sign for each thing or idea, which means, in practice, learning to read and write thousands of unique characters. The difficulty of acquiring this kind of literacy made it precious, and the people who acquired it joined a highly regarded elite. In Zhou China, they staffed each regional state's corps of administrators, judges, and tax assessors.

These officials were the mandarins, properly speaking. Scholars who made it into this office-holding elite administered everything "under heaven." To become a high-ranking mandarin was theoretically every young scholar's goal, although only a few could actually achieve it. Mandarin ministers put their best efforts into organizing civil society and fomenting agriculture and industry. Most used their learning for more everyday tasks. Scholars of the work-a-day variety—those who failed to make a high-enough score on the highly competitive imperial exams—kept records, wrote letters, composed poetry, and put together (then copied and recopied over centuries) treatises on statecraft and poetry, also on agriculture, arts, and industry. Even if the various jostling states within Zhou China feuded constantly, they were run internally by men whose expertise was not war. Meanwhile, Chinese peasant laborers were drafted by the state to drain wetlands, control the flow of rivers, terrace farmlands for irrigation, dig irrigation ditches, and engineer transportation canals. The population of Zhou China, with its burgeoning agricultural base, began to push toward twenty million in the last centuries before the Common Era.

Visions of Greatness

When, in 334 BCE, Alexander III of Macedon, a minor kingdom immediately north of Greece, set out to conquer the known world, neither China nor India was on his mind. His main adversary was the Persian Empire begun by Cyrus, which, under his imperial heirs, had already engrossed most of the eastern Mediterranean. By defeating the Persians, Alexander would dominate most of the world in one fell swoop, capturing the Persian emperor Xerxes and occupying the fabled city of Babylon. From there, Alexander's army went east, into Persia, toward India and Central Asia. By the time he reached those places, however, his army was unhappy, too long on campaign and too far from home. What was the point of conquering more? Given the mutinous spirit of Alexander's army in India, an expedition to China was out of the question. And then Alexander died—in Babylon—possibly of alcoholism or poisoned by his own men. He was thirty-two years old and had spent most of his adult life subjugating other people.

In terms of empire building, Alexander accomplished only the first step, conquest. He never got around to ruling, although he did establish twenty cities named after himself, the most famous being Alexandria, Egypt. He married his senior officers to conquered princesses along the way, also marrying one himself, a traditional method of ruling empires, but the marriages didn't last. Alexander also apparently considered himself semi-divine. His mother, who was one of his father's seven or eight wives, had encouraged that idea when he was young, and megalomania went with empire. Finally, Alexander greatly respected the culture of Athens, which is what we usually have in mind when envisioning ancient Greece. Legend has it that he was tutored by the famous philosopher Aristotle himself. As king of Macedon, Alexander's father had conceived a plan to attack the Persian Empire, and when Alexander succeeded his father as king, he took over the project. Supposedly he carried with him a copy of the *Iliad*, the story of his role model, the semi-divine warrior Achilles.

In emulating Achilles, Alexander succeeded beyond his wildest dreams. He became the most glorious warrior in a global chronicle studded with them. Alexander's life can be told as a string of battles and legendary deeds. For example, there's the classic prefiguring story, revealing something extraordinary about the hero's youth. In the story, the young Alexander manages to tame a horse that nobody else can, Bucephalus, the horse that will carry him to India. Eventually he will name a city after Bucephalus. In another legend, Alexander confronts a riddle, the impossibly tangled Gordian knot, which nobody can untie. He who undoes this knot, said the soothsayers, will rule Asia! Our hero severs it with a sword stroke, thereby "cutting the Gordian knot." Clever hero.

Alexander really was indubitably a great warrior, though. He invaded the Persian Empire in 334 BCE with an enormous army of the new Iron-Age variety, massed infantry with interlocking shields, bristling with spears. Chariots could do nothing against them. He swept through Anatolia, liberating it into his own control, offering death as an alternative. His toughest resistance came from the city of Tyre, a settlement of sea people, slightly off the eastern Mediterranean coast and strongly fortified. When Tyre fell, he slaughtered the male prisoners of fighting age and sold the women and children into slavery. The rulers of Egypt acted more appropriately towards him (in Alexander's view), pronouncing him a son of their god Amon. In Mesopotamia, Alexander's army defeated an even more enormous, but chariot-heavy, Persian army at Gaugamela. The Persian emperor fled the battlefield, and Alexander occupied the imperial capitals at Susa and Persepolis, which he later burned down, possibly by accident. Alexander's last campaign subjugated the far eastern reaches of what had been the Persian Empire, before his mutinous army forced him to turn back.

Despite rumors of divinity, Alexander turned out to be only too mortal. Following his sudden death without an heir in 323 BCE, his empire was divided among his generals and never reunited, making it one of the least durable great empires in world history. But Alexander had achieved undying personal fame, his principal goal. He definitively replaced Achilles as the most remembered Greek warrior hero.

Moreover, Alexander's attempt to propagate Greek culture throughout his conquests succeeded. Greek urbanism, language, and philosophy, literature and science, art and architecture—also

large-scale enslavement and virulent patriarchy—flourished for centuries in the cities that he had founded from Egypt to Central Asia.
This lasting influence of Greek culture in the eastern Mediterranean
region is known as Hellenism, Hellas being the ancient Greek name
of Greece. The Romans, who arrived in the eastern Mediterranean a
bit later, became enthusiastic adopters and propagators of Hellenism.
Julius Caesar thrilled to see his own face carved onto an equestrian
statue of Alexander. The Greek language continued to predomi-
nate in all the Alexandrias, even under Roman control. The famous
mosaic of Alexander that opens this chapter was partially preserved
for posterity because it graced a patrician home in the Roman city of
Pompeii when Mount Vesuvius erupted and buried it centuries after
the hero's death.   Alexander gained brief control over the original heartland of world civilization, but that control accomplished
relatively little. Alexander's conquests did nothing to change most
people's daily activities: the way they fed themselves, made clothing,
built houses, raised their children, experienced life and death. Imperial tempests continued to rage on the stormy surface of Eurasian
civilization in the hero's wake. New kings and emperors conquered,
imposed grim punishment on the vanquished, and rewarded their
warriors with plunder, only to be conquered and slaughtered in turn.
For two millennia, warrior monarchs and nobles lorded over peasants and serfs, extracted their wealth, and treated them like dirt.
Kingdoms and empires swelled, burst into pieces, and reconstituted
themselves in a ceaseless churn.

Meanwhile underlying social, economic currents moved slowly.
Material life—staple foods, the shape of a shoe, a shingle, a coin,
a loom, a plowshare—remained similar over many centuries. The
basic technological tool kit, patterns of farming and herding life, the
basic lifeways of villagers, the fundamental design of cities, clothing, tools, and weapons—were often shared throughout Eurasia.
Our species' self-destructive tendencies, our routine inability to treat
others without the consideration that we would like for ourselves and

our own families—these social pathologies had become civilizational norms as well.

Some things did change in the centuries after Alexander's death in 323 BCE, of course. Most hopeful was the rise of new, more ethical religions, the ones that would set enduring patterns, find adherents around the world, and define the spiritual life of humanity until only a global moment ago. Thus far, we have already noticed the prophet Zoroaster. He was only the beginning.

CHAPTER FIVE

Classical World

The Alexander the Great story, as told today, is riddled with legends, but we can be confident that the broad outlines are true. A Macedonian king by that name led an expedition of world conquest, won battles, founded cities, and died under murky circumstances. The same can be said about early kings in general. We can be pretty sure of their names, because of the inscriptions, statues, coins, and tombs that proclaimed their exalted status. Royal genealogies were carefully kept, if often amended. Very few other names and personal stories survive from several thousand years ago. What we have, mostly, to represent that distant past   STET are the legends.

Wang Zhaojun, who was born around 50 BCE near the Yangtze River, was so enchanting and beautiful, supposedly, that birds who heard her sing and play her instrument forgot to flap their wings and fell out of the sky. Sent to the imperial city of Chang'an to become the emperor's concubine and, possibly, one of his wives, she refused to bribe the royal portrait painter, according to the storytellers, and thus lost her chance at royal favor. The emperor sent her instead to marry a barbarian chieftain who wanted a Chinese alliance, so the great beauty went to live in a yurt. When her husband died, the emperor insisted that, in order to preserve the alliance, Wang Zhaojun should stay on the frigid steppe and marry another barbarian chieftain. The legend of this beautiful self-sacrificing woman lives on today. Many hundreds of songs, poems, stories, plays and, more recently, television series have paid tribute to Wang Zhaojun.

Sometimes we have a name when there is no direct historical evidence about the specific person with that name. That is true of many early philosophers, artists, and prophets, including some of the most important, such as the Persian prophet Zoroaster. Another striking case is that of Siddhartha Gautama, whose title "the Buddha" means the awakened or enlightened one.

The Buddha was "woke" to spiritual evils such as the caste system and the patriarchal subjugation of women. Reasonable guesses about when he lived range from 566 to 368 BCE. Born a Kshatriya, a member of the warrior caste, his legends say that he was a prince destined for kingly rule, but that he instead became a wandering holy man who slept in the forest, lived by begging, and spent his days meditating. According to the story, he meditated under one particular tree until he finally understood the great mystery of human existence: how all human beings should face illness, suffering, and death. Once he "awoke," he spent the rest of his life teaching other mendicant holy men, his disciples, the path to enlightenment. And they in turn taught others, so that Buddhism grew into one of the world's major religions. Yet we have not a single historical document that mentions, during his own lifetime, anyone named Siddhartha Gautama or called the Buddha. The story of the Buddha was not written down, apparently, until centuries after his death by his faithful followers, which is not the most reliable form of biographical information.

This situation is not uncommon. We have very little direct contemporary evidence, several hundred years later, of the prophecy and crucifixion of Jesus of Nazareth, though there is enough to verify his human existence. On the other hand, Gautama, like Zoroaster, may not have been a specific historical person at all. That, too, is a common situation for this time. Most literary scholars believe, for example, that Homer, the most famous bard of antiquity, supposedly author of the *Iliad* and the *Odyssey*, is a name given to an entire tradition. Homer, in other words, stands for a collective creation.

Confucius may be a similar case, as we will see. My intent here is not iconoclasm. I know nobody wants to think of their great prophet or sage as a collective author. For world history, however, what matters is not the creator, but the creation. Whether individuals or collectively, the thinkers whom we call Buddha and Confucius created two of the world's most influential ethical traditions.

This chapter covers the period from 500 BCE to 500 CE. By then, urban societies with writing, metallurgy, and a highly productive agricultural infrastructure stretched like a string of pearls across the middle latitudes of Eurasia. The Persian Empire had directly interconnected a considerable swath of this activity, and a few centuries later the conquests of Alexander intensified that connection. Silver and gold coins now greatly facilitated trade. People were regularly navigating the Mediterranean and Black Seas, the Indian Ocean, the South Pacific, and most intensely, the Malaysian archipelago between India and China. At the same time, patriarchy, kingship, and the warrior cult had grown steadily more intense with the creation of the first territorial states. Mega-states composed of many kingdoms were ruled by emperors who routinely advanced religious justifications for their preeminence. Only the world's remaining foragers still lived in fundamentally egalitarian societies.

Then, in societies across Eurasia, something happened to challenge the supposedly close ongoing relationship between kings and gods. Monarchy and organized religion had arisen in tandem and served primarily each other. But some religious thinkers began to criticize the behavior of royal warriors on ethical grounds. Actually, to label them simply "religious thinkers" is misleading. Some were prophets who wanted to hold the king responsible to the gods, as Zoroaster did in Persia. Some, on the other hand, were philosophers who wanted to replace gods and spirits in general with different models of reality. During this thousand-year period, prophets and philosophers across Eurasia changed the course of human society by speaking truth to power and pursuing ideals of rationality, universalism, and justice.

Their attempt at universality, above all, made them different. Among foragers, spirit work tends to be ad hoc, meant to serve the people whom the shaman attends, most frequently by a sort of exorcism. The earliest organized religions served warrior clans. Smite our enemies, oh Great Spirit! Universal religions, on the other hand, applied to everyone impartially, friends and enemies alike. Universal religions operate on the golden rule. Do unto others what you would have them do unto you. In other words, the universal religions worked against the mentality of "us vs. them" that we have identified at the heart of social exploitation in world history. Universality asks us to regard *all other people* as worthy of fairness and consideration. All this, in theory. It was not a message that empire builders readily embraced, however. An allegiance to humanity in general is subversive to the power and prestige of war-oriented leadership.

Jesus and Muhammad were the culmination of the new ethical tradition, but it started much earlier. Conventional dates for the life of the Buddha, the Old Testament prophet Isaiah, the pre-Socratic Greek philosopher Xenophanes, and the Chinese scholar Confucius—suggest that all five could have been alive (if they were all historical individuals) at the same time, between 550 and 480 BCE. Zoroaster would have lived even earlier. Zoroastrianism had already become the formal state religion of the Persian Empire, serving the needs of the rulers first and foremost. Empires rarely permit dissident holy men or philosophers to flourish, as the crucifixion of Jesus serves to illustrate.

Innovative thinkers and dissident prophets had more success in city-states or small territorial states where speaking truth to power was easier to get away with. In one small Hebrew kingdom under the Persian thumb, Isaiah raised a prophetic voice that denounced the ethical lapses of both king and people in the name of the god Jehovah. The free thinker Xenophanes left the Greek city of his birth on the Anatolian shore of the Aegean Sea when the Persians took it over, and traveled from one Greek city-state to another, challenging the existence of the misbehaving Olympian gods, whom he believed lacked the ethical orientation that gods ought to have. He argued in very modern fashion that people made gods in their own image. Self-centered people devised self-centered gods.

When the local oligarchs got riled, Xenophanes moved on to the next Greek-speaking city-state. The homelands of Confucius and of Siddhartha Gautama were likewise clusters of culturally similar, but chronically competing, territorial kingdoms, one in northern China and one in northern India. Before leaving Greece, though, let's recall that, when Athens acquired an empire, Socrates famously followed in the footsteps of Xenophanes as a speaker of truth to power. In 399 BCE, Socrates, who is considered the first important moral philosopher in the Western ethical tradition, was executed (ordered to commit suicide) for disrespecting the gods of Athens.

Buddha and Confucius

The Buddha similarly challenged the authority of India's Brahmins. How? He disparaged the importance of what they knew. The privilege of the Brahmin caste depended on the prestige of their priestly expertise, connected to the Vedic religion that Aryan barbarians had brought with them from the steppe. Brahmins were authorities on the caste system. They knew the sacred formulas and rituals that legitimated the power of kings. They knew, above all, the precise formulas for various animal sacrifices, the keystone of Vedic worship, particularly the great horse sacrifice. By the fifth century BCE, this was old-fashioned stuff in northern India, out of step with the urban society of the lower Ganges River valley.

To become the Buddha, according to the story, Prince Siddhartha joined other men who had renounced the normal expectations of society—to have a family, good clothing, a respectable, gainful activity, and a comfortable urban residence. These holy men, or ascetics, as we can call them in general terms, were seeking something different in life. Ascetic "renouncers" turned away from society to live outside villages and towns. They questioned the value of older religious traditions, preferring to seek the meaning of life directly. Ascetics valued physical privation (such as celibacy and hunger and cold) along with constant prayer as paths to spiritual strength and discovery. Eventually, such renunciation would inspire seekers in many religions—for example, Christian friars and Muslim sufis— but the phenomenon of wandering holy men who renounce civilized comforts seems to have originated in India. Paradoxically, it is a sign of affluence. A life of poverty and prayer can only exist in societies where people have food to give away. Spiritual seeking, like so many other cultural developments, depended on a reliable agricultural surplus.

After years living as an ascetic wanderer, Siddhartha sat under a tree and meditated for forty-nine days, until he believed he had discovered the solution to human suffering. As the Buddha, he taught that the solution was detachment. People suffer because they desire things. They suffer attempting to get them, suffer in the struggle to retain them, and finally, inevitably, suffer their loss. The Buddhist solution was not to desire the things of this world. Buddhists looked beyond earthly delights, to transcend the ego, to abandon the self, and to seek absorption into the great whirling unity of all life.

Samsara, the general Indian idea of reincarnation (and the transmigration of souls) was the background of Buddhist thought. The Buddha's own insight was his self-help method, the Eightfold Path, which includes rigorous meditation, self-discipline, and ethical behavior in all things. He taught his method of achieving enlightenment to his ascetic former companions, and then to anyone who would listen. Somewhat counterintuitively for us, the ultimate promise of Buddhist enlightenment is escape from the cycle of reincarnation, which is viewed as escape from suffering. After achieving enlightenment, the person will never again reincarnate but rather dissolve into the cosmos in blissful unity with the spirit of all life. This is "reaching nirvana."

The Buddha had no time for kings, the caste system, or Brahmin-prescribed animal sacrifices. Preaching the unity of all life, he was against killing in principle. He did not advocate the overthrow of kings or their replacement by anything different. He wasn't interested in anything that Brahmins or kings could do. He condemned them to irrelevance. His teachings spread quickly up the Ganges valley, finding adherents most especially in the cities among urban mercantile groups. As a spiritual exercise, the Eightfold Path was a hard slog, however, requiring total devotion. It was not for everybody. Because the Buddha had taught primarily a method, his teachings lent themselves to monasticism, the historical institution whereby sizable groups of men and women function as spiritually advanced practitioners on behalf of society at large. Men and women who devote their lives to advanced spiritual practice must normally be supported economically by a community—such as, for example, prosperous traders and professionals in northern Indian cities. Buddhism thrived in an urban environment. Within less than two hundred years, many cities in the Ganges valley had become predominantly Buddhist.

If that was not already the case by 321 BCE, the Mauryan Empire, born that year, made it so. India's history is characterized more by competing kingdoms than by long-lasting empires. The Mauryan Empire, which lasted less than 150 years, is one of the two biggest, longest-lasting homegrown empires in Indian history. Almost all traces of it have long since vanished from India's steamy landscape. Few written sources, particularly, have survived. Yet those that remain tell us about one of the most extraordinary moments in world history, with Buddhism at the very center.

The conquering army of Alexander the Great had reached as far west as the Indus River valley in 327–325 BCE. Although it lingered only briefly, it must have made a very considerable splash. And it appears that the founder of the Mauryan Empire was one of the many leaders inspired by Alexander's conquering exploits. This leader was Chandragupta Mori, who first gained control of the large Magadha kingdom on the lower Ganges, and then managed to dominate other kingdoms militarily. The Mauryan military seems to have been notably large and impressive. It included thousands of elephants that carried moving platforms of archers. The Mauryan Empire temporarily extended its influence over an enormous area including most of Afghanistan, Pakistan, India, and Bangladesh, but it was ruled by only one dynasty, the Mori family. (The name *Mauryan* comes from Mori). The family's empire reached its territorial height under its third emperor, Chandragupta's grandson Asoka.

Asoka's reign constituted not only the territorial apogee of the Mauryan Empire but also something more significant. We know about it because Asoka had inscriptions chiseled into stone columns and raised them throughout his dominions. Emperors like Asoka routinely used stone monuments to announce their conquests and their awesome power, but Asoka did something different. Instead of bragging rights, Asoka claimed regret and repentance for his particularly brutal (and therefore smashingly successful) 261 BCE conquest of the Kalinga kingdom, which had led to the deaths and displacement of hundreds of thousands of people. Asoka's inscriptions announced that he would rule, thenceforth, in accord with the principles of Buddhism, renouncing bloody conquests forever. Although strongly Buddhist in orientation, Asoka's edict promised free exercise of all religions in the Mauryan Empire, a truly astounding measure in an age when a state religion ranked beside a large standing army as a primary foundation of imperial rule.

Asoka promised to govern the Mauryan Empire with tolerance and justice for all people and respect for all living things. He asked his subjects to join him in reorganizing his empire on ethical principles. The message was inscribed in several languages, including the Greek and Aramaic spoken in the northwestern regions often visited by outsiders like Alexander.

Asoka's initiative seems wildly ahead of its time. There is nothing else like it in world history until the twentieth century. Asoka was addressing a very considerable portion of the civilized world, perhaps fifty or sixty million people then under Mauryan rule. On the other hand, our information, which comes entirely from Asoka's inscribed announcements, is entirely aspirational, telling us nothing about how his idea worked in practice. We do know that the Mauryan Empire did not last much beyond Asoka's death, and by 184 BCE the great experiment was over. It is safe to guess that it was much harder to institute than to dream up, yet no imperial dream in world history commands greater respect today.

China's imperial dream was less ambitious but more durable.

The Zhou ruling family continued to claim the Mandate of Heaven after 500 BCE, but it exercised limited influence. So, from 403 to 221 BCE, Chinese historians talk about a period of Warring States in which the Zhou, despite their imperial claims, were merely one player. Still, the idea of a divine mandate to rule all Chinese speaking people did not go away. It was shared by the seven rather similar warring kingdoms that had inherited a political culture and a scribal tradition from the Shang dynasty.

There was considerable diversity among the scholars who regarded themselves as the keepers of this tradition. They functioned as officials, both high and low, in the various warring kingdoms. Their independence of mind was encouraged by the diversity of their political opportunities, because the similarity of language and culture among the seven kingdoms facilitated movements from one to another. Refusing to be silenced by a disapproving king, dissident scholars simply moved on, just as philosophers like Xenophanes or religious teachers like the Buddha could do in their respective cultural spheres. The important result, for our consideration of social ethics in world history, was the so-called Hundred Schools of Thought. The most salient school, eventually, was Confucianism, which became the official ideology of the Chinese Empire by the beginning of the Common Era.

Confucius (if he was an individual) was probably born around 550 BCE. He served the rulers of various warring states as a scholar and bureaucrat—a rather disgruntled one, it seems, not particularly prominent or influential during his lifetime. While the acts of a historical man named Confucius are hard to discern, what his name stands for is crystal clear. Confucius stands for the classical tradition of literacy, scholarship, and government service that developed during China's disunited and bellicose Iron Age. More than that, he stands for the whole of classical Chinese culture, because he is traditionally viewed as the author or editor of the most revered ancient Chinese texts. And the Confucian approach was ethical from beginning to end. Confucian writings from half a millennium before Jesus of Nazareth include the golden rule verbatim. Humane treatment for all was among the first Confucian principles.

Confucius was obsessed with proper social order and behavior, sharply critical of rulers who were not wise and just, principled, and impartial. The Mandate of Heaven depended on the moral qualities of the ruler. Therefore, the incessant warring of the seven kingdoms could be attributed to the moral shortcomings of their rulers. The subjects of corrupt rulers had a right to overthrow them. These were old-fashioned ideas in China by Confucius's time, but Confucius was all about old-fashioned ideas. His definitions of proper behavior were extremely traditional, patriarchal, and authoritarian. Respect, obedience, even reverence toward parents and ancestors was proper behavior for everyone. Women were to obey men, younger siblings to obey older ones, and humble people to obey their social superiors, unquestioningly. Personal excellence lay in playing one's social role, and playing it well. The ethical check on hierarchy and patriarchy was rooted in the insistence that rulers and nobles ought to be held to a higher standard than humble people. Only striving conscientiously to be morally superior made a man fit for authority. This idea, present in all the world's great ethical traditions, is summed up by the old French expression "la noblesse oblige," nobility carries obligations.

Keepers of an ancient written tradition, China's later scholar-bureaucrats put the name Confucius on the best of that tradition. For example, collections of China's oldest poetry and rituals were attributed to Confucian authorship although he clearly didn't write them. The fallback position was to consider Confucius the definitive collector and editor of these texts, making him the imagined custodian of the entire Chinese classical tradition. Our term *Confucian-*

ism translates Chinese words meaning something more like "scholar thought." Confucius maintained that natural ability (and not wealth or nobility) was the best qualification for a scholarly calling. Eventually, and for thousands of years, there would be a national-level test that everybody had to pass for Chinese government work. Confucius proposed what the West later called an aristocracy of talent. Even women could enter this select group, but only under the most extreme conditions. Along those lines, the collection of China's oldest poetry includes one called "Speeding Chariot," by a woman, Lady Xu Mu. In addition to her talent as a writer, Xu Mu was a heroine of struggles against the northern barbarians. She had organized the defense of the Kingdom of Wei in 660 BCE, after her uncle and two of her brothers failed in the attempt.

By 221 BCE, Confucian scholar thought was on the rise, but ethical teachings meant little to the Qin dynasty that erupted across the North China scene in that year. Qin (pronounced Chin) had long been a leading kingdom. Its capital Chang'an had been the first Zhou dynasty capital eight hundred years earlier. It occupied a rich agricultural region and a communications hub connecting North China with regions farther south and west. The influence of the steppe was strong in Chang'an. As one of seven warring kingdoms, the kingdom of Qin enjoyed both a vigorous and innovative scholarly bureaucracy and a powerful army. This is the army represented by the famous terracotta warriors. Their real-life counterparts unified the Chinese Empire. In 221 BCE, Qin forces overwhelmed the other six warring kingdoms. The Qin king claimed the Mandate of Heaven and took the title Shi Huangdi, explicitly "emperor," rather than merely "king." He is remembered as the first emperor to govern all of China. It is his tomb that the terracotta warriors were molded to guard for all eternity. The tomb is reminiscent of those constructed by steppe barbarian kings (some Shang kings as well) who had sacrificed servants and horses buried with them. The terracotta army is, in fact, a civilized stand-in for battalions of sacrificed servants.

The Qin project was in most ways quintessentially Chinese. The

Qin mandarin bureaucracy was vigorous and ambitious, although not particularly Confucian. Qin scholars tended to emphasize strict laws and severe punishments rather than Confucian humaneness and self-improvement. In their warring kingdom, Qin mandarins had developed techniques of civil administration such as census-taking to guide the distribution of agricultural land. After 221 BCE, the bureaucracy of the Qin dynasty reproduced itself at the imperial level by standardizing the form of writing and the traditional texts that had circulated before unification. To further tighten the union of literacy and state power, books in private hands were burned. The Qin bureaucracy oversaw enormous public works, including canals, three thousand miles of wall along the northern border to keep out you-know-who, and an extensive system of roads to encourage trade and facilitate governance of its thirty-six imperial provinces. The Qin dynasty also took the precaution of bringing the former ruling families of the other six warring states to the imperial court to spend their days flattering the emperor rather than conspiring against him. Thus did the Chinese imperial court mold a loyal aristocracy. The Qin dynasty overreached itself, however, with its massive conscriptions of commoners for the army and public works. It was toppled from within after only fourteen years. Nonetheless, Qin was the effective beginning of Chinese imperial rule. The name China (Chin + a) comes from Qin.

The Qin were replaced in 206 BCE by the Han family, a new dynasty that governed for four centuries. In size, duration, and significance, Han China bears comparison with the roughly contemporaneous Roman Empire in the West. The comparison gains interest from the fact that, at their height, each empire was quite aware of the other's existence. Each had, not so much news, as persuasive physical evidence of the other—in small amounts of precious goods carried by relays of merchants, back and forth across Eurasia on what became called, for obvious reasons, the Silk Route. Both the Han and Romans brought together centuries of wider civilizational experience. The territory that each conquered was not merely controlled, but ultimately integrated, into each empire. In that sense, both the Han and the Romans could be inclusive.

In addition, as they approached the year 1 CE, the beginning of the Common Era, all the Old World civilizations had developed sophisticated ethical teachings based on universal moral principles that still inform human societies today. These teachings did not end the ruthless, routine exploitation of some people by others, however. That remained a routine aspect of civilized life.

Classical Empires of East and West

The new ethical teachings informed *classical* empires, establishing cultural models imitated for more than a thousand years afterward at their respective ends of Eurasia. China's Qin dynasty was quickly followed by the Han dynasty, which officially adopted Confucianism. At roughly the same time, the Hellenistic societies of the eastern Mediterranean Sea were engulfed by the rising power of Rome, which eventually adopted Christianity.

Rome began as one among many city-states near the shores of the Mediterranean Sea. The Romans and their neighbors had received the long-term influence of sea peoples like the Greeks and Phoenicians. Greek city-states to the south, also Etruscan city-states to the north, both limited Roman territorial aspirations until Celtic barbarians crushed the Etruscans around 390 BCE. Afterward, the Romans began their long and insanely successful career of military expansion. First, they subjugated other Latin-speaking people in central Italy and conscripted their men into the Roman army. Next, they conquered the Greek-speaking city-states of southern Italy and, in 264 BCE, began a series of wars against Carthage, a powerful city-state on the African coast.

Carthage was the chief city-state of the Phoenicians, that most seaworthy of sea peoples. The Phoenician alphabet eventually evolved into our own, but they left little other cultural legacy. Carthage was the dominant maritime power on the central and western Mediterranean Sea. To attack it, the Romans had to build a navy, which they used in a series of three wars spanning more than a century, first to take over Sicily, and finally to annihilate the Carthaginians, executing all the men and enslaving the women and children. It was in one of these wars that Hannibal invaded Italy with a Carthaginian army assembled in Spain, an army that famously had to march through the Alps with elephants. In the meantime, the Romans had invaded Greece (where they obliterated, in passing, the ancient city of Corinth) and occupied the entire eastern shore of the Mediterranean. Roman conquests did not stop there. They would eventually convert the Mediterranean into a Roman lake and engulf most of western Europe.

Roman military prowess impresses. Certainly, it was the Romans' favorite thing about themselves. Discussions of Rome's success in war often turn on its magnificent legions, massed infantry of the Iron-Age ilk—recruited, trained, equipped, provisioned, maintained, and deployed like a smoothly running machine. The Romans had a genius for engineering and creating systems of all kinds, and their war machine was a good example. The result was a style of fighting a bit like the Chinese, short on flamboyant heroics but full of deadly efficacy. The full-throated zeal of Roman war making constitutes another part of the winning formula. Conquest was enormously popular and vastly profitable. The triumphal homecomings of victorious Roman generals bringing spoils and slaves were ecstatic public festivals. The plunder and captured manpower that derived from each conquest fueled the next one. Victory in war, thought to reflect the favor of the gods, was an unfailing source of political prestige. (The original Roman gods, like the Greek gods, valued winning above all else.) Even emperors with no military chops routinely struck the pose of fearsome battlefield commander. The Roman Empire displayed, in a high degree, the warrior cult that characterized most post-foraging societies, particularly in the West.

In Han China, by contrast, the warrior cult played a lesser role. True, the Han dynasty expanded the Chinese Empire and maintained internal order with a vast army, one not dissimilar to the Roman legions in overall approach. The Han army's greatest sustained conflict was with steppe barbarians perennially lurking along the northern frontier. Around 1 CE, they were a people called the Xiongnu, among whom the legendary beauty Wang Zhaojun went to live forever. Against the Xiongnu, the Qin dynasty had initiated the long-term, never very effective, practice of building defensive border walls. The Han dynasty built additional walls. Han military action against the Xiongnu eventually repulsed them, sending a ripple effect west along the length of the steppe, as far as Europe. Thousands of miles away, the string of falling dominoes sent a steppe people called Huns surging into the Roman Empire. (Actually, Huns and Xiongnu may even have been closely related, even one and the same.) Han forces expanded the empire for the first time to the South China Sea, and these gains were permanent. In addition, the Han extended military control west, along the Silk Road. The core of Han control delineated the territory occupied, ever after, by ethnic Chinese. Today, the name *Han* defines that ethnicity. Han military expenses were great enough to cause serious internal unrest and lead to the dynasty's eventual downfall. And yet war and conquest did not drive the Han ideologically. Han emperors almost never set foot on a battlefield, nor did they pretend to do so.

The economic and demographic heartland of Han China lay in the northern and central regions—basically, the valley of Yellow River—that had formerly composed the seven warring states. While there was certainly diversity, the great majority of Han subjects shared a written language and, to a lesser extent, a spoken language. That sense of kinship contributed to the success of Han rule. Gradually, the Han extended their control south into the Yangtze River basin, which eventually became China's heartland, and beyond.

Rome, on the other hand, ruled *mostly* non-Romans. Early Roman culture—defined by the Latin language—was universally shared only in central Italy. The first stage of Roman expansion was among these Latin speakers, but after that the Romans arrived everywhere as aggressive outsiders everywhere they went. Most often, they arrived from across the sea. Over time, they incorporated subject peoples politically through the extension of Roman citizenship, but citizenship did not at first express a deep cultural affinity. So Roman control necessarily depended more on military force than did Han control, which rested more on cultural affinity and shared ideology, updating the Mandate of Heaven.

The Roman Empire overlaid Hellenistic civilization and adopted Greek customs, Greek literature, and Greek religion. Greek was the language spoken on the street in the Eastern Roman Empire. The intensely urban and public orientation of Roman life was typical of Mediterranean city-states. The Roman Empire was essentially a network of cities, systematically linked by superbly engineered roads and bridges, supplied by lengthy aqueducts, drained by subterranean sewers. "Citizen," which meant literally city-dweller, was the name Romans gave men with political membership in the empire. Citizenship, like civilization, was defined by cities.

Roman cities—with their civic forum and temples and theater and amphitheater and public baths and monuments and many public spaces for all sorts of gatherings and spectacles such as gladiator contests and chariot races—must have been more exciting places than their comparatively staid Han counterparts. Rome itself was a seething multistory city of more than a million. Chang'an and Luoyang, the Han capitals, were a third or a half of that, and sleepy by comparison. Despite the existence of large cities, Han China was overwhelmingly agrarian, and Han social life more circumscribed by domestic frameworks. The largest buildings in Han China were the palaces of the rich, basically larger and more lavish versions of a normal house. Compared with the taverns and fleshpots and extravagant public life of Rome's Mediterranean urban network, Han cities were less jumbled and polyglot, more spread out, more oriented toward the surrounding agrarian countryside. Han cities their wide, wide wind-blown streets deserted in the cold winter and their gated neighborhoods locked after dark, seem somehow more buttoned down than Roman ones.

Both Roman and Han societies were exceedingly patriarchal. The very term *patriarch* is of Roman origin, of course, and patriarchy was a keystone principle of Confucianism, which became official Han ideology. Both Roman and Han fathers exercised total control over everyone else in their families, most especially over everyone female. Upper-class women might learn to read and write among both Han and Romans. Overall, however, both societies were characterized by ideals of explicit, emphatic, almost absolute male dominance and sharp restriction of women's activities and movements outside the domestic sphere. That said, we must add that the lives of individual Roman and Han women—normally aristocratic dames whose distinction was birthing famous men—are historically documented much better than any of their predecessors. Sometimes we can even glimpse women who possessed distinction of their own. For example, consider Antonia, a Roman aristocrat who lived from 36 BCE to 37 CE. She owned property in Italy, Greece, and Egypt. She was a niece of the emperor Augustus, sister-in-law of the emperor Tiberius, mother of the emperor Claudius, grandmother of the emperor Caligula, and great-grandmother of the emperor Nero. She had a slave surnamed Caenis, also called Antonia, who was perhaps more interesting than her owner. Antonia Caenis was apparently a war captive, and not a domestic servant, but rather a literate secretary. Eventually a freedwoman, Caenis became the concubine of the emperor Vespasian until her death in 75 CE.

Another social axis of power in both classical empires was *seniority*, like patriarchy, a word of Roman origin. Elder males, especially the *pater familias*, "the father of the family," stood at the top, and the youngest girls, at the very bottom. Girls in both empires were often not even given formal first names and went instead by nicknames. Mothers and grandmothers commanded respect for their seniority, although decidedly less than senior males. In China, especially, birth order among siblings was a form of seniority routinely applied in daily life. You called your brother something different, for example, if he outranked you in age. If your uncle outranked your father in birth order, for another example, you had to address him with greater deference. The age rank of siblings is still routinely acknowledged in the basic kinship terms of modern Chinese languages, and so is the crucial fact of whether a particular uncle, aunt, or cousin is from your father's side, or from your mother's, which makes them traditionally less important.

These classical empires were powerfully hierarchical and authoritarian. In most ways they did not embody (what would today seem) enlightened rule.

Rome had a monarchy until around 500 BCE, and afterward became a *republic*, another word of Roman origin. The Roman *senate*, which bequeathed its name to governing bodies around the world today, was a gathering of rich and powerful elders. Other early Roman institutions of representative government were consuls and tribunes who represented the common good, as distinct from that of the nobles. These offices were quickly overshadowed by relatively unconstrained autocracy once the empire reached its full size. Thereafter, the explosive concentration of wealth and power totally outran the development of constraining institutions. Around the year 1 CE, the first emperor, Augustus, established the official semi-divinity of the emperor. It was a semi-divinity greatly doubted by those who saw the emperors up close. In addition to the famous cavortings of an unhinged emperor Nero, the stubborn mortality of Roman emperors continuously undercut the divine image. Of twenty-two emperors who ruled the Roman Empire at its apogee, fifteen were murdered or committed suicide. Fortune, a Roman goddess, was fickle, and she clearly outranked the emperor. She often gave her favors instead to the successful generals and elite guards in the imperial quarters who dominated the empire at its high point.

The Han emperor also claimed a special relationship with heaven, as we know, but it was more conditional. According to official ideas, the emperor's main purpose was to make his people prosper. This had absolutely nothing to do with empowering them to seek their own destinies, however. Instead, guided by a complex tradition of political and social thinking that Chinese scholars studied and glossed century after century, the sizable Han bureaucracy wanted to specify details of how life and work should be conducted under heaven. In practice, they were very far from being able to micromanage life around the empire. They began with a highly centralized model, which meant in a nutshell that appointees from the capital governed the provinces in the name of the emperor. Over the four centuries of Han rule, that centralization was mostly eroded, which meant that, in practice, local potentates still governed in the name of the emperor, but outside his control. Whether merit-based appointees from the capital or fortunate recipients of local patronage, the officials who governed China during its classical Han dynasty were more or less all supposed to be scholars. The model of mandarin rule, so closely linked to literacy, became a permanent dimension of all future Chinese empires. Not for nothing is China's official national language called Mandarin today.

Chinese scholars, especially those who became mandarins, were almost all men, of course. But perhaps the world's most influential early woman of letters was the Han scholar Ban Zhao, who was born at about the same time as the Roman concubine Caenis. Ban Zhao came from a family of scholars. She was no doubt literate by the age of fourteen, when she was married to a much older man. His death allowed her to pursue scholarship. Ban Zhao distinguished herself by completing the official history of the Han dynasty begun by her father. She became a trusted counselor to the imperial family and the librarian of the imperial court, training and supervising a staff that included men. Ban Zhao pursued astronomy and mathematics. She wrote poems, polemics, commentaries, and a book for her daughters, called *Lessons for Women*, that was still being read more than a thousand years after her death in 116 CE.

Her advice was mostly conventional: Humbly serve your husband.

Do not try to stand out or shine. When he dies, don't remarry. More notably, she insisted that well-born daughters should be educated. While her given reason was "so to better serve their husbands," her stance was still unusual. Ban Zhao also advised the royal family on "the arts of the bedchamber," not as a practitioner, however, but as one who had studied "The Dao of Loving," which was a little bit like the Kama Sutra. The objective was to improve health by "joining the essences," then balancing the yin and the yang. Female pleasure was an essential part of that process.

Finally, Ban Zhao had a great-aunt whom she never met, but whose memory probably inspired her. Her aunt had been an imperial consort, a third rank below wife and concubine, but she too had been a scholar and a poet. In 19 BCE the emperor's passions had turned to a pair of dancing girls, whom he promoted to the rank of chief concubines.

Both the Empress and Ban Zhao's great-aunt had objected. They were accused of casting spells on the newly favored concubines and were banished from court. Ban Zhao's great-aunt had made a spirited public defense of herself using Confucian precepts. The emperor, impressed, pardoned her, but she nonetheless left court to attend the banished empress.

The Chinese emphasis on civil bureaucracy contrasted the rough-and-ready Roman approach, which depended more on alliances with local elites and often left the countryside untouched. On the other hand, the Romans codified law, making comprehensive official law codes to replace traditional and customary law. This was a Roman innovation and achievement, the famous laws of Hammurabi having, in fact, not been a comprehensive code at all.

Han agriculture was founded on a free peasantry. At first, the empire taxed peasant households directly. As local landowning aristocracies gained influence, however, they made peasant farmers into landless tenants on their vast estates. As for taxes, landowning aristocracies found ways not to pay them. They also gradually coopted imperial power in the provinces. Slowly, the imperial center lost influence and, at the dawn of the Common Era, crop failures led to a fourteen-year interruption in Han rule. The interruption was led by an upstart emperor, Wang Mang, who reigned from 9 to 23 CE and redistributed land to the peasantry. The Yellow River changed course during his reign, causing stupendous destruction. No more Mandate of Heaven for Wang Mang, obviously.

During the later centuries of Han rule, continuing unrest among the peasantry disrupted the empire. Szechuan, a large and rich province, something of a land apart, almost broke away. The various Chinese peasant movements of this period responded to traditional ideas and imagery, often organized by Daoists. Compared with staid Confucianism, Daoism represents the mystical, "wild" side of Chinese spiritual thinking—in this case the belief in social justice. The rebels of the late Han dynasty, who tied yellow cloth on their heads as a kind of uniform, believed that hunger in the countryside represented a failure of the emperor's rule, an abrogation of the Mandate of Heaven. Their persistent uprisings eventually unseated the dynasty, but that did not bring the triumph of their fond dreams. For a time afterward, there was no emperor, and local potentates reigned supreme.

In many parts of the Roman Empire, the cities were Roman islands in a countryside that was not very Roman in customs or language. Italy, logically enough, had the most Romanized countryside, and plunder from the empire had made central Italy rich. One element of these "riches" was a large population of non-Roman slaves. Agriculture in the Roman heartland was founded on chattel slavery, rather than serfdom, in which the serfs are peasants rooted to the land. By establishing slave plantations, Romans were merely following the larger pattern of Hellenistically influenced Mediterranean societies. Roman conquests turned hundreds of thousands of war captives into slaves that were brought back to Italy to labor on commercial plantations. The Roman analogs of the Chinese peasant uprisings against the Han were the slave uprising led by the gladiator Spartacus in 73–71 BCE, and also a slightly later slave revolt in Sicily.

By gathering and consolidating the civilizational advances of a millennium—both east and west, at opposite ends of Eurasia—the classical empires created cultural paradigms, models that have been imitated ever since. They represent high artistic and intellectual achievements that have defined our world. On the other hand, they also embodied the basic flaws of most post-foraging societies: the glorification of war and warriors, steep social hierarchies and inequities, an extreme concentration of wealth, and a chronic confusion of megalomania with a divine right to rule. The classic empires allowed the rulers to torture and kill for their own amusement. New ethical systems embodying the golden rule condemned such inhumanities without preventing them.

Under Asoka, India's classical Mauryan Empire attempted to implement equity and tolerance officially, going so far as to renounce wars of conquest, but the Mauryan empire did not last very long as empires go. Confucian ethics became an official doctrine of the Chinese imperial government, which could interpret, apply, or ignore it at will. In general, imperial rule was ethical only when it suited the rulers. As for the early Roman Empire, it was not encumbered by an ethical ruling ideology, its official religion being of the old-fashioned, polytheistic, smite-my-enemies sort, until it finally became Christian.

Transcontinental Connections

By organizing market economies at the eastern and western ends of Eurasia, the classical empires stimulated transcontinental connections.

The Royal Road of the Persian Empire had blazed a good portion of the route. The Eurasian steppe had connected east and west since the domestication of horses. The steppe-barbarian Scythians roamed as far west as Ukraine and as far east as the modern Chinese border. They moved back and forth with ease, and their tombs contain two-thousand-year-old silk preserved by the permafrost.

Also intermediaries between east and west were the Sogdians, who spoke an Iranian language and lived surrounded by deserts east of the Aral Sea, where the Oxus River swelled annually with snow-melt from the flanks of the Himalayas, creating a large oasis of irri-gated agriculture famous for its grapes as well as horses and dancing girls. (Since then, a drying climate and human water-use have mostly evaporated the Aral Sea.) The Oxus region was Western civilization's nearest approach to China. It was halfway between the Roman and Han Empires. Between the Oxus region and the Chinese capital at Chang'an, lay vast expanses of desert. A Han expedition crossed the desert, found rich possibilities on the other side, and initiated a systematic, decades-long project to connect China with the Central Asia, a transportation corridor with military protection, reaching all the way from Chang'an to the Oxus region.

The result, by about 1 CE, was the Silk Road. The Silk Road is one of those misleading but irreplaceable names that require careful explanation. *Silk Road* is a modern term. It was, in fact, never a single road but rather a network of routes across Asia connecting east and west. Trade moved in stages, never (until much later) the whole east-west distance all at once. Nobody (that we know of) traveled all the way from ancient Rome to Chang'an or vice versa. While silk was the chief article, east-west trade included many other things, too. The Chinese were especially interested in getting Central Asian horses. This was a military interest, their chief motivation for creating the transportation corridor. As for Roman interest, it was piqued by Chinese silk for sale in the trade emporia of Syria. So much silk reached Roman aristocrats that moralists denounced it. (Sheer silk was too revealing! A woman might as well wear nothing at all!)

Another concern, because Rome produced nothing comparable to exchange, was the amount of gold flowing east to pay for silk. Roman glasswork was the world's finest, but delicate glass objects were not easily transportable for thousands of miles on a pack ani-mal. Fortunately for Roman glass exporters, the conquest of Egypt in 30 BCE connected Roman traders to sea links with India and beyond. A seaborne equivalent of the Silk Road began to operate along the southern coast of Asia, to and from China. That explains why archeologists have found Roman glassware in Guangdong Province (formerly called Canton in English), China's window on the South China Sea.

Eurasia had acquired a trading system. Arab traders were already making the monsoon crossing between Arabia and India's west coast in their small, seaworthy dhows. Meanwhile India's east coast was already connected to Malaysia by Indian and Malay (as well as Arab) traders. These traders were carrying Indian religious and political ideas into Southeast Asia, turning the Strait of Malacca into the world's most important commercial hub. Chinese traders handled the last leg, from Malaysia to Guangdong.

Then the Han dynasty lost control, and the Chinese Empire fragmented for a while. Rome, too, began to falter. Silk-buying Roman aristocrats disappeared from the scene. As a result of such changes, further outlined in the next chapter, east-west long-distance trade declined in Eurasia as a whole. Meanwhile, along with goods, the messages of the new, universalizing religions had begun to travel, too. In coming centuries, the world's great ethical religions would take center stage as organizing principles. Zoroastrianism had been the first ethical religion to gain wide sway and political significance. But it was specifically Persian and did not travel—and travel was a prerequisite for what we will call world religions. Buddhism, on the other hand, was a sturdy traveler. The biggest travelers of all were Christianity and Islam.

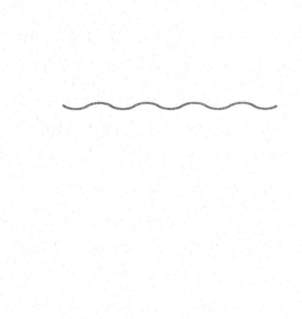

CHAPTER SIX

World of Faith

The decline of the classical empires loosened the links that had begun to connect Eurasia, east and west. The imperial elites of Rome and Han China had motivated a transcontinental trade in luxury goods. As Roman and Han urbanism dwindled, the transcontinental connections became more tenuous. In the meantime, the new ethical belief systems took on more prominent roles, spreading along trade routes far beyond their places of origin to become world religions. At the heart of each were basic principles that promised to reorganize life on Earth around the golden rule of ethical treatment for all.

Jesus of Nazareth, whose birth defines the beginning of the Common Era, was believed by his followers to be the son of God, a savior called Christ or the Messiah. A handful of references from his own time (and outside Christian tradition) confirm that Jesus was also a historical figure, a Jewish holy man whom the Romans considered a troublemaker and whom they executed by crucifixion. Crucifixion was a slow, painful death normally given to criminals like the two thieves who were executed alongside Jesus. The Romans meant to degrade Jesus by crucifixion, but the opposite happened. The Jewish followers of Jesus believed that he had risen from the dead and ascended into heaven, proving he was their Messiah. The apostles of Jesus founded a religion that eventually spread around the world.

Six hundred years later, beginning a few hundred miles south,

Muhammad and his followers launched a competing religious project. Muhammad and Jesus drew on shared cultural roots. For example, the angel who, in Muslim belief, appeared to Muhammad and gave him the Quran was the Archangel Gabriel. In Christian tradition, the Archangel Gabriel foretold the birth of Jesus. Both Islam and Christianity, along with Judaism, consider Abraham to be a founding patriarch. In Muslim tradition, Abraham constructed the Kaaba, the destination of the annual global pilgrimage to Mecca, visible in the illustration that heads this chapter. Likewise, Muslims consider Moses a great prophet, followed by Jesus, the last great prophet before Muhammad.

Metaphorically but unquestionably, Islam, Christianity, and Judaism, sometimes called the Abrahamic religions, are next of kin. It is not surprising that they became rivals, too, being so similar—intensely ethical and patriarchal. Today about a third of us are Christians, and about a quarter of us, Muslims, making these two the dominant world faiths. (Judaism, has too few followers to be comparable, nor does it seek converts.) This chapter focuses on the rise of Christianity and Islam, mostly between 500 and 1000 CE. During these years, Buddhism, the third world religion, spread throughout eastern Asia and redefined its cultures.

Christianity

Christianity was born *in* the Roman Empire, we could say, but not *of* it. Along with everyday devotion to modest household spirits, Roman religion at its zenith involved a pantheon of deities—the Greek pantheon, in fact, which the Romans adopted outright, giving each Greek god a name in Latin, so that Zeus became Jupiter, Athena became Minerva, and so on. Christianity arose in Roman-occupied Palestine among Aramaic-speaking Hebrews. The crucifixion of Jesus powerfully symbolized Christianity's oppositional relationship to Roman imperial power. For centuries thereafter, Christian believers dramatized their opposition by seeking martyrdom at the hands of Roman authorities in imitation of Jesus.

Christianity then developed and eventually spread throughout the Roman world. Jesus had preached in Aramaic, only to Jews. His early followers constituted, in effect, a dissident sect of Judaism. Only when the Christian message began to be disseminated in Greek did it spread more broadly among non-Jewish urban populations of the Eastern Roman Empire. Like the Buddhists, Christians scorned social prestige and looked to a transcendent reality. More than Buddhists, however, Christians reversed the signs of worldly prestige, proclaiming that "the last shall be first" in the kingdom of God.

Imperial authorities banned Christianity as a political threat.

Like Zoroastrians, Christians focused on people's ethical behavior in a cosmic struggle of good vs. evil. Nobody was presumed superior or more worthy than anybody else. The profession of the son of God? Carpenter, a respectable but never exalted trade. Christians, like Buddhists, welcomed everyone, including the enslaved and the poor, into the fold. Wealth and luxury were not only irrelevant to Christian godliness, they were actually an impediment to it. As in Buddhism, women participated in Christian worship from the first, a break with Jewish tradition. The Christian message must have had a powerful appeal among the urban plebeians of the slave-driven Roman Empire, where the emperor was officially a divine being. Nothing else can explain how Christianity spread so widely despite steady Roman disapproval, even if outright Roman repression was the exception rather than the rule. Christians worshiped in secret, although not in the underground tombs called catacombs, as legend has it.

Roman authorities executed hundreds of Christians, even feeding them to lions in public spectacles offered as holiday crowd-pleasers. Thus, a young Roman woman named Perpetua was executed in Roman Carthage, along with several others, to celebrate the emperor's birthday in about 203 CE. Perpetua was rich, married, and nursing a child at the time. The account of her martyrdom became an important early Christian text that circulated widely in the Roman world. Perpetua's father reportedly begged her to renounce her faith, and she refused, defying his patriarchal authority. A Christian slave named Felicitas was martyred during the same spectacle. Felicitas had been pregnant, but she gave birth in time to be martyred along with Perpetua.

Another famous early Christian martyr was Agnes of Rome. She was denounced as a Christian in 304 CE by a spurned suitor. Roman authorities condemned her to be dragged naked through the streets to a brothel where her haughty chastity would be defiled. According to her legend, the martyr's hair instantaneously grew to cover her nakedness as she was marched in shame through the streets of Rome. God struck the rapists blind for good measure. There is archeological evidence of her execution and of subsequent veneration on the spot. Her name has been forever afterward repeated as one of seven women's names in the Catholic mass. A piece of her skull is still conserved as a sacred relic.

Christians gradually gained ground, however, and their numbers were growing during these same years. Their rise was visible to everyone who entered the large Christian meeting halls called basilicas, that arose in Roman cities. These structures, the first purpose-built Christian churches, were patterned not on Roman temples with their dark, smoky altars for sacrificial offerings but rather on Roman courthouses, designed for large assemblies of people. Basilicas had internal columns that supported a high roof along a central nave, with overhead windows to admit natural light from above. The basilica defined the basic architecture of Roman Catholic churches for a thousand years afterward. Some basilicas could hold as many as a thousand congregants.

A famous story about the emperor Constantine describes the moment when Christianity finally gained official favor in the Roman Empire. On the eve of a battle in 312 CE, the emperor dreamed that a Christian insignia (two Greek letters signifying Christ) was the key to victory. He adopted the insignia for his army and won the battle, after which Christian bishops gained a valuable tax exemption. The name of *Constantine* helps reference not only the rise of Christianity within the declining Roman Empire, but also the east-west division that became part of the empire's decline. Constantine gave his name to Constantinople (today Istanbul), and Constantinople replaced Rome as the empire's most powerful city. Constantinople became the capital of the rising, Greek-speaking, Eastern Roman Empire, now the richest part. All roads led to Rome no longer.

Meanwhile, the Western Roman Empire continued to decline. As the Roman war machine ceased to provide the spoils of conquest, imperial power faded. Roman cities in the western provinces began to respond less to imperial directives and more to local influences. Roman administrative and military control waned, partly because of barbarian populations on the move. People arriving off the Eurasian steppe (the Huns) occupied large areas along the Rhine and Danube Rivers. Others (the Goths) rumbled through Greece, Italy, and southern Gaul. Still others moved into Roman Spain and from there to Roman cities on the northern coast of Africa. These were the Vandals, whose approach to civilization is commemorated in the word *vandalism*. These so-called barbarian invasions were less invasions than migrations of displaced (also armed and not-to-be-messed-with) people. Sometimes, the barbarians were offering military manpower that competing Roman generals recruited for their own purposes. But incoming migrants sometimes went rogue. A heavy blow came when a Roman emperor was defeated and killed in 378 CE. Gradually, the newcomers settled down and became Latin-speaking, Christian inhabitants of late Roman provincial societies, with ever less imperial control as the decades passed.

Augustine of Hippo, an early leader of the Roman church, lived during the Western Roman Empire's decline. Augustine was born to a well-off Roman family in what is today Algeria. For Augustine, Christianity was a choice, the religion of his mother but not of his father. Not yet a Christian, he studied in Carthage about a century after Perpetua was martyred there. He converted in 386 CE. His *Confessions*, an important early Christian text, depict a spiritual evolution that involved leaving his longtime mistress (at his mother's instigation) to marry a wealthy girl. Eventually he decided instead to become a celibate priest. Augustine was deeply influenced by Saint Anthony of the Desert, an early Christian ascetic who meditated for years in the Egyptian wilderness. Anthony is sometimes called the father of all monks. Augustine wrote his *City of God*, another landmark text of the early Roman church, after the Visigoths sacked Rome in 410 CE. And on the day that he died, now Bishop of Hippo, in 430 CE, Augustine's city was under siege by the Vandals. Saint Augustine greatly influenced the future practice of Christianity, especially in his emphasis on the sinfulness of sexuality and on the spiritual virtues of celibacy. Augustine's rigorous approach to combatting sin lent itself to monasticism. He inspired the Augustinian monastic order, which bears his name.

Finally, in 476 CE, the last Roman emperor of the west resigned.

The Eastern Roman Empire lived on for a thousand years. The name by which we usually call it is Byzantium. Serial name changes have somewhat obscured Byzantium's importance. Byzantium was a place where many elements of Roman civilization, including chariot races and bloody palace intrigue, were preserved in their entirety while the rest of Europe subsided into feudalism. Located at the intersection of Anatolia and Europe, on a waterway connecting the Mediterranean and Black Seas, Byzantium became a thriving walled trade center of a half million inhabitants. For centuries it continued to rule much of the old eastern empire. Moreover, the city founded by Constantine remained for almost a thousand years the greatest city of "Christendom," which now divided into eastern and western variants.

Byzantium became the center of the eastern (Greek Orthodox) variant of Christianity, whose leadership was Byzantine and whose liturgical language was Greek rather than Latin. From Byzantium, Orthodox Christianity spread into eastern Europe and Russia.

(Meanwhile, the Bishop of Rome retained primacy among Christians in the west—hence the name "Roman Catholic Church.") Just as Roman basilicas became the architectural template for future Catholic churches, Byzantine churches, especially the great Hagia Sophia cathedral, for centuries the most spectacular in the Christian world, became the model for Orthodox churches. It was in Byzantium that Roman civil law, arguably the empire's greatest legacy to later European civilization, was carefully preserved and codified during centuries when such activities had ceased in most of Christendom.

The former Western Roman Empire, meanwhile, disappeared. Barbarian peoples—speakers of Celtic, Slavic, and Germanic languages—finally settled down and founded a dozen kingdoms in formerly Roman territories. Among them were the Huns, effective warriors who may have been pushing other barbarians ahead of them as they arrived from the steppe. Unlike most of the barbarians who invaded the declining Roman Empire, but like the later Mongols, the Huns were rather East Asian in appearance. (Recall their close association with the Xiongnu of the northern Chinese borderlands.) By 453 CE, when their king Attila died suddenly, the Huns controlled much of Europe. As normally happened with nomadic conquests, however, the Hun Empire did not much outlast the death of its creator, Attila. The Huns did not settle in Europe, but other barbarian groups did. In France, Spain, and Italy, the newcomers eventually integrated themselves into an existing society, adopting provincial Roman language and customs. The modern French, Spanish, and Italian languages descend directly from the colloquial, usually called *vulgar*, Latin spoken in Roman times.

Gradually, Roman Christianity spread throughout western Europe. The progress of Christianity north of the Rhine (that is, beyond formerly Roman territory) can be charted by the foundation of monasteries that planted vineyards to make wine for communion, the most crucial Christian sacrament. The Viking pirates who swarmed so efficaciously over European coasts in the 800s and 900s CE were pagan descendants of the Neolithic battle-ax culture, not yet on board with the Christian program. Theirs was a famously uninhibited warrior cult, with their get-naked berserker battle frenzies, their pagan thunder god, Thor, and their vision of Valhalla (paradise) as a raucous eternal victory feast with wine, women, and song. Never was a culture more frankly and unabashedly war-oriented than that of the Vikings, starkly contrasting with their peace-loving Scandinavian descendants.

Trade shrank, in these so-called dark ages, and with it, cities. With shrinking cities, many other things declined—literacy, the arts, social institutions of all kinds, even an overall awareness of the larger world. The scale of life was reduced, becoming generally local, at most regional. Governance became more informal, structured at the top by feudal oaths of loyalty and obedience that warriors swore to each other. Writing became rare outside of monasteries, leaving us fewer sources to cast light on the situation. That's the reason for the old name *dark ages*. Lives more focused on subsistence were not necessarily darker than before, even if more limited. On the bright side, that ubiquitous keystone of Roman imperial society, slavery, vanished from European life. Despite their diversity, these small-scale societies all belonged to Christian churches, Roman in the west, Greek Orthodox in the east, which frowned on enslaving other Christians. Therefore, slaves were replaced by serfs, who were not technically enslaved chattel because they could not be bought and sold.

Gradually, the bishops of Rome were becoming recognized as the religious leaders of western Europe, the first popes. Overall, however, the west aspired to a restored imperial unity that never reappeared. In the year 800 CE, Charlemagne, a particularly successful Germanic warrior king, traveled to Rome to have the pope crown him "Emperor of the Romans." Charlemagne's effort to create a so-called Holy Roman Empire (neither holy, nor Roman, nor an empire, according to a famous quip) was a nostalgic last hurrah. Meanwhile, Byzantium consolidated itself as the capital of Greek Orthodox Christianity, even as it lost much of its old imperial ground to Muslim armies.

Islam

Charlemagne's 800 CE coronation responded partly to the rapid expansion of Islam. Muslim armies had conquered enormous territories in a very short time. In their initial expansion following Muhammad's prophecy, they had stormed across North Africa and soon occupied almost all of Iberia, which was to remain predominantly Muslim for centuries. Whereas both Buddha and Jesus had brought messages of personal salvation, Muhammad brought a vision of a godly society and specific guidelines concerning how to create it on Earth. Like Christianity and Buddhism, Islam extended its universal message to all people.

Like Christianity or Buddhism, Islam embodied an explicit program of social uplift, a set of rules to be followed by all those who surrender to the divine will. Unlike the Old Testament, a sort of anthology of Hebrew literature—also unlike the New Testament, which primarily recounts the story of Jesus and his apostles—the Quran is above all a guidebook for godly behavior. There is also a contrasting Muslim tradition, one that privileges the idea of a personal, ecstatic encounter with divinity, downplaying behavioral rules. That is the path followed by the distinctly minority Sufi tradition that has thrived at the margins of the Muslim world in Africa and South Asia. Sufi masters created separate communities of followers who often withdrew from society and lived from alms. But the spiritual work that Sufis did (and do) is part of a personal search for God and not (in the manner of Buddhist or Christian monasteries) a contribution to the society from which they have withdrawn. The majority Sunni tradition of Islam is very firmly about *not* withdrawing from, but rather, *molding* a righteous society. The Quran is the instruction manual.

Muhammad was born around 570 CE, in western Arabia, on the trade route between the Indian Ocean and the Mediterranean Sea. His native city, Mecca, was a distribution center for Asian trade goods. Muhammad's life is well documented compared to the lives of earlier prophets. He was not a prince or a carpenter, but a merchant. His was a world of faith, rich in religious possibilities, including those of Judaism and Christianity. Muhammad's revelation convinced him that he had marching orders from the one true God, and he set out to create the well-ordered society described in the Quran. Whereas Buddha and Jesus became wandering teachers, surrounding themselves with social marginals, Muhammad's prophecy involved community organizing from the outset, first in Mecca, and then in Medina, a nearby city where circumstances seemed more promising. Muhammad was a civil and, occasionally, military as well as spiritual leader. His proposals were not only for his followers, but for the whole community, whom Muhammad invited to submit to God's will. Both the word *Muslim* and the word *Islam* refer in Arabic to that submission.

The prophet Muhammad died in 632 CE, but by then he had inspired an entire society. It was primarily an Arab society, a society of herders, many of whom were still mobile pastoralists who retained the military vocation of Asia's lifelong horsemen. There were many Jews and Christians around as well, but they were unreceptive to Muhammad's prophecy. Muhammad's message was delivered to the wider world by galloping warriors possessed of a spiritual élan that swept away all opposition. Only a few years after Muhammad's death, most of Arabia was under Muslim control, and by 656 CE, Muslim warriors had overrun a large part of the Byzantine Empire. They had taken all of Egypt and Syria, along with about half the Mediterranean coast of Africa, also all of Arabia, Mesopotamia, and the Persian Gulf, along with the rest of Persia. A few more years, and they added Central Asia, Spain, and Portugal, too. For the time being, conquering Muslim armies often camped outside of existing cities, where they could remain apart and keep their new religion pure. Only gradually would the people who they had conquered become Muslims. In the meantime, the conquered would comprise subject populations who paid a special tax for their religious nonconformity.

Egypt, Syria, and Mesopotamia had been Byzantine or Persian

(which is to say Christian or Zoroastrian) until conquered by Muslim armies. They represented high cultures of the sort that usually absorbed conquering herders. And that is what happened here, yet again. The Hellenistic learning represented by the library at Alexandria, Egypt, for example, passed into respectful Muslim hands and was preserved. Persian became, and remained for centuries, the preeminent Muslim language of literature. Arabic gradually became the everyday language of Syria and Egypt and Mesopotamia, as well as Arabia. Damascus and then Baghdad became the seats of the prophet's successors, or caliphs, but in fact the effective power of the caliphate was never great. The caliphs were not religious leaders, and their authority was more theoretical than actual. Over time, the caliphate became irrelevant, fragmented, and disappeared. The caliphate's first dynasty, the Umayyads, were Arabs and governed from Damascus. The second dynasty, the Abbasids, who governed from Baghdad, were Persians, and their tenure marks the end of Arab dominance over the wider Muslim world. Arabic, the language of the Quran, remained the liturgical language, however. A basic part of serious religious training was to learn the Quran by heart in the original Arabic. Arabic-speaking Cairo, Damascus, and Baghdad remained the chief cities of the Muslim world. However, Persian, Turkish, Berber, and eventually Urdu, Bengali, and Malay became important Muslim languages as well. Beginning around 750 CE, the Abbasids presided over an evanescent golden age of Islamic culture. Baghdad become a world center of science, technology, engineering, mathematics, and medicine.

Now Muslim lands stretched from Spain to India, and eventually beyond, but their unity was almost entirely religious rather than political. Muslims don't do religious hierarchy, basically. There is no Muslim "church" organization, per se. The basic instructions are in the Quran, and they apply to everyone. Very unlike the Bible, the Quran was created all at once and, for some time after its creation, had no written form. (*Quran* means recitation.) Once you have the instructions, the rest is applying them. If ever there was a level playing field, it is the Muslim spiritual world. The most important rules are charity, frequent prayer, and stringent discipline over bodily appetites. Public performance of the cult is incessant but minimalist. It requires only a large clean space and a commitment to punctuality. After that, it's just you and your conscience, or for Muslim believers, you and your God, who is also everyone else's, because, according to the essential formula that defined Muslim belief, "there is no God but God, and Muhammad is his prophet."

The social emphasis of Muhammad's prophecy contrasted with the personal emphasis of both Buddha and Jesus. The focus of Muslim religious organizing was the whole community. Muslim religious authorities worried about controlling misbehavior, providing basic necessities, and overseeing the common good. The social emphasis of Muhammad's prophecy made secular authorities into mere enforcers. There was no really separate, complimentary sphere of secular governance. Christians could "render unto Caesar what is Caesar's," while rendering a different sort of tribute to God, on the presumption that Caesar and God demanded different things. In the Muslim world, secular authorities were also working for God and wanted the same things he wanted, at least officially.

Muslim common law, the much-misunderstood *sharia*, was based on an accretion of religious commentary by men of learning, collectively called the ulama. The ulama had no headquarters, academy, or leadership. Any man of sufficient religious learning could contribute, so sharia was extremely permeable to local pressures. Sharia is nothing if not comprehensive, covering even diet and personal hygiene, but English-language readers may equate it reductively with brutal punishments for women's sexual misconduct. Such punishments are local additions to sharia, reflecting the severe patriarchy of isolated herding communities a thousand years ago. Paradoxically, the open, democratic quality of sharia law, its lack of top-down, centralized control, has allowed conservative rural people to retain obsolete social norms that are not supported by the Quran.

Muslim religious scripture is also democratic. Under the Quran, a second tier of quasi-sacred Muslim scripture—comprising *hadith* and *sunna*—has been assembled by the ulama. Muhammad's words and deeds are not recorded in the Quran. From early times, Muhammad's living example (sunna) and his words (hadith) were preserved in oral traditions and eventually written down. More traditions were added to the collection gradually over the centuries, updating, filling in important gaps, adding evidence to one side or another of an ongoing interpretive debate in the ulama. As with sharia, there is no centralized control, and the only vetting process is open debate. It's as if Christian scholars established the words of Jesus by argument and evidence from oral tradition, citing the authentic provenance of this version or another, originally provided by an eyewitness, remembered and passed down a documented chain of reliable oral sources, before finally being committed to writing. Rather than a single collection of hadith, there are many.

Interestingly, women played a historically leading role in compiling and interpreting this second tier of Muslim scripture. At the outset, writing was not involved, and women were natural witnesses regarding the prophet's daily life and teachings. Women of Muhammad's household were key contributors. The prophet's third wife, Aisha, contributed more than two hundred hadith. But it wasn't only eyewitnesses of the first generation who were often women. Women's special role in the collection and transmission of hadith continued for a long time. Women who became recognized as authorities on specific collections of hadith might dictate them to male pupils and give public lectures about them. That seems to have been the case of Zaynab bint Sulayman, daughter of the governor of Basra, who lived during the brief golden age of the Abbasid caliphate and died in 759 CE. Another famous authority was Abidah al-Madaniyyah, who had begun her lifelong investigation as a slave girl in Medina. Abidah was still enslaved, living in Jerusalem, when a distinguished scholar of Muslim Spain passed through on his way to Mecca. Astounded by the slave's knowledge, he freed her and took her back to Spain. By the end of her life, she is said to have recorded ten thousand hadith.

Sunni Muslims, who are the large majority in Islam, accept a broad mainstream collection of hadith and sunna, but there are minority sects, especially Shia Muslims, who accept quite different traditional accounts. Their big differences do not concern Muhammad's prophecy but rather what happened afterward. Specifically, Shia Muslims believe that the rightful succession of Muhammad's worldly authority was lost quite early by the assassination of the rightful heir to the caliphate. Shia Muslims became a permanent minority opposition party. Their contrasting traditions, cultivated over centuries, as well as a historical narrative of grievances, are what separate Sunni and Shia. As the majority, Sunnis steadily exercised much greater institutional power. The caliphate, for example, was normally Sunni-controlled. Deprived of that power, with some exceptions, Shias turned to more charismatic leadership, the Imams, men believed to possess a special religious inspiration. Shias believed that a caliph of the rightful line might yet appear. They waited expectantly for this caliph-in-waiting, or "Hidden Imam." A few times, they believed he had appeared. Hence, Shia beliefs were not merely different from those of Sunnis. They were directly subversive of Sunni claims to righteousness.

In sum, Islam expanded suddenly in the 600s and 700s CE to become a transcontinental power and a world religion. It lacked political unity, but it defined a new major civilization. Practically overnight, so to speak, the Muslim world had joined Christendom as one of four chief civilizations spanning Eurasia. Indian and Chinese civilizations were undergoing changes, too.

Buddhism Hits the Silk Road

Buddhism, over a thousand years old at the time of Muhammad's prophecy, was only now spreading widely from its birthplace in the lower Ganges valley, becoming a world religion, too. Buddhism's urban vocation—its particular popularity among merchants and artisans—had carried it up the Ganges River, through the commercial cities of northern India, to Taxila, at the headwater of the Indus, not far from the Khyber Pass. Beyond the mountains, a couple of hundred miles north, was Central Asia—Bactria, Sogdiana, and the Silk Road cities of Bukhara and Samarkand. From there, one went east or west with equal facility. This is how Buddhism got to China. (The gargantuan bulk of the Himalayas blocks more direct travel between India and China.) From China, Buddhism spread to Korea and Japan. Directly from India it spread by sea to Southeast Asia, Buddhism's current demographic stronghold. Few other offshoots of India's multitudinous spiritual life—such as, for example, Jainism, which started at about the same time as Buddhism—have ever prospered outside of India. Buddhism's popularity among traders partly explains its peripatetic tendencies, no doubt, but only partly.

The Buddhist message explains the rest. Buddhism began among ascetics who had renounced the comforts of society to find the real meaning of life. The central emphasis lay on each person's imitation of the Buddha's search for enlightenment. Yet a universal religion must accommodate more than spiritual overachievers. There emerged, during the middle of the first millennium CE, a variant of Buddhism that held a more general appeal. It is called Mahayana, or the "greater vehicle," because it means to convey everyone to nirvana. Spiritual athletes can enter a monastery and apply themselves full time to the Buddha's demanding program of purification and self-improvement. For the weaker reeds among us, Mahayana provides compassionate spirits called Bodhisattvas to lend a helping hand.

Bodhisattvas are a bit like Catholic saints. Usually, Bodhisattvas began as people who achieved an unearthly spiritual perfection and no longer walk the Earth, but whose spirits have stayed to aid ordinary worshippers who beseech their intercession. Bodhisattvas have achieved enlightenment but postponed their own long-awaited reward. Most Bodhisattvas are gendered male, but the Bodhisattva called Tara (who probably descends from the Hindu goddess, Durga) promised she'd always be reborn female. Bodhisattvas like Tara are powerful, reassuring allies. Furthermore, in Mahayana belief, the

Buddha himself was no longer an ancient and long-gone teacher but rather a divine being to whom people could pray, seeking guidance. Helpful Bodhisattva spirits make Mahayana Buddhism warm and comforting. Charismatic warmth was a common characteristic of the emerging world religions.

Meanwhile, between 500 and 1000 BCE, Buddhism was beginning to wither in the land of its birth. The religious tradition today called Hinduism had undergone a profound transformation, developing very considerable warmth of its own. The earlier Vedic deities, brought by the Aryans, had been distant sky gods, and the signature Vedic religious act was an animal sacrifice. The great religious texts of the last millennium before the Common Era, following the Vedas, had been the Upanishads, abstruse treatises concerning the transmigration of souls. Only much later, around 500 CE, can we begin to see contours of Indian religious life as it currently exists, a brilliant cacophony of related but disparate Hindu traditions with no central authority.

Hindus share a common understanding of the spiritual world (involving karma, reincarnation, and the transmigration of souls) but locate themselves in diverse ways within it. Hindu deities are numberless. The great Hindu texts of this period were the Ramayana and Mahabharata, expansive narratives of fearsome demons and heroic deeds. These became the unifying texts of Hinduism as we know it today. The new focus was on attractive, sensual deities such as Krishna and Rama, mythological heroes who may have started out as real people and were later deified by tradition. Hindu belief in reincarnation makes it easy to weave together the threads of diffuse ancient mythologies. Krishna and Rama were added to the Hindu pantheon as new incarnations of the old-guard deity Vishnu. The jovial elephant god Ganesh, bringer of good luck, joined the pantheon as the son of old Shiva, the austere and awesome deity whose cosmic dance ends and restarts the universe. New gods added subplots to the cosmic story. The new version of Hinduism, much more than the older Vedic version, was a charismatic crowd pleaser.

Some things hadn't changed. Brahmins were still the arbiters of religious truth. That truth still involved the logic of caste, which became increasingly elaborate. The rise of charismatic Hinduism coincided with a reassertion of Brahmin power in Indian societies. Indian cities declined in this period, as happened in China and Europe as well. Buddhism, requiring urban wealth to fund its art and monasteries, declined proportionally. A more rural society was under the influence of village Brahmins to a greater extent. During the two hundred plus years from 320 to 550 CE, the Gupta Empire held sway across north India, partially recreating the earlier Mauryan Empire. This second great Indian empire, looming over the normal scrum of kingdoms, connected itself symbolically to the earlier Mauryans and shared their heartland. Several members of the new dynasty used the name of the first Mauryan emperor, Chandragupta. Unlike the Mauryans, however, the Gupta dynasty was Hindu, devoted to the god Vishnu. Its rise surely strengthened Brahmin authority. Among the best witnesses we have of the Gupta Empire were several Chinese Buddhists who had come to India to study and gather religious texts in the lower Ganges Buddhist holy land.

Buddhism had dribbled east—never west—on the Silk Road for some time. Why only east? To the west, Buddhism wasn't welcome in Zoroastrian or, later, Muslim Persia. To the east, however, lay China under the Tang dynasty (618–907), which lacked a strong state religion. The Chinese did not wait for Buddhism to drift their way. They imported it as part of a deliberate opening to the west. Under the Tang dynasty, as under the earlier Han, Chinese military power was extended to the Oxus region in Central Asia—the need for horses again being the main motivator. Iron-Age infantries no longer dominated Eurasian battlefields, having given way to horsemen, in part because mounted warriors now had stirrups. In both China and Europe, mounted warriors were likely to be aristocrats. (Only on the steppe were horses not an expensive luxury, a manifestation of unusual wealth.) Along with Persian horses, the Tang dynasty even imported the Persian sport of polo for peacetime practice. Sculptures of the Buddha and temples to serve a steady stream of pilgrims were carved into cliffs along the Silk Road. The Tang dynasty capital at Chang'an, the eastern terminus of the Silk Road, now became the biggest city in the world.

The Chinese Buddhist monk Xuanzang, after spending years collecting texts in India, returned with them to Chang'an, where he translated them into Chinese. Xuanzang worked in an early pagoda, which began as the Chinese version of a Buddhist *stupa*. Like Christianity, Buddhism used relics—fragments of a holy body—as powerful symbols. The most powerful were relics of the Buddha himself. According to tradition, his funeral ashes were divided and sent in all directions. A stupa was built to house each tiny bit of the Buddha's ashes. Asoka had thousands of stupas built. Chinese stupas turned out differently, so differently that they originated a new architectural form, the pagoda. Pagodas were much taller than Indian stupas, with tiers of tile roofing and a signature Chinese profile. China changed Buddhism, generating its own variant, called Chan, which in Japan became Zen. The jolly, bald Buddha statue most familiar in the west is strictly Chinese. Buddhism provided a religious application for the kind of wealth that empires generate for their upper classes. Thousands of Buddhist monasteries, tens of thousands of Buddhist monks and nuns, represented an enormous allocation of resources, as did works of art like China's many gigantic statues of the Buddha.

Buddhism gained a large place in Chinese life, but China never became unanimously Buddhist, far from it. There were always some elements of Buddhism that seemed more Indian than Chinese—such as celibacy and vegetarian diets. And besides, China had its own native religious ideas. The majority of Chinese religious practices were humble, intimate recognitions of local deities relating specifically to villagers' fields, hearths, and families. The homely quality of many folk devotions makes them easily pass unmentioned in discussion of capital-R Religion, despite their ubiquity in Chinese life.

The main Chinese competition for Buddhism was Daoism, a loose set of mystical traditions with beginnings that go right back to the

Zhou dynasty. Dao (formerly written Tao) has many elements, mostly not institutionalized. The small shrines by fields, roadsides, and in people's houses were loosely Dao. A major historical element of Dao was divination of the future. Another was the search for immortality, or at any rate, the unlimited extension of individual lives. More than one emperor poisoned himself in Daoist-inspired attempts to become immortal. Dao traditions also included lives of meditation and withdrawal from society to seek inspiration in nature, as we have seen elsewhere. Many elements of Dao were not too far from Buddhism and could easily meld with it. But Buddhists also competed with Daoists and sucked up their oxygen.

Wu Zeitan, whom we will call simply Empress Wu, favored Buddhism over Daoism. From 690 to 705 CE, after long being the power behind the scenes, Empress Wu donned the imperial yellow robe of absolute power. She was the only woman ever to do so, not as a place holder for a man, but rather in her own right. She had started as an imperial concubine and worked her way up, apparently though a love affair with the emperor's son, who kept her at the palace after his father's death. The concubines of a deceased emperor were normally shunted away to Buddhist convents if they had borne him no children. Official Chinese histories speak ill of Wu Zeitan (as they do, generally, of all powerful women), accusing her of murderous palace intrigue. She tried to break off the Tang dynasty and start her own, which did not go well.

Still, the Buddhist-curious Tang dynasty presided over brilliant cultural achievements. Tang China was unusually open to the world. Chinese commerce was expanding in the South China Sea as well as toward Central Asia. Chinese porcelain, in an early version, was being exported by sea. For example, around 826 CE, an Arab vessel went down in Indonesian seas heavily loaded with porcelain. In addition to Buddhists, Chang'an had tens of thousands of other foreign residents, including Persians and Sogdians, Koreans and Japanese, Zoroastrians, Christians, and eventually Muslims. When Xuanzang's pagoda collapsed, weighed down, perhaps, by the huge difficulty of translating all those sacred texts from Sanskrit to Chinese, Empress Wu had it rebuilt higher than before. The principal use of early woodblock printing, invented at this time, was making myriad copies of Buddhist texts—also poetry. Tang is the golden age of Chinese poetry and painting. School children have learned Tang dynasty poems by heart for over a thousand years.

The reign of Empress Wu was connected to these larger developments. Women of means spread their wings a bit in Tang China, wearing revealing clothing, even playing polo on horseback. It was all rather un-Confucian, but Tang times were un-Confucian times. Sophisticated courtesans like Japanese geishas were common, and the madams who ran houses of entertainment were respected public figures. Empress Wu, an upstart herself, naturally promoted the idea of careers open to talent. For aspiring scholars, she wanted competitive examinations, not political preferment, to be the principal path to government office. Empress Wu's attempt to found a new dynasty was short-lived, so her patronage of Buddhism and her encouragement of the official examination system proved temporary. Chinese traditions pushed back against Buddhism in the mid-800s. An economic motivation for the pushback appears in the imperial focus on dispossessing rich Buddhist monasteries and temples. Tang expansionism had empowered the military, and the military ran amok. In the An Lushan rebellion, a half-Sogdian frontier strongman brought his frontier army to menace Chang'an. Regional military governors began to supersede the influence of the emperor's mandarins, downplaying examinations, preferring scholars whose primary qualification was personal loyalty.

Overall, the years 500–1000 CE saw an incipient recovery of trade relationships across Eurasia. China was opening to the west, Islam to the east, and they were meeting in the middle. Traffic on the Silk Road intensified, renewing the trans-Asian connections of Roman-Han times. Muslim lands were not politically unified, but their political divisions did not prevent trade, and Muslim rulers provided an infrastructure that included roads, way stations, coins, markets, and an orderly social environment. Camels became the primary pack animals on the wide deserts of central and southwestern Asia. Baghdad, at the western terminus of the Silk Road, became, under the Abbasid caliphs, effectively the western counterpart of Chang'an.

Maritime trade also increased—in the Mediterranean, on the Atlantic coast of Europe, in the Indian Ocean, and on the South China Sea. The world's principal long-distance maritime trade still followed along coastal sea routes connecting Arabia to India to Malaysia to China. The Spice Route, as we will call it, had been open for centuries. For example, one of the first Chinese Buddhists to visit India hitched a ride with traders and was shipwrecked in Indonesia on his return trip. Arabs, especially, had been carriers of this trade even before they became Muslims. The mentioned vessel loaded with porcelain that sank in Indonesia in 826 CE (a characteristic Arab dhow) was bound for Oman in the Persian Gulf. It apparently traversed the whole route between Persian and China. That was unusual. Sailing vessels on the Spice Route, like caravans on the Silk Road, normally went back and forth on a limited segment.

Segmented trading patterns were linked to the winds. The Indian Ocean has patterns of seasonal winds called monsoons that have been a boon to sailors since Roman times. This was the world of the legendary Sinbad the Sailor, whose seven miraculous voyages eventually appeared in the *Thousand and One Nights*. The summer monsoon occurs when summer suns overheat the Asian landmass, drawing cooler, moist air in from the ocean, bringing rain. These winds blow reliably in one direction for months, and then, in winter, reverse direction as the landmass cools. Summer monsoon winds powered a marvelously fast and easy voyage from the mouth of the Red Sea to India, and steady winter monsoons powered a secure return. The South China Sea also has alternating monsoon winds to facilitate open-ocean crossings and returns.

Malaysia and South India were the crucial points of transshipment on the Spice Route. South India was taking off, 500–1000 CE, as probably the busiest long-distance commercial hub in the world.

The southern tip of India swarmed with traders from across Asia—Muslims, Jews, and Christians—all too busy trading to fight. By the 800s CE, there were sizable colonies of Muslim merchants at all Spice Route transshipment points, and also at Guangzhou, the eastern terminus of the Spice Route on the South China coast.

As South Asian maritime trade connected China and the Muslim world, Europe remained on the margins, connected to the larger network mostly through Muslim intermediaries. While there were now more ships sailing along European coasts, the most notable were Viking pirates, who plundered more than traded. Interregional trade in Europe was at a low point, and Europe's connections with other parts of the world were dwindling along with its urban network. In an age when Chang'an had more than a million inhabitants, and Baghdad almost as many, Paris and London, the principal cities of northern Europe, hovered in the vicinity of twenty thousand inhabitants each. Rome, which had boasted a million inhabitants in imperial days, was down to about thirty thousand. The largest European cities—Palermo, Cordoba, and Constantinople—were all linked somehow to great Asian trade routes, and only Constantinople was a Christian city.

Europeans found Chinese porcelains easy to admire but hard to acquire. Far eastern products were flowing abundantly into the Muslim world, but conflictive relations between Christians and Muslims did not facilitate trade. And that situation was about to get worse.

CHAPTER SEVEN

World of Woe

By the year 1000 CE, a millennium after the birth of Jesus, world religions organized most Eurasian societies. Disappointingly, however, the promise of the golden rule had not been fulfilled. A small minority truly lived by sacred principles of human brotherhood, while the majority twisted those principles to distinguish between "us" and "them," and then treated "them" (whoever that was) no better than before. The new ethical teachings had mitigated, but failed to undo, people's chronic inhumanity toward each other.

The young woman whom we call Joan of Arc was not yet twenty in 1431 when the English burned her alive, the way witches were burned, to get the devil out of them. Years before, the Archangel Michael had appeared to Joan in her father's garden and given her a mission—to drive out English invaders and assure the coronation of the French king Charles VII. Joan had also probably heard prophecies, which had circulated for a few generations, saying that English armies would be ultimately defeated by a young girl. Joan of Arc lived toward the end of the Hundred Years War, during which French and English kings struggled over parts of what is now France. At the time, claims of feudal loyalty and protection, personal oaths sworn between warriors, still over-shadowed incipient notions of nationality. English monarchs controlled as much territory in France as French monarchs did, and English control was increasing. Cutting off her hair and putting on men's clothes, the illiterate farm girl went to find the aspiring French prince, informed him of the angel's endorsement, and offered her support against the English.

Charles had little to lose. He saw that Joan was given a horse, a banner, and a second-hand suit of armor, and off she went to lift the siege of Orleans—which she did, within a week, merely by being present on the battlefield, waving her banner, and giving testimony that God backed Charles. The young woman's direct military potential was exactly nil, as she held her flag in a hail of arrows and bled from more than one. She wielded purely moral force, rooted in self-sacrifice. Not by accident had the archangel appeared to her accompanied by Saint Margaret and Saint Catherine, two early Christian martyrs. We know that Joan of Arc inspired others, too, especially because of the lifting of the siege of Orleans, obvious evidence of divine intervention.

Unfortunately for this plucky and slightly unhinged young woman, her success doomed her. The English needed to discredit her totally, which they did by reversing the signs of her story. Intervention yes, but hardly divine! Joan was captured by her enemies and put on trial for doing the work of the devil. Her diabolical habit of appearing as a man became evidence against her—a persuasive bit of spin at the time, because after all, what everyone knew about "the maiden of Orleans" was, precisely, that she had appeared on the battlefield, wearing armor, astride a warhorse, like a man. Even so, the English court martial had to ignore its own rules in order to confirm her guilt and execute her. After her death, she became a paragon of French nationalism and, ultimately, a Catholic saint.

As we can observe, royal claims to divine authorization were still de rigueur in 1431 Europe. Monarchs still ruled, supposedly, by the grace of God. The world religions had shown they could speak truth to power, but normally they avoided doing so. State power and organized religion were joined at the hip like conjoined twins between 1000 and 1500. Conflicts were framed increasingly in religious terms. For all their early promise—their ethical universalism, their intent to be an antidote against injustice—the world religions were being woven, warp and woof, into the fabric of patriarchal societies founded on exploitative state power. Woeful worldly struggles erupted within, and between, faiths.

Muslim World, Christian World

During the years 1000–1500, Muslim expansion slowed and, reaching approximately its current geographical extent, stopped. The Muslim golden age was ending. Meanwhile, the Christian golden age was still nowhere to be seen. Western Europe gave no hint of its coming development and eventual global power.

The Muslim caliphate fell apart. Bitter disputes over who should be caliph, let us recall, had created the deep and permanent rift between Sunni and Shia. The caliphate was generally a Sunni project, and from 750 to 1258 the seat of the caliphate was the purpose-built capital city of Baghdad. During that time, the caliph never exercised wide control over the sprawling realm of Muslim faithful. Moreover, he sometimes had direct rivals. A rival caliphate operated for over a century at the city of Cordoba in Muslim Spain, and another caliphate existed in Cairo for over two centuries. At moments there were three caliphs simultaneously, none recognizing the legitimacy of the others' claims. (Buddhism and Christianity were also fragmenting in 1000–1500, a period in which there were sometimes two rival papacies.)

This was the high point of Shia influence in the Muslim world. The Cairo caliphate, uniquely, was a Shia creation, and the Bagdad caliphate was controlled for a time by a Shia family. The Baghdad caliphate disappeared forever, though, when the invading Mongols flattened the city in 1258. By that time the Cordoba and Cairo caliphates were gone, too. Much later, the Ottoman Turks attempted to institute a caliphate in Istanbul, but most Muslims never recognized its authority. Between 1000 and 1500, Islam divided politically into three Muslim empires. Fragmentation and conflict among Muslims—Arabs, Persians, Turks, and Kurds—facilitated the invasion of crusading armies from Europe, and then, from Central Asia. The Mongols, when they arrived, would make the crusades look like child's play.

For three centuries, Christians, Jews, and other small sects had lived more or less peacefully under Muslim rule. Beginning around 1000 CE, Turkish migration into eastern Mediterranean lands put pressure on non-Muslim communities there. Conflicts erupted among Muslims, too, as we have seen. The famous Assassins, a radical Shia sect of Persian extraction, assassinated not Christians, for the most part, but Sunni Arabs or Turks. By Turks we mean various waves of Turkic-speaking people of Central Asia who were entering the Muslim world around 1000 CE. The Turks—specifically those who became the Ottoman Turks—began pushing into what remained of the Byzantine Empire. Despite the great schism between Eastern Orthodoxy and Western Catholicism, which occurred in 1054, the Byzantine emperor, who led the Orthodox Church, appealed to the head of the Roman Catholic Church for support against the Turks.

In 1095, the pope responded by calling for a crusade, a holy war, to establish Christian control over Jerusalem. Tens of thousands responded, especially from what are today France and Germany. Franks, the Muslims called those from France, and they applied the same name to all subsequent crusaders. Over the course of two centuries, crusaders mounted six transcontinental expeditions, traveling largely on foot from northwestern Europe to the eastern Mediterranean theater of war. The first crusade accomplished its mission of bringing Jerusalem under Christian control, amid an unbelievably indiscriminate slaughter of noncombatants. To say that the gutters of Jerusalem ran with blood in the name of God was not hyperbole, on that occasion, but rather a literal truth. The crusaders also claimed territory, built castles, and established "crusader states" in Syria and Palestine. A Frankish count Baldwin made himself King of Jerusalem. The seizure of Jerusalem, a city holy to Jews, Muslims, and Christians alike, gradually produced defensive unity among divided Muslims, and they found their leader in a Kurdish warrior named

Saladin. (Kurdistan, the land of the Kurds, has never had a sovereign state of its own, but it has never lacked fierce defenders. For readers who somehow missed the Kurds in history, meet their great warrior hero.) Saladin did not fight for the Kurds, however, nor for himself, but for Islam. His recapture of Jerusalem, respecting the lives of its Christian defenders, contrasted with the bloodbath committed by the crusaders there. When Saladin died in 1193, his remaining personal wealth was insufficient to pay for his funeral. Saladin's legendary probity won him grudging respect among his European enemies.

One of them was Richard the Lionhearted, king of England, a man of few words, a warrior's warrior, considerably less squeamish than Saladin about executing civilians. Richard proposed at one point that his sister marry Saladin's brother, with Jerusalem to be their wedding present. Richard's overall goal was to maintain crusader territorial claims in Syria, which was, broadly speaking, the main purpose of all crusades after the first one. Jerusalem, the original objective, was never retaken, but crusader territorial claims lived on.

Why did crusaders, not just land-grabbing barons, but the crusading rank and file, repeatedly make their dangerous journey? As in all wars, there was surely a variety of motivations. Crusaders won respect and prestige for "taking the cross," so they proudly wore a red cross sewn to their clothing. Crucially, they were promised God's "indulgence" of their sins as a reward. Official indulgences granted by the church supposedly protected sinners from divine punishment, a service that could come in handy for knights who spent considerable time brawling and carousing. The crusades remind us that Europe, no less than the Asian steppe, had developed a powerful warrior cult, and the Middle Ages were its zenith. At the same time, most crusaders clearly believed that they were doing something holy by taking the cross. Many left the satisfactions of normal life behind, and many never returned. It is not so easy, overall, to separate selfish motives from idealistic ones in projects like the crusades.

Richard the Lionhearted spent his reign at war rather than governing. Although born and raised in England, after becoming king he left England and spent the rest of his life mostly on crusade and in France, where he held many additional titles of nobility. In addition to king of England, Richard was Count of Poitiers, Anjou, and Nante, also Duke of Normandy, Gascony, and Aquitaine. Here was the divided control of France that continued into Joan of Arc's day. Richard had inherited a lot of French territory from his famous mother, Eleanor of Aquitaine, who was consecutively Queen of France, and then England, and one of the most powerful women of medieval Europe.

Eleanor's beauty was often praised but, interestingly, never described. She was, at any rate, quite well-educated for a medieval European lady. She could sing, dance, play the harp, and speak Latin, weave, spin, embroider, and do needlepoint, as well as ride horseback for hunting and falconry. Undoubtedly, however, her greatest appeal lay in the vast wealth that she inherited as Duchess of Aquitaine, making her perhaps the most marriageable young woman in Europe. No wonder that her first husband was Louis VII, the king of France, whom she accompanied on the second crusade when he was asked by the pope to help rescue the failing crusader states in Syria. Eleanor had a personal interest in the project because her uncle Raymond was a crusader with a stake in one of those failing states. The royal couple made a splash during their stay at Constantinople, but the second crusade ended in failure, and the royal marriage went on the rocks during the return voyage. Eleanor had borne two daughters but still, after fifteen years, no male heir.

Lack of male heirs was a deal breaker for royal marriages, and this one, like countless others, did not survive the queen's failure to produce one. With the cooperation of the pope, Louis had the marriage annulled on the grounds that he and Eleanor were too closely related. Eleanor's landholdings were restored to her, and despite her failure to produce an heir for Louis, they reinstated her incredible appeal as a marriage partner. Several high-ranking nobles considered abducting her and forcing her to marry them. Almost immediately, she married Henry II of England (also Duke of Normandy) who was eleven years younger than she (and more closely related to her than her first husband). Henry believed in her potential, and she gave him eight children, three of whom became kings.

Even as queen of England, Eleanor preferred to spend her time in France. There, around 1185, she and her ladies-in-waiting amused themselves with tales of romance and reportedly sat in judgement over lovers' quarrels. These activities are described in a contemporary tract entitled *The Art of Courtly Love*. Eleanor was at the center of an emerging phenomenon, more or less the beginnings of modern "romance." In a world where weddings normally responded to family imperatives, the idea of falling in love had little place in marriage choices. The new idea of courtly love (love among nobles at court) was not about marriage, not even about sex. It was the mystical idea of love, whereby one falls in love helplessly and eternally, with a soulmate *not* selected by one's parents, a celebration of personal idealism, uncluttered by mundane considerations. In fact, Eleanor's ladies reportedly viewed true love as next to impossible within marriage. Eleanor had various perspectives on this issue. Her husband did plenty of hands-on experimenting with courtly love. When she was accused of plotting against him, Henry had her imprisoned for many years, partly to keep her nose out of his notorious affairs.

The Turks, meanwhile, whose arrival had triggered the crusades, became the new masters of the eastern Mediterranean. Like all steppe people, they were natural soldiers, the combined result of their archery and horsemanship. A horse archer was a rider able to loose arrows accurately at a gallop. Only ceaseless practice and training made this possible, and boys on the steppe started very young. Once horse archers appeared in Muslim armies, they became the key to victory. The trick was to recruit boys who had been training informally all their young lives. Any kid from the steppe matched this description. Often, Turkish boys in Central Asia were sold to Arab or Persian recruiters who took them home to serve as *mamluks*. Mamluks formed corps of elite mercenaries, who continued to speak Turkish although living among Arabs. Turks also entered the Arab world in migrating groups, and behind them came the Mongols, the steppe warriors to end all steppe warriors. The Mongols did not stay in the region, but the Turks did, and became Muslims, the new war champions of the Sunni majority.

It was a specific group of Turks, the Ottoman Turks, who somewhat reunified the Arab world. Their Ottoman Empire lasted for over six hundred years and included not only Egypt, Syria, and Iraq, but also Anatolia, much of the North African coast, and eventually all southeastern Europe. The Ottoman capital Istanbul (formerly Constantinople, then Byzantium) was located in Europe, after all. Byzantium had become the center of Greek Orthodox Christianity and was still the most important city in the Christian world at the time of the crusades. Basically, over several hundred years, the Turks dismembered the Byzantine Empire and reassembled the pieces as the Ottoman Empire. The benchmark date was their dramatic conquest of the Byzantine capital, aided by impressive siege artillery, in 1453. The Turks had to defeat many Muslim armies in their quest for Mediterranean supremacy, but even more, they had to defeat Christian navies. To control the Black Sea and the eastern Mediterranean, the formerly steppe-dwelling Turks built a navy to confront Christian powers like Venice and Genoa. Venetian and Genoese galleys had become vital intermediaries between European markets and the Spice Route.

The Ottomans had many interactions with Christians. The great mosques of Istanbul developed an architectural style clearly influenced by the city's eastern Orthodox churches, chiefly the Hagia Sofia. Ottoman administration was innovative and rewarded talent. The Ottoman imperial family increasingly withdrew from public life into the luxurious Topkapi Palace, leaving much daily governance to a corps of rigorously selected and trained professional bureaucrats. Unsurprisingly, given their pastoral origins, the Turks employed many eunuchs in the imperial household, most especially in the palace harem. They also created and deployed another sort of imperial drone, called janissaries. Like mamluks, janissaries were boys taken from their families at a young age to be trained as an elite corps of mercenaries. Janissaries, however, were never Turks, but rather, converted Christians from Ottoman-controlled areas in the Balkans.

The Ottoman Turks were unifiers in a military sense, through conquest. In Central Asia and Afghanistan, other Turks were that kind of unifier, too. The fertile plains around the upper Ganges River attracted these dusty steppe warriors into northern India, where they formed a sultanate at Delhi. For a time, the Delhi sultanate was ruled by a Mamluk dynasty, just as mamluks had also formed a ruling dynasty in Egypt. From 1236 to 1240, Delhi was governed by a woman. Razia Sultana's father was a mamluk slave who, rising to rule Delhi, left his daughter in charge while away on campaign. He eventually left her his throne. She was killed in battle within four years.

Let us return to the clash between Muslims and Christians in the region of the Mediterranean Sea. The clash was framed by Ottoman advances from the east and Castilian advances in the west. Various small Christian kingdoms of northern Spain had resisted the Muslim invaders called Moors and slowly rolled back Moorish control between 1000 and 1500, crowding the Moors into the city-states of Seville, Cordoba, and finally, Granada, which fell in 1492. Seven centuries of conflict and coexistence on the Iberian Peninsula were over. By virtue of their historical proximity to Muslim traditions, Christians and Jews had normally been permitted to practice their own religions under Moorish rule, provided they paid the special tax on religious nonconformity. With the fall of Granada, the unifying kingdoms of Castile and Aragon, who had led the Christian reconquest, felt strong enough to expel their large Jewish community along with remaining Moors who declined to renounce Islam. Religious purity was the order of the day. The Spanish Inquisition did quality control, rooting out, torturing, and executing former Muslims or Jews who were suspected of continuing to practice their old religions.

The year 1492 marked more than the unification of Spain, of course. Fernando of Aragon and Isabel of Castile, the proudly Catholic monarchs of Spain, had also sponsored a voyage by a certain Genoese sea captain who proposed to sail west across the Atlantic to China. He never got to China, as will be disclosed in a later chapter. Much else needs to be revealed first, such as a lightning overview of the European civilization that produced Columbus.

Europe in the Middle Ages had approximately the same demographic weight as China, India, or the Muslim world. By several measures, when compared with the Roman Empire, Europe's Middle Ages represented a step backward. Medieval Europe certainly had a less impressive built environment, with fewer roads, sewers, and public buildings. It had many fewer slaves, too, almost none, but ordinary peasants were often serfs, tied to the land, required to labor for the landowner forever without pay. Education and literacy were more limited than under the Romans, as were trade, travel, and all expressions of high culture, such as theater, literature, painting, and sculpture. Medieval European society had, above all, narrower horizons than the Roman society that had spanned southern Europe, northern Africa, and the Middle East. Political organization was small-scale, a crazy quilt of kingdoms, principalities, duchies, counties, and city-states. The Italian peninsula, for example, was divided among several different kingdoms, the Papal-States, and city-states like Genoa and Venice. The Iberian Peninsula counted a half dozen kingdoms, and today's Germany, literally dozens of principalities. England was a single kingdom that had already conquered Wales, but not Scotland or any part of Ireland.

Life in medieval Europe was basically rural, intensely local, chronically violent. The normal social unit was a manor, the private estate of a noble family. The center of the manor was the noble's fortified residence, a castle. Peasants who lived on the estate as serfs, possibly for generations, owed rent to the noble family, delivered as a proportion of their crop, most of which was for subsistence rather than sale. Except for keeping record of rent payments, the landlord took little interest in farming. Unlike the ruling class of Rome, medieval European noblemen had only one calling: war. To be a nobleman was to be a knight. Unlike the Romans, knights in armor fought on horse-back. A knight's armor was so heavy that it required the strength of a horse just to move it around. Although mounted, all that most knights could actually do on the battlefield was hold their lances and spur their horses to charge. That was usually enough. The shock-force of such a charge could sweep away all opposition, scattering foot soldiers like bowling pins. Cavalry was useless against impreg-nable fortification, however, which is what made castles handy. A landscape littered with fortresses reveals the absence of centralized political control because strong castles could routinely resist royal power. Part of imposing centralized control, when that eventually took place, was banning the fortification of manor houses and the maintenance of private armies. In the meantime, all nobles had ret-inues of armed men.

After warfare and the warrior cult, the greatest pan-European social institution, by far, was the church. In medieval Europe, it was sufficient to say simply "the church" because the Roman Catholic Church, in the West, and the Greek Orthodox Church, in the East, permitted the existence of no other. *Catholic* means all-embracing. Far more than a shared creed, the church was an institution with centralized leadership, a clearly structured hierarchy, and meticu-lous record keeping, not to mention pervasive territorial coverage, vast material resources, and a profound hold on people's hearts and minds. Ecclesiastical Latin or Greek were the only pan-European languages. And aside from castles and city walls, the greatest con-structions by far were the gothic cathedrals that began going up all over western Europe during the lifetime of Eleanor of Aquitaine. As generation after generation of nobles left monetary bequests in hope of spiritual rewards, ecclesiastical land and wealth accumulated. In this, church property differed from family property, which was divided in each generation unless special primogeniture laws pre-vented division by giving all the inheritance to the eldest son.

In addition to parish clergy who served local congregations, monks, friars, and nuns entered proliferating holy orders, many living in monasteries and convents. The members of holy orders eventually outnumbered the parish clergy who ministered to congregations. Together, religious communities represented a substantial fraction of Europe's medieval population. Different orders had different requirements and missions. Some, most particularly the nuns, lived cloistered lives involving almost no social contact except with each other. Religious of both sexes took a vow of silence so as not to interrupt their meditation and prayer. Some took a vow of poverty and lived without a hint of creature comfort, using a block of wood for a pillow. Some provided social services, such as caring for the sick and educating the young. Not only health care and education, but also virtually all forms of written, artistic, and musical culture were in the hands of religious men and women. Inside the church, Latin scriptures were painstakingly copied and recopied. Meeting in Rome, churchmen from various parts of western Europe could converse in Latin. Outside the church, literacy was limited, even among nobles.

There was some tension between Europe's Christian churches and its feudal power structure. Unable to condone the sexual promiscuity of upper-class males, the clergy averted its eyes. The noble alpha males, for their part, scoffed at priests who wore cassocks instead of pants and learned how to read Latin instead of how to unhorse an adversary. Their knightly code of chivalry resonated more with pagan warriors past than with anything in the New Testament. When Christian precepts clashed with social realities, those precepts were often ignored. Warrior priests and bishops were not unknown. They used blunt weapons so as not to shed blood. A knight who had slaughtered, plundered, and raped not too egregiously might hope to set things right, before he faced God's judgement of his sins, by providing generous endowments to ecclesiastical entities. His saintly gesture would buy him indulgences, a specific number of masses celebrated in his honor, and hopefully, a sculpted crypt inside the church, close to the altar.

Song China and the Mongols

While Europeans were at the height of their knights-and-castles thing, something totally different was happening in China. The Tang dynasty had disappeared and the country become less, rather than more, militaristic. Meanwhile, China's economic and demographic center of gravity was shifting south.

Each ruling dynasty decided on the location of its capital city, but until the Song dynasty, 970–1279 CE, all ruling families had made their capitals in the northern heartland along the Yellow River, near the gateway to the steppe and the terminus of the Silk Road. All dynasties before Song had had mostly inland-facing, continental orientations. Song China, in contrast, had a more outward-facing, maritime orientation, at least initially. Its major cities were ports. Manufacturing and trade became more important than tribute or war. Song emperors made their capital in the southern city of Nanjing, on the vast Yangtze River, China's greatest transportation artery. The eastern plain along the lower Yangtze had become China's most populous and productive region. When China's capital eventually moved back north, its greatest wealth remained in the southeast.

Eastern China, along the lower Yangtze River, became the great center of economic activity. Access to water transportation made southeastern China the focus of large-scale manufacture and rice cultivation. Chinese porcelain, which requires special clay and extra-hot firing to achieve its glasslike perfection, was mass-produced and shipped to market safely and practically by canal boat. China now boasted a comprehensive network of canals linked to the great river system. The hydraulic canal lock, a necessary part of such a system, was invented by a Song engineer in 984. There would be nothing like it in Europe for a half millennium. Rice barges of a hundred tons carried staple food from southern paddies to northern cities. Chinese rivers, canals, and coastal waters swarmed with the surprisingly practical vessels called junks, which came in all sizes. Seagoing junks could be enormous, far larger than any European ship, and Chinese traders were busy sailing around the South China Sea, but without claiming any territories in the name of the emperor. If you had silk and porcelain to trade, after all, no further claims were necessary.

In stark contrast to medieval Europe, a market economy—also cities and literacy—flourished in Song China. The extraordinary volume of economic activity in China required more and more circulating currency. The Song solution was another Chinese invention: paper money. Meanwhile, the civil service examinations were made more truly competitive than ever, and more prestigious. The Song emperor himself supervised the final stages. A sure sign of widespread ability to read was the demand for popular literature. The first Chinese novels date from the Song dynasty, about five hundred years before their European counterparts. Moreover, the Song dynasty was much less militarist than the Tang dynasty had been. Imperial bureaucrats and centrally appointed magistrates ran the peaceable Song Empire.

Consider Zhao Mingcheng and Li Qingzhao, a celebrated urban couple of northern China, approximate contemporaries of Eleanor of Aquitaine. The couple were stylish and artsy, and both wrote poetry. Any elite Chinese wrote poetry, of course. The husband of the couple was a famous scholar, but the real excitement was his wife Qingzhao, who turned out to be not just a good, but a great, poet. These days Zhao Mingcheng is often called "husband of the famous Li Qingzhao." Mingcheng was a member of the mandarin elite whose passion was the study of ancient inscriptions, which Miingcheng collected, collated, and analyzed critically when not carrying out official duties. His thirty-volume magnum opus became a foundational study in the field. His wife Qingzhao shared his passion. Theirs was an amazingly companionate marriage. During their lives, the Song dynasty was losing its grip in the northern borderlands to yet another incursion of steppe horsemen. At one point, the couple had to flee south with fifteen cartloads of books and other possessions.

Mingcheng had been sent to a post as magistrate in a city on the lower Yangtze, and he died of dysentery on the way. In mourning, Qingzhao moved to nearby Hangzhou, where she continued to write poetry and later remarried.

The late Tang-dynasty reaction against Buddhism, including Buddhist empowerment of women, had continued in the Song dynasty. The wealth of Buddhist monasteries was progressively expropriated by the imperial government, which promoted a revival of earlier Confucian thought. Buddhist influence in China declined, without disappearing. In its place, however, severely patriarchal Confucianism regained official favor and totally dominated the great system of competitive exams that every would-be mandarin had to pass. Confucius had recommended that widows not remarry, so better to honor the memory of their departed husbands. Now, and not before, would the abhorrent custom of foot-binding become common among well-off families. Daoism, which had never lost its wide traditional following, also found renewed official favor in Song China.

China's Song dynasty finally collapsed because of the Mongol invasion. Mongolia is at the eastern end of the steppe, just north of China proper. The Mongolian language is probably related to Japanese, Korean, and Turkish. The Mongols were yet another group of yurt-dwelling, sheep-herding, shaman-consulting, horse-riding archers. To anyone who dared resist their onslaught, the Mongols became invincible enemies from hell. The Mongols made themselves felt, and more than just a little, at both ends of the Eurasian steppe.

The creation of a Mongol Empire, the largest land empire ever, is inseparable from the story of its creator, Temujin, who didn't even have a last name until he made himself Genghis Khan. A steppe warrior who rose from slavery to create the world's largest empire, Temujin was a simple man of his place and time. Pastoral people constantly raided each other's herds, and Temujin was enslaved in such a raid. He escaped and, after further adventures, finally married the bride to whom he had been betrothed at the age of ten. His bride was then kidnapped in another raid, but Temujin rescued her and even accepted her son conceived during her captivity. Although he later had five hundred consorts, she was his only wife ever.

In 1186, Temujin was elected khan (king) among the Mongols, but it took him twenty more years to become Genghis Khan (emperor) in 1206, by extending his control over related steppe peoples, many of them Turks. After becoming Genghis Khan in 1206, he turned his ambitions west and launched the most expansive conquests in world history. Genghis Khan was not a flamboyant battlefield commander. His personal contribution to his monotonous string of victories was planning, organization, and supply. On open ground suitable to the steppe warrior's tactics of speed and maneuver, the Mongols had no peers, except for other steppe warriors, such as the Turkic peoples of Central Asia, who largely joined the armies of Genghis Khan. When confronted with city walls, Genghis Khan deployed Chinese siege engineers whom he had captured elsewhere.

Mongol attack in 1220 turned Samarkand and Bukhara, the great Silk Road cities of Central Asia, into smoking ruins, their former inhabitants reduced to pyramids of skulls. The armies of Genghis Khan did something similar to Baghdad, as well. They also laid waste to the original center of Russia, including Kiev, opening the way for the eventual rise of Moscow. The largest land empire ever had been created in only a few years.

The armies of Genghis Khan basically didn't know how to lose. Habitually, they first offered their adversaries the opportunity to surrender and be spared. Those who accepted might be treated quite leniently. The Mongols eagerly recruited people with "civilized" skill sets—craftsmen and artisans and wise men of various kinds who had know-how that the Mongols lacked. The Mongols respected Daoist, Buddhist, Muslim, and Christian holy men and arranged debates among them. Resisting the Mongols was another matter entirely. Those who refused an opportunity to surrender inevitably saw their possessions pilfered and wasted, their men defeated and massacred, their women and children enslaved. This spectacular violence was

a tool of war, which the Mongols did not especially glorify or celebrate. For defeated enemies, the saving grace of Mongol domination
was its brevity. Among the skillsets that Mongol warriors had yet
to acquire was the administration of stable governing institutions.
They could conquer practically anything but govern practically nothing. Mongol conquests tended to be divided in each generation as
the conqueror's successors fought for control. By 1300, the vast area
dominated by the Mongols had been divided into four parts. One of
those parts was China.

The Mongols overthrew the Song dynasty and installed themselves
as the new rulers of China. Temujin's grandson, Kublai Khan, had
declared himself the first emperor of China's Yuan dynasty in 1271.
Steppe people had figured in Chinese history since earliest times.
Never before, however, had unassimilated outsiders seized all of
China. The Mongols moved the Chinese capital north to a new spot,
now called Beijing. Obviously nostalgic for the steppe, they reserved
a pasture within Beijing where they could spend time in yurts while
their horses grazed nearby, unmolested by the surrounding Chinese
population, who were forbidden to enter. This was the genesis of
today's Forbidden City palace compound on Tiananmen Square.
Ever pragmatic, Mongol rulers maintained the Song emphasis on
industry and trade, although they did not engage in these activities
themselves. The Song city Hangzhou had been among the world's
busiest ports. The Mongols governed through the existing imperial
structure, but without revering it. China's difficult-to-acquire literary culture was mostly lost on them, and rough-and-ready practi-
cality trumped mandarin prestige in Yuan dynasty governance. On
the other hand, Yuan rulers had a special taste for vernacular opera,
which did not require literacy to be appreciated.

These were not good times for China in most ways. The Mongols
were not gentle conquerors, and the Chinese chafed under foreign
domination. Moreover, the appearance of bubonic plague in remote
western China made matters much, much worse, causing catastrophic
population loss and hastening the end of the Yuan dynasty in 1368.

By then, the bubonic plague had roared across Europe as well. Its itinerary in the 1340s shows that it arrived on the Silk Road. Genoese and Venetian galleys that loaded Asian goods on the shores of the Black Sea transported plague-infected fleas with the Asian goods. The fleas infected both crew and travelers bound for Italian ports, as well as rats that lived permanently aboard ship. From Mediterranean ports, bubonic plague moved north along trade routes into the rest of Europe. The Black Death, as Europeans called bubonic plague, carried away its victims in less than a week, amid fevers, pustules, and bloody vomit—a horrifying and almost certain death. The plague's impact was enormous, and recent studies have revised estimates upward. It now seems probable that the epidemic killed approximately half of the European population, more in Mediterranean cities, less in the northern countryside.

By radically disrupting everything in its path, the bubonic plague cleared the way for new social, cultural, and economic developments, especially in Europe. An epidemic that killed half the population made the survivors—now viewed as essential workers—more precious, ipso facto. Common people began to get more respect. The apogee of Europe's warrior aristocracy now seemed a thing of the past. Knights and castles were becoming outmoded in a time of gunpowder, for neither steel armor nor stone walls could resist guns. The successful Turkish siege of Byzantium, deploying the heaviest artillery ever, up to that time, marked a turning point. As the warrior aristocracy lost influence, the post-medieval revival of cities and of trade within Europe accelerated.

Marco Polo, famous for his description of China under the Mongols, belonged to a Venetian trading family that had begun to explore the Silk Road in the late 1200s. Thousands of others were doing the same, but Polo wrote an influential account that made his name a household word. Dictated while Polo was imprisoned by Genoese competitors, his account seems to have been first intended as orientation for European traders who wanted to take advantage of the Pax Mongolica then reigning in Central Asia. The ghost author to whom

Polo dictated his account apparently took some liberties intended to give the book wider appeal, and it worked. In the early 1300s, after a quarter century of Asian adventures, this famous traveler returned to Venice permanently. In 1324, he died.

The following year, Ibn Battuta, a fellow son of the Mediterranean, began his own quarter century of travels. You could think of him as the Moroccan Marco Polo, because the two men's famous travels coincided rather closely, in both time and space. But Ibn Battuta was no trader, and his travels were much more extensive than Polo's. The first of his countless caravans took him across North Africa on a pilgrimage to Mecca, and his overall project was to provide a comprehensive account of the Muslim world. That included Muslim-controlled northern India, as well as sub-Saharan Africa and the Swahili coast, also Indian Ocean ports all the way to Sumatra—where Muslim sultanates were just beginning to take hold—not to mention Persia and Central Asia. Ibn Battuta found himself both impressed and challenged by the cultural diversity of the Muslim world whose fringes he explored. On more than one occasion he complained to far-flung local authorities that Muslim women really ought to wear more clothing. He returned home to a plague-ravaged Morocco in 1354.

"Medieval" India

Interestingly, India suffered neither Mongol invasion nor the plague. The continental Silk Road ran north of the Indian subcontinent, beyond high mountain barriers, leaving India outside the Mongol's terrestrial path of destruction. The maritime Spice Route, on the other hand, ran right through southern India. Comparable to Europe and China in demographic weight, India was one of the world's most successful societies when measured by the number of people it could feed.

The Gupta Empire had declined long before 1000 CE. Like Europe, India was mostly fragmented among many feuding kingdoms and principalities in the period 1000–1500. Minor Hindu empires controlled portions of it. Buddhism continued to decline in India, except for a last stronghold on the island of Sri Lanka. On the other hand, the wealth of India attracted many Muslim raiders from Central Asia in this period. Many stayed and settled down, spreading across northern India, which over five centuries became increasingly, although never exclusively, Muslim. The large unconverted Indian population under Muslim rule paid the customary Muslim tax on religious nonconformity. The invaders' most important center was Delhi, where Razia Sultan had ruled briefly. This was the society that eventually became the Mughal Empire.

Hindus resisted the incoming northern invasion long and hard, with partial success, over centuries. India's shifting regional standoff somewhat resembled the contemporaneous Muslim-Christian confrontations around the Mediterranean Sea. In the north of India, and most especially the northwest, Hindu resistance created a landscape of castles and a gamut of Hindu warrior sects like the Sikhs and the Bishnoi to champion the fight. Indians celebrate the memory of several warrior queens who defended their small kingdoms against Muslim expansionism. Rani Durgavati, a Hindu queen who ruled in the name of her young son, rode an elephant into the 1564 battle where, wounded, she committed suicide to escape capture. Another Indian warrior queen was Chand Bibi, a Shia Muslim woman, regent of Bijapur, a kingdom in west-central India, who died resisting a Mughal siege in 1599.

In the far south of India, the Muslim overlordship arrived only briefly. In general, Brahmins held onto religious control in the south, which meant, in India, political control also. The burgeoning maritime trade of southern India beckoned all comers. Southern India's pivotal role on the Spice Route was somewhat analogous to the one played by Central Asian oases on the Silk Road. Ports of the famous Malabar Coast, on the southwestern side of India, had traded with the Mediterranean region since Roman times and supported substantial communities of Muslim, Christian, and Jewish traders. On the southeastern side of India, the lesser-known Coromandel Coast was connected by trade to Malaysia and beyond. The Coromandel Coast was the scene of India's most notable sea power, the Tamil-speaking Chola Empire. At the height of its influence in 1000, the Chola Empire controlled Sri Lanka and carried out occasional military operations in Srivijaya on the island of Sumatra, a key point of transshipment in India-China trade. Chola wealth financed the construction of some of India's most impressive temples.

The trading advantages of the Chola Empire were inherited by its successor south Indian power, the Vijayanagara Empire, 1336–1646. Whereas the Chola focus had been coastal, Vijayanagara faced inland. It was, above all, a rallying point of Hindu resistance to Muslim conquests, founded on a site of Hindu pilgrimages, the traditional dwelling place of the monkey god Hanuman. The entire landscape of India, and all its rivers, are sacred to Hindus, but Vijayanagara was a special place even so. Long before the Vijayanagara Empire existed, according to the Ramayana epic, Lord Rama had visited the site to ask Hanuman for help in rescuing his abducted bride, Sita, from the clutches of evil. With its imposing stone-built capital at the southern end of India's central Deccan Plateau, facing the Delhi sultanates, Vijayanagara became the great citadel of embattled Hinduism. Vijayanagara attracted Hindus displaced from northern India, but also, in traditional Hindu style, treated religion, per se, as a matter of individual choice. The Vijayanagara Empire was not orthodox. It included both Jains and Muslims. It drew economic vitality from three hundred small ports operating on both coasts, not to mention its own production of spices and cotton cloth. The empire was visited by the flotillas of Chinese admiral Zheng He, during his exploration of the Indian Ocean in the early 1400s. In 1409, Zheng He erected a stone monument dedicated to peaceful trade, with Buddhist, Muslim, and Hindu blessings inscribed in Chinese, Persian, and Tamil, respectively.

Vijayanagara was rich and powerful, its capital was a teeming city with possibly a half million residents and a sophisticated water supply, graced by temples of Hindu deities, bristling with sculpture. Vijayanagara's main reason for being, however, was its truly enormous army. The city's very name stood for Victory. The gargantuan stables of the imperial war elephants stood not far from royal pavilions lacking external walls, where luxurious tapestries protected princes and princesses from prying eyes without impeding the breeze. The Delhi sultanates finally managed to destroy the Vijayanagara Empire and sacked its glittering capital city, which was never rebuilt. Today its carved stone temples, teeming with monkeys, have made it a UNESCO World Heritage Site.

South Indian cultural developments in this period merit mention. The Bhakti devotional movement, which developed first in southern India, infused Hindu religious practice with new fervor beginning in the 1400s. Meanwhile, southern Indian women exercised more freedom of movement and activity than did their northern sisters, partly because trade created more diverse opportunities. On the other hand, as in China and many other parts of the civilized world at this time, Hindu women who outlived their husbands suffered from increasing repression. Widows who chose to commit suicide by throwing themselves onto their husbands' funeral pyres were praised, and their proud families erected monuments to laud their self-sacrifice.

ACROSS THE EURASIA, peaceful religions had been appropriated by warlike societies. Reigning supreme as the organizing ideologies of world civilization, the great world religions had reinforced patriarchy and done little or nothing to diminish social hierarchy.

Meanwhile, a new Muslim dynasty, the Mughals, began to consolidate and extend the conquests already accomplished in northern India by the Delhi sultanates. In addition, the western monsoons were even then bringing more invaders to Indian shores. In 1500, Europe was recovering demographically from the bubonic plague and would soon enter its traumatic internal wars between Catholics and Protestants. China was recovering demographically from the plague, too, and turning its energies toward defense, as it faced new incursions from its northern borderland and from Japan. In 1500, the horse archers of the Eurasian steppe were finally ending their two-thousand-year stint as a continental loose cannon. Meanwhile, the world's oceans and seacoasts witnessed new activity. Camel caravans would soon give way to sailing ships as the primary vehicles of transcontinental trade. Parts of the world remote from Eurasia would now become connected to it.

The emergence, around 1500, of an interconnected world is an important moment in our story. So far, we have concentrated on the interconnected civilizations of Eurasia. Although long-distance trade had been historically limited, Eurasian societies had shared basic domesticated species (e.g., wheat and pigs), crucial technical innovations (e.g., the wheel and the plow), and key social institutions such as money and patriarchy. By putting the entire Silk Road between China and Europe under a single, trade-friendly administration, the Mongols had further facilitated Eurasian interconnectedness. Not all the results were favorable. One result was Europe's experience with the Black Death, which apparently passed from animals to human beings first in western China. Human interconnectedness means sharing microbes, along with innovations.

So while we see more interregional connections, it's hard to see much progress, thus far in our story, at creating fairer, more equitable societies. Steep social hierarchies characterized all the world's civilizations. Almost all were dominated by nobles and monarchs who regarded normal people as lower than themselves and displayed little commitment to the welfare of their subjects. As for the people not yet connected to civilized Eurasia, theirs was a different story.

CHAPTER EIGHT

Worlds Apart

Let us return here to our social ancestors, the foragers. Around the year 1500, most of the world's population lived in the major agricultural societies of Eurasia. The rest of the world was sparsely populated by comparison. As little as 1 percent of global population lived in North America, for example, and less than half of 1 percent in Australia. Comparatively few people lived in Siberia, sub-Saharan Africa, Southeast Asia, or most of South America—not to mention Antarctica. Much of the world was still occupied, around 1500, by foraging bands who maintained the ancestral lifestyle of us all. They had changed of course, over a hundred generations, but just how, we don't know. By preference, they lived outside the main flow of historical transformations.

Encountering civilization would be the worst thing that ever happened to the world's remaining foragers. For many, it was the last thing that ever happened to them. After 1500, foragers were mostly wiped off the map, their "other worlds" obliterated forever. Foraging populations were sometimes destroyed outright, whether quickly, by foreign microbes against which their bodies had no defense, or slowly, by enslavement, exploitation, and despair. The destruction of their societies robbed foragers of their ancestral cultures. Gradually, their bedraggled remnants were shifted onto the bottom rung of new social ladders erected by civilized newcomers.

On the margin of the story that we have told in recent chapters, there were other, alternative worlds still out there around 1500. For-agers inhabited many of these worlds apart. Many others already included agriculture and the warrior cult, which was not uniquely an Old World phenomenon. In the sub-Saharan Sahel region and Africa's rift valley, in central and southern Mexico, Central America, and the Andes—civilization and even empire building were recently in full swing. In the Aztec pantheon, Tezcatlipoca, a figure of ancient Olmec lineage (represented here carrying weapons and a shield) was a chief deity. Southeast Asia follows this pattern, too.

Around 1500, all these other worlds began to enter our main story. In this chapter we take a look at them before European colonization subsumed them into an interconnected *global* world.

The Sub-Arctic North

In the sub-Arctic north, the boreal forest (the northernmost ring of forest surrounding the Arctic Ocean) was a still largely a land of for-agers in 1500. The world's boreal forests are great expanses of a few species of conifers, often growing in permafrost, soil that is frozen permanently, year-round.

In Siberia, the boreal forest is called the taiga. The taiga is analo-gous to Canada's great north woods, but bigger. Three of the world's largest rivers, the Ob, the Yenisei, and the Lena, drain north across the taiga to the Arctic Ocean. Before they reach it, above the Arctic Circle, all trees disappear from the riverbanks, leaving a landscape of lichen-covered rocks. In addition to the bitter cold of winter, spring thaws engender swarms of biting insects of more-than-tropical pro-portions and create impossible transportation challenges. This is a land where agriculturalists simply cannot live. But a particular sort of herding is common there. The diverse foragers and herders who lived there had many names and spoke many languages. Names given them by outsiders were often slurs. Such is the case of similar subarc-tic populations in "Lapland," or rather northern Scandinavia. More properly, they are the Sami people. Many boreal populations share a unique adaptation. They are reindeer herders, although simple herding doesn't quite describe what they do, as you will see. In Siberia, the most numerous such group call themselves Nenet people.

People like the Nenets have lived in the frozen north for a very long time. Neanderthal mammoth hunters were there before *Homo sapiens*, already lighting fires for warmth and cooking, and using skins to make fur garments. The Nenets inherited the superior cultural equipment of Neolithic *Homo sapiens*, including crucial animal allies: reindeer and dogs. The dogs helped them hunt and herd, as dogs did everywhere. The reindeer were the distinctive key to this boreal way of life. The reindeer provided most of their food, as well as transportation when they pulled sleds—also their hides to protect the herders against the arctic frost. Migrating Nenets transported their gear, including their conical dwellings, on sleds of ancient design (which is not so different from modern design). The Nenets moved seasonally to accompany their herds on their annual transhumance. In spring, the reindeer migrated north out of the taiga, onto the tundra, to eat lichen, converting that abundant resource into meat, clothing, and muscle power for Nenets. This annual transhumance was determined by the animals, which, without it, cannot feed themselves. The Nenets accompany and live off the migrating reindeer, cooperatively hunting them en route. Around the beginning of the Common Era, each family acquired its own small herd of tamed animals that, like the wild reindeer, had to migrate at a certain time of year in order to eat.

The Nenets looked at their beloved taiga through animistic eyes. Like many foraging groups, the Nenets had social specialists in spirit work—shamans—who treated the sick, envisioned the future, and flew to distant locations in their visions. Large herds of reindeer guaranteed the Nenets an abundant livelihood. Some Nenet men were rich enough to afford more than one wife, although they did not have class distinctions or any sort of governance beyond the family. Nenet bands cooperated when it was in their mutual best interest and moved away from each other when conflict threatened. There was no scarcity of taiga, and no one else in the world wanted to live there, or knew how.

Even further north, along the coasts of what is today Alaska, Canada, and Greenland, other circumpolar inhabitants made a specialty of hunting sea mammals on the floating ice. These are the Inuit people, formerly called Eskimos. Their technically dazzling cultural adaptation to polar life was still comparatively new in 1500, but it signals the possibilities created by marine resources.

Further south, the coast of British Columbia was one of the few exceptions to the rule that hunters and gatherers can't settle down permanently. Marine resources, again, made it possible. These are the Native American people whose totem poles are recognized around the world. The secret of their permanent settlements was harvesting salmon runs, an almost unbelievably rich seasonal food resource that made migration unnecessary when people learned to smoke and store the salmon for year-round consumption. Quite rapidly, these sedentary, ex-foraging populations developed steep social hierarchies (even slavery) under hereditary leaders. They had stopped moving because the abundance of seafood allowed them to do so and because building and crewing their seagoing canoes required the participation of many. They did not develop any agriculture, though. Their coastal settlements remained small, their political arrangements simple, their trade minimal. The potlatch, in which surplus wealth was given away and ceremonially destroyed, was their most distinctive social institution. Their raiding parties tended to prey on the pacific agricultural people who lived to the south of them. In some ways, they were recapitulating the experience of early war-oriented societies elsewhere.

Overall, the difficulty of surviving in the sub-Arctic north kept its inhabitants isolated from the rest of the world until around 1500. A new global trade in animal skins would change that.

Australia

Australia's aboriginal foragers had their out-of-the-way continent to themselves. They believed that their spirits had sprung right out of that earth and would eventually go back into it. While not totally isolated from the rest of the world, they might as well have been. In the far north, coastal Australians clearly had some ongoing contact with Macassar islanders, who practiced horticulture. Nearby in New Guinea, other people farmed yams, taro, sugarcane, and bananas in a particularly Southeast Asian style of shifting horticulture. Yet on the mainland of Australia, the most arid of all continents, no one farmed. The land already provided abundantly for the people's modest needs. Before the arrival of Europeans, the greatest outside influence on Australian life during the last ten or twenty thousand years was the arrival of dogs.

Approximately a half million aboriginal Australians lived off the land. Although we imagine them in the desert, few of them lived there, preferring coastal and riverine woodlands. Most circulated in the same well-watered southeastern zones where Australia's population of European descent is concentrated today. Over tens of thousands of years, the material culture of aboriginal Australians had remained simple, but their social world had grown complex. They spoke hundreds of languages and dialects. Bands foraged in well-defined regions and met seasonally with others who spoke the same language. The more barren their territory, the more frequently they moved in search of food. Those who fished moved much less often. Their kinship systems and rules about who could marry whom were astoundingly complicated.

None of their hundreds of languages and dialects had a word for "aboriginal Australian," however. Speakers of different languages often regarded one another with suspicion. Yet most, if not all, shared a spiritual outlook. Like foragers the world over, they believed that plants, animals, and even rocks and rivers had spirits. These were not individual spirits, but totemic ones, representing whole species—the red kangaroo spirit, for example, or the kookaburra spirit. Particular physical features of the Australian landscape represented aboriginal creation myths: a striking ridge line was a recumbent giant turned to stone; fresh water flowed where an ancestor had cried rivers. Featureless plains might be the scenes of famous mythic events, now invisible but not totally gone. Aboriginal Australians encode their collective memories in a sacred geography much the way that Hindus do. But the Indian version has been written down for a thousand years and is preserved and performed by specialists, whereas individual aboriginal Australians take it upon themselves to preserve and repeat the part of the story that involves the particular totem with which they identify.

That brings us to the distinctively Australian twist called, in English, the Dreamtime. The Dreamtime was, above all, the transcendent moment when totem spirits walked the land and shaped it. That was long ago, but the Dreamtime is *not* just in the past. For foragers, time is not linear but circular, linked to recurring natural cycles. The rainy season is over, but the rains will return, just as the night has gone, but it will be back, over and over, forever. The ancestors or totem spirits that shaped the world are not done with us. To rouse and reinvigorate them, aboriginal Australians cultivate personal links with particular ancestors. A person linked to a particular totem must learn its "dreaming." Each totem has its dreaming, which is its story, or many stories, visible on the landscape in a series of physical features, such as orientational landmarks or, very especially in the desert, waterholes. These features are linked together, if only in the dreamer's mind, by a trail, called a song line. A thousand years ago, a tangle of song lines, visible only to the initiated, already covered the sunburnt face of Australia. They are still there, getting fainter all the time. What one does with a song line is sing it, which first requires being able to chart it. To do this people learned to sing special verses that would guide a walker along the song line, cuing necessary ritual actions along the way, just to keep the world working as it should. Aboriginal Australians who disappear occasionally to go walkabout are possibly tracing a song line. The song lines went on and on, passing from one language area to another, right across the continent. The same dreaming existed in many languages. Song lines also functioned as trade routes.

In 1500, the people of Australia had less than three centuries to take care of their ancestral homeland before outsiders turned it into someone else's private property and defined foragers as ignorant, lazy trespassers on it.

Africa

Although *Homo sapiens* evolved in Africa, that continent remains among the world's more sparsely populated, its regions radically diverse. Therefore, African history does not have a single outline. We will approach it one region at a time.

The north coast of Africa, along the Mediterranean Sea, participated culturally in the Old World, the continuous band of settlement linking Europe to China. Flying south over the unpopulated Saharan sea of sand, a third of the continent, we'll explore the southern edge of the desert, where agriculture becomes possible. This region, the Sahel, offered a limited interface between sub-Saharan Africa and the rest of the world before 1500. *Sahel* means shore. The Sahel "shore" faces north, so to speak, into a sea of sand, crisscrossed by camel caravans. Like the Eurasian steppe, the Sahel is a major crossroads of world history. Trans-Saharan caravans carried salt and gold across the sea of sand. The salt came from evaporation pans in the desert, the gold from the West African Gold Coast. The salt went south, and the gold went north. The fabled Timbuktu was the most important city of the Sahel. Timbuktu's great mosque of sunbaked brick, the world's largest such structure, annually replastered by cooperative voluntary labor, was an outpost of world religion. To trans-Saharan trade and the Sahel's natural productivity, add horses and, soon enough, gunpowder, not to mention the prestige, unifying power, and persuasiveness of a world religion—and poof, empires appear.

Expansive Muslim empires began to exist in the western Sahel in the centuries before 1500. But the empires of the Sahel were not particularly long-lasting, nor did they have very well-defined boundaries or institutions. Even the notable Male and Songay Empires disappeared without leaving much of a footprint. Africa could not be a land of durable empires because the economic and demographic base was not there. In the tropical forests south of the Sahel, people organized themselves on a very small scale, in villages often surrounded by wilderness, giving their societies a fluid, frontier quality.

Small-scale organization has always been the general strategy of *Homo sapiens* in tropical forests. Forest environments in the African tropics were extraordinarily challenging to our species because of endemic diseases such as malaria and schistosomiasis. Sickle cells, which cause anemia, seem to be a recent evolutionary defense against endemic malaria. The mounted empire-building armies of Eurasia could not penetrate the African tropics. There were no horses south of the Sahara until introduced by Europeans in the very far south because the African tsetse fly is deadly to Eurasia's beast of war. Agriculture expanded through the African tropics between 500 BCE and 500 CE, finding few regions of privileged productivity, the most notable exception being the Great Rift Valley of East Africa, the cradle of our species. Central Africa comprises one of Earth's great rainforests.

South of the Sahara, the spread of agriculture and iron working are generally associated with the so-called Bantu Expansion that occurred during the last millennium BCE. During that period, a family of languages, the Bantu languages, spread over much of the continent, starting from today's Nigeria and Cameroon. That is basically all that the evidence can tell us with certainty. The specifics are mostly a matter of logical inference. No doubt, this expansion was partly a migration of Bantu-speaking people who plunged into the rainforest and carved out new worlds there, displacing previous inhabitants like the foraging Pygmies. Alternatively, Bantu languages were adopted by previous inhabitants of the forests, possibly along with innovations like farming, iron-working, and various domestic animals. Linguistic clues allow us to know that Bantu speech moved south by two general routes: directly south into the Congo rainforest, and more southeast, into the lush, game-filled, grassy savannas of East Africa. Further south, Bantu speakers displaced foragers like the desert-dwelling San bushmen, whom we encountered in Chapter One.

On the grassy savannas of east Africa, Bantu speakers herded cattle, but overall, their importance for our story lay in their agriculture. They cultivated the Sahel's variety of millet and, in forest environments, root crops, practicing shifting cultivation. But the environment remained challenging, and Africa remained quite thinly populated, its Bantu farming villages widely scattered, virgin frontier land always available. Under those conditions, land has little monetary value. Livestock, and even more, people themselves, were the scarcest resource. As in most of the world, war captives were often enslaved.

Although pervasive, African slavery was more fluid than elsewhere, not lasting more than one lifetime. A captive's children were absorbed by the capturing community. This was another sign of the prevailing demographic vacuum. While they successfully populated some of the planet's hardest places for humans to live, Bantu peoples were unable to grow much more food than they needed, and therefore generated little surplus wealth, not enough to spur the creation of cities and empires.

Therefore, sub-Saharan African political organization was usually small-scale. Ethnic distinctions had a low profile in fluid societies where migration was frequent. Powerful men distributed their wealth and deployed influence to favor themselves, their kin, their followers, and their dependents. Hereditary kingships certainly existed in sub-Saharan Africa before 1500, but they were relatively limited. As a consequence, temples, palaces, fortifications, and public buildings were relatively few. Wars and warriors, too, played a comparatively minor role in African life. In 1500, Africa south of the Sahara was less a grid of kingdoms than a kaleidoscope of independent Bantu villages, with a scattering of pre-Bantu foragers, who had been pushed ever further south into wastelands such as the Kalahari Desert. Adaptability, the consummate human survival strategy, was a notable Bantu trait. It had to be. Marriage outside one's village often involved a change of customs and language. New villages might be constituted by individuals from various villages of origin, especially young men looking to carve out a place for themselves. Young people learned to recognize those from neighboring villages who belonged to their "age set," which might be the basis of future adaptive cooperation.

The arrival of Arabic traders characterized the Indian Ocean shores of East Africa—a place that we can call the Swahili coast, because Swahili, the world's most famous lingua franca, was created there. The years 1000–1500 had seen a general increase in Asian maritime trade, and Arab dhows were carrying a lot of it. The dhows rode the seasonal monsoons south of the Red Sea straight east to India, then returned west with the change of winds. For Arab sailors, the east coast of Africa was a familiar place, and they explored it further and further south, looking for ivory, gold, exotic animals, and slaves. They were likely to get what they wanted because they offered in return an opportunity for Africans to shop the Spice Route with a facility that Europeans would have envied, had they known about it. Today, tiny fragments of five-hundred-year-old Chinese porcelain still turn up in beach sands on the Swahili coast.

Swahili is the name given to the language that arose on that coast as Arabic-speakers and Bantu-speakers bartered the goods in trade. Swahili basically combines Bantu grammatical structures with Arabic vocabulary. A Swahili trading culture arose at trading ports, the most significant of which was Kilwa, a stone-built city whose mosque was the largest enclosed structure south of the Sahara. The presence of Kilwa and similar, smaller Swahili-speaking settlements stimulated inland trade. During Kilwa's 1000–1500 CE high point, the traders' intense interest in gold stimulated one of the continent's notable political projects at a place called Great Zimbabwe. Bolstered by control of local gold producers, the monarch of Great Zimbabwe (about whom we know little) constructed what appears to have been a royal palace encircled by vast stone walls. Social development in Bantu Africa was thus following familiar global patterns, although on a smaller scale. All in all, it was still one of the least conflictive, least exploitative worlds apart.

Japan

Japan, too, showed familiar patterns, the warrior culture of the steppe on the one hand, and the steady, millenarian influence of China on the other. Still, in 1500 the Japanese islands remained more otherworldly, more isolated from mainland East Asia than one might expect, given the nearby Chinese Empire's already two-thousand-year history.

The earliest known inhabitants of Japan had established a few fully sedentary fishing communities without agriculture, something we also saw among the totem-pole builders across the Pacific Ocean. They also invented the world's first known pottery, by covering baskets with clay to make pots for boiling seafood. They were probably the ancestors of the Ainu, aboriginal people who still inhabit remote northern islands of the Japanese archipelago. They were eventually displaced by the ancestors of the current Japanese population, who crossed the sea from Korea around 250 BCE. The successful invaders were agricultural people, but not city builders. Their lingering lack of political organization seems partly a function of isolation. China, already unified and organized by the Han dynasty, was close enough to exert an influence but too far away to interfere. (Chinese interference has historically applied only to countries bordering China—Korea, Vietnam, Tibet, Mongolia.) A Chinese traveler to this still wild-and-wooly Japan reported communities ruled by female shamans in the early Common Era. Patriarchy was nowhere to be seen. For a thousand years, Japanese developments remained out of phase regarding those in China. For a long time, Japan had no written language and barter remained the chief means of exchange.

Then, around 250 CE, horse-riding warriors invaded Japan from Korea. They established a bridgehead on Kyushu, the southernmost island. Their main installation remained in the far south but, very slowly, they spread northward up the thousand-mile Japanese island chain. They were clearly related to horse-riding warriors of the steppe and, like the steppe nomads, they admired Chinese civilization. They created their own Chinese-style ritual monarchy in which the monarch reigned but did not rule. They called their ritual monarch "emperor," possibly another Chinese influence. Their capital city—first at a placed called Nara, and then, Kyoto—was, not accidentally, a miniature version of the Tang capital at Chang'an. To write, the Japanese adapted the Chinese system, adopting many basic characters outright. They tried to impose China's system of census-based land distribution and its finely graduated ranks of imperial nobility. They adopted Chinese variants of Buddhism. Chinese furnishings, Chinese clothing, Chinese painting, and Chinese poetry defined their idea of good taste. Around 1000, a tiny, leisured elite circulated in carriages around Kyoto and Tokyo, to see and be seen. Murasaki Shikibu, a Japanese courtier, became the world's first novelist when she created *The Tale of Genji* at that time. The novel chronicles the courtly love affairs of Genji, Murasaki's irresistibly attractive princely protagonist.

Novels by women aside, the warrior cult had more prominence in Japan than in China. In China, the emperor reigned and mandarins ruled. Warriors mostly followed orders. In Japan, mandarin-style bureaucrats were few. After 1000 CE, the Japanese emperor reigned and warriors ruled. Centralized power (when it existed in Japan) lay in the hands of a military leader called the shogun. The minimal governance of the emperor had allowed warriors called samurais the opportunity to control their localities. As in medieval Europe, warriors held sway, generally, over a small-scale, minimally urbanized society. Their war-oriented culture—its technique, weapons, armor, fortification—underwent endless elaboration. Appropriating sophisticated Chinese metallurgy, they made swords from thin layers of alternating higher- and lower-carbon steel to produce a blade both flexible and sharp. Japanese warriors, with their bellicose Lotus Sect, appropriated even Zen Buddhism's emphasis on meditative self-discipline. The shogun was a very worldly leader, a samurai "first among equals" with none of the emperor's hereditary, ritual reverberations. The shogun's influence therefore depended greatly on circumstances, on the qualities of the individual man, and on the strength of his allies and adversaries. Therefore, the shogun was sometimes strong, sometimes weak, other times absent altogether. The result was a somewhat anarchic period labeled, in Japanese history, the country at war.

This grim situation had a positive impact on European attempts to colonize Japan. It stopped them cold. The land of the rising sun was defended also, of course, by its peripheral location. For whatever reason, the Japanese people were able to resist colonization with unusual success, as we will see.

The Americas

North and South America were the most isolated of all the worlds apart. Foragers still predominated territorially across both continents around 1500. The globe's Western Hemisphere had produced a robust Agricultural Revolution all its own, though its fauna had fewer animals that could be domesticated. The Americas also produced their own warrior cults, their own dance of empire building, their own cities with temples elevated atop pyramids somewhat resembling ziggurats—all with a time lag of several thousand years vis-a-vis the Old World.

The Olmecs of southern Mexico and the Norte Chico society of Peru had been succeeded by other city-dwelling people. By 1500,

Olmec cultural ideas and practices had diffused through central Mexico and northern Central America, giving rise to the increasingly more developed Mayan, Toltec, and Aztec civilizations. At the same time, the Incas, highland Peruvian successors to the Norte Chico civilization, were expanding in the Andes. The Incan Empire that eventually arose in the Andes was the most extensive and ambitious polity in native America.

As in Eurasia, Native American cities had arisen at sites characterized by highly productive agriculture. Andean agriculturalists terraced slopes near a water source for irrigation, and they learned to apply natural fertilizer that came not from cow manure—there being no cows in native America—but rather, seabird guano. In central Mexico, native people constructed garden platforms in highland lake waters and built dikes and sluices to control their level and replenish the garden soil with alluvium. Southern Mexico and Guatemala (together sometimes called Mesoamerica) also saw the development of the mixed-farming, *milpa* system, in which corn, squash, and beans are planted together, interacting beneficially as they grow. Intensive Native American agriculture centered on a grain crop—corn. Andeans had also domesticated potatoes, which they preserved by freeze-drying in the high mountain air. Mesoamerica, particularly, abounded in domesticated plants—beans, chocolate, peppers, avocado, tomatoes. This was partly because many wild versions were available there to be domesticated. Partly, though, the people of Mesoamerica seem to have been unusually skillful at identifying candidates for domestication. The long road of prehistoric immigration from Asia to the Americas had crossed countless climatic zones, requiring the migrating foragers constantly to identify new edible plants. Animals were a different matter. The ancestors of Asian domestic animals were totally absent from the Americas. Because of their isolation from Eurasia, Native American civilizations lacked not only cows, horses, donkeys, water buffalo, pigs, sheep, goats, and chickens, but also iron metallurgy, the plow, wheeled vehicles, and alphabetic writing—basic shared elements of the Eurasian civilizational kit.

As in ancient Mesopotamia, Mesoamerican cities normally surrounded ceremonial centers, step-pyramids where priests made sacrifices to the gods. Central Mexico's Pyramid of the Sun, focal point of the city called Teotihuacan, a city built more than a thousand years before the Spanish arrived, was the world's largest pyramid. Mesoamerican pyramids look enough like Mesopotamian ziggurats that some have mistakenly supposed this parallel to represent a historical connection. Atop both were the temples of local gods, and both were constructed in stages, gradually rising higher with the passage of time. Mesoamerican city-states were often surrounded by others of shared language and culture. The Mayan city-states competed so fiercely that fighting among them is believed to be a major reason that the biggest ones vanished long before 1500. The large central buildings of the Andean city of Cuzco were built of stones that interlocked like puzzle pieces, protecting them against earthquakes. But the most spectacular American city was surely Tenochtitlan, with its bustling marketplaces and blood-stained pyramids, capital of the Aztec Empire in 1500. Traversed by canals like Venice, more populous than London, Tenochtitlan rose from a highland lake. As in early civilizations around the world, these indigenous populations were divided into nobles, commoners, and slaves. They adored godlike emperors, celebrated warriors, and subordinated women—all in familiar fashion.

In 1500, agriculture was spreading to new parts of North America. Corn traveled particularly well. It had spread from Mesoamerica north to New Mexico, enabling the creation of the large multidwelling structures called pueblos. Corn had spread, too, up the river bottoms of the Great Plains and into forests east of the Mississippi River. Moreover, North American woodlands had been modified by burning to produce a generally more open, parklike landscape, interspersed by clearings where early Native American agriculturalists had begun to plant corn. During the years when the Mongols were creating the world's largest-ever land empire in Eurasia, indigenous people of what is called Mississippian cultures were planting corn, beans, and squash and raising large ceremonial mounds inspired by Mesoamerican pyramids. The population surrounding Cahokia, a ceremonial center on the Mississippi River at what is today St. Louis, Missouri, became, for a while, the largest urban conglomeration in the current United States. Cahokia's principal mound constitutes a smaller, earthen version of Teotihuacan's Pyramid of the Sun.

Corn had spread to South America, as well. And in the densely forested Amazon basin (about half of the continent) a different crop had taken root—a root crop called manioc, which became the indigenous staple east of the Andes. Manioc was a crop suited for shifting cultivation—the clearing, temporary use, and eventual abandonment of successive garden plots, as practiced by the Yanomami, as well as by Bantus and by the Southeast Asian hill dwellers whom we will meet shortly. Indigenous Amazonians practiced "un-natural selection" by systematically favoring certain species of fruit-bearing trees in the forest. They built dikes to control seasonal flooding and improved the soil in permanent garden plots along riverbanks, supporting substantial populations that were later swept away by European diseases. Impressive extensions of artificially improved soils long went unnoticed and are only now being mapped.

In Mesoamerica and the Andes (as earlier in Mesopotamia and China), the rulers of urban populations began to generate imperial projects. As in ancient Egypt, they identified their emperors with the sun. The Mayan zone comprised feuding city-states and lacked imperial unity. The two largest indigenous empires, the Aztec and Inca Empires, arose only in the last centuries before the European invasion. The native political organization of America was thus truncated after 1492, just as it began to gather momentum.

The rise of the Aztecs and the Incas repeated yet more familiar patterns. The Aztecs arrived from the arid plains of northern Mexico as barbarians who took over the millennial, Olmec-derived civilization of southern Mexico. Aztec warriors fought their aristocratic adversaries one-on-one, like Bronze-Age charioteers or medieval knights.

Their main goal was to capture a prestigious enemy, who would then be sacrificed to the Hummingbird God or, once a year, to the warrior deity Tezcatlipoca, atop the great pyramid of Tenochtitlan. A young warrior representing Tezcatlipoca was pampered for a year by the inhabitants of the Aztec capital, fed delicacies, and wed to four maidens, meeting several times with the emperor, before his chest was opened and his heart extracted in tribute to the warlike god. If the supply of captives ran low, ceremonial contests called flowery wars were staged among competing city-states. The Aztec emperor was both his city's high priest and its commander in chief, a semi-divine presence upon whom ordinary people dared not look. The awesome public spectacle of human sacrifice, sometimes in very large numbers, supposedly kept the sun in the sky, but in reality served to cement Aztec control over their terrorized empire. Inca emperors, too, were regarded—and regarded themselves—as semi-divine. They claimed descent from a principal deity, the sun god, Inti, and administered an equally complex, though less violent, ceremonial world. To prevent the dilution of their royal blood, brothers sometimes married sisters, as among Egyptian pharaohs. At death, Inca emperors were mummified but, rather than being entombed, continued to play a ritual role.

Early American civilizations were surprisingly similar to their Eurasian counterparts, the main differences being a several-thousand-year time-lag and the Native Americans' paucity of domestic animals. The Aztec and Inca Empires were rapidly expanding in 1500, but their days were numbered.

Southeast Asia

Southeast Asia was the least isolated of our worlds apart. Southeast Asia contains the world's largest and most complex archipelago, with an ancient seafaring tradition connecting the Indian and Pacific

Oceans, a global crossroads since the beginning of the Common Era. The mainland portion of Southeast Asia, on the other hand, is covered with steep, tropically forested mountains that pose immense transportation difficulties. Around 1500, mainland Southeast Asia had a sixth of India's population density and a seventh of China's. It was Asia's analog of Central America or Central Africa, an under-populated tropical region.

Southeast Asia originated a distinct agricultural tradition. The world's earliest centers of agriculture all combined an arid climate with the facility of irrigation. The chief early crops in much of the world were grains, which are grass seeds. Grasses thrive in semi-arid environments such as the Indus and Yellow River valleys. Weeds and pests were fewer and easier to control in semi-arid climates. Responding to their humid tropical environment, Southeast Asians originated a horticultural tradition better adapted to rainy forests. The people planting yams, taro, sugarcane, and bananas in New Guinea (mentioned a bit earlier) were part of this tradition, and their chief crops are typical because they are grown from cuttings, not seeds. In addition, they are quite large plants, easier to cultivate in a garden clearing carved out of the forest. Unlike seeds, which are sown in dry soil and later activated by the presence of water, cuttings must be planted in reliably moist soil. They are perfect for a monsoon climate.

For several reasons, grain—which can be easily stored, distributed, and taxed—lends itself to large-scale production and state control. The basis of kingship in Southeast Asia, beginning in earnest around 500 CE, was highly labor-intensive irrigated rice. In a land of few people, intensive agricultural labor was unnecessary, less a way feed people than a way to enrich the state. Therefore, intensive agriculture in Southeast Asia was normally done by unfree labor. Each kingdom occupied the flat bottom of a single river valley, ideal for rice paddies capable of feeding a capital city: its army and workforce, its temples and monasteries. Southeast Asian kings could not control the steep, forest-clad mountains that surrounded their valley kingdoms. Kings marched into the mountains or attacked one another's capital cities largely to capture a workforce.

Southeast Asian kings claimed divine sanction, of course, as did kings everywhere, but interestingly, they made their claims using written Sanskrit, the sacred language of India, rather than local languages. The earliest Southeast Asian kings had imported Brahmin advisors. They had appropriated an ancient Indian ideology of kingship, called *devaraja*, and with it, adopted the official worship of Hindu deities such as Shiva. The salient example is Cambodia, formerly the Khmer Kingdom, which coalesced around the lower Mekong River, the region's largest. The Khmer Kingdom expanded for a time to become the Khmer Empire, boasting one of world's most bustling ceremonial centers around Angkor Wat during its twelfth-century apogee. By that time, however, Southeast Asian religion had turned more Buddhist than Hindu.

Cultural diversity was the inescapable result of the region's location at a global crossroads. Vietnam, a small river valley kingdom bordering China, spilled down the coast of the South China Sea, developing strong maritime trade links with China. Vietnam is culturally as well as geographically close to southern China. It suffered a thousand-year occupation by China, however, and regards its looming northern neighbor warily. All continental Southeast Asia has close cultural links to China. Many Southeast Asian languages are related to Chinese, and many ethnic groups in mainland Southeast Asia migrated there from historical homelands in China. Many of the region's ethnic minorities—lumped together in common parlance as hill people—came from China as well. The existence of these ethnic minorities attracted world attention during the US-Vietnam war, when the ethnic Hmong minority fought for the United States.

Often living in steep, isolated country, these ethnic minorities can also be found in India and China, but the sparsely populated highlands of Southeast Asia became their continental refuge and redoubt. China's thousand-year expansion south and west from Yellow River origins spread the Han ethnicity by absorbing and displacing populations already there. Hill people are thus usually historical refugees, communities who have habitually fled armies and tax collectors, preferring to fend for themselves on isolated mountainsides.

In their mountain fastness, Southeast Asian hill people practiced shifting cultivation of roots like taro and yams, and, after 1500, sweet potatoes and manioc from the Americas—crops that stay in the ground until ready to eat, crops that were therefore difficult for the soldiers of valley kingdoms to steal or destroy. People like the Hmong formed fluid, rough-and-ready, cooperative, and egalitarian societies in opposition to the rice-growing, temple cities in the river valleys—normally speaking a different language and practicing a different religion. In the past, hill people tended to be animists. Today they are often Christians, always glad to be different and "in the face" of their historical enemies, the valley people.

Malaysia, Indonesia, and the Philippines comprise another side of Southeast Asia—a slender peninsula and an infinity of islands, scene of humanity's oldest major seafaring tradition. Indian cultural and trade influence arrived here early in the Common Era. Bali preserves vividly Hindu cultural elements down to the present day. The great Indian epics, Ramayana and Mahabharata, supplied the raw material for the region's popular art forms, such as shadow puppetry. Of the major islands—Sumatra, Borneo, Java, New Guinea, and Luzon—only Java developed large-scale paddy agriculture, along with its attendant kingdoms and occasional empires. Javanese kingdoms resembled those of mainland Southeast Asia. The dominant social mode of the archipelago before 1500, though, was Malay seafaring. Malay seafaring culture extended from Madagascar, off the coast of Africa, east more than halfway around the world, to Easter Island, off the coast of South America. Malay sailors, like their contemporaries, the Vikings, were pirates who traded or raided, according to the occasion. Like Vikings, they were military as well as naval specialists. Malay warriors sometimes experienced a trancelike battle frenzy, "running amok," another similarity with the Vikings, who were known for "going berserk." Malay raiders might hire themselves out as the coast guard of some one-valley rice-paddy kingdom. The Malay seafaring tradition thus enabled (but also complicated) the region's role as a pivotal transshipment point on the Spice Route.

Buddhism, rather than Hindu *devaraja* ideology, became India's more significant religious export to Southeast Asia. Buddhist culture (like Muslim culture, somewhat later) arrived informally, carried by traders. It struck much deeper social roots than had state-sponsored Hindu culture. Javanese kings built large, striking Buddhist temple complexes like those in Cambodia's Khmer Kingdom. Java's rice-paddy-based Majapahit kingdom became a forerunner of today's Indonesia. On the other hand, several ports in the great archipelago became naval and trading powers without any appreciable agricultural hinterland, rather like Carthage or later, Venice, in the Mediterranean.

The most significant of these landless sea powers was Srivijaya, on the island of Sumatra. Srivijaya's Sanskrit-sounding name indicates early Indian influences and, roughly in the years 700–1100 CE, Srivijaya was a principal center for the dissemination of Buddhism in Southeast Asia. Srivijaya controlled the Malacca Strait, the essential route linking India and China. In its heyday, Srivijaya extended its power over Sumatra, the Malay Peninsula, and even Java, raiding the Khmer and Vietnamese, and, incredibly, even organizing a mass migration to Madagascar, off the coast of Africa, 3,300 miles away, apparently around 830 CE.

Many mysteries remain about Srivijaya. Srivijaya disappeared in the thirteenth century, leaving so little trace that locals forgot it had ever existed. Like other tropical port cities, it must have been very lightly built. Many of its structures probably floated in a complex of rivers and estuaries. Today, aerial photographs reveal the outlines of vanished canals, ponds, moats, and artificial islands near the Sumatran city of Palembang, probably the remaining visual footprint of Srivijaya. Interestingly, while they built little in the Sumatran hinterland, Srivijayan monarchs built many stone monuments in Java.

They even added some finishing touches to Java's great Buddhist monument at Borobudur. Bas relief at Borobudur shows the kind of ships involved in this ancient, and mostly forgotten, maritime tradition. They show outriggers for enhanced seaworthiness, and the timbers of the ships' hulls are apparently sewn together with cables rather than being nailed, for greater flexibility on large ocean swells. (An image of such ships, based on a Borobudur carving, opens the next chapter.) Srivijaya remained Buddhist even after the transforming effect of Muhammad's prophecy began to be felt along the full length of South Asian trade routes in the 700s. Muslim ideas gradually superseded Buddhist and Hindu ideas in trade-saturated areas of the Southeast Asian archipelago. Buddhist Srivijaya was replaced, as a regional power, by Muslim Malacca in the early 1400s.

This was the setting of the seven famous naval expeditions led by the Chinese admiral Zheng He between 1405 and 1433. These were huge and costly imperial enterprises, involving the construction of many hundreds of ships, some of them enormous. Each voyage took several years, and together they covered the entire Spice Route, from the mouth of the Yangtze River to Java and Malaya, India, and Arabia, and even to the Swahili coast beyond. The routes, shared by Arabs, Indians, and Chinese, had been well known for a thousand years. Zheng He was not, for the most part, exploring. He arrived in Malacca to find a Chinese merchant community already thriving there. The Chinese admiral's perusal of the Spice Route was more a combination fact-finding mission and diplomatic charm offensive. Chinese diplomacy consisted primarily in a dazzling show of wealth and generosity, a flurry of gift-giving among new royal friends. Zheng He's great naval expeditions were vast undertakings when compared with the European voyages we will talk about shortly. They were not unsuccessful, but they were discontinued forever when Chinese diplomatic concerns returned, as they always did, sooner to later, to the empire's northern borderland, where a last group of steppe warriors jostled for its impending debut on the world stage.

In 1500, people on the margin of Eurasian civilization lived diverse lives: the Nenets following their reindeer, the aboriginal Australians patrolling their song lines, the Bantus organizing their inter-village age sets, the Japanese refining their warrior cult, the Malays living afloat, the hill people steering clear of rice paddies, the Native Americans foraging, planting corn, founding their theocratic empires. But they had some things in common. They were satisfied with their way of life, whatever it was. They had scant knowledge of, or interest in, anything European. And like the Europeans themselves, they were totally unprepared for what was about to happen.

Premodern World.

Indicating chief early cities, civilizations, and trade routes, as well as important geographical features discussed in the text.

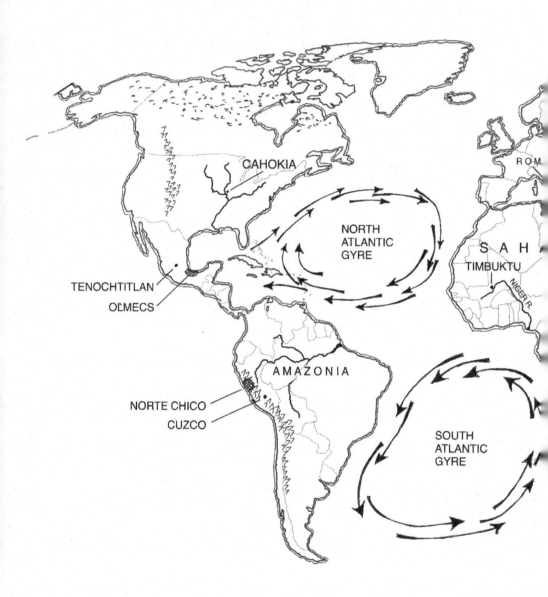

Part II

CHAPTER NINE

New World

We have arrived at that famous turning point in world history, the rise of the West. Magellan's famous circumnavigation of the globe aptly symbolizes the change. Transoceanic voyaging quickly began to play a determining role in world history. Double outriggers like those of Srivijaya, pictured here, had already made transoceanic voyages. So had Viking longships, Arab dhows, and double-hulled Polynesian canoes. But such voyaging had never really been routine before Western Europeans explored the rest of the world. The well-known trigger for this transformation was an Otonopoly over trans-Asian trade at its western end.

In 1453, the Ottomans captured the great walled city of Byzantium. By 1500, the Ottoman Empire was nearing its apogee. Its greatest emperor, Suleiman the Lawgiver (whom Europeans called "the Magnificent") was still a boy. Under Suleiman, the Ottomans would extend their empire west into Persia, east along the North African coast, and north into Europe, annexing Bulgarians, Croats, Serbs, and Hungarians, until they were finally thwarted at the second siege of Vienna in 1532. Suleiman spoke five languages and ruled over twenty-five million subjects. He reportedly felt inspired by Alexander the Great. None of his languages was European, but he famously made a red-haired European harem slave one of his two wives. As Lawgiver, he promulgated legal codes very different from sharia common law. He renovated the Kaaba in Mecca, built the Dome of the Rock, added the current city walls to Jerusalem, and erected the breathtaking Suleimaniye Mosque in Istanbul. The European terminus of the Silk Road and Spice Route now lay in Ottoman hands. As masters of the eastern Mediterranean Sea, the Black Sea, and the Red Sea, the Ottomans could completely block Venetian and Genoese middlemen's access to Asian trade. The Ottomans also conducted naval operations in the Indian Ocean. The Ottoman presence clearly motivated European voyages of exploration, seeking a way around it. Those voyages remain a surprising development, nonetheless.

In Europe, as across Eurasia, dynastic life went on as usual, a ceaseless chronicle of noble avarice and royal greed. The best efforts of prophets and religious reformers had produced little in the way of heaven on Earth as, for example, Henry VIII famously led England out of the Catholic Church because the pope would not allow him to divorce his wife, then beheaded his way through a string of wives in pursuit of a male heir. Religious protests had permanently shattered the Catholic unity of Europe. The resulting Protestant sects were of various kinds. Some of the first ones were primarily assertions of sovereignty (the English case, just mentioned, for example). Other Protestants made radical attempts to recover the basic elements of early Christianity, such as the charismatic engagement of the faithful. Protestants wanted to strip away later Catholic innovations, such as elaborate ritual, liturgy, and the cult of saints. Protestant sects arose primarily in northern and western Europe in a process called the Reformation. The beginning of the Reformation, in 1517, was the work of a disgruntled German clergyman named Martin Luther, whose most notable complaint was the church's sale of indulgences by which rich sinners could supposedly buy their way clear of hell's gates. Protestants like Luther wanted all believers to read the Bible, which therefore had to be translated into many languages. Luther himself translated the Bible into German, helping establish the standard form of the modern German language.

Unsurprisingly, for scrappy Europe, Catholics and Protestants came to blows very quickly. Spain, newly unified after the final victory of its Christian reconquest, championed the Catholic cause. England defended Protestantism. The Spanish Armada, an aborted 1588 attempt to invade England, and the Spanish Inquisition, charged with policing religious conformity, are famous manifestations of the epoch's religious conflict. France, divided between majority Catholics and minority Protestants, was the scene of bitter internal feuding. An extreme, but not unrepresentative, example is the 1572 Saint Bartholomew's Day massacre when, by secret prior arrangement, Catholic Parisians abruptly began to murder Protestant Parisians in the name of religious truth. A famous point of contention was whether communion bread and wine merely symbolized or *actually turned into* the body and blood of Christ. It seems an inadequate reason for Christians to slaughter one another, yet the dispute spread throughout France, leaving a death toll in the thousands. Luther's disruption of European religion proved most disruptive in the north, where the glorious wars of religion culminated in a Thirty Years War (1618–1648), an awesome cataclysm that swept away millions of souls in a vortex of disease, famine, destruction, and death.

Meanwhile, there was also an intellectual, artistic, and literary "rebirth" happening, too. A central element in this "Renaissance" was the recuperation of texts in Latin and Greek, "classical" wisdom that had been lost in Europe during the Middle Ages but was meanwhile preserved in Muslim libraries. Moreover, Renaissance humanists like Erasmus of Rotterdam, who were reading the recovered wisdom, gained a much wider understanding of the world. Erasmus had a strong critique of religion, but he did not abandon Christianity or even become a Protestant. Instead, he proposed that all truth was *not* religious truth, that non-Christians were *not* all in league with the devil, and that Christian scripture was *not* the only thing worth reading. In full perspective, the idea of a European Renaissance applies mostly to art history. Most Europeans never heard of "the Renaissance" while it was happening. It's capital-R reputation comes from later scholars who have looked back in admiration at artistic geniuses like Michelangelo or da Vinci. The Renaissance was, in fact, a much smaller phenomenon than the Reformation, affecting mostly intellectuals, painters, sculptors, architects, and wealthy patrons. The intellectual opening that we see in Erasmus lighted the way of the future, however.

Bottom line: Europe hardly seemed poised for geopolitical breakout in 1500. The European countries with rocky Atlantic shorelines had always been, historically, on the receiving end of Eurasian influences. Moreover, Christendom seemed to be losing its centuries-long contest against the Ottoman Turks. To understand the voyages of discovery and the rise of Europe after 1500, leading to the unparalleled colonization of the globe by Europeans, one must see it not as an event, but as a *process*. That is because a Europe capable of world colonization did not yet exist in 1500. It came into existence only gradually after 1500, as Europeans learned from and built on their initial discoveries, bringing colonization abroad, industrialization at home, and eventually, world hegemony.

The unexpected appearance of three or four previously unknown continents—a significant discovery indeed—radically changed European thinking about the world and eventually triggered a scientific revolution as part of the colonizing project. Europeans displaced and despoiled the indigenous inhabitants of the Americas. Europe became, by the mid-1800s, unquestionably the dominant world region. Before Europeans could grasp the world and make it their oyster, however, they had to get their hands around it. That was something that had never been done before, the source of their crucial advantage.

Let's look at Europe's so-called "Age of Exploration" to observe the initial steps of the process.

The European Breakout

Little Portugal was able to outflank the Ottoman presence and directly access the Spice Route. Then Spain destroyed the Aztec and Inca Empires. That's the skinny—the same basic stuff children learn about in primary school, expressed here without the habitual myth-making. Instead of cheerleading, we'll try to understand the hows and whys of the process.

Portugal was precocious among European kingdoms in the 1400s. The Portuguese monarchy had gained social heft from its centuries-long crusade against the Moors. Its leading role in the reconquest of Iberia helps explain why little Portugal was first to circumnavigate Africa. After expelling Moors (and Jews) who refused conversion to Christianity in 1496, the crusading energies of the Portuguese crown pursued the defeated Muslims back to North Africa. The Portuguese king Sebastian died there, personally leading a charge into Muslim lines. Sebastian's body was never recovered, and desperate rumors of his miraculous survival circulated for years in Portugal.

The Ottoman Empire stood at its high point, and the Portuguese regarded themselves as the advance guard of Christendom. These details shed light on Portuguese promotion of a long-term explora-tion project intended, in part, to join forces with a mythical Christian monarch whose kingdom supposedly lay in sub-Saharan Africa.

This project, Portugal's exploration of the Atlantic coast of Africa in the later 1400s, was begun by the man known to history as Henry the Navigator. A Portuguese prince who never became king, this "navigator" was not a sailor. Henry was a royal booster who fore-grounded the idea of religious mission, but he had more on his mind. Africa seemed to him a promising field for Portuguese enrichment. The small but steady flow of gold brought from south of the Sahara by the caravan trade had not escaped his attention. He devoted his life to collecting information, drawing maps, and funding expe-ditions. The project was to sail south, down the Atlantic coast of Africa, to see what was there. Presumably, Africa had a southern tip that could be rounded, allowing one to sail from the Atlantic into the Indian Ocean—but nobody knew for sure. The problem wasn't getting the hunch or daring to try, however. Prevailing head-winds (blowing north) made sailing south along the coast practically impossible. As a result, the Portuguese began to rig their ships with the triangular sails used by Arab dhows, which enabled better progress against a headwind, but it was still slow going. One Portuguese expedition after another turned back in frustration.

When Henry died, the Portuguese crown sold this project to a consortium of Lisbon investors who made it more profitable. Having eventually progressed south of the Sahara, Portuguese explorers had begun to finance themselves by stopping along the African coast to procure gold dust and black slaves. Outright chattel slavery, the buying and selling of people, had disappeared from Europe after Roman times. Therefore, black African slaves were now marketed in Portugal and Spain as exotic novelty items for the aristocracy. The profits of slaving led the Portuguese crown to reassume control of African explorations, and in 1487 a Portuguese sea captain named Bartholomew Dias finally found the trick to sailing around Africa. It was as follows: The predominant winds of the South Atlantic blow in a counterclockwise gyre, northward up the African coast, across to South America and down the South American coast, and then back across the ocean to the southern tip of Africa, completing the cycle. It was lengthy and indirect but *easy* to ride the gyre from the Canary Islands to the Cape of Good Hope, which is what Dias did. No one had ever imagined such a thing before. The European road to India was open.

In 1497, a four-ship Portuguese expedition repeated the Dias feat. The expedition's leader was Vasco da Gama, a Portuguese noble with royal connections but little experience in maritime adventures. His expedition rounded the Cape of Good Hope and sailed up the eastern "Swahili" coast of Africa. By then, da Gama was well-oriented, and back in the "known world." Arab traders predominated along the Swahili coast, and da Gama found monsoon pilots willing to guide an open-ocean crossing to India. His little Portuguese fleet landed on the Malabar Coast at Calicut, a Hindu trading kingdom associated with the Vijayanagara Empire. If the Portuguese wanted to join the Spice Route, they had come to the right place, but da Gama's diplomacy failed to impress. The Arab traders who worked the Malabar Coast suggested to the local king that the Portuguese gifts, ordinary trade goods of mediocre quality, were laughable. Four red cloaks, seven brass vessels, a box of cane sugar, and two barrels of olive oil? Where were the silks, spices, jewels and precious metals? Da Gama pushed his luck by demanding special trading privileges. When his gambit was refused, he kidnapped several local people and left in a huff. His impromptu attempt to retrace his steps to Africa was not correctly timed to ride the monsoon, and disaster ensued. Instead of 23 days, the Indian Ocean crossing took 132. Starvation, scurvy, and lack of water killed half of da Gama's crewmen and debilitated the rest. Only half his ships made it back to Lisbon. Even so, their cargoes of spices were valuable enough to make a large profit from the voyage. Da Gama was a hero.

In 1500, another Portuguese flotilla left for India. This time, however, the fleet rode the South Atlantic gyre *too far* west and bumped into Brazil. Compared with India, Brazil had little or nothing to offer in trade, so after claiming these previously "undiscovered" territories for Portugal, the fleet's unimpressed admiral continued to Calicut, where he hoped to establish an exclusive Portuguese commercial base. Local Arab traders were not having it, though. Conflict irrupted, and as many as seventy Portuguese died. The Portuguese blamed the king of Calicut and ended up bombarding his city with their naval artillery, a weapon that did not yet exist in Asia.

In 1502, Vasco da Gama led a war fleet of twenty ships back to Calicut to teach its insolent inhabitants some respect. "Respect" was not the lesson that they learned, however. Da Gama failed to take Calicut and had to be content with terrorizing coastal traders by capturing undefended trading vessels and cutting off the crew's hands, ears, and noses. The recipients of these lessons were largely Muslims, da Gama's chief mercantile competitors. Before bombarding Calicut, da Gama offered its king the chance to surrender the local population of Arab traders, but the king declined. So, da Gama seized a ship full of several hundred mostly male pilgrims leaving Calicut in the direction of Mecca and killed them all—locking them below decks and torching their ship—in a fit of pique.

The next year, in 1503, the annual Portuguese India fleet harassed Calicut and got permission from a rival king to build a fortified trading post nearby. A young warrior who distinguished himself that year returned in 1506 to attack the Spice Route itself. This was Afonso de Albuquerque (for whom the capital of New Mexico is named), the most renowned European colonizer of Asia. Albuquerque had cut his teeth fighting Muslims in North Africa, and his attack on the Spice Route was a rancorous crusade against hereditary enemies. Albuquerque tried but failed to close the Red Sea to Asian trade by fortifying and putting artillery at its narrow southern mouth. He then tried to strangle access to the Persian Gulf by capturing Ormuz from the Persians, and there he succeeded. His capture of Ormuz began a string of brilliant victories. Continuing to India, Albuquerque seized the trading port of Goa, which remained a Portuguese base on the Malabar Coast for more than four centuries.

In 1511, Albuquerque led an assault on the biggest Asian city that the Portuguese ever captured. This was Malacca, a Muslim city on the Malaysian Peninsula. The Strait of Malacca was the Spice Route's crucial pinch point between the Indian Ocean and the South China Sea. Under the trade-oriented Sultanate of Malacca, the Spice Route had become a highly diverse enterprise, involving Arabs, Indians, and Chinese as well as Malays. Albuquerque intended that Malacca should become Christian and Portuguese. He saw killing Muslims in Malaysia as a strike at Mecca and Istanbul. The capture of Malacca provided rich plunder and constituted an essential step in the Portuguese takeover of the Spice Route. The last step, establishing a Portuguese base in South China, would take a little longer.

Time was of the essence, or so it seemed. Spain, a much bigger and more powerful kingdom than Portugal, had become a sudden contender for Asian trade in 1492 by funding the first trans-Atlantic voyage by a Genoese freelance explorer named Christopher Columbus. Spain did not have much experience in Atlantic exploration, but Columbus did. He had connections to Atlantic exploration projects through his Portuguese wife, his years of residence in Lisbon, and his many voyages up and down the African coast as far as Ghana. Soon after Bartholomew Dias found and rode the South Atlantic gyre to the tip of Africa, Columbus proposed his alternative plan to reach China and India, the great fountainheads of Asian trade, by sailing west instead of east, without knowing what winds would bring him back, without knowing, either, about the North and South American continents that stood in the way. The Portuguese, who already had a wind road to Asia, weren't interested in funding the proposed voyage. The Spanish took a chance on Columbus, becoming the second European country to seek a back door to the Spice Route.

Columbus did not find a back door to the Spice Route—but he always believed he had, which is why he called the American natives "Indians." Still, his Spanish backers were well pleased. Now both Spain and Portugal were making claims to sovereignty over faraway "islands," as they called newly discovered lands outside of Europe. Both kingdoms' claims had the same religious justification. God was on their side. As Christians bringing the only true religion, both Spanish and Portuguese claimed a God-given right to dispossess pagans and heathens who resisted their control. To keep his two exemplary Catholic powers from stepping on each other's toes, the pope formally divided the world outside of Europe into two parts—the future Spanish part and the future Portuguese part. The famous Tordesillas Line separating future Spanish and Portuguese claims was hardly ever honored by anybody, although it remained, for decades, a "fact" in European diplomacy. It exemplifies the Age of Exploration mindset.

From their advanced base at Goa, the Portuguese confidently projected saving the souls of all East Asia. Yes, their resources were stretched thin by ambitious commercial endeavors, but they felt confident of God's help in spreading Catholicism around the world. Portuguese Jesuits established missions in Japan in the 1550s and made thousands of converts there. The Jesuit order functioned as a sort of evangelizing Catholic vanguard. The Jesuit specialty was studying the societies that they hoped to evangelize, learning their languages and customs. The Spanish, who took over large populations in the Americas, evangelized indigenous Americans on a continental scale. From California and New Mexico to Peru and Paraguay, Jesuits, Franciscans, and members of other Catholic orders staffed mission settlements in the "wilderness." A notable side effect of moving indigenous people into mission villages was the death of a large portion of them from European epidemic diseases. Still, from their own official perspectives, the two Iberian kingdoms were engaged in laudable undertakings, bringing the "true religion," and with it, eternal life, to brutes were otherwise doomed to burn eternally in hell.

Europe's temporary world takeover was driven by a mix of motivations. Official rhetoric was ideological, about saving souls or, later, about bringing benighted peoples to civilization. The mouthpieces of burgeoning empires dismissed the material fruits of their military victories as mere fringe benefits, a soothing sign of God's favor. On the other hand, most people left Europe to explore and colonize the world and, above all, to seek their personal fortunes. Saving souls was the least of their concerns, and founding colonies, the next least. Imperialist ideologies are always, first and foremost, excuses for self-aggrandizement. Loudly proclaiming laudable imperial motivations salves guilty consciences and redirects pliant ones. Official folderol must be recognized as such, but not brushed off. Imperialist ideologies, even when brandishing "true religions," are above all tools of aggression.

Columbus had focused his exploration on the large Caribbean islands, and the very first focus of settlement was the large island of Hispaniola, today divided between Haiti and the Dominican Republic. The native Arawak people, who practiced shifting agriculture, were generally unwarlike and posed no resistance. Columbus reported that they could be easily conquered and evangelized, possessing, so far as he cared to observe, no religion of their own.

They did, unfortunately for them, have gold earrings, and the Spanish pursuit of that gold eventually destroyed the Arawaks. Other than precious metals, the Spanish saw nothing that they wanted to acquire from their hosts, and they were getting impatient. By 1502, the year in which Vasco da Gama made his second voyage to India, the situation had deteriorated on Hispaniola. In that year, a young Spaniard named Bartolomé de las Casas joined the colony. The Spanish had begun to requisition indigenous labor, as well as food, and the natives were resisting. Las Casas, who received his own grant of Indian labor, personally witnessed, and later denounced, the horrors practiced by Spanish colonizers against indigenous people whose tribute they deemed insufficient. Sick of the abuse, las Casas became a Catholic priest in 1510, the first one ordained in America. He was right about what he had seen. The Spanish attempt to monetize the native people of the Caribbean exterminated them completely within only a few years.

Las Casas chronicled that genocide in his *Brief Account of the Destruction of the Indies*. His life's work was trying to prevent its repetition. Truly believing in Spain's religion, he nonetheless regarded actual Spanish treatment of indigenous Americans as a crime against God and humanity. The basic cause of this situation was not in doubt. The Spanish invasion of the Americas, like the Portuguese incursion in the Spice Route, was driven by creditors and investors. Creditors and investors had to be repaid. The Spanish conquistadors were determined, according to las Casas, to profit by raising themselves up to a high social rank that bore no relation to their humble origins in Spain. In accordance with its religious ideology, the Spanish monarchy rewarded each conquistador by granting him the labor of a specific group of Indians.

By this logic, the Indians were now subjects of the Spanish king, who parceled them out like livestock and entrusted their forced Christianization to the gentle mercies of his conquering vanguard of military contractors. This labor grant, called *encomienda*, allowed European conquerors to live like European nobles, surrounded by servants, masters of agricultural estates that were worked by forced labor. A violent takeover of indigenous America had allowed Spanish conquerors to make the native people into something like serfs. Conquered natives were forced to labor for generations to repay their conquerors' rapine and pillage. From the large islands of the Caribbean, the Spanish exploration of the Americas proceeded to the mainland, always in search of new populations whose future labor could repay the cost of subjugating them.

The highlands of central Mexico, seat of the Aztec Empire, were probably the most densely populated place in the Western Hemisphere. Once landed on the coast of Mexico in 1519, a Spanish force numbering only in the hundreds was invited to Tenochtitlan, but it gathered thousands of allies among the Aztecs' rival states, particularly one called Tlaxcala. The late Aztec Empire amounted to a reign of terror, and many of its subject cities were eager to challenge Aztec rule. Welcomed into Tenochtitlan, the Spanish made a hostage of the Aztec emperor Montezuma and, when invited to an annual festival honoring the deity Tezcatlipoca, the Spanish attended with concealed weapons and slaughtered their hosts in a surprise attack. Long story short: aided by thousands of Indian allies, the Spanish leveled Tenochtitlan, and then built their own new capital city on the same site. The Cathedral of Mexico replaced the Aztec great pyramid at the city's center. Many of the former tributaries of the Aztec Empire accepted these new imperial masters, just as eventually they would accept the conquerors' religion as well.

In Peru, seat of the Inca Empire, the Spaniards used what they had learned elsewhere. Atahualpa, the Inca emperor, was taken hostage after admitting them to his presence. The Spaniards demanded an emperor's ransom and, having received it, killed Atahualpa. Confusion ensued. As in Mexico, Indian allies swelled the Spanish side. Rival claimants to the Inca throne had already started a civil war, even before the outsiders arrived. Now rival claimants aided the Spanish until, when they realized their error, it was too late. By 1533, the Inca capital was in Spanish hands. As in Mexico, a small number of Spanish adventurers had assumed control of dense agricultural populations by taking over an indigenous empire semi-intact.

While the Aztec and Incan overlords had been co-opted or swept away, many daily elements of indigenous life remained in place. Eurasia's enormously greater endowment of domestic animals had resulted over the millennia in zoonotic diseases that had never, until now, reached the Americas. European diseases ravaged indigenous populations who had no inherited resistance to them. The resulting death tolls in native America resembled those of the bubonic plague in Europe. The Spanish invaders were mostly unaffected. Nonetheless, native people remained the bulk of the population, while people of European descent became a new ruling class. Most elite Mexicans and Peruvians have looked European, and most poor ones, indigenous, ever since.

Overall, Spanish ambitions resembled Portuguese ambitions. They played out differently because of contrasting circumstances. The Portuguese had crashed into the middle of the Spice Route and used their naval artillery to get what they wanted. Fortified ports on coasts and offshore islands were their preferred situation for Asian trade. From there, they could begin sending vastly profitable spice shipments back to Europe, gradually engrossing more and more South Asian trade. The Spanish had found nothing remotely similar in America. Recouping their investment required them to push inland. The indigenous people of America wore gold jewelry, and their ruling class had treasures that the Europeans could pilfer. But the long-term profitability of conquest would have to come from indigenous labor. Spanish territorial control expanded gradually, whereas the Portuguese mostly stuck to their coastal installations and offshore entrepôts.

Portugal's pioneering seaborne empire was basically a global trading network. Portuguese overseas installations were ports, wharves, warehouses, and fortified naval bases at critical junctures along the Spice Route, steppingstones to China, frequently islands: Ormuz, Goa, Malacca, Macao. Even this limited trading empire, because of its vast reach, put enormous strains on tiny Portugal, which lacked sufficient population to crew all its ships. A basic element of the Portuguese seaborne empire was the trade in enslaved Africans. Portugal had started the European slave trade to profit from its exploration of the African coast. Slave trading expanded and remained a Portuguese monopoly through the 1500s. African slaves became essential to European plantation colonies all over the Americas. The trans-Atlantic slave trade became the initial keystone of global commerce, connecting both coasts of Africa with the Americas. The slave trade also spurred Portugal to begin colonizing African source areas such as Angola and Mozambique. Brazil was the pioneering plantation colony that became a model for later ones run by the Spanish, Dutch, English, and French.

Portugal's 1500 "discovery" of Brazil had, in the short term, produced only small profits. Portugal lacked sufficient population to settle a large land area. In contrast to Spanish territories in America, Portuguese Brazil remained, for a long time, primarily coastal. For several decades, Portuguese merchants traded steel ax heads to the Indians for logs of dye wood, a raw material for European cloth making. But Portugal's Brazilian claims remained vulnerable to European interlopers such as the French, who founded a short-lived colony called Antarctic France (later known as Rio de Janeiro) until they were expelled by Portuguese soldiers in 1567. The Portuguese had not encountered indigenous empires that might be defeated all at once, bringing millions of laboring subjects under their control, as the Spanish had done with the Aztecs and Incas. Instead, the Portuguese found only foragers and indigenous villagers practicing shifting agriculture. These people could not be fixed in place and taxed as the Spanish were doing in lands formerly ruled by Incas and Aztecs. To appropriate their labor, it would be necessary to defeat and enslave them piecemeal—or get rid of them and bring slaves from Africa.

By the early 1530s, a few thousand Spanish and Portuguese adventurers and their financial backers had established the outlines of the eventual European world takeover. It involved breaking with established trade routes, venturing into unknown waters. It also involved plenty of small-scale war making. Early victories paid enormous dividends and fueled previously unimaginable further efforts. The learning process was underway.

A Global System Emerges

By the early 1530s, then, a few thousand Spanish and Portuguese adventurers had begun to sail around the world. Gradually, other European monarchies began to enter the game, too, sponsoring expeditions of their own. Sponsoring rarely meant full financing, however. The financing was generally private and commercial. European exploration of the world was emphatically a for-profit enterprise. By sponsoring a voyage, a European sovereign lent it not so much money, as credibility, making it easier to find investors and empowering explorers to claim sovereignty over "newly discovered islands." Bit by bit, European sailors were creating a global communication system. To find their way around the world, they had to understand its continents, seas, and winds.

Magellan, the voyager who led the first-ever circumnavigation of the globe, 1519–1521, had sailed Portugal's wind road to India and had been present at Albuquerque's capture of Malacca. Magellan located the source of rich spices in the nearby Molucca Islands, and he proposed to find a quicker route there from Europe. When the Portuguese king declined to sponsor him, Magellan sailed instead, as had Columbus, for the Spanish crown. Magellan's idea was to sail west from Spain, then south around (or, possibly, *through*) the continent that Columbus had discovered, thereby approaching the Moluccas from the east. Magellan succeeded—although not personally, because he died in the Philippine Islands, trying to force baptism on a group of refractory locals. The Pacific Ocean had turned out to be much larger than he expected. His crossing took three months and twenty days. Only 18 or 19 of his original crew of 270 made it back to Europe. But they had reached the Spice Islands, which Spain now claimed, along with the Philippines. Magellan's route around the stormy southern tip of South America (through the Strait of Magellan, which therefore bears his name) was never practical for regular shipping. Spanish contact with the Philippines was maintained only by an annual trans-Pacific roundtrip voyage between Manila and Acapulco.

Eventually, both France and England sponsored voyages of exploration to inspect the Atlantic coast of North America and, hopefully, get past it and onward to China. To pay for their expeditions, they used a new financial tool, the joint stock company. No less than individual lenders, however, joint-stock investors wanted a quick return. French- and British-sponsored voyages lurked briefly along the North American coast, but they found no Spice Route to join. Nor did they find dense, well-organized farming populations that could be subjected to European rule and taxation. Colonial *settlement* projects, involving major transfers of European population, would take several generations to gather momentum. In the meantime, the English and the French saw only one way to monetize their claims to portions of the Atlantic coast: the fur trade. The pelts of beavers and other fur-bearing animals of northern forests brought an excellent price in Europe, where they combined comfort with fashion and prestige. Furs were easy to acquire in trade from the native people and not difficult to transport. The explorers identified various water roads into the interior of the continent: Chesapeake Bay, the Hudson River, and the Saint Laurence River. Hudson's Bay, in the far north, became the center of the North American fur trade.

It is difficult, today, for us to appreciate how *un*inviting the North American coast appeared to sixteenth-century Europeans looking to turn a quick profit. Forests with snowy winters; populations that practiced semi-sedentary, shifting agriculture; ample investment opportunities for the fur trade—all existed in abundance much closer to Europe, in Siberia. The Atlantic coast of North America seemed climatically rather like Europe, which was not encouraging, either. At this point, the Europeans were more interested in tropical climates that produced exotic goods. Still trying to find a back door to the

Spice Route, French- and English-commissioned voyages searched stubbornly for a fabled northern sea route around North America, the so-called Northwest Passage. In fact, the Northwest Passage did not then exist. The Arctic Ocean was impassable year-round because of ice. Yet the lure of the idea was such that "Northwest Passage" is still written with capital letters. Unhappily, global warming is now making Arctic navigation more feasible just when we don't need it.

Meanwhile, Russian territorial explorations eastward across Siberia greatly extended European knowledge of northern Asia. The resulting claims configured a continental Russian Empire. The original center of Russia had been Kiev, a stopover on the Vikings' river road from the Baltic Sea to the Black Sea. Then came the Mongols, Lithuanians, Poles, Swedes, and Germans, who sequentially dominated Kiev, so that Moscow, instead, became Russia's capital. Moscow was more isolated. Whereas Kiev faced west, so to speak, into Europe, Moscow faced east, into the Siberian frontier.

Muscovy was a forested place dotted with log cabins, even log churches. From the 1400s to the 1600s, insistent Russian expeditions mapped and extended Russian claims all the way across Siberia to the Pacific Ocean. Like other forms of European exploration and expansionism, this one had a clear economic motivation, the fur trade.

For a century, Portugal had no European competitors for Asian trade. But in the 1600s, another small, unexpected European country partially displaced it—the Netherlands, often known abroad as Holland because North and South Holland are the chief maritime trading provinces of the Netherlands. By 1600, the Netherlands had developed a vocation for trade because of the country's location at the mouth of the Rhine River. The major axis of medieval European trade had connected the manufacturing cities of northern Italy with the trading cities at the mouth of the Rhine. The Dutch did not have much territory, which is the reason that they had already launched their signature wind-mill-powered drainage projects, but they had location, location, location—also seafaring know-how and, like most peoples in Europe, considerable military experience. Dutch warships followed Portuguese vessels to their overseas bases, picked them off, and took over their trade routes.

The Dutch, who had become Protestants, had no intention of obeying the pope's division of the colonizable world into Spanish and Portuguese halves. Dutch interlopers took possession of the Moluccas, which had remained in Portuguese hands despite Magellan's hopes. Also capturing Portuguese bases in Brazil, Africa, and Malaysia, and even occupying part of Taiwan, the Dutch established their own global trading empire. The Indonesian archipelago, centered on the populous island of Java, became a long-time European colony, jewel of the so-called Dutch East Indies. In 1602, the Dutch introduced a new, soon-to-be-standard element of European seaborne colonization. They organized their colonization as a strictly commercial project, the Dutch East India Company. It was soon the biggest company in Europe. The Dutch also developed a new sea route to get spices back to Europe. Detaching themselves from the coastal monsoon traffic of the Spice Route, Dutch ships sailed due west, straight across the Indian Ocean from Indonesia to the Cape of Good Hope, which they took from the Portuguese, making it a Dutch colony. Between Indonesia and the Cape stretched a very long open-ocean crossing, unlike the mostly coastal Spice Route. Eventually, European access to the rest of the world involved many such long open-ocean crossings, the most famous and important being those pioneered by Columbus. This kind of voyage required new navigational tools.

People had studied the stars for thousands of years, of course. It wasn't hard to do a rough astronomical calculation of latitude. The height of the sun at midday gives an easy indication. Sailors also knew that certain stars remain always in the northern part of the sky. As one sails south, for example, the North Star sinks toward the horizon.

Squinting at the North Star, mariners could estimate its distance from the horizon by extending their arms and using "rule of thumb." Various sorts of sighting instruments could help them. But there is no West Star or East Star, and, because of the planet's rotation, no simple way to measure longitude by the stars. Sailors had to try to keep track of distance traveled east or west, day after day. They could tether a bulky floating object to a knotted cord and measure how quickly the cord unspooled as the ship sailed away from it, giving a speed in number of knots. Such calculations were not very accurate, though. Dutch East India vessels sailing straight across the southern Indian Ocean from the Cape of Good Hope often underestimated their progress and broke up at night on the west coast of Australia.

To calculate longitude by the stars required controlling for Earth's rotation, i.e., controlling for the passage of time. For that, global navigators needed an accurate clock, but in those days, clockwork called for a pendulum, which would emphatically not work at sea. This engineering challenge would not be solved until the eighteenth century, after the Dutch, French, Spanish, and British governments had all offered prizes to anyone who could invent a reliable method of calculating longitude at sea. Only after long and concerted effort was an appropriate chronometer invented. Far from enabling early European maritime success, precision celestial navigation arose out of it.

Europeans had not taken over the world by 1600, far from it. Yet they took a long step in that direction when they learned to circumnavigate the globe routinely. The crucial word here is *routinely*. By becoming world travelers, Europeans gained a much more comprehensive understanding of the planet. Going half-way around the world, then returning home, repeatedly, transporting tons of goods, all sorts of animals, and thousands of people—Europeans created a global transportation system that far transcended and would gradually replace both the Silk Road and the Spice Route. The new trade routes converged on western Europe from all points of the globe. Now thousands of men, mostly European, could boast of world-girdling travels rivaling those of Ibn Battuta or Marco Polo.

The impact of this transformation was gradual but telling. European claims over the Americas, not to mention Asia, remained highly contested, but they grew steadily. In 1600, Europeans had yet not managed to reorient world trade, only to access its main trunk. Gradually, though, they did reorient global commerce, as generations of Portuguese, Spaniards, Dutchmen, and Englishmen braved the waves to exploit overseas trading empires. Outsiders to Europe, on the other hand, visited there less often, and they always arrived on European ships. Until the 1500s, Atlantic Europe had been on the periphery of Eurasian civilization—on the periphery, we could say, of the global communications network, if such a thing existed. Now such a thing certainly did exist, with western Europe at its heart. No other place on Earth received regular news and information from so many diverse, distant locations. As a result, Europe's North Atlantic shore would become, for a while, the center of the world economy. The profits would be enormous.

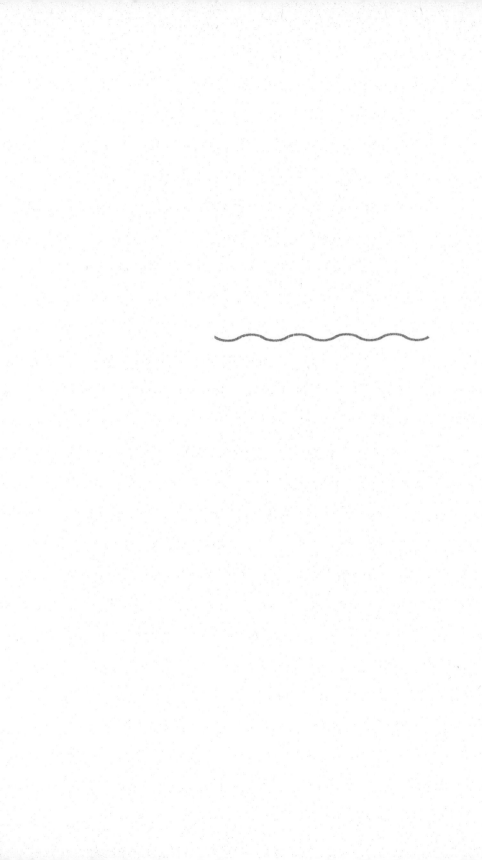

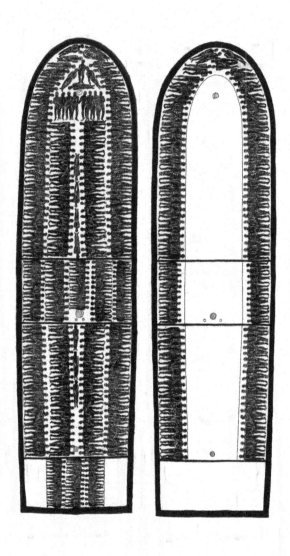

CHAPTER TEN

Colonized World

Foragers and tribes, kingdoms and empires, reacted variably to the unprecedented wave of European intruders. Asians, who shared with Europeans the common heritage of Eurasian civilization, were generally unimpressed. They resisted the intruders quite successfully at first. For the people of Australia and the Americas, however, resistance seemed futile. For them, the Europeans arrived swathed in something like the Black Death—pandemic diseases that swept away a large portion of aboriginal populations, killing natives while leaving Europeans unharmed. Moreover, most of Australia and the Americas was inhabited by foragers whose only defense was flight. The result was "settler colonialism," which cleared and replaced previous inhabitants of colonized lands, rather than taking them over.

Whatever the mode of colonization, however, its results were never mutually beneficial for colonizers and colonized. Almost always, sooner or later, the result was some sort of unfree labor. The salient example was the trans-Atlantic slave trade, which transported millions of human beings, packed like sardines in a can, from Africa to the Americas, where their fate, and their children's fate, was gang labor on plantations. About a million of these enslaved passengers died in transit. The imprint of European colonialism is still plainly visible in our world, even generations after the last formal empire closed shop. European colonialism shaped our world by connecting pretty much everything to a global economy centered on Europe. Today, that economy still exists, though Westerners no longer monopolize it. This chapter shows how the global economy first took shape.

East Asia

For Chinese people, the Europeans arrived at the height of the Ming dynasty (1368–1644). After more than a century of Mongol occupation, the imperial ruling family was again Chinese. The Mongols had governed from the north, close to Mongolia. Ming rule arose in the south and returned the Chinese capital to Nanjing, also in the south.

The overriding initial purpose of Ming rule was to rebuild traditional Chinese institutions. Emblematic of this purpose was its dominant intellectual current, neo-Confucianism, which now became a quasi-religion. The Mongols had neglected Chinese literary culture and the imperial system of administrative exams. Ming rulers set out to restore them. Moreover, Ming rulers returned the Grand Canal, the principal north-south communications artery, to working order, and did a lot of wall building on the northern border. The familiar Great Wall images of today represent recently restored portions of Ming-era wall. In southern China, where many millions had been integrated over the last thousand years to become Han, ethnic Chinese, many other millions had escaped integration—or repented of it—and now revolted. Many moved south to become Southeast Asian hill people. Partly to quell such rebellions, the Ming dynasty maintained a standing army a million strong, along with the world's largest naval shipyard.

Ming China doubled down on tradition. China continued to have the world's largest and most diverse economy. The region of the Yangtze Delta, starting point of the north-south Grand Canal, was now a hub of pre-mechanized manufactures such as porcelain and silk. And yet, in accord with the conservative overall Ming approach, the dynasty emphasized that most Chinese of activities, agriculture.

Whereas the Song dynasty had promoted trade, the Ming tax base returned to the countryside. In addition, Ming imperial government grew enormous. Its mandarin civil service was based on restored official examinations and on a particularly large corps of palace eunuchs, as many as a hundred thousand strong. While many were domestic servants to the imperial family, the eunuchs of Ming China also had large administrative responsibilities. An example was Zheng He, the admiral who commanded a string of famous Ming naval expeditions in the early 1400s.

As its wall building and large army indicated, the Ming state had powerful adversaries. The Mongols had been expelled, but they were not the only pastoral steppe people lurking along the northern border of China. Another challenge was posed by the Manchu people who lived north of Korea. A more novel but no less persistent menace now loomed on China's seacoast, pirates who operated from the southern Japanese coast and a scattering of small islands in the East China Sea. The coast of China was their prime target, but these pirates were in business for themselves and sometimes raided Japanese targets as well. Eventually, they had settlements on the mainland coast and Taiwan. No part of the Chinese coast was safe from pirates during the first century of the Ming dynasty. And then things got worse, when Japan launched a powerful invasion force, 150,000 strong, mostly into Korea, but also into Shandong Province, a heartland of traditional China. A Ming counterattack was successful, but Japanese military adventures in northeast Asia had only just begun.

Meanwhile, Portuguese merchants appeared at Guangdong in the 1510s. By then, Admiral Zheng He's famous voyages had been discontinued as the Ming dynasty struggled to suppress piracy and regain control of China's coastline through, among other measures, a general ban on overseas trade. The Portuguese merchants wanted silk. They were not disposed to accept the ban and became confrontational until the Ming navy chased them back to Malacca. Portuguese pirates then joined the other pirates still lurking along China's southern coast. Finally, the intruders reached an accommodation with the imperial government. Accommodation meant sharing profits with local Chinese actors powerful enough to pull imperial strings. By this means, in the 1550s, the Portuguese finally received permission to trade—but only at one place, a bit of land near the mouth of the Pearl River, where they constructed permanent warehouses. Macau, that bit of land, eventually became a Portuguese enclave and still today exercises a mild sort of extraterritoriality, allowing it to figure internally as "China's Las Vegas." Macau was the original template for Hong Kong, which was established nearby by the British several centuries later.

Portuguese commercial ambitions were thwarted by the strength of the Ming state. Europeans very much desired Chinese silk and porcelain and tea, but China as a whole, and most particularly its imperial state, wanted little that Europe had to offer. European trade would benefit Chinese producers and Guangdong merchants, on the other hand, and very much so. Consequently, local Chinese governors encouraged Portuguese mercantile ambitions on the sly, in return for a cut of the profits. But every so often, the emperor sent a "new broom" to sweep away local corruption, and the European traders had to regroup.

The most notable aspect of this global encounter lay in the collaboration between Xu Guangqi, a Chinese scholar, and Matteo Ricci, an Italian-born Jesuit who was probably the first European ever to master classical Chinese. After joining the Portuguese Jesuit mission to Asia, Ricci began to study Chinese language and culture at Macau. Xu Guangqi was thirty-eight years old when he met this Western wise man who dressed and spoke like a Chinese. Xu was quite impressed, no doubt. Xu was a scholar whose rise into the ranks of the imperial mandarin bureaucracy had stalled when he failed to pass the national-level test. This was a common disappointment. Failed candidates like Xu Guangqi usually went home to use their educations as a provincial intelligentsia. Xu met Ricci in Nanjing in 1582, when Ricci had been in China for almost twenty years.

As a prelude to proselytizing the Chinese, Ricci wanted to show that he understood and respected them. This was a good approach to take with the Chinese, who thought of China as the center of the world. Ricci learned to speak several regional variants of vernacular Chinese, and to read and write the classical language, which differed as much from vernacular Chinese as classical Latin differed from vernacular Italian. Ricci made himself, in effect, an authentic Confucian scholar. He worked on tools to help Europeans learn Chinese, including a dictionary and a phonetic form of writing that followed Chinese tonal pronunciation. For the benefit of his hosts, Ricci made the first European-style map of the world with place names in Chinese. But what got him invited to the imperial palace was the way he predicted solar eclipses. As Son of Heaven, it seems, the Ming Emperor gave astronomical knowledge a high priority.

Xu Guangqi and Ricci became friends. Xu converted to Christianity. Together, the two scholars translated Western classics into Chinese, and Chinese classics into Latin. Xu looked for practical ways in which China could learn from the West, such as the introduction of new crops and the adoption of European artillery. Mateo Ricci lived in China for twenty-eight years and never returned home. Or rather, China became his home. According to Chinese regulations, a sort of spiritual quarantine, outsiders like Ricci were supposed to be buried at the foreign enclave of Macau. But when Ricci died, the Chinese made an exception and interred him in Beijing. Such a relationship of mutual respect and reciprocal benefit was not common in the colonial world. It did not really promote colonization.

The Dutch, sailing in the Portuguese wake, took a more direct approach. But the Dutch, too, failed to impose themselves in Ming China militarily. Unable to win a Macau-style trading foothold on the mainland in the 1620s, the Dutch created an unauthorized foothold off the Chinese coast, in southern Taiwan, which was not Ming territory and had served generations of pirate raiders as a base. The Dutch were joined within a few years, on the northern side of the island, by a similar (though briefer) encampment of Spanish adventurers, who were hoping to build on Spain's new claim in the Philippines. Dutch occupation of Taiwan lasted four decades, but they never penetrated the Chinese market and finally gave up, contenting themselves with sole possession of the Dutch East Indies.

These bracing encounters with the strong Ming state contrasted the Portuguese experience in Japan. Japan lacked a strong unifying state in its internally divided, country-at-war period. When the Portuguese initiated contact in 1549, the power of both emperor and shogun were at a low ebb. Regional rulerships called daimyos, headed by samurai lords, dominated southern Japan—perpetually feuding, a picture not unlike that of mediaeval Europe. Europeans entered Japan much more easily than China because competing daimyos did not present a unified front. They viewed the Europeans less as a threat than as an opportunity—potential allies against their neighbors. The samurai leaders very especially noticed the utility of European firearms. Gunpowder had been first invented in China, of course, making European guns more impressive than horrifying in East Asian eyes. Japanese copies of European guns appeared almost as soon as the Japanese could lay their hands on samples to reproduce. Before long they were mounting light artillery on Japanese boats.

Eventually, the Portuguese received the protection of the shogun, who needed allies, too. Then European guns became a weapon to be used by Japanese state-builders against disobedient daimyos. The arrival of Europeans in Japan thus eventually strengthened central power, resulting in the mentioned 1592 invasion of northern China and Korea. By the 1630s, the shogun was strong enough to dispense with his European ace in the hole. The threat posed by outsiders had grown. The Dutch and Spanish had arrived in Japan, as well, and the shogun did not want things to get out of hand. After several generations of proselytizing, Portuguese Jesuits, accompanied now by Spanish Franciscans, had converted about three hundred thousand Japanese to Christianity. Several had traveled to Europe and returned with a global perspective. The Japanese now knew that the Spanish had colonized both the nearby Philippine Islands and, further away, an entire continent called America. Seeing that it had more to lose than to gain from the Europeans, the newly invigorated Japanese state slammed the door shut. Expelling all Europeans and executing thousands of their converts, the former country at war became the "closed country." Japan would remain closed to the outside world for two centuries.

India and Southeast Asia

In India, Europeans would find countless opportunities to play local powers one against another. Just two dynasties had ever ruled most of India, each for only a few generations. However, the teeming kingdoms and principalities of the South Asian subcontinent were hardly, for that reason, insubstantial. The economic production of the subcontinent was just under a quarter of global output, exceeded only by Ming China, which India would surpass in the 1700s. India (today the world's least-urbanized major country) was more urban than Europe then, mostly because India also had more manufacturing. It produced especially textiles, using above all cotton, the Indian domesticate that was destined to be, from then on, the world's preferred clothing fiber for hot climates. When Vasco da Gama appeared on the Malabar Coast around 1500, small kingdoms and principalities had dominated India for nine hundred years or so. And just as the Europeans began arriving in strength on the southern coasts, powerful imperial invaders entered from the north as well. These were the Mughals.

Yes, the word *Mughal* derives from *Mongol*, but the Mughals were not Mongols. You could think of them as ethnically Turkic heirs of Genghis Khan's empire, Muslims who wrote poetry in Persian, prayed in Arabic, and ate Indian food. As steppe warriors, they had helped forge the Mongol Empire and put on conquering airs. Once they took over most of northern India, they never left. Culturally, the Mughals were initially oriented toward Persia and Persians, whose superior refinement they did their best to imitate. The Mughals gradually made themselves at home in India, though, and after generations there, it really was their home. Eventually they abandoned Turkish and Persian to speak Urdu, a language descended from Sanskrit, quite similar to Hindi. (Today, Urdu is the national language of Pakistan.) Inside its impregnable walls, the Mughal imperial residence in Delhi was composed, in a very Indian style, of pavilions without walls, like those of Vijayanagara.

The Mughals entered the Ganges valley from the northwest around 1500. They expanded east to Bengal, then progressively south. They occupied India's central Deccan Plateau, including Vijayanagara. Southern India remained generally outside Mughal control. Meanwhile, the trading stations of the Portuguese were joined by those of new European imperial contenders along both southern coasts. The single most important spice in their trade was black pepper, and the principal source of black pepper was southern India itself. Moreover, southern India was a major point of transshipment on the Spice Route where goods changed hands. Cargos arriving by sea from the east, such as clove and nutmeg from Indonesia, were traditionally landed at trading emporia on the southeast coast and transferred to the southwest coast by their buyers, there to await transshipment to the Persian Gulf or the Red Sea.

The Portuguese quickly established a string of trading stations, including Goa, on the Malabar Coast. In addition, they took over the island of Sri Lanka, the world's main source of cinnamon. From these places, in combination with their other trading stations on the coasts of Africa, Arabia, Malaysia, and China, the Portuguese established themselves as major carriers on the Spice Route.

During the early 1600s, an Indian warrior queen named Abbakka Chowta resisted the Portuguese takeover of the Spice Route on the Malabar Coast. Chowta became a popular heroine whose charisma can still be felt today. A contemporary described her dark skin and humble clothing, which is the way she is depicted still. Chowta mingled with her followers, and she resembled them. But Chowta was not a Hindu or a Muslim—or a Christian or a Jew. Instead, she belonged to another of India's many small religious groups, the Jains, who profess respect for all forms of life. Jains have always been a small, typically urban, minority, and religious diversity was their natural milieu. As queen of a small kingdom south of Goa, Chowta allied herself with Hindus like da Gama's old nemesis, the king of Calicut, and with local Muslims of the Malabar trading community. Abbakka Chowta died, still resisting the Portuguese, around 1625.

Her contemporary Mumtaz Mahal died in 1631. Mumtaz Mahal was no warrior, although she died in childbirth while accompanying her husband on a military campaign. Her husband, Shah Jahan, ruled the Mughal Empire from 1628–1658, a period that is often considered its pinnacle, although the empire continued to expand territorially until around 1700. Like most Mughals, Mumtaz had been born in India. Her father was Persian, which gave her an added air of sophistication, and she was beautiful. She gave Shah Jahan many warrior sons. Shah Jahan ignored his other wives and was grief-stricken when Mumtaz died delivering their fourteenth child. In tribute to her, he built the world's most beautiful mausoleum, the Taj Mahal, so large and grand that in photographs many people today mistake it for a palace. His reign was more notable in cultural than military terms. He encouraged peaceful coexistence between Muslims and Hindus.

Although it also controlled Afghanistan, the Mughal Empire was Indian at heart by the 1600s. Its capital was Delhi. Its rulers were locals. Its way of life, although Muslim and imbued with Persian literary culture, was unlike anything outside of India. Perhaps it is good to underline that we are *not* referring to the entire subcontinent here. The most Muslim parts of Mughal India were those that today have become Pakistan and Bangladesh. The Mughal Empire was an old-fashioned territorial empire, with no navy and little interest in maritime trade. The energy of its economy and the refinement of its high culture, however, were second to none.

Meanwhile, around 1700, in neighboring Persia—which we ought to begin to call now by its modern name, Iran—the Safavid dynasty was also declining. The Safavids were unique in the Muslim world, an imperial family whose early prestige was rooted first in Sufism, and later, in Shiism, both marginalized by mainstream Sunnis. Simultaneously, a third Muslim empire, that of the Ottoman Turks, declined as well after its golden age under Suleiman the Lawgiver. A second Ottoman attempt to capture Hapsburg Vienna, in 1683, had ended in disaster. Ottoman arms would never again make territorial inroads in Europe. A few Muslim regimes were still expanding in Southeast Asia. Overall, however, the period of Muslim territorial empire building had ended, overtaken by Christian empire building of the new seaborne trading variety.

In the 1600s, the Dutch, French, and English sailed into the Indian Ocean and challenged the Portuguese by establishing coastal trading stations of their own. The Dutch snatched Sri Lanka from the Portuguese and, for a time, the main European competitors in India were the Dutch East India Company and the English East India Company. England and the Netherlands became great rivals in the East India trade—a rivalry that has disappeared from our historical consciousness today, though preserved in peevish English expressions like *going Dutch* and *Dutch treat*. Initially, the Dutch seemed to have won the competition, in 1688, when a Dutch noble, William of Orange, became king of England. As a result, the Netherlands took the lead in the spice trade, expanding its control over the Dutch East Indies. England, meanwhile, concentrated on India's textile trade, which turned out to be the richer prize in the long run. The British started by importing Indian cotton prints, which appealed not only because of their colors and patterns, but also as a novelty, because cotton had not previously been so available in Europe.

English influence waxed as Mughal power waned in 1700s India. Hindu leaders in central India, the Marathas, went on the offensive against the Mughals militarily. Now the French East India Company developed its own trading stations on the eastern Coromandel Coast. Next, England and France fought a war for empire, a war sparked by conflicts on the North American frontier, which is why Americans know it as the French and Indian War. The war for empire ended in 1763 with substantial British gains against France in both North

America and India. Britain now dominated the entire Coromandel Coast, from its southern tip to Bengal, India's major textile production and ship-building center. Bengal was a particularly rich prize for the British East India Company. Its base at Calcutta became the new command post of an emerging British colonial project, firmly under parliamentary supervision by the end of the 1780s. Loss of English colonies in America added urgency to British military operations against remaining Mughal territories. Now British colonizers, setting out from Bengal, pushed inland, gradually extending control over the entire subcontinent in the name of East India Company stockholders.

The colonization of Southeast Asia, too, was gradually consolidated in the 1600s and 1700s. The Dutch East India Company had started its operation in Indonesia as a string of trading stations, but in the late 1600s it began to expand its control over the large island of Java, the region's agricultural heartland. Successfully wresting Malacca from the Portuguese, the Dutch nonetheless failed, after several attempts, to take Manila from the Spanish. Operating from Manila's superb harbor, the Spanish used the Philippines for sporadic attempts at entering the China trade. The Spanish exercised little active control over most of the Philippine Islands until after the British occupied the Philippines in 1762–1763, during the war for empire. Returning to Spanish control, the Philippines gradually became the scene of Caribbean-style plantation agriculture, producing sugar, tobacco, and hemp. In the early 1800s, the British took Malacca from the Dutch, and eventually added other trading stations, one of which was Singapore. In contrast, mainland Southeast Asia (today's Myanmar, Thailand, Cambodia, Laos, and Vietnam) avoided European colonization until the 1850s and 1860s. French military intervention in the region followed the presence of Catholic missionaries—Jesuits, as in Japan and China—who had begun activities in Vietnam many years earlier. Vietnam, Laos, and Cambodia eventually became a French "protectorate" called Indochina. Then Myanmar passed into British control, leaving Thailand the only uncolonized part of Southeast Asia.

European penetration of Asia was slow and cumulative, quite unlike the sudden, sweeping Spanish takeover in the Americas. Nor did Europeans introduce unfamiliar epidemic diseases to Asia, as they had done in the Americas, because Asians and Europeans shared Old World microbes. European state trading companies were not bashful about using violence to establish themselves, obviously, but they worked in partnership with local Asian elites. Native populations remained largely intact. In sum, the establishment of European trading empires in Asia involved little European immigration or direct territorial colonization of the sort that occurred in the Americas and, as we are about to see, elsewhere.

The Emergence of Neo-European Societies

The Spanish aspired to rule Native American populations, while others—the English particularly—aspired to populate their American colonies with European people. The result there (as later in Australia and South Africa) was a different kind of colonialism, often not recognized as such. European settlers often had the willful idea that their new home had been somehow previously uninhabited, or inhabited by people too few or too primitive to matter. Often these unfortunates were foragers. Incoming settlers wanted to recreate a European lifestyle outside of Europe, importing the crops and livestock for a European diet, and maintaining their European language and religion. Only removal or extermination of native people allowed settler societies to approximate European ones. As a result, the original residents had to be destroyed, swept aside, or incorporated by settler society as a separate caste of unfree rural laborers. This sort of settler colonialism resulted in neo-European societies, which aimed to recreate European life by introducing European people, animals, and plants to replace whatever was there previously. This enormous, violent displacement is still remembered in patriotic myth as the peopling of a new Eden. Mythic visions cloud any clear-eyed under-standing of settler colonialism, however.

At heart, modern colonialism was always a for-profit undertaking. The most basic fact about any version of neo-Europe was what it exported for profit. Settlement was very expensive, and settler colonies had to pay their way. Export products defined a colony's earning power with respect to the mother country. Export products also defined the colony's internal development. Compared to conquest, settlement took much, much longer. Settlement required a large trans-Atlantic transfer of population, and the settlers had to learn to feed themselves in a new environment. While these settler populations would be largely self-sufficient, they also wanted an ongoing connection to their societies of origin in Europe. Spaniards wanted to drink Spanish wine, and English people wanted to wear English clothing. Only a profitable export product could provide settlers with imported European goods. Only a profitable export product could repay investors and creditors. Therefore, a colony's export activity defined its economic and social relations. In plantation colonies, the plantation owners dominated. In mining colonies, mine owners did, and so on.

What kind of societies resulted? Any sort of neo-Europe was a land of opportunity for Europeans, which is why so many migrated there. Farmland was much more easily available to settlers over-seas than in their European homelands. Poor European migrants improved their social status by becoming colonial landowners. The elimination of existing populations created frontier abundance for incoming settlers. Social relations within settler populations were therefore more egalitarian than those of the European mother country. This was the rough equality much celebrated in the early United States. However, this more egalitarian spirit *excluded* native people and newly imported slaves. No matter how much the colony might prosper, natives and slaves never enjoyed the benefits of prosperity. On the contrary, plantation slaves normally had to work longer hours when the price of tobacco, cotton, or sugar was high—earning no more, of course, since they earned nothing anyway. Overall, colonies with large non-European populations were less egalitarian than countries in Europe.

No neo-European colony better reproduced its sending society than did New England. Let's begin as school children do in the United States, in 1621, at the Plymouth Colony of Massachusetts. A ship called the Mayflower has unloaded its cargo of religious dissidents on the western shore of Cape Cod Bay. Their voyage has been backed by one of England's new joint stock companies, eager to make a profit by funding overseas colonization, but their own mostly religious purpose is commemorated in the name *Pilgrim*. These Pilgrims were Protestants who had left England, and often left the Church of England, for religious reasons. They intended never to return. Instead, they proposed to create a new and better society guided by Protestant ideas, but they were also required to repay the investors who had funded their colony. They had not been, for the most part, farmers at home, and they were ill prepared to survive in Massachusetts. Half of them died during the first hard winter. Fortunately for them, they got help from a native man who befriended them and helped them prepare to survive the second winter.

His name was Tisquantum, but our schoolchildren learn to call him Squanto. We learn about him in primary school around the harvest celebration that has become our Thanksgiving holiday. We learn that Squanto showed the Pilgrims how to plant corn, that they then had a good harvest, and that they therefore gratefully invited him and other Indian friends to a feast. And this feast was the first Thanksgiving. In the good old days, it seems, everybody got along. But, no, the story of harmonious beginnings evaporates when you drill down a bit. For example, Tisquantum was a Patuxet, the name of the tribe that had lived there in Plymouth until European diseases wiped them off the face of the Earth, just a year or two before the Pilgrims arrived, leaving their cleared fields unplanted. Tisquantum had survived only because he was not there. A bit earlier, in 1614, he had been lured aboard a passing English ship and kidnapped, along with twenty-six other unfortunate Patuxets, and then sold into slavery in Spain. Spanish clergy rescued him from slavery, and he somehow made his way home to Massachusetts, to find that his Patuxet community no longer existed. Tisquantum lived at the Plymouth Colony for twenty months, providing his famous advice about how to plant corn—in the Mesoamerican way, together with beans and squash. Also notably, he connected the anxious Pilgrims to the fur trade, their primary way of satisfying pushy investors.

The Indians who attended the first Thanksgiving in 1621 were mostly of a related group, the Wampanoags, ninety of them, with their chief Massasoit. They stayed for several days and hunted five deer for the festivities. Although problems arose after the first Thanksgiving, the Wampanoags' good relations with the English colonists lasted until Massasoit's death. Massasoit's son and successor, Metacomet, took the ceremonial name Philip in tribute to his father's friendship with the English. When Metacomet's people felt crowded by the growth of English settlements, conflict erupted, and the colonists mobilized. King Philip's War, 1675–78, became the major conflagration of early New England. Many English settlements were attacked, and many were destroyed. The native population of the region was cut in half. The Pilgrims' Indian friends from the first Thanksgiving were then exterminated altogether by the next generation of settlers.

The 1607 colonization at Jamestown, Virginia, was the beginning of permanent English settlement in what is now the United States. Its story is less inspirational. In Jamestown, settlers had no religious or civic motive to speak of. At Jamestown, the commercial bottom line of all European colonization stood nakedly obvious and unadorned. An indigenous drug, tobacco, which native people used ceremonially, found an avid market in Europe, where it was used recreationally. Recreationally, tobacco is highly addictive, and after a prolonged taste, practically markets itself. Therefore, tobacco became Virginia's legendary early export crop, its lucrative way of paying off London Company investors. In Massachusetts, where there was no such opportunity, settlers farmed principally for their own subsistence, becoming independent small landowners.

The profitability of tobacco turned Virginia into a plantation colony, run by "planters." A Virginia planter used his wealth or credit to launch a relatively large-scale commercial operation. Such a gentleman almost never worked in the fields of his own plantation. He needed many laborers, by far the most expensive part of his operation. The planter's profits depended partly on his paying his workers very little. In a plantation colony, things are arranged to favor the planters, and planters need cheap, fixed labor. So, Virginia settlers often arrived from England as contract laborers—indentured servants—who slaved on plantations for years to repay the cost of their trip to Virginia. Indentured servitude was no way to make a fortune, and indentured European servants did not last long as an agricultural labor force. Tobacco planters replaced them with Africans for sale in the Atlantic slave trade. English settlements south of Virginia, too, followed the plantation model. South Carolina saw the most intense application of its basic principles. In the rice-plantation lowlands, enslaved African settlers far outnumbered the free European ones. Charleston, South Carolina, became a wealthy colonial city, full of urban slaves.

Plantations constituted a major form of settler colonialism in the Americas. And from Virginia and Maryland to Cuba and Brazil, plantation labor was always slave labor. The Atlantic slave trade existed primarily to supply labor to profitable plantation colonies. Human cargos were embarked on the African coasts, where European slave traders bought war captives by the hundred. The main market for slaves lay in plantation colonies like Virginia, many of which were created in the 1600s and 1700s. So, the ancient practice of enslavement, humanity's old crime against humanity, expanded marvelously, becoming a principal motor of the Atlantic economy and a cornerstone of new global trading patterns. Slave trading became big business—perhaps the biggest business—in Europe's new seaborne empires. More than twelve million or so human beings enslaved in the African interior were marched in chains to the coast and sold to European traders. (Our figures enumerate only those who survived the hellish weeks of the trans-Atlantic Middle Passage across the Atlantic. Millions died at sea during the four hundred years of this killer trade.) The traders were the usual seaborne empire-building suspects. By volume of human cargos, the perp walk was led by Portugal, followed by England, France, Spain, and the Netherlands. Even pious New Englanders bought human cargos in Africa, swapping them for plantation sugar in the Caribbean, which they then carried to New England to be distilled into rum. There, loaded with rum and tobacco, they sailed to Africa again to trade for more slaves. This triangular trade enriched the original Yankee traders.

Very different societies resulted from New England settlement as compared to Virginia settlement. New England was the neo-Europe that most closely approximated the original. New England settlements responded, overall, to shared community and religious aspirations, not just profitability. They were able to satisfy creditors and investors by exporting furs and rum without exploiting large populations of unfree laborers directly. New Englanders owned family farms that served mostly to feed the farmers' families. After King Philip's War, there were no more Indians to infringe the settlers' property rights. Lumber-rich New England began to build ships and make a killing in the triangular slave trade. New England society participated in the Atlantic economy much as English society did, becoming more broadly prosperous as a result. Other colonies north of Virginia, particularly New York and Pennsylvania, somewhat resembled New England in that regard. All these colonies attracted European settlers who were eager to have their own subsistence farms. None became a major plantation colony—partly because of the colder climates, partly for other reasons. Pennsylvania and Georgia also responded initially to visions of benevolent social reform and opportunity. Maryland, which did have plantations, was founded to be a haven for English Catholics.

Neo-Europe was never an inclusive project, though. White supremacy was in its DNA. Settler colonies always displaced and marginalized (or sometimes annihilated) the original population. Plantation colonies produced the worst social outcomes. The legacy of protracted, violent exploitation was lasting trauma and social pathology. The master-slave syndrome created yawning disparities of wealth, power, and privilege, souring social relations for centuries. Large populations of slaves on commercial plantations were like nothing since the Roman Empire. Plantation societies with intense slave regimes sometimes had an African majority, often preserving elements of African language, music, and religion. Inevitably, the result was cultural mixture that flew in the face of colonizing aspirations. Plantation societies just could not, in truth, be very neo-European. Rich planters still wanted to be as English (or Portuguese, or Spanish, or French, or Dutch) as possible, and their wealth made it possible for them to import fancy glassware, fine linens, and specialized hardware from the old country, often sending their sons to be educated there. But their children were raised by enslaved nannies and lived surrounded by slaves, who often became their childhood companions, long-term confidants, and sexual partners.

Plantations clustered on the coasts of the Caribbean Sea, most particularly on its largest islands—and in Brazil, the mother of all plantation colonies. Haiti and Jamaica were French and English plantation colonies, both located on large islands snatched from Spain. The Dutch, too, had their sweet Caribbean footholds snatched from Spain. Moreover, the main imperial contenders had further plantation colonies on the South American mainland: French Guiana, (formerly British) Guyana, and (formerly Dutch) Surinam. Sugar was the great export crop in the Caribbean region, as in Brazil.

Sugar plantations soon eliminated the indigenous people who had welcomed the first Europeans, leaving only white settlers, their black slaves, and lots of brown people in the middle. The presence of the brown people signals race mixture and social fluidity. In plantation colonies, European colonists were likely to arrive as men alone. They normally had children with enslaved women, whether consensually or not. Often, they granted freedom to their own children born as slaves. Moreover, slaves could sometimes earn and save money, too, occasionally enough to buy their freedom. Most plantation societies developed a sort of middling class composed of free people of mixed race. The result was to create somewhat softer, more harmonious (although still unequal) relations among racially diverse people. The Portuguese and the French became known for mixing comfortably with the colonized people around them. The English and Dutch, not so much.

Brazil practically invented the sugar plantation, and sugar plantations practically invented Brazil. Sugar grew best in the soils of Brazil's narrow coastal plain, especially on the northeastern bulge around the settlements of Recife and Salvador. Whereas silver deposits had quickly drawn Spanish colonization inland, Portuguese settlement clung to the Brazilian coast from the 1500s to the 1700s. The discovery of gold (and even some diamonds) far from the coast finally beckoned irresistibly. For the most part, however, the interior of Brazil remained a sparsely settled frontier of indigenous people and slave hunters. Meanwhile, natives mostly vanished from the coastal plains. They literally could not survive plantation slavery. Disease and despair wiped them out. The most powerful families in the Portuguese colony were large sugar plantation owners whose operations required hundreds of slaves. Brazil became the biggest buyer, the most frequent destination of the slave trade. About half of the millions who survived the trans-Atlantic crossing as human cargo landed in Brazil. Massive, forced migration over centuries gave strength and continuity to Brazil's African culture.

And Brazil is roomy. When they escaped from a plantation, Brazilian slaves often formed their own societies nearby. The most famous of these was Palmares, which lasted for almost a hundred years in the northeastern Pernambuco region. The last leader of Palmares was Zumbi, an African king born in Brazil, defeated, beheaded, his kingdom lost, and his head displayed on a pike in 1695. Zumbi's kingdom in the backlands of northeastern Brazil had consisted, at its height, of possibly thirty thousand people in eleven villages, occupying highlands away from the sugar plantations along the coast. The Palmares settlements consisted especially of ex-slaves, who at first called the place Little Angola. Palmares was a *quilombo*—an African-style social organization that gathers dispersed population of diverse origins to form a new group. (The famous Angolan *imbangalas* of the 1600s, new communities formed by alliances of young warriors from many villages, did something similar.) The people of Palmares farmed, traded, and also raided to supply themselves. On raids, they took slaves as well as cattle. Portuguese authorities had repeatedly failed to destroy Palmares before the 1690s. The colonial authorities succeeded in 1695 by sending, not a Portuguese militia, but a force of backlands slave-hunters, largely of indigenous descent, against Palmares.

From about 1580 to 1640, the Dutch interlopers occupied the most prosperous region of Brazil and learned to do the sugar-and-slaves drill. Finally expelled from Brazil, the Dutch introduced sugar cultivation to the Caribbean region by colonizing Surinam, Aruba, and Curaçao. In the mid-1600s, England and France made their own island claims in the Caribbean, also to grow sugar. The Spanish were the last to create large-scale sugar plantations there, distracted by the glittering possibilities of Mexico and Peru. Nonetheless, the Spanish colony of Cuba would eventually become the world's preeminent slave-driving sugar factory.

Mexico and Peru were not plantation colonies, though both had some plantations. Mexico and Peru exported precious metals, the world's most valuable commodity. The first installment was gold from Aztec and Inca imperial treasures, but the great mines of Mexico and Peru were silver mines. Silver was in demand. Silver, not gold, was the European key to trade with China, where European products found few buyers. Ming China's outsized domestic economy was restrained for lack of circulating currency, as earlier Chinese economies had been, as well. Money facilitates exchange. That is its great importance for a market economy. China's long-term need for currency had already led it to introduce paper money, but silver was safer. Silver was what China wanted from European traders in return for its products. For centuries, silver from American mines flowed to Spain, and then quickly beyond, to pay for Chinese silks, tea, and porcelain.

Silver exports turned Mexico and Peru into Spain's richest colonies by far. The entire Spanish colonial project in the Americas was organized to support the mining and exportation of silver bullion. The Spanish crown took a 20 percent cut, termed "the royal fifth," of total output. Spanish treasure ships, towering galleons deeply laden with bullion, conveyed it to Spain in an annual fleet. English, French, and Dutch pirates swarmed around it like flies.

Spanish America, viewed as a whole, contrasts all the other European colonies discussed so far. The conquistadors had conquered not just treasure and territory, but labor, lots of it. Mexico and Peru had been the most densely populated and politically consolidated areas of indigenous America. Now the former subjects of the Aztec and Inca Empires became subjects of the Spanish monarchy and were incorporated into colonial society as a laboring class. By the tens of thousands, they became silver miners, the ones who dug the deep shaft mines, extracted the ore, smelted and minted it, transported it from the highlands to the coast, and loaded it onto ships for the annual treasure fleet. The farming villagers who had once worked for Aztec and Inca overlords now worked the same fields for Spanish overlords. Thus, indigenous ancestry still characterizes Mexico and Peru today. Many native people still conserve traditional dress and customs, and many indigenous languages are still spoken. Mixed heritage is the norm. By the 1600s, the wealth of silver and abundance of labor had made possible impressive fortifications, public buildings, and universities. The mining economy of Mexico and Peru was the heart of Spain's colonial project.

During the 1500s, conquistadors had scrambled over huge swaths of North and South America in search of precious metals and opportunities for conquest. They had founded a far-flung network of cities, laying claim to, without really controlling, vast hinterlands. Areas without mine or a lucrative plantation crop found little to export. They attracted few settlers, imported few slaves, made little progress at subjugating local tribes, and generally languished as colonial backwaters. Spanish American colonies in the Caribbean developed profitable sugar plantations once the mining economy had begun to decline there. That's why Cuba, the Dominican Republic, and Puerto Rico have modern populations of African descent and prominent racial mixture.

As for the French colonial project in America, it left a relatively small footprint. Sugar-producing Haiti was its richest jewel. Meanwhile, France made enormous claims in North America. French claims comprised New Brunswick, Nova Scotia, and Newfoundland—settlements of coastal, maritime orientation. The principle French claim in North America sprawled inland from its Atlantic entryway at the St. Lawrence River to the Great Lakes and beyond. It was all about the fur trade. The fur trapping was done by native people. French colonists traveled and worked closely with them, ranging across the enormous French-claimed territories from the Great Lakes, west across the entire Mississippi Valley, and south to New Orleans, in canoe journeys of many months. Actual French settlement existed only at the St. Lawrence River, around Quebec and Montreal, where French is still spoken.

The French crown subsidized French settlers, but it expected them to provide indentured agricultural labor. Few Frenchmen willingly crossed the Atlantic to bend their backs for a landlord in the Americas. Except for its fur trade, French colonization in that part of the globe was always more aspiration than reality. The fur trade itself generated only scant French settlement, a few isolated trading posts perched on the banks of rivers, great and small. The sprawling French claim on the map was inhabited by native people who had rarely laid eyes on anyone French, unless perhaps they had once spotted a few *coureurs des bois*, or forest brokers, as traveling fur-trade operatives were called.

The fur trade was consolidated in 1627 by the Company of New France, and the coureurs des bois were its commercial agents in the Great Lakes and Mississippi Valley. Coureurs des bois often lived with native women and spoke indigenous languages. They recognized Iroquois adversaries as well as Huron or Algonquin friends. Coureurs des bois inhabited a native world, and although they disrupted it by their mere presence, they did less to destroy it than agents of any other European colonial project.

Not only the Americas experienced settler colonialism.

Consider Australia. Beginning with the arrival of the first British fleet at Sydney in 1788, Australia became a British penal colony. Here, unusually, was an official program of colonization sponsored by the government rather than by private investors. Early colonists were convicts who chose "transportation" to Australia rather than incarceration in Britain. No lure of a profitable connection to the world economy was necessary to motivate these settlers, and they found none in Australia. They *did* find a continent's worth of "unclaimed" land for the taking because the British government refused to recognize any aboriginal land rights at all. The land mattered little, though, until European sheep were added. Wool, one of Europe's own early export commodities, could now link the continent of Australia securely to the world economy.

Aboriginal Australians were utterly dispossessed by British colonization. They resisted the loss of their world, of course. But they won no victories. The invaders made no treaty, not even the kind that soon proves worthless, with the aboriginal people. The colonizers explained (to one another) that foragers are ipso facto primitive savages who do not own land or have leaders with whom civilized people can make treaties. Settlers were given legal title to lands that aboriginal people had traversed with their song lines from time immemorial. Settlement of Australia didn't take over just the temperate and well-

watered southeast coast. Settlers took the entire continent. Sometimes title-owning, gun-wielding settlers tolerated the presence of
native people on lands traversed by their song lines, sometimes not.
So relentlessly were the foragers swept aside that the Australian colony became the very model of neo-Europe.

South Africa, too, became a settler colony, by a combined neo-
European effort. The Portuguese arrived first but settled not at all.
Then South Africa's strategic location led to permanent colonization
by the Dutch East India Company in 1652, because South Africa was
the place to catch the winds for a long voyage due east across the
open Indian Ocean to the Dutch East Indies. Dutch colonization of
South Africa began, like the Portuguese installation it replaced, as a
maritime way station at Cape Town. The hinterland suited European
settlement. This is the origin of the Afrikaans-speaking Boer population. (Afrikaans is basically local Dutch, and *Boer* means farmer
in Dutch.) Imperial tussling among Dutch, French, and British contenders delivered the Cape Town colony into British hands officially
in 1815. In reaction, Afrikaans-speaking inhabitants of the former
Dutch colony began to travel northward to escape British control,
leaving coastal settlements far behind. Their journeys across the
South African grassland added the word *trek* to the English language.
Antipathy to British control of the Cape Colony led the dissident
trekkers to create their own independent Boer settler republics that
lasted for several decades. Settler colonialism did encounter obstacles
in South Africa, such as the eruption of Zulu power under the great
leader Shaka, between 1816 and 1828. The native African population
was simply too large for South Africa to be effectively neo-European,
even with extraordinary measures that eventually coalesced in the
formal regime of white supremacy called apartheid.

The European penetration and partition of most of Africa
occurred very late, on the eve of the twentieth century. European
colonialism is too big a story to fit in one chapter of world history. It
was said that the sun never set on the British Empire, back when it
included India, Canada, Australia, and South Africa. Little England

had assembled the world's largest empire ever. Mongolia lost bragging rights. And taking together all parts of the world colonized by Europeans, the result was undeniably dramatic. Very few places on Earth were able to escape European colonization. China escaped nominally, but endured over a century of humiliation. Only Japan, Ethiopia, and Thailand escaped entirely.

The West had risen.

CHAPTER ELEVEN

Modern World

Before 1800, Europeans had begun colonizing all the world's continents except for Antarctica. Their overall control was still quite limited, however. At first, Europeans occupied coastal enclaves connected to their respective mother countries by dangerous, protracted, inevitably erratic voyages at the mercy of winds and currents. European explorers had traversed, but not yet populated, the interiors of North and South America, Africa, and Asia. Europeans controlled the world's principal trade routes, but they imported much more than they exported. During the 1800s, that changed.

During the 1700s, the incipient world economy already spanned the globe, but it involved only a tiny amount of world production and consumption. Most people in the world, the overwhelming majority, were farmers or herders or foragers who subsisted on what they gathered, hunted, or raised themselves. They wore homemade clothes. They traded for salt monthly, an iron tool every few years, perhaps a piece of jewelry once in a lifetime. They were 90–95 percent involved in their subsistence economy, one could say, and only 5–10 percent in a money economy. Prevailing commodity markets were local or regional. International commercial circuits had gained global reach, but they carried low-voltage current, so to speak.

During the 1800s, the voltage surged, and new world economy increasingly impacted people's lives. The market that had spanned the world with gossamer threads, carrying silk and silver and spices, expanded to include bulky staple goods and heavy raw materials. Gossamer threads were replaced by steel rails and copper wires. People gradually abandoned or lost direct access to a subsistence economy. *Homo sapiens*, especially urban dwellers, lived more and more submerged in a market economy. That meant they needed more money to buy things that they had formerly grown or made for themselves. Even some basic necessities now came from overseas. By the 1900s, when the girl pictured here worked in a southern US cotton mill, almost everybody lived up to their eyeballs in the new global economy. It had become the key to wealth and power everywhere. This deepening and intensification of the world economy materially transformed life on Earth.

Industrialization, in a word, drove the change. Mechanized production vastly expanded the volume of world trade. At its most basic, industrialization involved taking traditional subsistence activities— such as the spinning of thread and yarn—out of the home. Investors accumulated capital, gathered workers, disciplined their activities, purchased raw materials, sold the product, and pocketed the profits. In a few industries, such as flour milling, Europeans had long harnessed the power of water wheels turned by river power. Manufacture of Chinese porcelain already occurred in mass-production facilities and with a minutely specialized division of labor. Europe's Industrial Revolution accelerated because of its increasing mechanization and its appropriation of new forms of energy. Coal-generated steam and, eventually, electrical power drove a vast leap in manufacturing *quantity*. Mechanized production could not approach a skilled craftsman's quality, but in sheer volume the machines won with no contest. Tireless machines tended to saturate any market eventually, making export markets crucial to industrialization.

Industrialization compounded the European commercial advantage. Raw materials and commodities, not only finished goods, began to travel long distances. North Atlantic factories had a special relationship with the plantation system because their first major product was cotton cloth. European colonies had enriched the colonizers commercially since the 1500s, of course. European control of shipping, finance, and marketing already constituted enormous leverage in world trade. But Europe had long remained a net *importer* of manufactured goods, with a chronic trade imbalance regarding India and, especially, China. Europe's Industrial Revolution gradually reversed that relationship. After the middle of the 1800s, Europeans had become the chief exporters of manufactured goods to the rest of the world, including China. Opening markets to "free trade" became the mantra. Therefore, although the mechanization of production occurred in only a few places, the impact was global.

Making the World Modern

Europe's Industrial Revolution, and the world's, started in England for various reasons. England had coal and iron, both of which were crucial. England was politically unified. England had long exported wool, so it already had export markets and some necessary infrastructure (such as ports, canals, banks, and insurers) for the textile trade.

The new surge of industrialization was all about textiles. England's own East India Company disrupted the textile market by importing cloth from India as a supplement to its spice trade, beginning in the late 1600s. Indian print calico fabrics were inexpensive and appealing. English weavers successfully had the Indian imports banned, and local entrepreneurs rose to the challenge of supplying English demand themselves.

During the 1700s, English industrialists constructed the first modern textile mills, usually water powered at first, bringing together hundreds of workers in structures unlike any that had previously existed. Decades of tinkering allowed spinners and weavers to connect their spinning wheels and looms mechanically to the force of the river.

Generations of schoolchildren later learned the names of particularly transformative pieces of textile manufacturing machinery, such as Richard Hargreaves's famous early invention, the spinning jenny. The spinning jenny accelerated production by twisting many threads at once. Hargreaves was an illiterate hand-loom weaver from northern England who worked not in a factory but at home. Such work was often done by women, which is the reason that Hargreaves named his contraption "jenny." Hargreaves made some of the first spinning jennies for his friends, who were enthusiastic until they saw the price of their product tumble as a result. Somehow, mechanization meant that workers could produce more and earn less. Some workers understandably became anti-mechanization Luddites who wanted to get rid of the machines. The workers almost never profited personally from accelerating mass production. Those who profited were the factory owners. That's why Richard Arkwright, the "father of the factory system," died quite rich, whereas Hargreaves continued to work with his hands.

Arkwright assembled the necessary capital to connect many such machines to a water wheel of the kind that had long been used to mill flour. That's why the factory that he built in 1771 was called Cromford *Mill*. Assembling the workers around a large mechanical power source—*that* was the innovation that enriched Arkwright and future capitalists. Arkwright recruited entire families of displaced rural people and built worker housing at his "mill." Later, he built more mills. At one point, he had 1,150 employees, around two-thirds of them children. They worked around the clock in two thirteen-hour shifts. The overlap meant that the machines never had to stop, even for a few minutes.

Time had become money, and high production values were not needed for the mass market. In 1803, England had 2,400 looms. In 1833, it had 100,000. And that was only the beginning. English cotton cloth became the 1800s' most basic stock in trade internationally—what silk and spices and porcelain had been in earlier centuries. Cotton fabric, rather than woolen, was the great product of English textile mills, despite the cool English climate and wooly English traditions.

The rise of the English textile mills was the defining event of the Industrial Revolution. It occurred just as the British Empire expanded, and not by accident. It ended with English mills spinning and weaving Indian cotton to sell internationally—including, especially, in India. The Indian looms of Mughal days now disappeared. The de-industrialization of India was not merely simultaneous with the rise of the English mills: it was the obverse of the same story. The supply of raw material was totally imported from overseas colonies at first—from India and from plantation colonies in the Americas. In the Americas, enslaved Africans grew a South Asian crop to supply raw materials for English factories that exported in bulk around the world. The critical word here is *bulk*.

England also debuted modern industrialization's impact on the countryside. Overall, in human history, the mass of any population had foraged, farmed, or herded, living necessarily close to the land, while only few people lived urban lives, disconnected from the land, as merchants, servants, artisans, warriors, or bureaucrats. In the world's traditional societies, cities rarely represented a tenth of the population. Then the Industrial Revolution of the 1700s and 1800s began, indirectly, to depopulate the English countryside in a process called enclosure. Enclosure was the erection of fences or hedges around the private property of great landowners. England's nobles, in practice, owned most of the country, in return for their loyal vassalage to the king. English peasants, like other European peasants, had lived as serfs on these lands for generations, and the nobles had supposedly taken good care of them. Common lands provided shared access to subsistence. But the relation between noble and serf was old-fashioned stuff in a world reorganizing itself around market relationships.

The new industrial demand for textile fibers made a change. Now landlords maximized wool production. Herds of sheep required only a few full-time shepherds, whose skill was commonplace and inexpensive to hire. Well-enclosed pastures minimized the need for workers and facilitated experimentation with selective breeding and

pedigrees. Great landowners became "gentleman farmers" who practiced "scientific husbandry," selecting particularly meaty or wooly
male animals to sire their herds, creating livestock custom-designed
to produce abundant wool and mutton. They planted alfalfa as a
special fodder. Scientific husbandry dictated a new logic of rural life.

Enclosure made many rural people "redundant." A lot of hungry children, cousins, grandparents, and what have you, were simply
more mouths to feed. Anything that the ex-serfs had formerly provided to their ex-lord could be bought by him with the new profits
of wool production. As a result, the rural population was no longer
tied to the land, as in medieval times. The former peasantry now
had every opportunity to leave—people were asked to leave, in fact,
after umpteen generations, whether or not they had anywhere to
go. Enclosure emptied the English countryside of its former workforce just as English cotton mills began to hire more workers in the
industrial cities.

Urbanization accelerated. The cities' new inhabitants would have
to find a connection to the global economy or be confined to a poor-
house. Factories were usually urban, and certain English cities—
such as Manchester and Birmingham—famously grew up around
the mills. But even cities without many factories swelled quickly in
industrializing economies as the countryside occupied fewer workers.
Large port cities became especially important with the rapid expansion of maritime trade. Rapid urbanization became part of the new
model of industrialized economies.

Model is the wrong word, though. England's Industrial Revolution was not really a model that others might adopt. Yes, it accelerated the expansion of Britain's seaborne trading empire, the
world's largest. Yes, it gave England, for the first time, a dominant
export product to deploy in world trade. The very last thing that
the industrialists wanted, however, was to inspire imitators around
the world. They regarded their technical innovations as trade secrets
and guarded them closely. Moreover, England's Industrial Revolution required more than a series of technical innovations. It emerged

from a particular historical situation, a set of opportunities presented by England's new, privileged position in world trade. Therefore, England's Industrial Revolution spread very little. It was spatially concentrated (toward the northwest) even in England. It spread to southern Scotland, a bit, but no further, not even to Ireland or Wales.

In continental Europe, only Germany (most especially its Ruhr Valley) and, to some extent, Belgium and the Netherlands industrialized significantly during the 1800s. The Netherlands' leading role in world trade aided it, obviously. Northern Germany, too, with its medieval Hanseatic trading league, already played a large role in European trade, and like northern England, northern Germany was well endowed with coal and iron deposits, which were critical to this phase of industrialization. Other parts of Europe fed the new industries, and bought from them, without industrializing much themselves. A striking thing about early industrialization as a global phenomenon was its extreme spatial concentration, even within Europe.

The other place where industrialization occurred by the early 1800s was New England. Rather than copying England's developments, New Englanders roughly co-invented mechanized manufacturing. New Englanders had already become active participants in Atlantic trade. Also, New England was full of the same sorts of Protestant dissenters who animated English industries. New Englanders began building cotton mills almost as soon as Old Englanders did. Until the American Revolution of 1776, most American colonials considered themselves loyal English subjects. Unsurprisingly, mill engineers took their expertise back and forth between England and New England. The all-important cotton gin, a machine that enabled the fully mechanized spinning and weaving of cotton fiber by removing the seeds from it, was invented by a New Englander visiting a Georgia plantation in 1793.

England, northern Germany, New England and, gradually, other northeastern areas of the United States—such as New York, Pennsylvania, and Ohio, where large coal reserves awaited—comprised the core of world industrialization in the 1800s. This was the world of steam, steel, and electricity, chief elements of a second stage of industrialization that began around 1850. This world ran on coal at first. Its landscapes and not a few of its people were blackened by coal dust. On the eve of the World War One, the United States, England, and Germany mined 93 percent of the world's coal.

Coal might appear grimy and unattractive today, but let's remember that before coal, most power was muscle power, whether of humans or domesticated animals. Like petroleum, coal is a fossil fuel that represents the concentrated energy of millions of years of photosynthesis occurring in the distant past. Coal-burning steam engines powered factories without the location constraints of waterpower. The highly concentrated energy of coal made it an ideal power source for vehicles. And that would be even more true of oil, which eventually replaced coal. In 1859, Pennsylvania entrepreneurs drilled the first commercial oil well. Modern industrial economies were born and have always thrived in close association with fossil fuels.

Meanwhile, Europeans actively discouraged industrialization elsewhere. In the context of global colonialism, Europe's industrialists aimed not to rival the weavers of India, for example, but to drive them out of business. Before World War Two, modern industrialization spread hardly at all outside of its original core area. Outside of Europe and the United States, only Japan truly joined the industrial club. Mechanization transformed production in the world's industrial core. It literally energized the capitalist world economy, and *that* transformed the entire world. English cotton textiles were spun and woven in England, but every fiber of the raw material had to be shipped from outside of Europe. In response, the world's colonial plantations doubled down to produce food and raw materials to feed European industrialization.

In sum, the Industrial Revolution defined the center of the emerging global economy in 1800s. The center lay in western Europe and the northeastern United States. England had already become the world's most globally connected country. Now it became the cutting-edge manufacturer, too. Before 1700, the luxury trade in silver, silk, and porcelain had integrated only a small part of the world's population economically. Now, the emerging global economy moved vastly larger quantities of goods: manufactured articles of mass consumption, raw materials, minerals, fibers, and food.

It also moved people. The industrializing global economy stimulated the greatest long-distance mass migrations in history. Some were forced migrations. The trans-Atlantic slave trade continued until the mid-1800s, and so did an east-bound trade of African slaves to Muslim countries, also involving large numbers. These flows were joined in the late 1700s by a century and a half of mass migration by Europeans. The largest exporters of people were Britain, the Netherlands, Spain, and Portugal—the usual suspects when it comes to seaborne empires, excluding the French, who emigrated much less. French Canada was populated mostly by indigenous people, and French Caribbean colonies, mostly by African slaves and people of mixed race.

It took truly massive migrations to create viable homesteading populations on the other side of the world. England produced the most migrants expecting to farm. They became settlers in the United States, Canada, Australia, or South Africa. Overall, European migrants experienced more the pull of opportunity than the push of displacement. But there was plenty of push, too. The Irish potato famine of the 1840s was an exceptional shove, and the migrants who flooded out were truly refugees. Enclosure and industrialization themselves displaced millions of English people, some of whom found no workable alternatives. Accumulating poverty and prison crowding inspired the search for penal colonies like Australia. Also more pushed than pulled, obviously, was the migration of (European) Russians into Siberian exile. Germans and Italians, displaced by European wars of national consolidation, were likewise pushed to the Americas.

Contract laborers, another set of migrants, left India and China—some more pushed, others more pulled. Many of the Indians, for example, had been weavers before losing their livelihood to the Industrial Revolution. Contract laborers crossed oceans to do heavy work, normally gang labor, especially on tropical plantations, but also mining and railroad building under British direction. Many were indentured laborers, bound to work for years to repay the cost of their transportation. Indians traveled to South Africa, Guyana, Trinidad, Jamaica, Malaysia, and Fiji. Many were meant to replace the labor of former slaves who refused to work on plantations after emancipation. Chinese workers tried their luck in South Africa, Peru, Cuba, Australia, Malaysia, Hawaii, and California. Whether mining, doing plantation labor, or building railroads, they were constructing a world economy. After the Opium War opened China to British activities, many of the Chinese workers were indentured "coolies," gang laborers without legal rights. Coolies came from the poorest of the poor and were often abducted or contracted against their wills. Most Chinese emigrants were not coolies, however. Free Chinese laborers who paid for their own transportation chose more promising destinations. California and Australia attracted free Chinese contract workers. Some migrated to Southeast Asia (Thailand, the Philippines, Java, Malaysia), the historical center of China's maritime trade diaspora. Chinese residents in Southeast Asia had become a prosperous middle class of traders and entrepreneurs. Only in Southeast Asia did Chinese migrants establish permanent, substantial communities. On average, Chinese emigrants returned home more often than those of any other major sending country.

All this interconnection required more and better communications. Outside of the industrial core of the world economy, the arrival of a locomotive or a steamship was the most tangible sign of global industrialization. The advantages of the new technology were enormous, most especially regarding land transportation. In an era when most people hand-carried loads, drove pack mules or, in a few places, heaved carts and wagons down muddy roads using animal traction, covering only a few miles a day, railroads provided a previously unimaginable gain in ease, speed, and carrying capacity. Railroads were difficult and expensive to build, however, requiring enormous labor and material inputs. Train tracks can climb, descend, or turn only very gradually, so laying track requires a lot of planning, tunneling, and trestle-building. Steamships (with a steam engine attached to a paddle wheel or an underwater propeller) moved faster than sailing ships, but the biggest gains were in cargo capacity and reliability. Steam power freed sailors from the tyranny of tides and winds. Ships that never needed to await the wind could, for the first time, sail on tight schedules. Steam power was coupled with iron construction. Although it sounds counterintuitive, iron-hulled ships could be much larger and more seaworthy than wooden ships. But big, new iron-hulled steamers required larger and deeper port facilities. The telegraph, forerunner of the telephone, sent a very simple electric signal over copper wire. Short and long signals, written as a sequence of dots and dashes, corresponded to letters of the alphabet in the once-famous Morse code. The telegraph was a long-distance system never distributed to individual households, but telegraph cables laid across the ocean floor in the 1870s could transmit news, such as fluctuations in commodity prices across the Atlantic, in a few minutes.

Interconnection wrought change, but the rate and degree of change were hugely variable from place to place. Remote interior provinces and inaccessible mountain villages would long remain isolated from the world economy. To visit them was like a journey into the past. Meanwhile, port cities well served by railroads began to share their lifestyles internationally. Globalization accelerated. Overall, as the market expanded inexorably through the 1800s, the world economy would structure life more and more. In material terms, the modern world was shaped by accumulated money, which is to say, by capital.

It is time we called capitalism by its name.

Experiencing Capitalism

Capital is accumulated money. Capitalism happens when money rules, displacing other sorts of authority, further empowering money.

We've just laid out the origins and overall shape of the world capital-ist economy. Now let's look at its internal logic, the way it was expe-rienced, and the overall impact on people's lives, both at the center of the world economy and in its peripheral regions.

During the 1800s, the logic of the market, in which human rela-tions were mediated by money and exchange, loomed ever larger. A growing obsession with money was then widely criticized as "the root of all evil." Money had become a more central preoccupation for many. It happened naturally as they deepened their participation in a market. Historically, people who grew their own food, made their own clothes, didn't pay rent, and didn't live in a consumer econ-omy, had little use for money. The more that competitive market relationships replaced cooperative subsistence relationships, how-ever, the larger money's role. People who found cooperative subsis-tence replaced by the competitive market often felt that the world had become a crueler, harder place. For example, neighbors who used to share and now sold things to each other felt less solidarity when they did so. Often, the capitalist world market was experienced as an out-side intrusion that upset traditional social relationships. "We used to trust each other, you see, but now . . ." If a new scope and efficiency of exchange was the bright side of capitalist globalization, this was the dark side: the corrosive loss of community reciprocity. Society as a whole suffered, but modern entrepreneurs making a killing could more easily overlook the loss of traditional cooperative and recipro-cal relationships. Displaced rural people were more inclined to miss the old days.

Particularly outside the capitalist core regions, many potential laborers resisted participating in the market economy, to the frus-tration of the entrepreneurs, who considered such behavior a sign of stupidity. After all, who wouldn't want more nice stuff? But native people who could grow their own food and make their own clothes often had to be tricked into buying things that they did not want or need. Colonial authorities sometimes dumped unwanted goods on them and then collected payment by force. Likewise, without a desire to consume European goods, Latin American or Southeast Asian peasants often did not accept wage labor on plantations if they could avoid it.

In the colonized world, therefore, capitalist entrepreneurs in the countryside often had to coerce their laborers. One general "recruiting" tactic was to deprive potential employees of access to traditional subsistence activities. Another was to make wage employment a legal requirement for rural people. Those who lived off the land in the old style could be imprisoned for vagrancy or conscripted into the colonial army. Sometimes, landlords bought up all the land, so that people could find nowhere to grow their own food. Sometimes they advanced a month's wages to workers, who then couldn't leave the plantation until the debt was repaid. But sometimes the wages were so low, and the prices so high, that a worker's debt couldn't easily be repaid. Sometimes workers could get food and supplies only at a high-priced company store. Called debt peonage, this system of permanent indebtedness has existed all over the world in modern times. "You load sixteen tons and what do you get? Another day older and deeper in debt. Saint Peter don't you call me, 'cause I can't go. I owe my soul to the company store." These song lyrics describe the system in early twentieth-century Kentucky coal mines.

Widely shared wealth was generally *not* an attribute of early capitalist enterprise.

Early factories everywhere were famously grim places for industrial workers. Their long hours, low pay, and dangerous working conditions sometimes compared unfavorably to those of plantation slaves. The worst abuses were probably in the countryside, where profit-driven plantations replaced small-scale, pre-capitalist subsistence farming. Although quite unequal and exploitative, the precapitalist arrangements had been at least predictable and minimally adequate for survival. The poor—especially poor subsistence farmers—rarely prospered before the plantations came, but they usually didn't starve. The threat of hunger, in contrast, was a basic feature of colonial capitalism. Consequently, the market-driven dissolution of traditional social arrangements produced considerable angst around the world. The benefits of agrarian capitalism accrued mostly to large landowners and to the colonizing mother countries.

The United States of America, home to both factories and plantations, pretty much defined the capitalist experience. It must be accounted the world's salient capitalist success story, but the dark side is not absent. Very early industrialization had occurred in New England, followed by New York, Pennsylvania, and the southern shores of the Great Lakes—while the South and West remained agricultural or pastoral. In the US South, the slave plantation, not mechanized industry, was still the defining economic institution. Kept separate, plantation and factory were, in fact, part of the same system. Those white-columned mansions surrounded by slave quarters and cotton fields? They reflected industrial globalization as much as did the redbrick factories with their armies of machine-tending workers. Industry to some extent followed the covered wagons of pioneer farmers west from Ohio, but only in the northern latitudes, where slavery was banned. The master-and-slave society of the cotton south could not mix with a society of subsistence farmers, entrepreneurs, and free, rootless industrial workers. It might give the slaves uppity ideas. Nonetheless, North and South were complementary parts of world capitalism, which is how they coexisted under the US Constitution for two enslaved generations.

The US Civil War of 1860–1865 finally ended the slave-plantation system in the capitalist heartland. It was the world's first truly industrialized war, involving railroads, iron-clad warships, even multi-barreled proto machine-guns—and it was no contest. The industrial North inexorably overwhelmed the plantation South, whose only consolation was to make a cult of its doomed military glory. Southern master-slave society lost its legal basis, and the ex-slaves refused to do gang labor on plantations ever again. But the ex-masters still owned everything except the ex-slaves' bodies. Ex-masters and ex-slaves had little choice but to grow cotton together. Plantation societies, having coalesced around a single export crop, always have a hard time finding new employment. An ex-slave could keep half the cotton that he raised on ex-plantation land, while the ex-master kept the other half. This was share-cropping, a good deal for the ex-master who risked little and himself might do no work except owning. It was not so good for the ex-slave, who profited little and commonly did all the work. Without land of his own, however, he had no alternative. A crop failure would expose his family to starvation, unless the ex-master lent him more money, but at least he could live in his own house, have his own family, and control his own time. Remaking a plantation society into something better would take many generations. Following the Civil War, the ex-slave-owning US South entered a century of share-cropping and economic decline.

Meanwhile, industrialization accelerated in the northern United States. European immigrants poured into that part of the country after the US Civil War. They were almost all Europeans, but most spoke languages and practiced religions that were relatively new to the United States. Many were Catholics, whereas US religion had remained primarily Protestant from the beginning of colonization, and anti-Catholic attitudes were historically strong among English-speaking people. War production of the 1860s had boosted industrial growth in the North, whereas fighting and destruction had taken place almost completely in the South. The two contrasting societies remained as distinct as before, if not more. And now there was another US region aborning, the West. Railroad-building advanced on a scale not seen elsewhere in the world, completely crossing the continent by 1869, and within a few more years, completing a national rail network. It took an awful lot of steel.

The ribbons of steel ended the isolation of the last remaining free-roaming Indians of the Great Plains. Professional buffalo hunters began the systematic slaughter of the vast herds of bison upon which the indigenous peoples of the Great Plains depended. Shooting from trains was one buffalo-hunting technique. The shooters had no use for the wounded or dead animals. Aside from sport, the shooters' principal purpose was exterminating the herds so that the Indians would have to depend on reservations for food. In that, the buffalo shooters succeeded. In the 1880s, the unraveling indigenous tribes of the West succumbed to a prophetic vision that promised salvation: the settlers' disappearance and the buffalo's return. Indigenous people facing the destruction of their world began to participate in marathon religious "ghost dances," seeking to save themselves and set the world right. Ghost dancing "fanatics" were a frightening threat to civilization, and they were slaughtered by unsympathetic settlers and soldiers. The hundreds of women and children infamously massacred at Wounded Knee (on the Pine Ridge Indian Reservation in South Dakota) were ghost dancers. The destruction of native tribes was frankly welcomed by settlers flowing west from St. Louis. In their eyes, according to the sadly memorable racist ditty, the "only good Indian was a dead Indian." Many settlers hoped that they could farm the prairies of the West, but that proved over-optimistic because of the semi-arid climate, and most farming homesteads eventually failed. Other settlers trekked northwest in trains of covered wagons to claim excellent farmland in Oregon. Cattle were the more viable option for the plains themselves. Cattle to feed the hungry industrial workers were driven north from Texas to a railhead in Dodge City.

Meanwhile, the propellers of North Atlantic industrialization strongly stirred the coastal waters of Latin America. In fact, the independence of most countries south of the United States occurred between 1810 and 1825, partly as a response to that stimulus. Let us now examine the impact of capitalism in Latin America. Industrialization and middle-class prosperity did not arrive in Latin America, overall, until the mid-twentieth century. Latin American participation in the capitalist world economy resembled that of the US South or West: extractive economies, harshly exploitative plantation or frontier societies, often stratified by racial hierarchies.

Through the 1700s, colonial Latin America's primary links with the world market had been sugar and silver. The sugar and silver did not stay in the colonizing mother countries, however. Rather, it flowed through them to other destinations. What colonial Latin

Americans most wanted to import were English cotton textiles, but the Spanish and Portuguese empires were closed, monopoly trading systems. Only Spanish or Portuguese ships were welcome in their colonial ports, and foreign traders were locked out. English manufactures arrived only through intermediaries, with a limited selection and a hefty markup. Through the 1700s, seaborne empires competed commercially with one another to maintain a positive balance of payments and accumulate capital, a rivalry known as mercantilism. Capitalism had now become a primary medium of global power.

Then came the French Revolution and Napoleonic Wars, which are discussed in the next chapter. That crisis in Europe gave Latin American elites the opportunity to escape from closed mercantilist trading systems. Many were eager to do so. Britain responded by favoring the Latin American independence movements diplomatically. Many insurgent leaders operated from London exile. Simon Bolivar's famous Jamaica Letter was a plea for British assistance, with bright visions of future commercial opportunities for Britain in Latin America. A few thousand British mercenaries traveled to join Bolivar in Venezuela. Opening their ports to British trade was one of the first things Latin American countries did upon eventually winning independence. The United States eventually played a similar role in Mexico and the Caribbean.

In Brazil, the dramatic opening to direct British trade happened even before independence. Britain helped the king of Portugal escape a French invasion in 1807. Escorted to Brazil by a British fleet, the king showed his gratitude, upon arrival, by immediately opening Brazilian ports to English textiles. Brazil then moved into the English trading orbit more smoothly than any other emerging nation of the region. Partly, this was because Brazil was already a plantation colony exporting food and raw materials to Europe. Brazilian cotton helped supply English textile mills. In addition to sugar, which lost value on the world market as more and more plantation colonies produced it, Brazilian slave plantations began cultivating coffee. After independence, coffee became Brazil's chief export commodity. For about a century, Brazil became a coffee kingdom in the sense that the antebellum US South has been called a cotton kingdom. Slave-owning coffee planters became its ruling class. By the late 1800s, Brazilian slaves were producing most of the coffee on the world market.

Most Latin American countries relied on a single export crop, but Brazil had several. Brazil's coffee-growing region lay in the southeast of the country, around Rio de Janeiro and São Paulo. Other regions of Brazil had their own tropical export products. In the Amazon basin the export product was rubber, the congealed sap of a rainforest tree. Elsewhere, it was cocoa beans, i.e., chocolate. Booming plantations were slow to let go of slavery, which continued to dominate plantation agriculture in Brazil until the 1880s, longer than anywhere else in the world, although Cuban sugar and coffee plantations were slave-powered almost as long.

Argentina and Chile, isolated in the distant south, long colonial backwaters without sugar or silver, contained prosperous frontier societies in the 1800s. Their late integration into the world market proved advantageous. Like neighboring Uruguay, Argentina and Chile did not contain large populations of oppressed plantation laborers or exploited miners. Their tiny populations created better opportunities for post-colonial immigration. A climate similar to Europe's also made these countries more attractive to European immigrants, many of whom wanted to plant a European crop, wheat. Some of the new immigrants were Spaniards, as one might expect, also English and Irish during the mid-1800s, but eventually most were peasants "pushed" out of the Italian countryside by globalizing changes. European immigrants were "pulled," too, by high wages and the easy availability of beef from the sprawling ranches of the Argentine pampa. As a result, the southernmost countries of South America became notably more neo-European that those in the tropics. Lest we overlook a crucial fact, however, Argentina, Chile, and Uruguay, like the United States and Canada, could prosper as neo-European societies because they had dispossessed their indigenous people so thoroughly. The prosperity of neo-European societies generally benefit the displaced indigenous population not at all. It came strictly at their cost, just as prosperity in plantation societies came at the expense of the enslaved workforce.

In Asia, capitalism took longer to transform people's lives, and when that finally did happen, it was more under their own control, which may be why it ultimately turned out better. Pre-industrial Europe had produced very few high-value goods for Asian trade. Asians were less temped than neo-Europeans by the mechanized manufactures of the Industrial Revolution. Asian states had, in general, not yet fallen under European tutelage. Asians wanted access to global trade, but they had no desire to become completely submerged in a world economy that had been created by, and was still controlled by, Europeans. Therefore, capitalism found it harder to penetrate Asian societies, which preferred to deal with the West through designated windows and doorways.

Overall, the emerging world economy always had a major trade imbalance, created by the superior demand for Chinese goods. By the late 1700s, as a result of British imperial expansion, imports from China had taken an emblematic place in England and, to a lesser degree, throughout Europe and neo-Europe. "Tea time! Get out the good china!" Also, recall the Chinese economy's outsized need for silver currency. Silver from the great mines of Mexico and Peru had long flowed massively to Spain—and from there to other European countries that needed silver to pay for silk and porcelain and tea. By another route, starting in the Philippine Islands, the so-called Manila Galleon had made a single trans-Pacific roundtrip voyage per year (over 250 years), carrying Chinese manufactures to Mexico, and Mexican silver to Chinese merchants on the return trip.

Other distinctive products of traditional Chinese manufacture, such as lacquerware, played ancillary roles in the European vogue for all things "Oriental." Porcelain, like silk, was something uniquely Chinese until finally copied elsewhere by forced technology transfer.

Around 1800, tea had become the most valuable Chinese export, and the need to pay for Chinese tea in silver had become highly inconvenient for British merchants and imperial officials.

What to do? China and Japan had, for the most part, kept the Europeans out, or kept them at arm's length, as we have seen. Japan's shogun had expelled them entirely in the early 1600s. China had tolerated a strictly limited trade with Europeans, mostly at Guangdong. Around 1800, traders of many nations had converged on Guangdong. They were not really allowed to enter the country, only to conduct deals with Chinese merchants at the port of Guangzhou. The British thought China needed "opening." Unofficially, English traders had become aware of a strong demand for opium in China, which the Chinese government regarded as a social problem. To limit opium use, the Chinese imperial government discouraged its production in China, making the illegal trade that much more profitable. Shrewd British traders saw the opium habit as a means to correct their annoying trade imbalance. What if opium, instead of silver, could be used to trade for tea? Eureka! The British began to cultivate and process opium poppies in their Indian colony and then trade opium illegally for Chinese tea. Outraged, the Chinese emperor stopped the trade and sent a letter of protest to the Queen Victoria of England, receiving no response. The Chinese government then took forceful measures, including the confiscation of existing illegal stocks of opium in possession of British traders at Guangzhou. Now it was the British turn to be outraged.

The result was the Opium War of 1839–1841, followed by a Second Opium War of 1856–1860, in which European military incursions, organized and spearheaded by the British Empire, forcibly opened China to free trade, British-supplied opium being the main component of this "freedom." British military power also established privileged status for European merchants in Chinese ports, five of which were now opened permanently to European traders. In Guangdong, the British rewarded themselves for their efforts by establishing a permanent trading enclave similar to Macao: Hong Kong. In the new, commercially inflected style of imperialism, colonial assets like Hong Kong could be acquired by force of arms, then secured by lease at favorable rates. The Opium Wars signaled a growing European advantage in military technology and a growing weakness of China. By this time, the Ming dynasty had been replaced by the Qing dynasty, a problem in itself, because the Qing were not exactly Chinese.

The Qing family, China's last imperial dynasty (1636–1912) came from Manchuria, a land beyond China's northern border. Like the Xiongnu and the Mongols before them, the Manchus were warriors above all. They expanded the Chinese Empire to its greatest size ever. At this point China had the world's largest economy, and it governed about a third of the world's population. The Qing insisted that Chinese men adopt the Manchu hairstyle, pulled back from the forehead, with a long braid in back. All government officials were required to wear Manchu clothing, too. Chinese resentment of the Qing dynasty, and their consequent lack of devotion to it, helps explain why the British Empire triumphed over China so quickly and thoroughly in the Opium Wars. Several other enormous upheavals also gave notice of Qing weakness. The Taiping Rebellion of the 1850s and 1860s, which left possibly twenty million dead, was the largest peasant rebellion in world history.

By the late 1800s, China was being integrated in the world economy piecemeal, in a manner mostly managed by predatory outsiders. As a result, the world's oldest existing empire was starting to wobble. India underwent a similarly precipitous decline under capitalism in the 1800s.

In 1750, Mughal India was still the world's leading weaver of cotton cloth and represented about a quarter of world manufacturing output. Cotton is native to India, so the raw material was near at hand. The center of the Indian textile industry was Bengal, at the mouth of the Ganges River. British military superiority was established by the small-scale conquest of Bengal in 1757. English traders had been paying for the products of Indian spinners and weavers with silver and gold. But as English colonization advanced up India's east coast, and then clawed its way inland up the valley of Ganges, the colonizers suppressed the weavers and exported their raw material to English factories. Then they brought the finished product back to sell in India, completing their execution-style capitalist triumph.

Thereafter, the Indian colony was administered as a vast for-profit enterprise, producing untold wealth for the investors and functionaries of the British East India Company. The general approach was to work with the subcontinent's own ruling classes, pressing them to extract as much wealth as possible from the Indian people, and then skimming the cream off the top. In 1857, Indians rose in rebellion and made a bid for independence. The rebellion was crushed, and to prevent a repetition, the colonizers intensified their colonial governance by making Queen Victoria officially empress of India. The British planned a new colonial capital in Delhi, former seat of the displaced Mughals, and set about transforming the subcontinent into the mother of all imperial cash cows.

To that end, the British supervised the construction of an extensive railroad system and instituted English-language government institutions. Everything was done to augment the efficiency of colonial oversight, the extraction of food and raw materials, and the distribution of good English manufactures. Agricultural policies were geared to facilitate taxation and encourage cash crops rather than support subsistence, an innovation that normally brought malnutrition to traditional peasantries. Partly owing to ongoing "improvements," a severe famine wracked Bengal in the 1870s. The Bengal famine fixed images of poverty and pestilence—bodies stacked like cord wood in the street—in the modern European imagination. Meanwhile, the British East India Company continued to report profits that even some in parliament judged to be obscene. India's share of global manufacturing dwindled to around 2 percent by 1900.

BY 1900, much had changed, shall we say, since the days when Indians and Chinese had swatted aside European traders like bothersome mosquitoes. Modernity had eclipsed all the old centers of world civilization. Meanwhile, European trading empires had successfully colonized much of the world and harnessed it to a capitalist world economy.

Europe (and neo-Europe) was the chief beneficiary of capitalist growth, not only because of colonial trade, but also because capitalist financial mechanisms such as joint stock companies, stock markets, and banks were normally located in the imperial hub. Asian shipping did not disappear from the coastal routes it had served for many hundreds of years, but most shipping was now done by Europeans. Industrialization was the final European advantage, reversing the earlier, long-term Chinese advantage. As capitalism burgeoned, its rising tide lifted primarily European (and neo-European) boats. And burgeon, it did. Earlier long-distance trade had carried only small quantities of high-value goods consumed by elites. New commodities like tea, sugar, and tobacco were consumed, eventually, by the middle classes, even to some degree by the poor. The volume of world trade therefore increased greatly in the 1700s, then even more in the 1800s. In addition, industrial manufacturing produced more inexpensive consumer goods than had ever existed previously, which meant more people could have them. The daily rhythms of life around the world were changing. For consumers, many changes were enriching, but most people outside of the capitalist core regions could hardly be called consumers.

The modern world of 1900 was not fully a capitalist world, but one was on the way. Like dynamite, industrial capitalism could move mountains. But the love of money still struck many people as an abomination, the root of all evil. Capitalist wealth, capitalism itself, was morally suspect in their eyes. "Money-grubbing bankers" everywhere had a bad smell for traditionalists on the losing end of capitalist transformations. Therefore, traditional values rooted in religious ideas slowed the advance of a modern capitalist outlook and often encouraged resistance to it. Moreover, several modern ideologies emerged along with capitalism, whether to support or to oppose it, part of a wave of new thinking that would gradually challenge old habits and verities around the world.

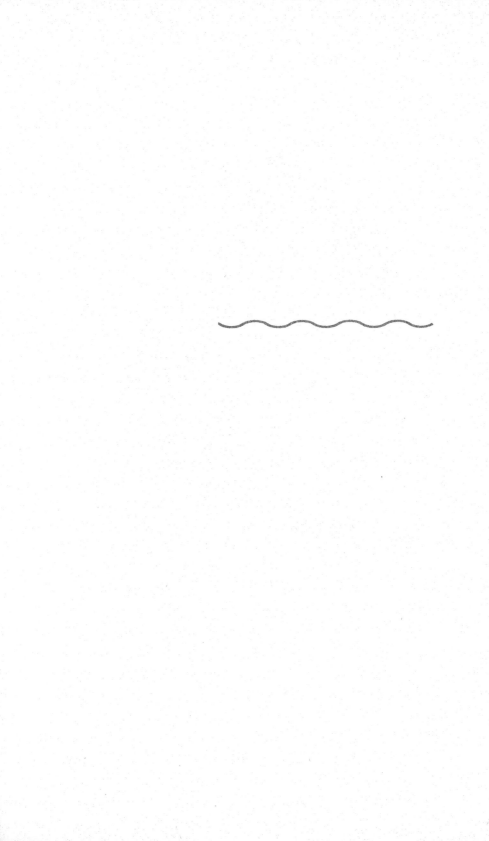

CHAPTER TWELVE

Liberty

The first new idea was Liberty. To explain its origins and impact, we must describe its emergence over time and in context. By the late 1700s, experimentation was laying the groundwork for modern astronomy, biology, geology, and physics, as well as politics.

The eclipse of traditional authority drove this change in European thinking. The change responded to practical needs created by European colonization, such as the need to sail around the world, deal with its diversity, and grapple with previously unimagined phenomena. The new challenges could not be addressed by reference to authoritative old books, previously believed to contain everything worth knowing. The traditional placement of Earth at the center of creation, with heaven above and hell below, for example, failed completely to account for what could be seen through Galileo's telescope. Galileo's insistence that Earth orbited the sun got him in big trouble with the Church, which officially silenced him. Yet today we recognize him as the father of modern science. When traditional sources of knowledge, such as sacred scriptures, proved unable to explain new data, modern thinkers put aside ancient texts and relied on evidence and logic. If microbes caused communicable diseases, handwashing and quarantine would control them better than a sprinkling of holy water. Galileo's university at Padua, near Venice, Italy's great center of maritime trade, created a botanical garden to study plants newly discovered overseas. Ultimately, the entire style of

European education would change to downplay rote memorization and argument from ancient authority. The modern emphasis turned toward solving practical problems through data collection, hypothesis, and empiricism.

Modern ideas arose in, and responded to, a rapidly changing world. Modern thinkers assumed that change was natural, inevitable, and something to be embraced, not resisted. Modern ideas became the voice of change, a direct challenge to ancient authority of various kinds. Whereas premodern thinking revered tradition, modern thinkers believed that tradition got in the way of improvement. The divine right of kings and the superiority of a blue-blooded nobility, for example, were founded on old belief systems that prized a stable social hierarchy. Modern political thinkers believed a person's worth should not depend on wealth and bloodline. They believed that everyone deserved an equal chance, that no one should be born owning, and no one, born owing. The modern world was supposed to offer equal opportunity to all. This basic idea, the baseline of modern political thought, was encoded in the word *liberty*. New York's famous Statue of Liberty, holding her torch to guide "the wretched masses yearning to breathe free," is a personification of this idea. So is Marianne, who holds the French revolutionary tricolor in the famous Delacroix painting, calling the people to revolt against aristocrats and kings.

Liberty was a revolutionary idea around 1800. Liberty contradicted social hierarchy and rule by divine right. Modernity and tradition had become adversaries. Traditional royal claims to rule by the mandate of heaven had been discredited by modern thinkers, who believed that henceforward religion and governance should be separate.

In rethinking the basis of state power, however, modern political thinkers pointed in different directions. One direction, the most strongly individualistic, has become known as liberalism. Liberalism produced a "liberal democratic state" with a limited, pluralist government "of the people, by the people, and for the people." A liberal democratic state guarantees free elections and a free press, rights of property and contract, rule of law, an independent judiciary, and so on. For liberals, the best government is that which benefits the most individuals. Individual liberties are the starting point of liberal thought.

Nationalism and socialism, two alternative directions of modern political thought, have a different starting point: the idea of community. Nationalists evoke a community of people who share a homeland, a history, a language, and a religion. The great object of nationalist action is to consolidate one's own national community and to defend it against others. Socialists defend a different sort of community, the "common people" of all nations who, for thousands of years, have been victimized by kings and nobles, and more recently, by billionaire capitalist tycoons. They want the exploited masses everywhere to realize their shared predicament and work together against their victimizers. Socialists call for revolutionary change to raise up the downtrodden of every nation and reorganize the world to eliminate social inequality.

Modern thinkers called *philosophes* promoted liberalism by questioning traditional wisdom about religion, government, and society in 1700s imperial France. The most famous of all was Voltaire, who publicly criticized both the church and the opulent nobility that clustered at the royal court of Versailles. Voltaire corresponded with other thinkers participating in an intellectual awakening that, retrospectively, we call the Enlightenment. Like the Renaissance, the Enlightenment often gets blown out of proportion. The Enlightenment occurred mostly in the northwestern European centers of social, religious, and economic transformation, particularly France. Another philosophe, Diderot, set out to edit the first *Encyclopedia*, a bold systematization of new knowledge. Diderot also published a critical analysis of European colonialism in "the two Indies," as the (American) West Indies and the (Asian) East Indies were then called. Yet another philosophe, Rousseau, wrote a *Discourse of Inequality* that challenged the supposed superiority of nobles over commoners. In one influential text, *The Social Contract*, Rousseau established a modern understanding of the state. Kings, according to the philosophes, were not actually handpicked by God. But, if kings did not rule by divine right, then what? The idea of a social contract means that the state is empowered by society, not the other way around. Legitimate power flows, not down from God, but *up* from the governed. Governments that don't rule by consent of the governed are tyrannies. Only majority support confers the right to rule. In England, the ideas of Locke and Hobbes covered similar ground, reasoning from rational premises and invoking a similar idea of social contract.

Gradually, modern political concepts like liberty, nation, and revolution upstaged the millenarian traditions of Buddha, Confucius, Jesus, and Muhammad. Although retaining some potential to challenge the self-serving power of the state, the established world religions had functioned chiefly, over a millennium, to buttress "the powers that be." Only exceptionally did religions become vehicles of social equality. More routinely, they justified old inequities by retelling ancient myths about how things came to be. Liberty, Nation, and Revolution burst on the scene as new, replacement myths, representing modern political values, taking direct aim at ancient injustices.

This chapter traces the rise of the first of these new replacement myths—Liberty—which developed into liberalism. Initially, liberals were the political prophets of all things modern, the ideologues of the new capitalist order. They founded new republics and promoted industrialization. Liberalism became the overall theme of the French Revolution, the founding ideology of the United States of America, the unofficial creed of the British Empire, and the guiding light of democratic pluralism. Liberalism changed people's experience of family and community. It became a new way of living, one particularly suited to the new capitalist order.

The Spirit of 1776

The French and American Revolutions were globally foundational events of political modernity and world liberalism. Both drew on new political ideas, unfurled the banner of liberty, and invoked the natural right of people to enjoy political equality. Both replaced a king who claimed divine right with a constitutional republic that ruled, theoretically, by consent of the governed.

The French Revolution was a thoroughgoing attempt to redesign society and governance. Although resentments of specific royal abuses and taxes got the revolutionaries started, they soon went far beyond their initial intentions. To raise money for huge imperial military expenses, the French king had called a meeting of the Estates General, a body representing nobles, clergy, and commoners, the explicitly unequal components of the old French feudal system. Along with the king, the nobles and clergy basically owned and operated France for their own benefit, while commoners—the huge majority, who also paid most of the taxes—had almost no power or rights. During the single, truly revolutionary year 1789, all that changed. The commoners rejected the royal agenda that had called them to Paris and, meeting without nobles or clergy, declared themselves to be a National Assembly, not representing feudal estates anymore, but instead, the French People as a whole.

The French revolutionaries of 1789 put the feudal system on trial, strung it up, laid it out, and drove a wooden stake through its heart. They established the principle of popular sovereignty and abolished the feudal privileges that had allowed dukes, counts, barons, and marquises to rule Europe for forty generations. They imprisoned and executed their reigning king and the famously out-of-touch, cordially hated, let-them-eat-cake Queen Marie Antoinette. They promulgated a universal bill of rights that eventually became the preamble to a written constitution. They systematically dismantled the power of the Catholic Church in France, confiscating its wealth and turning the clergy into public employees under the thumb of the state. They also brought many traditionally church-run activities, such as education, firmly under public control. For a while, they even tried to replace Catholicism with a state-operated "Cult of Reason," but pushback forced them to proclaim instead a sort of deity *du jour*, an all-in-one "Cult of the Supreme Being." They removed from the public calendar the many Catholic holidays, such as Christmas, Holy Week and Easter, along with the feast days of hundreds of saints, replacing them with civic holidays. The French Revolution spun out of control in the mid-1790s, executing thousands of presumed counterrevolutionaries by guillotine in a period aptly called the Terror. Within a few more years, it succumbed to the dictatorial and not-very-revolutionary military expansionism of Napoleon Bonaparte, who introduced a cult of personality and crowned himself emperor.

The independence of the United States, on the eve of these events, was less revolutionary. The American Revolution was directed by the colonial ruling class, many of them plantation owners, and it never escaped their tutelage. It was revolutionary mainly in replacing a king with a republic: the born-liberal United States of America, with its federal organization, periodic elections, bicameral legislature, and separation of powers to guarantee the rule of law. Its large population of enslaved laborers did create contradictions that we consider later, but somehow the spirit of 1776 became, for a time, the world's most successful national project, the very definition of a liberal democratic state. The early United States of America became an inspirational model much imitated by later republics around the world.

Revolutionary liberalism arose in opposition to something: an old regime built on traditions, religious ideas, and a power structure of noble families. Europe's position in the new world economy favored merchants, financiers, artisans, and industrialists who traditionally had held little political power. Liberalism became, in very general terms, the political ideology of these emerging middle classes, who stood socially between the landowning nobility and the landless peasantry. Both nobility and peasantry were rooted in the countryside, local in orientation, whereas the new middle classes were predominantly urban, firmly embedded in the wider market economy. Urban industrialists, artisans, and merchants had gotten out of step with a medieval Christianity that discouraged lending money at interest, frowned on the pursuit of wealth for its own sake, preached communal limits on private property, and maintained that a fair price—for a loaf of bread, for example—did *not* depend on what the market would bear. In the traditional Christian view, pricing was a moral, not an economic, matter. To counter these ideas, liberals advanced the logic of the marketplace, what we think of today as the basic principles of free market economics.

The canonical statement of free market principles is *The Wealth of Nations*, published in 1776 by Adam Smith, who has been called the father of capitalism. Smith was a professor at the University of Glasgow in Scotland, a raving liberal long before the word had been coined. He was a professor of moral philosophy, a field that examined people's behavior towards each other. Smith was a famous lecturer and an absent-minded professor who talked to himself and once stumbled into a hole while expostulating on free trade. He wrote about, and advocated, social relationships mediated by the market. He made history's most influential statement of what is now called market-oriented rationalism. In so doing, he invented classical economics. To possess market-oriented rationalism would be a personal advantage, from now on, for participants in a capitalist economy. Smith described the market as a self-regulating mechanism, highlighted the crucial role of individual self-interest, and advocated breaking complex tasks into simple repetitive ones, the basic modern industrial division of labor.

Liberals envisioned new models of society and self. The protagonists of a market-oriented society were individuals, not families. Individual choice mattered more as social arrangements became more fluid. In practice, modern individualism loosened many old social ties, encouraging young people to ignore traditional customs, go to the city, and reinvent themselves, adopting new styles of dress and comportment. Marriage choices were not to be made, anymore, by parents for familial purposes, but instead by modern individuals, based on romantic preference, a matter of unfettered personal choice. To harness the "acquisitive materialism" of modern individuals, liberals, most especially the English ones, declared the sanctity of private property. To motivate people's industriousness, their private possession of the fruit of their labors must be absolutely guaranteed. Otherwise, it was assumed, they would rationally not work so hard. Material selfishness was consequently assumed, even condoned. Liberals often wanted to limit political power to the owners of significant property, especially real estate. These property-owning individuals had a personal stake in the system, so they could be counted on to preserve it.

Liberalism, shaped by new economic realities, became the political arm of industrial capitalism. Liberalism encouraged both production and consumption. Traditional societies had rarely valued the endless acquisition of more and more stuff. Traditionally, only nobles and royals possessed large houses or more than a few changes of clothes. The Industrial Revolution changed human societies by democratizing the possession of material goods. The rather bare interiors of European houses in the 1700s began to overflow, in the 1800s, with rugs, wallpaper, bric-a-brac, and overstuffed furniture. Because mass production favored quantity over quality, overproduction was a constant threat, leading to industrial recession. Trading empires took on a new function: to provide an outlet for goods that could not be consumed domestically. The search for new markets became a geopolitical imperative. A common critique of non-European people was their lack of desire to acquire so many possessions. The greatest offenders in this regard were, of course, the world's dwindling populations of foragers, who never bought anything at all. Eventually, with the invention of advertisements, capitalist societies engineered the perpetual stimulation of desire, giving birth to consumer societies with a seemingly limitless potential to consume. This did not happen until the twentieth century, but it could never have happened without the new, positive value placed on acquisitive materialism in the 1700s and 1800s.

"Early to bed and early to rise, makes a man healthy, wealthy, and wise!" The homely virtues of Benjamin Franklin, most famously in *Poor Richard's Almanac*, a colonial bestseller (and most explicitly in his *Advice to a Young Tradesman*) were all about getting ahead. Franklin was the son of a soap and candle maker who became a printer's apprentice, ran away to Philadelphia, and started his own newspaper. Franklin was a tireless publicist for reason and liberty. "To see by Faith," he wrote, "is to shut the eye of Reason." Franklin also provided readers of his almanac with helpful "hints to those who would be rich." Patiently and in plain language, Franklin explained the economic concept called "opportunity cost," and the importance of establishing good credit. Time is money, the smart set began to say. As a printer, Franklin embodied another central current of early liberalism, its close association with the press. Newspapers of the 1700s and 1800s were often a single folded sheet published by a single man, the editor, typically a passionate liberal. Newspaper editors regarded themselves as part of a network committed to the dissemination of knowledge in the modern world. Typically, editors exchanged papers with one another by means of newly established mail services and reprinted many articles from other publications that served as their far-flung correspondents. Most editors wrote most of each issue themselves. Political and economic news was the main element. Modern progress was the main theme. Franklin's promotion of lending libraries and a public post office should be viewed in this light.

Liberalism soon dominated educational institutions in the industrialized world. Liberals considered public education crucial for self-governance. How could ignorant people rule themselves, after all, except badly? The gold standard of elite social achievement for English-speaking gentlemen was a "liberal education." A liberal education tried to instill a broad, modern understanding of the world, including the basics of physics, chemistry, and biology, as well as literature, history, and Earth science. The first two years of general education requirements at US universities are what remains, today, of the old liberal education. It aimed to instill a broad humanistic empathy, affirming the unity of human experience. Liberal educational institutions gradually accepted women. To be a schoolteacher became one of the first respectable middle-class professions for women. Conservatives still considered most formal education inappropriate for female minds, but liberals were committed to educating girls. Because ideas of discovery, reason, and individual choice were so central to liberalism, a true liberal became a voracious reader. Novels, which normally turned on the matter of marriage choice and were read especially by women, presented new models of romantic love that flew boldly in the face of conservative patriarchy.

Tied to education, liberal culture was often elite culture. A liberal education conferred a powerful sort of cultural capital. A person who could confidently use Greek and Latin words, discuss opera as well as recent scientific discoveries, and express an informed opinion on national and international events was a modern person. And "modern" was already the opposite of "backward." Moreover, liberal culture was associated with dominant social groups, especially Protestant ones. The acronym WASP (for White Anglo-Saxon Protestant) was used to name the dominant ethnicity of the United States, and of course, most especially, of New England. The Protestant denominational colleges scattered across the United States championed the "liberal arts," a term preserved today only in academic settings. Especially in the United States, there was always a countercurrent to liberalism, a popular mistrust of over-educated professorial eggheads. Nonetheless, by the mid-1800s, the commanding heights of national culture in the entire English-speaking world were in the hands of proudly self-styled liberals. So were the commanding heights of national economies. "Self-made" entrepreneurs might sneer at effete college boys, but not at liberalism.

Liberal culture was also a key to success for the upwardly mobile. Manipulating credit to maximum advantage, as Benjamin Franklin instructed young tradesmen to do, was likely to improve their lifetime profit margin. So was thrift, industry, rationality, efficiency, planning, and the carefully calculated deferment of gratification. Liberal culture provided the software, so to speak, appropriate to operate a capitalist, industrial economy. The writings of Franklin were Exhibit A for the famous theory concerning a Protestant work ethic associated with early capitalism. "Time is money" was an idea that had begun with a managerial elite, but it gradually spread to all those with ambitions of upward mobility. The liberal mindset expressed itself in widely influential habits of mind that progressive parents eagerly taught their children. Early to bed and early to rise makes a man healthy, wealthy, and wise! Public schooling, more than any other thing, spread this version of cultural modernity from elite families to non-elite ones in the United States. From then on, better-educated people tended to be more liberal.

The social software for a capitalist manufacturing economy arose together with the industrial hardware, the factories themselves, in the centers of world capitalism, even as these centers colonized South America, Africa, and Asia. The outlook and skills that adapted people to modern economic life became part of European cultures in general, more rapidly in the Atlantic north than in the Mediterranean south. Neo-European populations, such as those of the United States, Canada, South Africa, and Australia also inherited this mindset, this technology, these skills. And, beginning in the second half of the 1900s, the elite classes of Asian, African, and Latin American countries—having been firmly integrated into the world market—learned French or English and began to acquire the same cultural repertoire. Liberalism disseminated somewhat, in the colonized world, as the sons and daughters of Asian, African, and Latin American elites became business partners, joined rotary clubs, and earned advanced degrees at US and European universities. For the most part, however, liberal culture was not available (if desired, which was certainly not always the case) to ordinary people in the colonized world, even as it became the key to personal prosperity.

During the first century of industrial globalization, world living standards became radically unequal. Great Britain and the Netherlands were the world's most productive countries per capita, and European countries had achieved, in general, a high standard of living. On the eve of World War One, the European centers of liberal culture were four or five times wealthier than other parts of the world, something emphatically not true during earlier historical periods. The largest private fortunes, by far, were accumulated in the United States. Among the greatest was that of the industrialist, steelmaker, and, ultimately, philanthropist Andrew Carnegie, a Scottish immigrant who endowed workingmen's lending libraries. By 1919, he had funded construction of nearly half the libraries in the United States. Even countries with comparatively little industry, such as Argentina and Australia, could eventually enjoy a European standard of living because they shared the requisite cultural programming.

Free and open elections, with votes honestly tallied, became the acid test of the liberal democratic state. Elections and voting rights gradually expanded in the world's handful of rich, industrialized societies. Initial property qualifications were removed, elections were made more direct, and the right to vote was eventually extended to women. Gradually the insurgent liberal spirit of 1776 had morphed into a dominant form of elite culture. By the time of World War One, liberalism had become the quasi-official ideology of the world's most powerful states.

Elsewhere, however, in most of the world's societies, tradition and religion still held sway. The world economy had penetrated daily life almost everywhere, damaging at least as many people as it benefited. There are always winners and losers caused by capitalist disruptions. Liberty was the political soundtrack of the intruding marketplace, so it inspired winners much more than losers. Avowed liberals "liberated" a continent's worth of Spanish and Portuguese colonies in the 1820s, but liberalism held limited appeal among those diverse populations.

The Americas

When early capitalism facilitated the rise of merchants and industrialists, eclipsing royals and nobles, the liberal emphasis on equality facilitated that eclipse, as we have seen. Overall, the premise that "all men are created equal" challenged social privilege and hierarchy. But equality had its limits, too. People whose mental horizons are configured by home and family, religion and tradition, normally feel comfortable with familiar social inequalities. That is how God made the world, they say. What are we going to do about it? This is doubly true of traditional ruling classes who embrace privilege, benefit from hierarchy, and exploit their "inferiors" with an untroubled heart. Liberal principles did not, in many cases, result in liberal practice. Traditionminded societies tended to stonewall the radical implications of liberalism. In practice, liberal political systems usually failed to achieve true equality and worked around the idea, instead, by defining some people out of the political community altogether. Slave owners in the southern United States are an obvious example.

Liberty, equality, and fraternity (the values of the French Revolution) applied to everyone—*except those to whom they didn't apply.* Problem arbitrarily solved! Thus, women were not included in the magic circle of full citizenship rights, nor were people of non-European race, not to mention slaves. Race and gender became basic principles of exclusion. And not only in France of course, but in the United States, and in wannabe liberal democracies throughout the Americas, systemic racism offered a pervasive workaround, a legal proviso concerning classes of people who could be excluded on principle from the magic circle of equal consideration.

Imagine the framers of the US Constitution in the 1780s, trying to determine whether, or to what extent, slaves should be counted as people. Holding human beings as property obviously contradicted liberal values ("all men are created equal . . ."); therefore, the US Constitution could logically make no reference to slavery. And yet, the ruling class of the southern United States, including George Washington and Thomas Jefferson, were slave-owning agribusinessmen grown wealthy in the colonial plantation system. By staying mum about human bondage, the Constitution allowed the plantation owners to remain firmly in control of their enslaved workers. Slaves? What slaves? Next, another decision for the constitutional convention, the famous three-fifths compromise. At issue was the number of elected representatives whom the plantation owners would be able to send to the US Congress. Slaves would never vote in congressional elections, nor would their modest interests be represented in any way whatsoever. But if their slaves were counted as people, engrossing the population of southern states, powerful southern slave owners would gain congressional clout vis-a-vis their non-slave-owning northern counterparts. Oh, *those* slaves! As a compromise, slaves, discretely referred to in the text as "other persons," were to be counted, or rather *dis*counted, at 3/5 the rate of "free persons."

Liberal states typically dealt with social inequality, not by eliminating it, but by *finessing* it, often keeping it legally invisible. Latin America, the main global region into which liberalism spread in the 1820s and 1830s, offers salient examples. Liberalism took hold in Latin America because of the new ideology's contemporary prestige throughout the Western world. Latin America's new republics were among the world's first liberal states. In many ways, it was not a good fit. The new republics possessed historically influential religious establishments. Overall, their populations were highly traditionminded. All Latin American societies had export-oriented economies substantially powered by unfree labor. All were controlled by white landowning elites and had overall populations largely *not* of European descent. All had developed a complex caste system as a result of European colonization. People purely of African or indigenous descent ranked at the bottom of this system, people of purely European descent at the top.

Around the region, racial discrimination justified the long-term

subjugation of the Latin American masses, often under liberal republican rule. The great exception was the Republic of Haiti, which had
been among the world's most brutal and productive sugar plantation
colonies until the French Revolution. The virus of Liberty, Equality, and Fraternity spread quickly to the French colony and triggered
an upheaval, one of the world's most famous slave rebellions, in
which the planter class was permanently subtracted from the equa-
tion. Haiti became the great cautionary tale for American and Latin
American slave owners during the 1800s, the example of what can
happen when you babble carelessly about equality in front of the
help. Overall, Latin America's new republics voided the old caste
laws that plainly contradicted their liberal constitutions, but that did
not erase the shadow of the caste system, which can be felt in behavior and attitudes right down to today. Overall, the new republics
proclaimed liberal principles while refusing to apply them to people
whom they considered ineligible for equality.

Like their political models, the United States above all, Latin
American republics were liberal democratic states in theory. To create a liberal democratic state, one required, theoretically, an elected
constituent assembly to write a constitution and then establish various state institutions, such as courts, an army, a legislature, and a
president. When liberal states were established in landscapes of plantations worked by slaves or downtrodden peasants, guarantees of
liberal democracy became mere stylish window dressing. The owners
of great estates and their city cousins tended to become, in practical terms, the entire citizenry. Poor, rural majorities did not vote
or, unable to represent their own interests, merely played the role
of loyal followers, casting ballots given them by their landowners.
Excluded from the polity, the dark-skinned majority population of
Latin America was pronounced "not yet ready for self-government"
by the light-skinned elite. It was true to a degree. The peasantries of
Latin America had no schooling whatsoever. They would certainly
need some education to become effective citizens of a liberal repub-

lic, observed their "betters," who were in a great hurry to do nothing about it. Most Latin Americans would have no access to public education for more than a century.

Public schooling was certainly no priority for Pedro I, the leader of Brazilian independence in 1822, for example. He was an old-fashioned royal with an autocratic temperament. He aspired, however, to be a modern ruler, which meant inevitably a liberal one. So, in a fit of impatience, he dissolved the assembly that was trying to write a liberal constitution and wrote it himself, creating a new, specifically Brazilian nobility and a senate with lifetime tenure, as well as high property qualifications for voting in the country's regular elections. He left Brazil's enormous enslaved population enormously enslaved, though. Brazilian planters felt that they simply couldn't do without their slaves and, from their perspective, educating slaves was asking for trouble. Pedro II, who ruled from the 1840s to the 1880s, freed his own slaves in a sincerely liberal gesture, and, unlike his father, he did believe in the transformative power of education. But slave owners still controlled the coffee kingdom, and public schools served only their sons, not their slaves. Brazil's collective investment in slavery declined only after 1850, when the British Empire had outgrown the slave trade, then banned it, and used its navy to intervene in the Brazilian traffic. As British industries saturated market after market in the Americas, slavery had begun to limit profits rather than guarantee them. Free workers would presumably consume more British imports. Moreover, as the commercial calculus reversed, British abolitionists had succeeded in making slavery more visibly repugnant to liberal sensibilities everywhere. Brazil finally abolished slavery in 1888.

Circa 1900, European racial science functioned systematically to facilitate violation of liberal principles. A generation of European scientists had been cataloguing and classifying human specimens on a global scale. Now scientific ideas were turned to the grand purpose of invidious comparison. Global exploration and colonialism had led Europeans to create a taxonomy of human beings as a series of subspecies termed *races*. They did so intellectually as part of the larger project called Natural History, a scientific attempt to understand the entire history of our planet, and life on it, including people. Inevitably, European racial scientists identified themselves, along with their families and compatriots, as superior specimens of human being. (Nothing so disposes *Homo sapiens* to errors in judgement, it seems, as self-love.) European racial theorists put the people who least resembled Europeans at the bottom of the racial totem pole. The familiar language of chauvinist bigotry—the color-coded racial system that divided "mankind" into black, white, red, and yellow—emerged in this context. Two centuries later, we understand that a genome of awesome variability configures human diversity, which can by no means be reduced to a four-color scheme. At the time, however, racism was (supposedly) science, making "not yet ready for self-rule" a permanent judgement against non-Europeans around the world.

The science of white supremacy encouraged and excused the betrayal of core liberal principles. It is not coincidence to find white supremacy invoked most often in the English-speaking world, which had particularly enshrined those principles. In the post-plantation United States, former slave-owning elites regained control after the Civil War, and then launched a vigilante reign of terror that nullified the voting rights of their ex-slaves for a half century. Meanwhile, also because of their supposed racial inferiority, the indigenous tribes of the Great Plains had been reduced to submission and misery, and the Chinese workers who had built US railroads were declared permanently unwelcome in the United States. Liberalism's stress on the legal protections of equal citizenship encouraged total exclusion of those deemed racially unfit for it.

The late 1800s even spawned a science of so-called racial improvement, eugenics, which later became a Nazi specialty. Eugenicists, who existed in Europe, the United States, and Latin America, tried to limit the reproductive rights of people they considered inferior stock. People with "high quality" genes, as indicated by their achievements or racial type, should have many children, according to eugenicists, while those without the right pedigree should disappear completely. Settler colonies applied eugenics to the decimated remnants of native populations. Some colonized people were considered currently unfit, but perhaps culturally "redeemable." Indigenous Americans, Canadians, and Australians were sent to special schools, deprived of their native roots to make them fit for citizenship. Others were considered hopeless, irredeemable candidates for forced sterilization, their hypothetical grandchildren slated for oblivion. Liberal Argentina and Brazil encouraged European immigration in this period, hoping darker-skinned Argentines and Brazilians would be outpaced reproductively by the newcomers, thereby "whitening" the host populations.

Liberal guilt, a nagging awareness of racist hypocrisy, could easily arise in these situations, but it usually didn't. Liberal guilt was, for the most part, not yet a thing. White supremacists, who envisioned a global contest among races around 1900, sneered at liberal guilt as soft-headed weakness. It was natural and necessary, in their opinion, that the master races triumph. Meanwhile, liberalization was no option for the colonized, or nearly colonized, areas of Asia. Colonialism plainly contradicted the spirit of Liberty, after all.

Asia

Liberalism was prominently absent from colonized Asia. Europeans mostly refrained from propagating ideas of liberty, equality, and fraternity there. In Asia, European political philosophy held little appeal, anyway. When Asians embraced capitalist modernity, they generally did so in the spirit of fighting fire with fire.

Never-colonized Japan is the most prominent example. Beginning in the 1630s, when the proliferation of Christian coverts began to seem threatening, Japan's ruling shogun had suppressed Christianity completely. Then, for more than two hundred years, the Japanese closed Japan to outside influences, whether material or cultural. They banned all foreigners, including traders. They even forbade the return of Japanese traders who had lived abroad and had presumably been infected by European ideas. This was a complete rejection of liberal thinking—roughly its authoritarian opposite. The result, in terms of social development, was positive. Internal trade grew, and Edo, the city that would become Tokyo, developed a thriving society of artisans and small-scale merchants. Then, in the 1850s, naval vessels from the United States appeared in Japanese harbors, refusing to leave, making a noisy display of their naval artillery, and commencing to survey coastal waters for their future operations. Japan was going to open itself to the world economy, or else.

The Japanese response was a reversal of Its two centuries of self-imposed isolation. The Japanese now embraced the economic dimensions of liberal modernity with unusual alacrity. It was a replay of what had happened around 1600, when the Japanese had very quickly adopted European-style firearms, then used them to expel the Europeans. Japanese modernization was not an embrace of Western values, however. It was modernization in self-defense. The elements that mattered most were industrial and military. Both elements combined in constructing battleships. Iron-clad, steam-powered battle fleets firing explosive shells were the military backbone of seaborne empires by 1900. The British had used their far superior mobility on the coast and on China's great rivers to humiliate Qing forces in the Opium Wars of 1839–1842 and 1856–1860. Any aspiring world power wanted to have a competitive high-seas battle fleet, and, by the 1890s, the Japanese had built one.

Following its humiliation, China's Qing dynasty imitated its humiliators, likewise modernizing in self-defense. The Qing had little choice but to modernize because the Opium Wars had forced them to open their territory to the commercial and ideological penetration of the West. Even the limited circulation of Christian tracts had helped inspire the vast and destructive Taiping Rebellion. Like indigenous ghost dancers in the western United States, the Taiping Rebellion suggested a psychic crisis affecting millions, something highly menacing to Qing authority. After the Opium Wars, Christian missionaries could go anywhere they pleased in China, traveling far into the Yangtze basin on European river steamers, and now Catholic missionaries were joined by less culturally sensitive Protestants. After putting down several midcentury rebellions, the Qing dynasty set out to build a modern arms industry and an armored, steam-powered battle fleet with guns that fired exploding shells. The Qing manufactured ammunition for their imported Remington rifles and Krupp artillery. Then they manufactured the weapons themselves. They established an English-style cotton mill in Shanghai and a Chinese Merchant Steamship Line to compete with foreign carriers of coastal and river traffic. They strung telegraph lines communicating the provinces with Beijing. They were more ambivalent about building the greatest, and most costly, element of transportation infrastructure: railroads. Qing authorities bought the very first, short rail line in 1877, and dismantled it. By 1896, when Japan had 2,300 miles of track, China still had only 370 miles.

It was the speed and thoroughness of Japanese self-defense modernization that had made it so successful. The world's main antidote to European colonization was nationalism, and nationalism—*not* liberalism—was the keynote of the transformative period called the Mejii Restoration. Japanese modernizers were restoring the authority of the imperial family as they downplayed Buddhism and promoted Japan's ancient animism, Shinto, as a national cult. Japan's modern armed forces bolstered nationalist pride. The acid test was the Russo-Japanese War of 1904–1905, in which the rising Asian power handily defeated the battle fleet of a European imperial power. Unfortunately, Japan's modern armed forces were used for the time-honored purpose of aggression to enhance "national greatness." Japanese military and industrial leaders wanted to join the European race for empire. As the British gradually absorbed all of India, the United States extended its sway over the Caribbean, and assorted European powers expanded their claims in Africa and China—Japanese nationalists began to eye Korea and China as possible locations for a Japanese Empire.

China's attempt at self-defense modernization was much less successful than Japan's. Building and deploying a large fleet of battleships required more than technical capacity. It required institutional vigor and focus that the Qing dynasty no longer possessed. The last dynasty of imperial China had been shaken to its core by midcentury rebellions and foreign incursions. Its sovereignty had been significantly compromised. The Qing knew they had to do things differently, but their position was shaky. After all, they were a Manchurian family and, inside China, still widely identified as outsiders. In the late 1800s, the Empress Cixi governed as a regent in the name of unfit male relatives, and a regency spells weakness for any monarchy. Meanwhile, Europeans wanted to liberalize Chinese laws and governance because that would favor their informal colonization projects. Following the Opium Wars, China was divided into various zones of foreign influence. In each zone, particular European powers held privileged commercial concessions. Only the late-coming United States renounced any desire for its own slice of the pie, proclaiming instead that all imperial powers should enjoy equal access to China, the so-called Open Door Policy.

After 1900, Qing prestige continued to decline despite efforts at reform. When the young Emperor Guangxu was allowed to make policy, which was not usually, he promoted vocational schools and downgraded the importance of poetry and calligraphy in the traditional state examinations. In addition, the imperial government had begun to encourage foreign language study, and many Chinese students were traveling to Japan, Europe, and the United States to gain industrial know-how and advanced degrees.

Around 1900, the Empress Cixi sent a group of five learned men—two of them Chinese, and three of them Manchu—to study modern political systems in Japan, Europe, and the United States. Upon their return, they recommended the Japanese model: modernization *without* liberalization. But it was not to be. Cixi and Guangxu died in 1908. The only plausible Qing heir was still a child, and his regents were all

Manchurian. The legitimacy of Qing rule was in tatters. In 1909, lib-eral provincial assemblies were elected, the first such in Chinese history.

The manner of the final Qing collapse, ending the ancient impe-rial system, helps reveal the forces in play. By 1912, Chinese railroad building had begun in earnest, carried out by foreign companies, responding to foreign initiatives and loans. The result was a rail sys-tem designed, not to consolidate Chinese national development, but rather to make a profit for foreign companies—all to be paid by the impoverished Chinese people. Chinese control of the new railroads became an urgent nationalist demand. China's new military was another focus for nationalist feeling. Soldiers became enthusiastic supporters of Chinese nationalism. On one famous occasion, a Qing general had harangued his troops, standing in formation before him, commanding those guilty of protesting against foreign control of railways take one step forward, so to be identified and punished. The guilty soldiers obeyed, but simultaneously, all their comrades in arms stepped forward, too. This impressive show of rank-and-file solidar-ity led the general to abandon his demand. Such fervent nationalism explains why the mutiny of various army units around the major rail-and-river transportation hub at Wuhan could gain momentum and spread—then spread further and further—without anyone's taking effective action to stop them. The spontaneous uprising of 1912 that toppled the Qing dynasty and formed a republic was not a triumph of liberalism, however, and it carried little momentum.

Asian women's lives, a few of them, anyway, offered a toehold for liberal ideology. Early liberals were largely not feminists. The basic idea that all men were created equal did not apply to women except peripherally. Patriarchy remained alive and well in liberal Europe and the United States. However, the modern feminist critique did clearly emerge among some liberal nonconformists during the 1800s, most often in women's education. That was true as well in Asia.

Women in the world's largest traditional societies had much need of new thinking. Since Neolithic times, the world's most populous societies had tended to become more hierarchical and oppressive.

The place of women had deteriorated in both China and India. In both countries, widows (of any age) were occasionally expected by the most devout, conservative religious, to sacrifice their own lives to the memory of deceased husbands. Forget remarriage. It was now considered disrespectful for a woman to take a second husband after her first one died. Foot-binding, to create an image of impossibly tiny feet, had emerged in China, first among rich families, as a stylish body modification for girls. It basically turned them into cripples who could hardly walk on their tiny, crumpled feet. Some men found this attractive, also sexually provocative, apparently. Girls with bound feet had a lifetime to sit quietly and read classic advice in the obligatory *Four Books for Women*, urging them to practice "reverent submission" to men. The Indian extreme of outrageous oppression was the practice of *sati*, in which a widow was urged to immolate herself on her husband's funeral pyre. Both foot binding and sati were practices imposed on women, partly by other women. Mothers bound their daughters' feet to make them more appealing wives for rich husbands. The draconian limitations on women's freedom sometimes embodied in Muslim sharia flowed from similarly backward traditions.

In this setting, liberal ideas often brought an improvement. Stylish Western women might wear whalebone corsets to create the image of impossibly tiny "wasp" waists, but at least many of them got a liberal education, not necessarily limited to the needlework and devotional training preferred by conservatives. Liberal societies had a tradition of female literacy originating partly in Protestant ideas about the importance of reading religious texts. As public education expanded in industrializing countries, the new teachers were primarily women. An interest in educating girls was an aspect of liberal culture that colonizers did not check at the door, so to speak, when dealing with colonized populations. It was a relatively small gesture, but quite meaningful to the women whose lives it touched.

British colonization of India had little to recommend it in humanitarian terms. Mostly, it was imperial self-aggrandizement that enriched Britons and impoverished the people of the subcontinent.

And yet, regarding the welfare of women, British rule was a tad liberal. Anandi Gopa Joshi would certainly have said so. Colonialism or no, Empress Victoria's young Indian subject studied medicine the United States in the 1880s, becoming the first South Asian woman to earn a medical degree anywhere.

Chendramukhi Basu (University of Calcutta, class of 1883) came from a Bengali Christian family that educated all its daughters. Basu was one of the first two colonial girls to earn a university degree in the entire British Empire—excluding the homeland, of course. Less typical, and more inspirational, is the story of Savitribai Phule. Daughter of a rural family in Maharashtra, Savitribai Phule was married at the age of nine, to a boy three years older than her. Both she and her husband had to grow up before they could consummate their marriage or become teachers and open India's first school for girls, disregarding caste status. Today Savitribai's picture is on an Indian postage stamp. None of this is so surprising. Women have always been more easily absorbed by colonizers than have men, and education has been at the heart of the liberal project since the beginning.

Bookish liberalism has always thrived at school, after all. As a University of London law student, Mohandas Gandhi even got the idea that liberal principles could, and should, be applied to the subject population of the British Empire as a whole. Law degree in hand, Gandhi meant to establish a law practice in South Africa, where the British were ramping up their colonial presence in the late 1800s. South Africa's settler population was still largely Afrikaans-speaking, part of the Dutch imperial legacy, not on the best terms with the new colonial rulers. For manpower, the British had begun transporting Indian contract laborers to South Africa, as we have seen, treating them as a portable, equally inferior, "black." The British used the slur "nigger" in their empire as liberally as did whites in the US South. In 1893, they applied it to twenty-three-year-old Gandhi, who had taken a job as a lawyer in South Africa. Gandhi, a true citizen of the empire, had said that he felt British first and Indian second. British officials set him straight, throwing him off a train when he dared to purchase a first-class ticket, kicking him off the sidewalks where blacks were forbidden to tread. Gandhi stayed in South Africa until the eve of World War One, struggling for civil rights within the British Empire, developing the ideas about nonviolent civil disobedience that he applied later so famously in India.

LIBERALISM, the first modern political ideology, had shown itself to be a transformative force overall. The affirmation that all "men" were created equal eventually applied to all people. On the other hand, affirmations and realities are not the same thing at all.

Liberalism's equivalent of the Golden Rule was often ignored in practice, as we have seen. Any ideology of rule becomes, in part, a tool of social control. Ruling classes with hierarchy in their hearts could turn liberalism's promise of equality into a principle of racist exclusion. All shall be equal, except those who are certified inferior and should have their tubes tied. Nor was liberalism a particularly *popular* ideology, ever, anywhere. Highly illiberal religious or traditionalist ideas retained a much stronger hold on most people's thinking. That was true not only outside of the core areas of industrial capitalist development but also within them.

Liberal challenges to traditional thinking were hard for many people to absorb. Meanwhile, liberalism soon had to compete with other modern political ideologies. One of them, nationalism, proved to be a more reliable crowd pleaser. Nationalism defined a specific group of people to treat with equal consideration, the members of one's own "national family." Creating viable national families was a challenge, but much easier to accept, for most people, than equal consideration for all the world's diverse tribes, without distinction. Nationalism offered politically unifying opportunities to focus animosity on outsiders. Rather than challenging old traditions and prejudices, nationalism often manipulated them and built on them. Its usefulness to decolonizers and demagogues alike made it the most potent political ideology of the modern world.

CHAPTER THIRTEEN

Nations

Was India one nation, or many? The subcontinent had rarely been unified politically. Indians speak scores of languages. Around 1900, the language most widely understood in distant parts of the country was the English spoken by the colonizers and their Indian collaborators, a tiny fraction of the population. Indians practice diverse religions. Hinduism itself is not unified, and only recently, under political influence, have Indians considered their variegated spiritual practices to constitute a single, shared religion. The term *Hinduism* was, in fact, first applied by British colonizers as a way of indicating "all local Indian religious practices," excluding Muslims. Muslims represented a sizable minority of the population, an influential minority, given the recent Mughal past. Even after Pakistan and Bangladesh were carved from India's main trunk, the remnant would still be the world's most diverse society in religion, language, and general conditions of life. Arguably, to free itself of colonial ignominy, India needed a dose of nationalism.

To explain the power of modern nationalism, we must explain what a nation *is* exactly. Nation suggests kinship, the most powerful of human bonds. The word *nation* derives from a (Latin) root meaning birth. One is born into a nation, as one is born into a family. A nation is a group of people who regard themselves as a big family, connected somehow by blood, history, and culture. All members of a family matter. All belong. And yet, the metaphor of family also suggests patriarchy and inequality. Parents, not children, control families, after all. In any conflict with the broader world, though, family members are normally unified. After all, nobody but *me* can beat up my little brother! Nationalism is more often a producer, than a product, of unity. It produces unity by invoking the idea of an external threat to the family.

Indian society was built like a honeycomb, thousands of separate cells nestled closely together. The British had managed to take over the subcontinent by expanding their control a few cells at a time. They left Mughal royalty on a Delhi throne until eventually appropriating the throne for themselves. India's supposed unity under its empress Queen Victoria updated the country's supposed unity under the Mughal Empire, not a warm and fuzzy image for most Indians. In sum, political unity is an old challenge in India.

The most unifying thing about the Indian National Congress, by far, was what it *opposed*: British colonialism. Shared opposition is an excellent unifier because the opposers need to agree only about their mutual enemy. After all, the enemy of my enemy is my friend. The Indian National Congress that Gandhi led after 1920 defined itself primarily through shared opposition to British colonization. Gandhi now defined his Indian identity against the colonizers by adopting non-Western dress. The London-educated lawyer who had proudly worn formal British attire for most of his life took off his coat and tie and dressed ever after in the minimal, loose-fitting garments of a simple Indian villager. His British interlocutors sneered at Gandhi's "half-nakedness," but India's humble villagers didn't.

By tapping a feeling of kinship, nationalists draw on primordial human emotions. If we regard all fellow citizens as worthy of the same consideration we give our siblings, the result is a strongly unified nation. Essentially, nationalists want to scale up the emotional solidarity of a foraging band for societies of millions. But most members of a nation will never meet one another. Any kinship they feel must transcend direct experience. National feeling is something that they learn about in school, something they glimpse at public events like state funerals and international sports competitions. Nationalism is orchestrated rather than spontaneous. Nations don't just arise, they are created. They are political projects. In the early twentieth century, the Indian National Congress embarked on just such a project.

Another thing about nations. Although they evoke feelings of primordial identity, nations are *modern*. Today, every bit of territory on Earth belongs to one nation or another. A hundred years ago, however, there were few such clearly constituted nations anywhere. Most of the world, by far, was controlled by monarchs. Ethnicity was not yet a key political principle. A monarch and his subjects often had little ethnic or national affinity. Europe's Habsburg emperors, for example, had subjects all over the continent, speaking a variety of languages, belonging to a variety of vaguely defined ethnic groups, all owing loyalty to the Hapsburg dynasty rather than to each other. Therefore, nations were entirely secondary things in a world of kings and emperors. In a world of republics, though, nations overshadowed monarchy.

The basic elements of nationalist ideology are few and simple: First, a nation demands *primary* loyalty. We expect people to lay down their lives to defend the nation. Second, a nation is tied to territory. Third, all nations should be sovereign, independent, and self-governing. Ideally, all members of a particular nation should reside under the aegis of a state organization that defends their collective interests and expresses their collective will. In other words, each nation should have its own state. It should be a *nation-state*. As these basic principles became universally accepted during the last two centuries, nationalism became the great, global empire-buster. Today's division of the world into nation-states shows the universal appeal of basic nationalist principles.

Nationalism also has other, less laudable uses beyond empire-busting, however. The dynamics of human interaction in large social groups make it easiest to build national solidarity on negative emotions like mistrust, resentment, and fear of outsiders. Stoking animosity and focusing resentment is basic to the nationalist tool kit. Your family is threatened! Defend your own! Nationalism's call to arms functions like a fire alarm in the night, rousing us from daily concerns to confront a deadly emergency. Responding to a fire alarm, we don't try to decide for ourselves whether there really is a fire or not. First comes adrenalin-driven action, reflection only later, if at all. Nationalist calls to arms work that way, too. That's why panic drives so many nationalist appeals.

In sum, rather than a full theory of governance, nationalism is an tactic, a unifying banner, a way to rally political support. All too frequently, nationalist leaders play to prejudices and self-regard. Nationalism's dark side lends itself to demagoguery.

The Emergence of Modern Nationalism

Modern nationalism emerged alongside liberalism in the late 1700s. Both were present in the American and French revolutions, which espoused the idea that political power should flow *up* from the people of a sovereign nation to their chosen rulers. We have already seen how liberalism emphasized elections and constitutions written by the people's representatives. Nationalists, on the other hand, worry less about "people," a motley crew of diverse individuals, than about "the People," a mythic entity with one voice. Nationalists speak of "the will of the People." In real life, diverse groups are never unanimous and never speak with one voice. Only in a limited, rhetorical way, after all, could the framers of the US Constitution speak as "We, the People." Nonetheless, nationalist leaders cannot do without this fiction. Modern demagogues boast a quasi-mystical rapport that allows them to speak for the entire nation.

Modern nationalism arose, not from some deep social impulse, but from political expediency. Nations were not crying out to be born. Rather, political leaders sired them by impregnating societies in turmoil. After 1800, Napoleon turned the French Revolution in nationalist directions by "liberating" much of Europe into the French

Empire. Other European nations resisted French imperialism, often invoking French revolutionary principles to do so. Liberalism and nationalism interacted in the resulting scuffle. Invaded by France in 1807, Spaniards wrote a liberal constitution to resist invasion. Spanish resistance to Napoleon became the first modern war of national liberation, fought in the name of the Spanish People. Military mobilization across Europe brought a surge of nationalist feeling during the Napoleonic Wars.

Outside of Europe, modern nationalism gained momentum in the early 1800s as the antidote to European colonialism. Nationalism's first major field of operation was the Americas. Shock waves were felt across the Atlantic as Spanish liberals fighting Napoleon called for aid from Spain's colonies. Spanish colonies resisted colonial status, however, and, in the 1820s, established a dozen newly minted republics, a landmark event in the history of world nationalism. All these new republics were still aspirational nations rather than consolidated ones. The feeling of national belonging—the heart of nationhood—was still quite limited in these societies. Latin American populations descended from both oppressed and oppressors. Ex-slaves and ex-slave owners may be blood relations, but they generally don't feel much like family. And even in the best situations, it typically takes several generations to build a nation in people's minds.

Through the 1800s, Latin American countries were ruled by their landowning classes with limited participation by anyone else. At election time, rural laborers (the majority) might act as loyal followers, voting or carrying weapons, but they did so at the direction of their patrons, not in their own interest. Their patrons, meanwhile, listened to Italian opera, read French literature. They paid attention to London commodity prices and Paris fashions. They cringed at Latin America's authentic cultural heritage, an embarrassing reminder of non-European roots that they had no desire to cultivate. Rather than create good schools at home, they sent their children to study abroad. Latin America's export-oriented economies required little social infrastructure, little political development, and no mass mobilization at all. Nationalism, that preeminent instrument of political mass mobilization, languished in the toolbox, mostly unused in the 1800s.

As Latin American societies gradually urbanized and industrialized after 1900, political leaders pulled nationalism out of the toolbox. Urban workers generally live in communication with each other and the wider world. When contrasted with peasants, urban people are less linked to sources of traditional patronage, more likely to know their rights. The way to engage industrial workers politically (but without letting them set the agenda) is to offer them a symbolic seat at the national table, the dignity of public respect and full citizenship. After 1900, Latin American nationalists abandoned the liberal "not yet ready for self-governance" rhetoric and actively courted majority populations of African and Native American descent. The era of mass politics had finally arrived, and nationalism was the charm. Scientific racism went out the window, and non-European race defined new national identities. Painters created murals full of indigenous peasants who were brown and beautiful. Mixed-race musicians adopted rhythms and instruments brought from Africa by slaves. Essayists explored the idea that Latin American cultures, like Latin American populations, are of mixed origins. Unlike the racial scientists, they declared mixture to be the region's true genius. The old racist slur on Latin American populations, their "mongrelism," was turned on its head and made a badge of pride. National novels, now taught in school, depicted star-crossed lovers facing, and often overcoming, social and racial contrasts. Race mixing became patriotic.

In the 1910s and 1920s, the region's nationalist leaders reached out to new, brownish constituencies and got an enthusiastic response. Europhile liberal parties that had governed across the region collapsed in country after country as the world economic system faltered in 1929. In Brazil and Argentina, also Mexico, Chile, and Colombia, significant industrialization occurred during the 1930s, and nationalist leaders rode a wave of worker and middle-class support. Charismatic nationalist presidents gave thunderous speeches at enthusiastic rallies and on the radio, declaring "economic independence" from the "neocolonial" capitalist order. Unfortunately, many nationalist strongmen were populist demagogues who freely abused their authority. But their nationalism found a devoted broad-based following and changed the contours of political power. Labor politicians from the mid-twentieth century won presidential elections for a half century thereafter in Argentina and Brazil.

Globally, by the time of the First World War, the spirt of liberty had lost revolutionary appeal, upstaged by the nationalist spirit of inclusiveness and self-determination. In Latin America, the search for national identity became a powerful cultural movement. Artists highlighted the distinctiveness of historical experience, folklore, and traditions. Popular music and dance, such as tango and samba, became highly successful emblems of Latin American national cultures. Nationalist composers made classic music with folk themes, nationalist painters depicted simple-but-worthy peasants, cookbook writers collected rustic regional recipes for national cuisines. By demonstrating the strength and vitality of their national identities, all made the case for self-determination, ipso facto.

In 1900, all the world's empires were vulnerable to secessionist movements with a nationalist soundtrack. And empires still ruled the world, but not for much longer.

Toward a World of Nations

Around 1900, liberal republics were still quite rare in Europe, Asia, and Africa. Outside the Americas, monarchies and empires dominated the map. A global wave of nationalist movements finally changed that. Only in the twentieth century did power go really to "the People," in principle at least.

It is easy to forget the general supremacy of kings and emperors until so recently. The mostly democratic Europe of today was still a liberal pipe dream during the 1800s. While the Napoleonic Wars had created republics across Europe, conservative reaction at the

1814 Congress of Vienna had restored the old monarchies. Europe was home to the British, French, Dutch, Spanish, Portuguese, Russian, Habsburg, and Ottoman Empires. There were a few constitutional monarchies, but free and open elections were still a thing of the future just about everywhere.

Obviously, we cannot give a blow-by-blow depiction of worldwide political events. The overall trend is what we need, and it is clear enough. As empires struggled against each other (and against their colonial subjects) in the late 1800s, they awakened nationalist reactions. Nationalists invoked the basic principle that every nation has the right to rule itself. This principle has come to seem self-evident now, but two hundred years ago that was not yet so. Little or no nation-building had ever happened in many parts of the globe. Rather than a map of single-colored nations with clear borders, visualize a swirling kaleidoscope of cultures and power arrangements. Eastern Europe, for example, was a crazy quilt of ethnicities and languages where empires had ebbed and flowed over the centuries. Many Slavic ethnicities—Poles, Serbs, Czechs, Slovaks—inhabited the Habsburg or Russian Empires, scattered across villages and regions, intermarrying sometimes and not others, a shifting archipelago of ethnicities. These ethnic identities were ambiguous and fluid, as cultural identities normally are, before nations sharpen and fix them with laws, administration, and public schools.

Again, nationalists made nations, instead of the other way around. Nationalists call on us to be loyal to something bigger than ourselves, then they make that thing up. This is true of all nations, to varying degrees. Thus did nationalist artists and writers go to work defining specific national identities in Eastern Europe, as they also did in Latin America and elsewhere. Music provides a salient example. Classical composers like Liszt and Chopin wrote sonatas and rhapsodies based on Hungarian or Polish folk songs. They regarded traditional peasant culture as a repository of national authenticity. Eastern Europeans who lived under imperial rule came up with a new expression of nationalism as young men gathered to practice calisthenics and paramilitary exercises in a patriotic spirit. They were imagining themselves as patriot rebels in training, informal militias ready to subvert imperial overlords in the name of their nation. The Poles, for example, reminded themselves of their earlier, glorious history of independence from the Russian Empire that now ruled them. Remembrance of former independence inspired revolts in the 1830s and 1860s. The Serbs had their own glorious history and their own language, but, frustratingly, no nation-state of their own. Instead, they were divided between the Ottoman Empire to the south and the Habsburg Empire to the north. The Ottomans let go in 1878, but a spark from the continuing Serbian struggle, a terrorist assassination, ignited the First World War. We will return to that in a moment.

The big nationalist story of the mid-1800s, in Europe, anyway, was the unification of Germany and Italy. Neither had been a unified state in modern times. Ethnic nationalism was invoked to construct these two large and populous nation-states from a welter of minor kingdoms, duchies, and principalities. Nationalist historians in Germany promoted the idea that Prussia, one of Europe's many German-speaking areas, embodied the German national spirit. That leant credibility to Bismarck's bid to unify German speakers into a nation-state under Prussian rule. An important moment occurred when Prussia defeated France in 1871 and annexed the disputed province of Alsace-Lorraine, inhabited by speakers of both German and French. After that, generations of French schoolchildren were exhorted to avenge this outrage to the French nation. Italy, like Germany, had previously been a culture area rather than a political unit. Part of Italy was ruled by the pope, other parts by various princes and monarchs. Not until 1861 did Garibaldi's nationalist movement create a unified kingdom of Italy, recruiting an available monarch from the northwestern part of the country. The Germans, too, had established a Reich, a kingdom rather than a republic, but a national one. The unification of both Germany and Italy involved considerable fighting. The later 1800s saw the rise of German militarism.

Prussian-unified Germany replaced France as the continent's most dangerous neighbor.

Outside of Europe, nationalism found less scope for development during the mid-1800s, partly because so many potential nation-states were securely colonized by Europeans. The major European empires now proposed that non-Europeans were not yet ready for self-rule of any kind. The British Empire, with a deep commitment to white supremacy, stood at its apogee, the biggest empire ever. The French Empire had bulked up its claims substantially in the 1800s. It now controlled large parts of Africa and, since the middle of the century, Vietnam, which in conjunction with contiguous territories, had become French Indochina. While Spain was slipping from the ranks of imperial powers, Portugal and the Netherlands were not. Indonesia was still the Dutch East Indies. The Ottoman Empire was moribund. The Chinese Empire was defunct, but its corpse had not been interred. India, a major center of world civilization, had been turned into a British financial asset.

Even the United States, while formally encouraging liberal republicanism abroad, had swallowed its shining-house-on-a-hill scruples and joined the race for empire. Surging US industrial production threatened a crisis of overproduction, suggesting the need to find new markets overseas for US manufactured goods. The US construction of a transoceanic canal across the Isthmus of Panama obeyed that impulse, as did ongoing US occupation of the Philippine Islands, with their incomparable deep-water harbor at Manila Bay, on the doorstep of the fabled East Asian market. The United States seized Cuba, Puerto Rico, and the Philippines in a brief 1898 war with Spain. That allowed the creation of US naval bases and coaling stations—such as Guantanamo Bay, on the island of Cuba—to facilitate the projection of US naval and commercial power. Germany, Russia, and Japan, too, were reaching for empire. The 1880s saw a final surge of imperialist predation on remaining areas that had never been colonized by Europeans.

An 1884 conference in Berlin initiated an undignified international "scramble for Africa." Although the Spanish, French, Portuguese, Dutch, English, and French had all already established trading enclaves along the African coast, the African interior was the part of the Earth least known to European powers when they agreed amicably in Berlin on how to partition Africa among them. Within about twenty years, they had done the deed. Around 1900 European flags flew from virtually every flagpole in Africa. Although the basic principles of nationalism—the right of self-determination, the right to have a nation-state—were not questioned, they seemed simply not to apply in Africa. These supposedly universal principles of human political organization were bracketed in European treatment of Africans, as had been the case for slaves in the early United States or indigenous peasants in Mexico and Peru. France, building on French settlement in Algeria going back decades, claimed the largest territory, although a sizable part was Sahara Desert. The Belgian King Leopold acquired and operated the so-called Belgian Congo as a personal money-making venture. Within a few years, his African claims, organized around the forced collection of rainforest rubber, led to the death of millions.

Meanwhile, the newly unified German Empire conducted the most concerted imperial strategy in Africa. Like the militarist industrialists of Japan, those of Germany were hungry for empire. Not for nothing had the 1884 Berlin Conference been hosted in Berlin. Beginning in 1884, Germany launched colonial projects in three widely separated parts of Africa, six attempts in all, four of them lasting ones (Cameroon, Namibia, Tanzania, Togo). Meanwhile, Italy registered its own imperial aspirations by occupying Libya, Eritrea, and part of Somaliland. And the British, having occupied Egypt, used it as base for incursions into Sudan and further south, areas it would eventually annex. That left only lofty, arid Ethiopia, a less enticing or more forbidding prize, alone on the African continent, uncolonized.

In Asia, as in Africa, nationalism would be mostly a twentieth-century story. The great exception was the rise of an industrialized Japan, possessed of modern weaponry, able to defend itself against would-be European colonizers. The Japanese had retained—also reinvigorated—their traditional monarchy as a nationalist talisman. By 1895, the Japanese extended control over Korea, launching their own drive for empire. The Chinese Empire, a mere shadow of its former self, resisted Japan's upstart imperialism, but to no avail. To drive home their point, the Japanese annexed the Chinese province of Taiwan. Russians contested Japanese imperialism, too, and were similarly humiliated. The Japanese fleet won an easy victory over Russian battleships in 1905. By the eve of World War One, the strength of the Japanese battle fleet was exceeded only by those of Britain, the world hegemon, and its principal naval challenger, Germany.

Meanwhile, the nationalist potential of the Chinese people was clear enough. The non-Chinese origins (and resulting unpopularity) of the Qing dynasty had contributed to its demise. Nationalist sentiments were evident in Chinese protests against Japanese aggression in 1895. They were evident in the anti-foreign spirit of the Boxer Rebellion of 1898–1899 that targeted European missionaries. The rebels were termed Boxers because they practiced paramilitary calisthenics, which meant, in China, martial arts. To put down the Boxer Rebellion, intervening European armed forces, entrenched in their zones of influence, turned their guns on the Chinese people. Then they punished the Chinese nation by imposing disproportionate reparations for the crime of patriotic rebellion. Rising nationalist feelings were evident in the 1905 boycott that protested racist mistreatment of Chinese people in the United States. There was a microscopic liberal opposition in China—or rather, mostly in exile—led by mild-mannered, US-educated Sun-Yat Sen. Sun-Yat Sen organized a movement, first in Japan, then among Southeast Asia's overseas Chinese community, finally around the world. He was strongly oriented towards the United States, and even accepted the liberal idea that ordinary Chinese were not ready for self-rule. When the Qing dynasty finally collapsed, making Sun Yat-Sen the provisional president of a new Chinese republic, his leadership became irrelevant. Nationalist fervor now manifested itself in the army and in mass demonstrations favoring Chinese ownership of the new railway network. And they were particularly manifest when, after World War One, German concessions in China were transferred to Japan by the Versailles treaty. Chinese students, expecting a different outcome, initiated a movement named for the day when they received the news, the 1919 May Fourth Movement.

The May Fourth Movement initiated a protracted period of nationalist soul-searching and a growing resolve to challenge imperialist privileges in China. The imperial powers that had won concessions in China were determined to maintain their privileges, and they did not hesitate to guarantee them with deadly force. When workers in Shanghai demonstrated against a lockout by their Japanese employers, British troops fired on them, killing dozens. When workers in Hong Kong protested that massacre, British soldiers fired on them, too. The ever-increasing incursions of Japanese imperialism into China constituted the greatest irritant of all.

In India, as in China, nationalism reached relatively few people but was influential, nonetheless. Returning to the subcontinent from South Africa in 1915, Gandhi had joined the Indian National Congress. The congress had begun as a sort of liberal debating society formed under British auspices to give graduates of the University of Calcutta a forum for their opinions. By this time, however, Gandhi had little use for liberalism anymore. He formulated his program using Indian words and concepts: *ahimsa*, non-violence; *satyagraha*, civil disobedience; *swaraj*, self-rule. He contrasted Western materialism against Indian spiritualism. Perhaps he never really said, when asked his opinion of Western civilization, that he thought "it would be a good idea," but it sounds like him. The popular response to Gandhi's nationalism frightened the colonial government, which massacred groups practicing nonviolent civil disobedience in 1919.

From then on, Gandhi made the Indian National Congress into a real force for decolonization.

Swadeshi, nonparticipation in the colonial economy, became Gandhi's most flamboyant tactic. Gandhi led a boycott against British cloth, suggesting that Indians should instead develop their domestic economy, become self-sufficient, even spin their own cloth as a meditative spiritual exercise. It was at this point that Gandhi adopted Indian peasant costume, wearing a simple piece of cotton fabric he spun and wove himself. Another brilliant gesture, this one in 1930, was to march with scores of followers 250 miles to the sea, declaring his intention to make salt without paying the colonial salt tax. On their way to the sea, his followers were beaten by colonial law enforcement without offering any resistance. Such provocative tactics got Gandhi thrown in prison for two years during the 1930s. Then came World War Two, and Indians were asked, or rather instructed, to defend the British Empire.

The world wars are vivid, meaningful scenes in the theater of our contemporary imaginations: a day that will live in infamy, London under the blitz, the rape of Nanjing, the siege of Leningrad—ringing phrases, defining moments, life-and-death dramas, peopled by heroes and villains. We remember the world wars of the twentieth century as contests between nations. At the level of world history, however, what matters is the bigger picture. Both world wars were above all contests between empires.

World Wars

Both world wars pitted would-be empires against already established ones. The imperial aspirations of German and Japanese militarists were loudly proclaimed and clear to see. They wanted what the better-established British, US, French, Dutch, Portuguese, and Russian Empires already possessed. But the existing empires were determined to curb the expansion of their upstart rivals who, after the scramble for Africa, could expand only at *their* imperial expense. By that time, the Chinese and Ottoman Empires were already trudging toward the chopping block. The British Empire was at its apogee, the most expansive political entity ever, about a fifth of the world's land area. The United States habitually disavowed imperial ambitions, but it had subjugated its Indian nations, annexed Puerto Rico, Hawaii, and Alaska (not to mention Texas, New Mexico, Arizona, and California), occupied the Philippine Islands for decades, repeatedly invaded Cuba, Haiti, the Dominican Republic, Nicaragua, and Panama, and sent its great white battle fleet sailing around the world to show the flag of US power at the beginning of the twentieth century.

As for the wannabes, around 1900 Japan and Germany had become lead contenders, along with Great Britain and the United States, in a great naval arms race. Given that the contestants all operated seaborne empires—or aspired to do so—it makes sense that navies were their weapon of choice. Maritime empires had sea routes, installations, and coaling stations to protect. They needed to show the flag regularly to overawe brown people in this port or that, or, if awe were insufficient, to show imperial displeasure by bombarding the misbehavers from offshore with naval artillery, a behavior nicknamed gunboat diplomacy. The age of sail had ended, and the battleships of the day were coal-burning, armored behemoths studded with swiveling gun turrets. The long-range artillery on the biggest battleships could hit targets over the horizon with explosive shells too heavy for sailors to load without winches. Construction of modern naval vessels required heavy industry, advanced technology, enormous investment. The largest of the new battleships were thought to be invincible. Observers of the imperial arms race kept score, tallying the number, tonnage, and firepower of battleships launched year by year.

On the eve of the World War One, empires and imperial wannabes had established a precarious balance of interlocking alliances in Europe. German imperialists wanted to expand at the expense of the Ottoman and Russian Empires. They also eyed British and French claims in Africa. After occupying both Korea and Taiwan, Japanese forces were ready to jump the imperial claims of Britain, France, the Netherlands, and the United States in Southeast Asia. The disintegrating Ottoman Empire was losing ground in the Balkans, and both the Habsburg and Russian Empires hoped to expand there.

Serbian nationalists, resisting Habsburg encroachment, assassinated a Habsburg noble in Sarajevo, prompting competitive intervention as Habsburgs and Russians went toe to toe. When neither empire blinked, they activated their military alliances with other imperial powers. Voilà, World War One. Imperialism set it up, nationalism triggered it, industrialism made in hell on Earth.

Launched in a frenzy of patriotic hoopla, World War One (1914–1918) became a contest of endurance and industrial capacity. German armies captured territory to the west, in France, and to the east, in Russia. But initial advances stalled, in part, because heavy machine-gun and artillery emplacements favored defenders over attackers. The military technology of attack—tanks, warplanes, submarines, and aircraft carriers—was gradually elaborated during the war, but not in time to overcome the existing advantages of defense. Both sides had dug in deeply. The brunt of the fighting in World War One was a contest of brute strength and grim attrition in which battles lasted months. Modern empires were industrialized, by definition. To triumph in war, they required strategic depth, which meant more ships, more guns, more young men, and more supplies and ammunition to replace what the enemy destroyed each month. World War One's main theater of operations, in northern France, consisted of stationary battle lines and deep, sheltering trenches separated by a no man's land where artillery, machine guns, and poison gas churned gore, rotting uniforms, and rusting barbed wire into the mud, year after year. No battle was decisive; only the cumulative outcome would determine victory or defeat. Which empire would be the first to run out of weaponry, munitions, supplies, or young men? German generals decided to stop the carnage and surrender when defeat became inevitable in World War One.

This was not a war of national liberation. Yet nationalism and patriotic hoopla were the prime mobilizing theme on all sides, called forth by the universal need for mass mobilization. The surge of nationalism also validated the basic principle that every nation deserves to be a nation-state. Therefore, following the butchery that destroyed a generation, national self-determination became a major theme of the post-World War One peace conference. The beginnings of a world government emerged from the conference, and, significantly, it took the form of a League of Nations. The League of Nations embodied the aspiration that all sovereign states could be equally represented on a one-nation, one-vote basis. The League of Nations did not reflect the reality that European empires still girdled the globe. Out of sync with the realities of global power, the League of Nations did not outlast the 1930s.

Meanwhile, would-be empires were still trying to be born. Heavy war reparations had impeded Germany's ability to prosper economically after World War One. The result was widespread acceptance within Germany of the nationalist narrative of resentment advanced by Hitler. Hitler claimed that Germany had been betrayed, rather than defeated militarily, and then victimized by Jewish financial machinations. Hitler's projected Nazi empire was to include, first, all areas inhabited by German speakers; next, the Slavic lands of Eastern Europe, which would be prepared for German settlers by ethnic cleansing; and finally, the rest of the world. Nazi claims to national greatness were especially virulent, but not at all unique. Japanese imperialist aggression masqueraded as the construction of a Greater East Asia Co-Prosperity Sphere. The Japanese were annexing more of China and developing a formal nationalist ideology meant to draw on resentment of European imperialism and, simultaneously, establish Japanese racial and cultural superiority within Asia. In Italy, meanwhile, another strongman leader, Mussolini, spoke the same language of national greatness. Mussolini suggested that the new Italian nation, too, could have an empire, and thereby fulfill the imperial destiny bequeathed it by its Roman forebears. Italy had already assumed control of Libya when the receding Ottoman Empire let it go in 1912. In 1936, an Italian attack on Ethiopia finally turned it briefly into a new European colony, Italian East Africa.

Fascism, an -ism named for Mussolini's movement in Italy, was a term applied to all three rising would-be empires. Rather than a distinct ideology, fascism is a pattern exemplified by three desperate mid-twentieth century lunges toward national greatness. Fascism is basically an ultra-violent, extreme form of nationalism that strongly focuses resentment on national enemies, both internal and external. Franco's Spain, a German ally, also fit the pattern. It is about empire-building rather than empire-busting. In the hands of German, Italian, or Japanese imperialists, national self-determination applied mostly to "superior" nations—or rather, deluded empire-building "master races" like themselves.

World War Two (1939–1945) likewise pitted rising empires against existing ones.

The near collapse of world capitalism during the 1930s had seriously weakened Britain and the United States. Liberalism entered eclipse worldwide, validating fascist imperial ambitions. Proudly illiberal German and Japanese nationalists—loosely allied in theory, but never effectively so—made parallel bids for empire at that moment. Japan occupied most of the French and Dutch claims in Asia, along with Korea, the US-controlled Philippine Islands, and much of China. Hitler repeated Napoleon's feat of dominating the entire European continent and Napoleon's error of trying to conquer the Russian Empire, as well. The British Empire was still the world's largest, however, and by then the United States had become the world's leading industrial power. These were joined eventually by no-less-imperial Soviet Russia, which bore the brunt of the German assault and finally turned the tide at the Battle of Stalingrad. The allied victory over both Germany and Japan was already clearly defined in 1945, when the United States used its new atomic bombs to speed Japanese surrender.

The postwar exposure of fascist war crimes gave racist imperialism a bad smell that lasted for decades. It also ended a century of European racial science, which was discredited internationally by its close association with Nazi mass murder in the Holocaust. Within the United States, the new global stink of white supremacy encouraged disenfranchised African Americans to create a civil rights move-

ment. In Asia, it facilitated the independence of Indonesia. Before
being incorporated by force into the short-lived Japanese Empire,
Indonesia had been for centuries the world's second most populous
and profitable European colony. When the defeated Japanese occupiers of the Dutch East Indies withdrew in 1945, local patriots easily
succeeded in preventing the effective reassertion of Dutch imperialism. As a result, the Dutch East Indies shed its colonial status quickly
after World War Two. Major European "possessions" overseas were
soon to be a thing of the past. The formal decolonization of the world
occurred within a couple of decades following World War Two.

Nationalism, *not* the imperialist lust for national greatness, but
the basic right of national self-determination, was now on a roll.
India, the world's largest and most lucrative colony ever, became the
world's largest electoral democracy shortly after Indonesian independence. India had contributed 2.5 million fighters to the British
war effort, and 87,000 Indians had died for it, not counting those
who starved to death. Embattled Britain had been too distracted
to facilitate Indian anti-famine efforts during the Bengal famine of
1943, which consumed over two million people. Incensed, Gandhi
had demanded that Britain "Quit India," and the British had imprisoned him. After World War Two, the inhabitants of British India
were in no mood to wait for independence, and the British were in
no position to make them wait. British rule ended, but the end was
tragic. India's enormous Muslim minority was fearful of its fate, and
when decolonization finally occurred in 1947, that fear led to partition into predominantly Muslim Pakistan (and Bangladesh) and
predominantly Hindu India. Partition displaced over ten million
people and led to enormous suffering, but it finally decolonized the
Indian subcontinent.

Rapid wholesale decolonization after World War Two represented
a decisive triumph of the core nationalist idea, whereby every nation
deserves self-determination. Africa, fully colonized in the 1880s,
began to decolonize in the 1950s, without upheaval. A wave of independence movements swept over the middle part of Africa, meeting

little resistance from European colonizers who had found these most recent colonies to be less profitable than they had imagined during their imperialist scramble of the 1880s. Also notably, in the wake of the World War Two, with its industrialized murder of millions of European Jews, Zionists managed to create the modern state of Israel in territories inhabited two thousand years earlier by the Biblical Hebrews. The Zionists were adamant that the land had been given to them by God himself. Unfortunately, their remembered homeland had since become Palestine, inhabited in post-Biblical times by Muslims who claimed it, too. Rather than a religious confrontation, this was a nationalist show down, a single territory disputed between two nations, separate and antagonistic, a zero-sum situation with no compromise imaginable. The British Empire had finally dissolved, and many former British colonies, now independent nations, joined a looser association with Britain, the Commonwealth.

Nationalism faded from the global scene in the 1970s and 1980s. Partly, it was a victim of its own success. Formal colonialism was over. Fascist brutality had disgraced nationalist demagoguery worldwide, at least for a while. The victorious wartime liberal-socialist alliance against fascism ended after the war, however. The United States and the Soviet Union emerged as the world's chief postwar powers. Both exercised imperial sway over other nations, yet neither officially believed in imperialism. Both rationalized their de facto imperial domination as a matter of universal principles. Both were supposedly trying to make a better world, not just aggrandize themselves. The United States had become the undisputed world capital of liberalism. Its opponent, the Soviet Union, had become the global standard bearer of revolutionary socialism.

The global dual between liberalism and socialism would define world affairs in the post-World War Two decades. Socialism, so far unexamined in these pages, has many meanings. Like liberalism and nationalism, it deserves a chapter of its own.

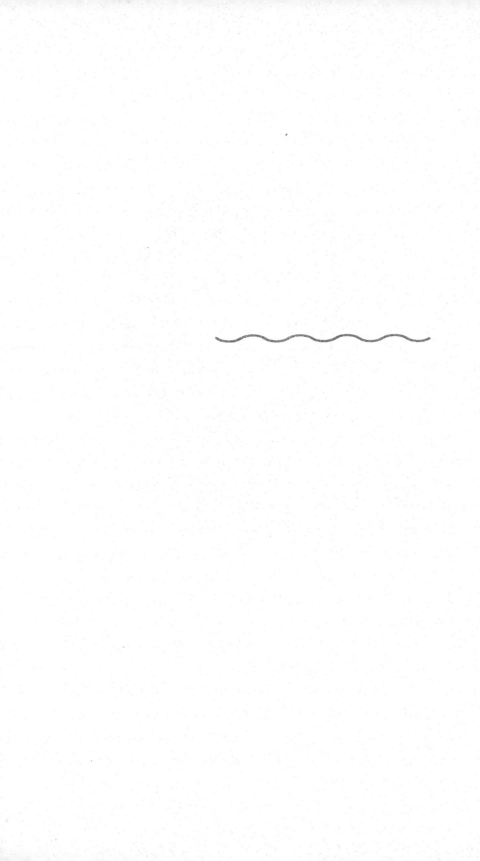

CHAPTER FOURTEEN

Revolution

After World War Two, the world belonged, no longer to empires, but to nation-states. That was the idea, anyway. In fact, the war's victors—especially the United States and Russia—still exercised quasi-imperial sway over many other countries. The two were no longer allies after the war, and they espoused diametrically conflicting ideologies. They quickly became enemies. Therefore, the post-World War Two world moved quickly into a new confrontation that was both a geopolitical and an ideological contest.

With the stated goal of preventing future wars, the victors of World War Two instituted a second major attempt at democratic world governance, the United Nations. Like the League of Nations of the 1920s and 1930s, the United Nations was founded on the principle that all nations were created equal. In the United Nations, unlike the earlier League of Nations, however, some nations were to be more equal than others. The victors of World War Two became the five members of its Security Council and held sweeping veto powers. All five of the Security Council members in fact represented empires of one kind or another. When the United Nations was formed, Britain and France still had colonies around the world. The Soviet Union and the People's Republic of China had inherited colonial empires from the Romanov and Qing dynasties. While denouncing imperialism, Russian and Chinese revolutionaries ruled Estonians, Mongols, Tibetans, Kazaks, Lithuanians, Uyghurs, and many others. Russian soldiers had occupied Eastern Europe at the end of the war, and they stayed for decades. The United States, for its part, made its wartime mobilization quasi-permanent, retaining military bases and alliances and exercising political tutelage in scores of countries around the world. As old-style colonial empires disappeared, the global contest between postwar capitalism and revolutionary socialism took center stage.

Socialism foregrounds the idea, basic to all modern political thought, that enlightened governance can make societies better. More than liberals or nationalists, however, socialists envision *revolutionary* improvement—rapid, purposeful, and profound. A socialist revolution aims at redesigning society to achieve specific ideals and objectives. In contrast to liberalism, socialism privileges the collective over the individual. Socialism was born as an ideology of resistance against the industrial capitalist order championed by liberals. Socialism therefore became liberalism's archenemy.

Early socialists noticed that early industrialism had exacerbated poverty, rather than eliminating it. Liberals tended to consider this a regrettable failure of the impoverished individuals in question. It was the workers' fault, in other words, that they had become poor. This was a gospel that industrial workers did not find empowering. Classical liberalism inspired highly motivated, upwardly mobile managers and merchants, not bone-tired cotton-mill workers pulling ten-hour shifts.

Socialists, on the other hand, took the side of the bone-tired workers. Theirs was the most idealistic and ambitious political goal ever: a completely equitable society without conflict or exploitation. Socialists had many different ideas about how to achieve this goal. Karl Marx, ultimately the most influential socialist thinker, thought that capital—accumulations of private wealth—had become the chief driver of inequality in the modern world. Capitalism, in Marx's view, amounted to rule for money's sake, rule by millionaire plutocrats whose main concern was always their own private fortunes. Marx believed that a revolution would be necessary to overthrow the capitalist ruling class.

Socialism found its principal constituency, at first, among workers in the newly established factories. Early generations of industrial workers embraced the socialist critique of capitalism and viewed the millionaire plutocrats as their victimizers. Socialism, in many international variations, became their creed. Not all these socialists were revolutionaries. The most fundamental tactic of the powerless many, employees of the powerful few, was to band together. In union there was strength. Labor unions represented their membership in negotiations with company management, and beyond the workplace, the labor movement regarded itself as a socialist counterweight to capitalist power. During the twentieth century, labor movements pressured liberal democracies to extend civil rights and public welfare, softening the hard edges of capitalism.

Among the many variations of socialism, were some scorned by Marxists as utopian. These so-called utopian socialists believed society could be reformed by "demonstration effect" alone, without a revolution. To show what they had in mind, utopian socialists formed intentional communities (especially in France, England, and the United States) organized around the idea of economic equality, cooperation, and the inherent dignity of labor, which industrialism had destroyed. They perceived capitalism as a spiritual, not just an economic, problem. In their rejection of the new capitalist order, the utopian socialists created communities a bit like the countercultural hippie communes of the 1960s. Extraordinarily, some utopian socialists of the mid-1800s went so far as to repudiate patriarchy and even endorse free love. Some hippie communes were, in fact, directly copying utopian socialist precedents. Another example of socialism without revolution was La Commune, which governed Paris for about two months in 1871. During that time, excited Parisians organized mutual aid groups and built barricades in the streets to protect themselves against the army, which was directed by the

French government to slaughter them patriotically. For over a century, socialism became the go-to philosophy for people on the losing end of capitalist disruptions.

Marxian revolutionary socialism became the most influential variety. The mid-century publication of Marx's vast historical study, *Capital* (first volume published in 1867), had an impact as significant, in its way, as that of Darwin's natural history study *On the Origin of Species* (1859). By 1900, revolutionary socialist radicals were commonplace in Europe—but often in exile like Marx himself. The bookish German philosopher researched and wrote his famous study at the library of the British Museum. Marx's disciple and associate, Fredrick Engels, also German (but not, like Marx, Jewish), was the scion of a rich industrialist family. Marx was not particularly influential in England, however. English socialists focused on organizing industrial workers into unions rather than on overthrowing the government. Unionizers encountered violent resistance, but gradually they won the right to organize.

Labor unionization became a widespread form of *non-revolutionary* socialist organization. By the twentieth century, no major industrialized nation lacked a labor movement. The Labor Party of the United Kingdom outpaced the country's dominant Liberal Party in the 1920s. In the United States, too, and generally throughout the industrial capitalist world, socialists and other radicals were at the forefront of movements to protect the public's health and welfare, civil rights, and social security. The most famous socialist leader of the early twentieth century United States was Eugene V. Debs, who had worked on the railroad and, when unemployed, became a tramp who hopped freights looking for work. Debs often went to jail for organizing workers and supporting strikes. He read Marx in jail without becoming a revolutionary. He ran several times for president as a socialist candidate, complaining that money should not rule and that socialism was a simple recognition of human equality.

Especially in the United States, the labor movement did not challenge the capitalist system, focusing instead on collective bargaining for wages and benefits. Yet violent repression of socialists and labor leaders remained normal in capitalist societies until the 1920s. President Franklin Roosevelt's New Deal—which critics condemned as socialist—finally reversed government attempts to suppress labor unions in the United States. The New Deal maintained the political guarantees of liberal democracy while introducing a new sense of social responsibility.

Non-revolutionary socialism is democratic socialism. Although the New Deal is certainly an example, democratic socialism has existed mostly in Europe. European social democracy, as in Sweden or Denmark today, has set the world's highest national standards of health, education, and welfare in the period after World War Two. Most countries in Europe today embody a social democratic orientation, to some degree, leading to a more equitable distribution of wealth, high-quality public education, comprehensive national health care systems, generous social security provisions, and so on. The main problem with such things is paying for them. Democratic socialism's contribution to a higher national quality of life is unquestionable, but it was overshadowed in the twentieth century by revolutionary socialism.

The revolutionary project to destroy the capitalist system and establish a "dictatorship of the people" looms large in world history. Marxist regimes in twentieth-century Russia and China regarded democracy as something possible only in a perfect future, when revolutionary dictatorship would no longer be necessary. In the meantime, their assault on capitalism put them on a permanent war footing, especially regarding internal enemies. This was the authoritarian variant of socialism properly called *Communism*.

All forms of socialism favor community and cooperation over individualism and the market. This aligns socialists with many traditional value systems around the world. Therefore, as industrial capitalism produced an ever-deeper penetration of the world market into African, Asian, and South American societies after World War

Two, many peasant movements embraced socialism, too—the revolutionary kind. Marxism provided an antidote for blame-the-victim explanations of poverty and underdevelopment. In Asia and Africa, adopting socialist ideology could bring aid from the Soviet Union, just as adopting liberal ideology brought aid from the United States. In Latin America, numerous guerrilla armies and even a few revolutionary regimes—most notably Cuba's—adopted socialist ideology to counteract US influence. Latin American states did not feel much affinity with revolutionary Russia or China, though, and they rarely received help from either. Cuba was the notable exception.

Our big twentieth-century story starts in imperial Russia.

The Union of Soviet Socialist Republics

Russia in 1917 was a land of contrasts. It had developed its own version of Orthodox Christianity, withstood the Mongols, and built a vast inland empire in Central Asia and Siberia. During the early 1700s, Czar Peter the Great had encouraged cultural and economic currents from France, England, Germany, and the Netherlands. But Russia had retained quite autocratic political traditions, including an all-powerful czar. Muscovite monarchs ruled with an iron hand. Russian aristocrats—the oligarchs of another era—conversed in French while making countless Russian peasants into serfs, obliged to work eternally for great landowners. Russia's late-onset serfdom developed after serfs had mostly disappeared from the rest of Europe. At the same time, Russia's textile industry, using domestic cotton, flax, and wool, had expanded rapidly. So had a major coal-mining and steel-making region in eastern Ukraine, not then an independent country. An ambitious program of railway construction tried to knit together this contrasting mix of old and new. Still, a first crack in the autocratic edifice occurred in 1905, when Russian liberals won some representation in an elected legislature, the Duma. At the same time, socialist radicals began organizing local councils, called soviets, made up primarily of soldiers and industrial workers.

Russian losses in World War One undercut the czar's control of his empire. The liberals who replaced him soon lost control, as well. In February 1917, liberals from the Duma formed a provisional government, but socialist revolutionaries opposed them, cobbling their network of local soviets into a parallel power structure. The majority party in the soviets was the Bolshevik Party, led by the Marxist revolutionary Lenin. In October of the same year, following further war losses, Lenin and his Bolsheviks took power in an armed uprising, beginning the Russian Revolution. The new "red" Russian government pulled out of the war and defeated a challenge from a "white" Russian anti-socialist alliance of liberals and monarchists. In the early 1920s, the Bolsheviks began to consolidate a new Communist order. For the first time, Marxist revolutionaries had the chance to transform an entire society.

The hammer and sickle, symbol of the Russian Revolution, has become world famous. Together, the sickle for harvesting grain and the metalworker's hammer represented a desired alliance between peasants and industrial workers. Peasants and industrial workers were logical allies, in Bolshevik thinking, because both were victimized by capitalist exploitation. In practice, however, rural and urban workers tended to live in different worlds. In Russia and elsewhere, rural and urban people have normally found it difficult to make common cause. Tradition-minded Russian peasants tended to be quite conservative. Systematic requisitions of their harvests turned them against Bolshevik rule. Recognizing that the peasantry could be pushed too far, Lenin instituted a moderate New Economic Policy that allowed rural producers some freedom to market their own crops. But Lenin's death in 1924 left control of the Russian Revolution to Stalin, whose determination to reshape society knew no bounds. The great goal of all twentieth-century revolutionaries, once they had consolidated power, was to catch up industrially with the centers of world capitalism. It was a heavy lift.

Between 1927 and 1953, Stalin presided over a drastic attempt to minimize free market forces in Russian life. The alternative was a command economy, in which the state determined prices and wages and set production quotas. Unlike the utopian socialists, these Marxist revolutionaries had no qualms about industrialism. So long as factories were controlled by the state, meaning that they were collectively owned by the Russian people, mass production would benefit everyone. The people's collective ownership and benefit, however, turned out to be highly theoretical. Meanwhile, the sacrifices demanded by the revolutionary state were brutal and incessant. Workers sacrificed their health and safety (not to mention their free time) to meet arbitrary production quotas organized into ambitious five-year plans. The revolutionary state directed all possible resources to the construction of a new urban, industrial Russia. This was the command economy in action. Production soared. Educational opportunities expanded. Russia retained control of the sprawling land empire created under the czars, which stretched from Europe to the Pacific Ocean. Rather than an empire, it had theoretically become a voluntary confederation of equal partners, the Union of Soviet Socialist Republics, or USSR.

Meanwhile, the revolution failed miserably in the countryside. Stalin's five-year plans called for the creation of large collective farms, each bringing together dozens of peasant families. The collective farms would gain the advantages of scale associated with mechanization and modern, large-field agribusiness. Revolutionary farm laborers would theoretically work together in the spirit of joint ownership, believing that their efforts promised a better future for all the USSR's diverse peoples. But in practice the peasants were skeptical, especially the better off among them, and many resisted joining collective farms. Some even preferred to slaughter their livestock rather than turn it over to the Bolsheviks. Collectivization of agriculture proceeded anyway, though, and resistance to it was manifested in chronically inadequate harvests and dwindling herds. Still, Stalin wanted to export grain to pay for industrial machinery, leading peasants to hoard grain and officials to requisition it arbitrarily. The command economy again. The most devastated region was Ukraine, whose climate and soils made it naturally the USSR's breadbasket. During the 1920s and 1930s, famines in Ukraine killed millions of people.

Then came World War Two, which was fought mostly on Russian soil. Today, Russians remember the "Great Patriotic War" as their defining national experience. Stalin's factories proved equal to the test of industrial strength. The USSR's strategic depth ultimately turned the Nazi tide. The effort cost the lives of twenty million Russians. As a result, the now-socialist Russian Empire added new territory and extended its control over Eastern Europe. The Russian military-industrial complex was on a postwar roll. By 1950, Russian scientists had tested an atomic bomb, and in 1957 they launched the first manmade orbital satellite, *sputnik*. Soon they attempted the world's first manned space flight. Russia had become the leader of the socialist world, which had squared off against the liberal, capitalist "free" world in the Cold War. Russian science and industry competed successfully in a great arms race—the creation of atomic and then hydrogen bombs and delivery systems, including strategic bombers, nuclear submarines, and intercontinental ballistic missiles, all in just a few years. The creation of massive nuclear arsenals was an enormously costly undertaking. Only a few states ever tested a nuclear device, much less maintained intercontinental missiles and bombers at constant readiness, as occurred during the height of the Cold War. Envisioned by both sides as a global ideological contest, the Cold War was also a duel between two imperial powers, Russia and the United States.

What the USSR's revolutionary state never did—and could not afford to do during the Cold War—was satisfy the daily desires of Russian consumers. This was the Soviet Union's fatal flaw. Chronically inadequate housing, pervasive scarcities and rationing, eternal lines to buy a sausage or a loaf of bread—caused discontent among Russians who saw colorful advertisements of unprecedented consumer abundance in the postwar United States. Even relatively privileged professionals and managers in the Soviet Union did not enjoy the material wealth on display in Hollywood movies. When tensions in the political system led to restructuring in the 1980s, the urban people of the USSR quickly abandoned efforts towards socialist revolution. Their discontent seemed unanimous and overwhelming. No doubt it had been habitually concealed for decades in the wake of Stalinist purges. The Soviet Union dissolved without fighting in 1991, allowing its constituent republics—the Baltic states, Belorussia, Ukraine, Kazakhstan, and other Central Asia countries—to recover independent sovereignty in a matter of months.

At the time, there was surprisingly little resistance to the end of USSR. The Communists had totally transformed Russian life, but they had not instilled deep loyalty to their ideology, despite several generations of systematic indoctrination. Even during the subsequent transition to a market economy in the 1990s, when a handful of new capitalist oligarchs appropriated the lion's share of Russia's national wealth, few Russians wished to see the socialist system restored. In general, ex-Soviet citizens responded more to old-fashioned nationalism. When the USSR crumbled, people's main regret on the street in Moscow seemed to be the loss of the Russian Empire.

Whatever its idealistic goals, and despite its impressive achievements in science, industry, and the arts, the Russian Revolution had resulted in millions of unjustifiable deaths. The exact numbers of lives crushed by the revolutionary state cannot be established, but it is huge, numbering many millions. Stalin and his minions became arbiters of life and death, always in the name of the greater good, always in the name of "the People." Liberalism's individual rights and guarantees were totally absent under Communism. Government abuses were relentless, but this was not corruption in the old-fashioned sense—not, for the most part, a way for leaders to amass great fortunes. Instead, the principal abuses of power in the Soviet Union were the work of misguided ideologues who believed too much in their own ideals. Anyone who disagreed with them was "reeducated" or purged. The Great Purge of 1937, which victimized thousands, was one of countless such. The network of Siberian labor camps called the *gulag* had begun under the czars, but it radically expanded under

Soviet rule. The greatest work of anti-Soviet protest, *A Day in the Life of Ivan Denisovich*, was a narrative of gulag life from a prisoner's perspective. Stalin's cult of personality was supposed to give the revolution a human face, but it helped create the modern nightmare of "big brother" dictatorship.

As with colonial, slave-owning liberalism, revolutionary socialism in practice looked quite different from the theory. Communist dictatorship fell far short of its lofty goals. The Russian Revolution is only one case, of course. The military triumph of the Chinese Communist Party, beginning in 1948, inaugurated the second major case. Communist triumph in the world's most populous country, just as the USSR was acquiring nuclear weapons, seemed a major advance for the Marxist vision of world revolution. The loss of China precipitated panic among world reactionaries.

The People's Republic of China

For China, the Communist takeover was the beginning of a world-class national recovery. After defeat, humiliation, and partition by outsiders, followed by the 1912 Qing collapse, the world's greatest remaining traditional empire had dwindled into a failed state for a couple of decades.

A Chinese republic was proclaimed, but centralized governance effectively vanished, leaving real political control in the hands of regional warlords. Meanwhile, Japanese imperialists occupied more and more of eastern China economically and militarily. In 1931, the Japanese annexed Manchuria, the Qing homeland, which had been ruled from Beijing for several centuries. Manchuria was resource-rich and had seen significant industrialization in recent decades. Surpassing the concessions that had been imposed on China by the other imperial powers, Japan became the most aggressive invader of all.

Various political projects were swirling in the air of 1920s China. Significant industrialization was taking place in coastal cities, most especially in Shanghai and Guangzhou. In coastal China, a Nationalist party arose—the Guomindang. Its ideology was somewhat liberal and basically friendly toward the West. The Nationalist leader was (like Sun Yat-Sen) a man from Guangdong, Chiang Kai-Shek, whose salient skill was bending regional warlords to his purposes. Opposing the Guomindang was the Chinese Communist Party under its eventual supreme leader Mao. Mao was a provincial idealist who had been inspired by the May Fourth Movement and the Russian Revolution. While Chiang Kai-Shek was trying to cobble together a government that could interact with warlords and imperial powers, Mao began organizing peasant soviets in the countryside. According to Marxist theory and the Russian experience of a few years earlier, Communist revolutions were supposed to begin among industrial workers.

Chinese revolutionaries, however, got their first secure toehold among peasants.

The Communists and the Nationalist disliked each other almost as much as they disliked the Japanese. Nonetheless, when the Japanese invaded the Chinese mainland in the 1930s, Communists and Nationalist allied to resist the invaders. The Guomindang had the support of the United States, naturally, given Chiang Kai-Shek's pro-capitalist, pro-US attitudes. In addition, Chiang and his wife were Christians, which also helped attract US sympathies. Despite the supposed Nationalist-Communist truce, Nationalist troops continued to attack Communist strongholds in the countryside, forcing Mao's revolutionaries to make their celebrated long march, a strategic retreat of several thousand miles into the remote backcountry of northwest China. Meanwhile, the Nationalists received significant wartime support from the United States and, at the time of the Japanese surrender, the United States further aided Chiang's efforts to finish off Mao's Communists. But it was not to be. After the Japanese withdrawal, the People's Liberation Army decisively defeated the Guomindang. Chiang's forces then fled mainland China to the island of Taiwan—still, with US encouragement, refusing to accept defeat. On Taiwan, the Guomindang established a would-be government in exile that entitled itself the Republic of China but actually governed only the island. Thanks to continuing US favor, the Taiwan-based Guomindang occupied China's seat on the United Nations Security Council for more than twenty years. Meanwhile, in fact-based reality, the Chinese Communist Party governed the world's largest sovereign state, the People's Republic of China, starting October 1, 1949.

This was only the beginning of the Chinese Revolution. An actual revolution, in Communist terms, was not simply seizing control but also transforming society. It was not to be a minor transformation, not merely an ad hoc repair to an existing social edifice. Communist revolutionaries planned demolition, redesign, and rebuilding from the ground up. In the 1950s and 1960s, a generation after the Soviet Union, the People's Republic of China entered the redesign phase. Chinese revolutionaries wanted to rewrite all the rules, dethrone the old ruling class, accelerate industrialization, completely reorganize agriculture, even retool human behavior. They believed that true socialists must be idealists who put society's needs before their individual ambitions. True socialists should not work for their own gain. Instead, they should devote most of their efforts to the common good. The revolution's main practical undertakings were the collectivization of agriculture and an all-out drive to jumpstart heavy industry. Success or failure rested on a radical attempt to remake Chinese life. The revolutionaries broke up large landholdings and then created enormous collective farms. They encouraged people to try to smelt iron in their backyards and then built gargantuan industries run by the army. The revolutionaries launched one personal/ethical/social improvement program after another, campaigns to make everyone more serious and honest, less selfish, more public spirited. The exemplar to be imitated was found in the *Diary of Lei Feng*, a young revolutionary who thought only of the party and the People, never of himself. This utterly selfless behavior is understandable because, by all appearances, Lei Feng didn't really exist, his diary being an idealized creation of revolutionary propagandists.

Just as had happened in the Soviet Union, Communist efforts to change human nature produced limited success. All the practical innovations that depended on making people better failed conspicuously. The so-called Great Leap Forward produced a famine that, in the early 1960s, claimed the lives of many millions. The collectivization of agriculture was a debacle, just as it had been in the Soviet Union, and the incessant campaigns of moral uplift were spectacularly unedifying. In the mid-1960s, after the famine precipitated by the Great Leap Forward, Mao inaugurated a last-ditch attempt to transform Chinese society and wipe away all traces of corrupt, old-style, traditionalist and capitalist thinking. Because all previous attempts had failed, he appealed now to students, asking them to discipline their elders and root out stubborn corruption and old-style thinking. The new targets, sadly, were the first-generation of revolutionaries who, in Mao's eyes, had strayed from the righteous path. This was the Cultural Revolution, in which frantic crowds of students made their teachers wear dunce caps. Many committed revolutionary veterans were publicly disgraced and then imprisoned or exiled to the countryside to learn simple virtues from the peasantry. Mao's attempt to reach out to the people directly produced another cult of personality—the proliferation of his image, the dissemination of his ideas to everybody in a famous little red book.

On the other hand, Chinese leaders had regained control of their own country after a century of outside intervention. In a few more decades, China would recover its long-lost prominence in world affairs. Meanwhile, the whole world had become embroiled in the ideological conflict between Liberalism and Communism, which was also a conflict between two new-style empires that exercised global power without establishing colonies.

Cold War Battles

The nuclear arms race between the Soviet Union and the United States characterized the Cold War, but large, permanent deployments of Russian and US armed forces also confronted one another in post-

World War Two Europe. The US government opposed revolutionary change in principle and interpreted Marxist ideas anywhere as evidence of Russian meddling. Meanwhile, US multinational corporations expanded globally, and Marxism became a standard element of revolutionary movements throughout the decolonizing world. The stage was set for conflict.

Marxism was then arriving at an apogee of world influence. The Soviet victory over Hitler had been followed by Soviet occupation of Eastern Europe, by Soviet detonation of an atomic device, by the triumph of the Chinese Communist Party, and finally, by various Soviet "firsts" in the space race. For the most part, however, Marxist influence did not radiate from the USSR or the People's Republic. Instead, revolutionary decolonizers (of different stripes) adopted Marxism because it served their own purposes. Marxism aligned them with a powerful global cause. Disappointingly for needy world revolutionaries, they received little material aid from the USSR or the People's Republic. Russia could project military power internationally, but its capacity to offer economic aid was strictly limited. An undeveloped China could do nothing to help revolutionary allies far from its borders. Still, writers, intellectuals, and artists in the developing world found inspiration in the idea of social revolution. Marxism offered a persuasive rationale for rebellion against a liberal, capitalist power structure, and World War Two had established such a power structure globally. At its apex was the United States, which had emerged from the war incomparably stronger, in economic terms, than any other country. That is why the United States could attempt to "contain" socialist revolutionaries worldwide. International containment of socialism was the official policy of all US governments for decades.

Perhaps more than ever before in world history, the dueling great powers of the Cold War projected their imperium ideologically as leaders of opposing causes. American leaders talked about defending freedom and democracy everywhere. Russian leaders talked about supporting the uprisings of oppressed people anywhere. Both modern empires exercised a self-serving sway over other countries, but without formally colonizing them. Both were, in fact, idols with feet of clay, many of whose actions belied their idealistic claims. Each responded above all to its own national and imperial interests. The USSR wanted to maintain control over the Asian territories that it had inherited from the czars, also over the countries of Eastern Europe that had been occupied by the Red Army at the end of World War Two. Soviet territorial imperialism didn't advance much further than that, however. The American empire was more modest in formal, territorial terms. After the war, Americans even relinquished US control of the Philippines in an explicitly anti-imperialist gesture. American empire was embodied less in specific colonies than in American hegemony worldwide. Multinational corporations headquartered in the United States began, during the 1950s and 1960s, to accelerate their postwar march around the globe. After World War Two, the United States assumed the place formerly occupied by Great Britain at the center of international affairs militarily, economically, and culturally. There was heady talk about an American Century.

The Cold War was cold in the sense that it included little or no direct combat between the United States and the Soviet Union. It was a war because of its scope and deadly seriousness. The creation of vast arsenals of nuclear weapons permanently targeted on major population centers, ready to be launched at a moment's notice, constituted the most costly and ominous arms race ever. It was a war, moreover, because both sides formulated their struggle as an irreconcilable clash of ideologies, with the fate of the world hanging in the balance. Both ruled out compromise on principle. It was a war, finally, because proxies representing the United States and the Soviet Union *were* involved in physical combat.

Africans, Asians, and South Americans, socialist revolutionaries without any direct connection to the USSR, and on the other side, army and police officers of anti-Communist governments supported by the United States—these were the actual combatants of the Cold War. They fought battles sporadically and indecisively from the

1950s to the 1980s. There were also several full-scale shooting wars fought partly by third-party surrogates.

The Korean War (1950–1951) was the first such. Destruction of the Japanese Empire, which had annexed Korea, put that suffering country up for grabs after World War Two. Two Korean forces that had resisted the Japanese occupation now competed for control of an independent Korea. Some were Communists with links to China, others were anti-Communists with links to the United States. Korea was divided into north and south as a temporary measure, but the struggle continued. The Korean War developed into a conventional hot war involving large armies on both sides. The United States, officially acting in the name of the United Nations, led an international "police action" to contain the Communists. It was a US initiative, though, and the troops representing the UN were largely US soldiers. On the other side, the fledgling People's Republic of China unofficially sent large numbers of troops to help the Communists. The Korean War reached a stalemate within two years, the fighting stopped without a formal peace treaty, and South Korea became, and remained for decades, a permanent US military outpost.

French Indochina—which is to say, Vietnam—became the scene of the most significant Cold War battle, and it was a hot one. The Japanese had occupied the French colony during World War Two: one empire poaching colonies from another. After Japan's defeat, France reasserted its imperial control, but it encountered staunch, ultimately successful, nationalist resistance. The leader of this independence movement was Ho Chi Minh, who had become a Marxist while studying in France during the 1920s. By 1954, Ho's followers had defeated the French colonizers and taken control of northern Vietnam. The US oversaw a north-south partition, as in Korea, erecting a liberal, capitalist regime in southern Vietnam. But without outside support, an independent South Vietnam could not compete. Whereas North Vietnam was the product of a successful nationalist uprising, South Vietnam was the product of US intervention. Elec-

tions to reunite Vietnam were scheduled, but—given the clear like-
lihood of a popular victory for Ho Chi Minh—never held in the
south. So, during the late 1950s and early 1960s, North Vietnam
conducted a guerrilla war against the south, which continued to
receive US support, advisors, and, by 1964, combat troops. Although
North Vietnamese soldiers were involved, most of the combatants on
the Communist side were lightly armed peasants. On the other side
were the well-armed troops, helicopter fleets, and strategic bombers
of the world's premier military power. US officials explained that a
victory anywhere in the world might give dangerous momentum to
Communism—the slippery-slope logic of containment. The Vietnam
War became an international symbol, one generally unflattering to
the anti-Communist cause. The massive bombing of North Vietnamese cities, using more tonnage than all of World War Two's myriad
bombing campaigns put together, failed to defeat the Vietnamese revolutionaries. The lightly armed peasants not only survived, but they
also emerged victorious from the clouds of napalm and defoliant.

Cold War battles were fought completely by proxy in Africa,
where neither Russians nor Americans ever ventured. Most African
countries had decolonized quickly, early in the Cold War, but there
were some exceptions. The older European "possessions" proved
harder to liberate than those acquired in the 1880s scramble to colonize Africa. Algeria, a white settler colony that had been granted the
status of "overseas France," theoretically equivalent to French provinces in Europe, was decolonized by a prototypic, socialist-inspired
National Liberation Front in a bitter 1954–1962 war. In the far south
of Africa, European dominion had been more firmly implanted than
anywhere else outside of Algeria. Rhodesia, a colony named for its
English founder, had a large white settler population that took the
precaution of leading the nation into independence under a new,
appropriately African name, Zimbabwe. It then faced two revolutionary challenges, one affiliated with the USSR and one with China.
In 1980, Zimbabwe became a socialist state.

Africa's two major Portuguese colonies, Angola and Mozambique also felt the nationalist breezes of 1960, when more than a dozen African nations became independent all at once. The right-wing Portuguese dictator Salazar held out militarily against decolonization, however. Not until he was overthrown in 1974 did the Portuguese government accept the independence of Angola and Mozambique. Nationalist movements that had been formed to fight the Portuguese struggled among themselves for almost two decades in both Angola and Mozambique. To help define the outcome, the United States supported two armed groups in Angola. Notably, revolutionary Cuba sent soldiers to fight on the other side in Angola, its outstanding international venture of the Cold War.

Latin America was another principal venue of Cold War struggle. In Latin America, the Cold War manifested differently, however. Latin America comprised a score of nation-states from the first wave of world decolonization. Yet much had *not* been accomplished, in terms of national consolidation, since their wars of independence in the 1820s. In some ways, the end of Spanish and Portuguese imperial control had left Latin America's majority populations of dark-skinned people internally colonized by their own lighter-skinned ruling classes. Here's the background relevant to understanding how Latin America became a major Cold War battleground.

Latin America remained, in some ways, one big plantation. Only a few of the largest countries had industrialized, and those, only partially. After a hundred years of rule by the landowning classes, populist leaders with an urban, working-class base had come on the scene in the 1930s and 1940s, notably in Brazil and Argentina. Overall, however, the region's main connection to the international market was still the exportation of food and raw materials. Poor and oppressed peasantries composed the brunt of national populations in many countries. Meanwhile, weak Latin American states had offered rich opportunities to international capital. As the local contacts of visiting gringo entrepreneurs, Latin American elites cooperated and profited richly. European and US businessmen found elite families (who staffed the weak states as administrators, lawmakers, and judges) reassuringly white and hospitable, overall. Bright visions of modernization animated many, but the results were never beneficial for Latin American majorities.

Cold War ideologies put Latin America fully in play. The USSR was remote and disconnected from the region. Revolutionary socialism never became a majority persuasion there, far from it. Yet Marxism provided both a common cause and a compelling explanation of Latin American realities. Harsh class exploitation, cozy alliances between local oligarchs and foreign imperialists—these commonplaces of Marxist rhetoric truly resembled Latin America. Latin American intellectuals, artists, and university students frequently adopted Marxist attitudes during the Cold War. It was easy for them to view the United States as an imperialist foe. For a century, the people of the United States had treated Latin Americans with explicitly racist disdain. Until the 1930s, when it adopted a Good Neighbor Policy in preparation for a world war, the United States had scornfully invaded and occupied small Caribbean nations to "police" them for the benefit of outside creditors. Several small states, such as Nicaragua, Haiti, and the Dominican Republic, were deposited by US marines in the hands of reliably pro-US dictators who abused their countries for decades with US backing. After World War Two, US policy makers wanted Latin America to go back to its pre-1930s economic role, trading food and raw materials for manufactured goods. Latin American nationalists, in contrast, wanted to industrialize. The response was an overall anti-American atmosphere that facilitated an embrace of revolutionary socialism.

Modern socialist ideas had first entered Latin America with the Mexican Revolution of 1910–1920, a pivotal event. Afterward, an avowedly socialist and revolutionary, anti-imperialist party, the PRI (for Institutional Revolutionary Party), ruled Mexico for the rest of the 1900s. PRI imagery presented the revolution as the true decolonization of Mexico, the triumph of indigenous and racially mixed Mexicans over the legacy of Spanish conquest. This was mostly rhetoric, a matter of nationalist slogans and images of mustachioed equestrian heroes like Emiliano Zapata and Pancho Villa. In truth, the Mexican Revolution did not remake society, but it did revolutionize the country's public culture. Zapata and Villa became official national heroes. Some farmland was distributed to the landless, in the form of village common lands to be worked cooperatively, an experiment in collective agriculture not unlike those then occurring in the USSR. In 1938, the PRI expropriated the country's oil industry, creating a precedent that major Latin American countries would eventually follow. PRI Mexico welcomed left-wing refugees, among them revolutionaries like Leon Trotsky and, later, writers like Gabriel Garcia Marquez. Consequently, during the Cold War, the USSR treated Mexico as a socialist sister state, refusing to aid any insurgent groups that opposed the PRI.

Latin American labor movements were notable players in the Cold War. In Brazil, Getulio Vargas brought his country into the age of heavy industry, put labor politics at the center of his winning coalition, and then committed suicide in 1954 amid a storm of controversy. Juan and Eva Peron won the undying love of Argentina's urban workers and the hatred of its ruling classes. Both Vargas and Peron rejected the socialist label and had no objection to capitalism, but their appeal to workers marked them as "pink," if not red, in the eyes of US policymakers. The movements created by Vargas and Peron at mid-century joined revolutionary socialist currents during the Cold War. All the major Latin American countries had politically potent labor movements.

Meanwhile, the United States incorporated Latin American armed forces into a permanent postwar military alliance. All the countries of Latin America had become US allies during World War Two. A 1948 Rio Pact kept the wartime alliance ongoing. It remained in place even as many of the region's elected governments gradually became antagonistic to the United States in the 1950s and 1960s. US trainers imbued allied Latin American army officers with their stark Cold War vision of a worldwide struggle to contain Communism. Latin American militaries found themselves on the front lines of the struggle. US forces, for their part, would stop Soviet tanks and bombs, explained the trainers. The Cold War mission of Latin American militaries was to police their own countries' universities, labor movements, and poor neighborhoods, to root out socialist revolutionaries before they became strong enough to endanger the free world. US military aid included antipersonnel weapons and training in "enhanced interrogation techniques," still known as torture at the time, to extract information from captured urban guerrillas whose only defense was secrecy. Informed of these unsavory details, US officials were publicly shocked, *shocked*—and denied it was happening.

Each of Latin America's Cold War battles reflected the experience of a particular country, but the basic patterns repeated themselves. In 1954, Guatemala's reformist socialist government was the first to be overthrown by its own US-trained military. The overthrow was orchestrated by the CIA, which armed and launched a special Guatemalan proxy force for the task. Among the international socialist revolutionaries who fled to Mexico from Guatemala was a young Argentine physician who had been helping organize the Guatemalan land reform. This was Che Guevara, whose countenance became an international icon of revolution. In Mexico, Che met Fidel Castro, a Cuban law student and revolutionary leader who was then exiled in Mexico after a failed attempt to overthrow the US-supported Cuban government. Before the 1950s were over, Che and Fidel had gathered a few dozen like-minded young Cubans, invaded the island using an old yacht named the Granma to launch their pinprick assault, created a "liberated territory" in eastern Cuba, marched west to defeat the dictator's army, and, amazingly, entered Havana victorious on New Year's Day, 1959.

The Cuban Revolution was Latin America's greatest socialist experiment, lionized by the Left, vilified by the Right. It was Communist and truly revolutionary. Cuban revolutionaries drove out the former ruling class, collectivized agriculture, abolished private ownership of land (and all real estate), and eliminated the private sector altogether. They made showcase advances in education and public health. Che Guevara envisioned a new, less selfish sort of person—a New Man—the kind of socialist citizen needed to make the new system work. The Cubans emphasized voluntarism and high production goals as methods of socialist self-improvement, just as Chinese revolutionaries were also doing during the 1960s. Overall, their economic program failed, but aid from the USSR kept the Cuban state afloat. Soviet involvement was immeasurably greater in Cuba than elsewhere in Latin America. In response, a CIA proxy force of Cuban dissidents was armed and trained in south Florida and launched, unsuccessfully, onto Cuban beaches at a place called the Bay of Pigs in 1961. To prevent a second attempt, Cuban revolutionaries invited the placement of nuclear-armed Soviet missiles on the island, but these were removed after the tense 1962 US-Soviet standoff called the Cuban missile crisis, probably the closest that the world has come, so far, to a nuclear exchange. The Cubans encouraged the organization of like-minded guerrilla movements in other Latin American countries, but Cuba never intervened in them directly.

Meanwhile, as had occurred initially in 1954 Guatemala, a series of US-supported military takeovers toppled non-Communist constitutional governments that US policymakers nonetheless considered too "pink." One of these was the government of Brazil, whose president was a political heir of Vargas. The 1964 Brazilian coup that overthrew him was organized by Brazilian and US officers who enjoyed a close working relationship in their permanent military alliance. The US ambassador to Brazil was one member of this fraternity. The new de facto military president of Brazil was another. The coup installed a right-wing Brazilian military regime that ruled for two decades by decree, while maintaining constitutional appearances, repeating mantras of national greatness, and constructing some of the world's largest hydroelectric dams. Argentina's military likewise governed that country during most of the Cold War, worried that free elections would inevitably favor Peron. Peron was no Communist, but his sway among working class Argentines reeked with revolutionary potential. The anti-insurgency "dirty war" waged by the US-backed Argentine military was the region's worst political violence in the late twentieth century.

The dirty war—which affected Argentina, Brazil, Uruguay, and Chile—was the way that the armed forces of these countries fulfilled their alliance with the United States. The dirty war involved death squads, normally police or soldiers out of uniform who executed student leaders or union organizers considered intolerably "pink." Death squads "policed" universities, labor unions, poor neighborhoods, to destroy socialist revolutionaries "unofficially." To do so, they violated their own laws and made *disappeared* into a transitive verb. Soldiers in plain clothes snatched their victims without explanation, simply "disappearing" them, in what became common parlance.

Those forcibly disappeared were taken from their beds (the famous "midnight knock on the door") or perhaps pushed into a waiting car as they left their places of study or employment, and never heard from again. Frantic family visits to the police station were fruitless. No, I'm sorry, there was no record of an arrest. Reports could be filed, but investigations went nowhere. Meanwhile, the disappeared loved ones were being interrogated under torture on a military base, using a variety of ghoulish enhanced techniques. Who were their contacts? Where were they hiding? The interrogators commonly concealed their gross violations of basic human rights by executing their informants after torturing them. And as if that weren't dirty enough, the children of murdered mothers were sometimes adopted by their murderers.

The dirty war was a response to urban guerrillas whose one advantage was their hidden proximity to targets. In urban environments, they could kidnap and ambush agents of state power with ease. The Tupamaro guerrillas of Uruguay offered an emblematic example. Tupamaros once kidnapped an industrialist "class enemy" for abusing his workers, and then, following protests in the newspapers, kidnapped a cardiologist to take care of his heart condition. They kept "the people's prisoners" (including a US counterinsurgency instructor) in a hidden underground cell in a residential district of the capital. Eventually, however, systematic interrogation (under various forms of psychological and physical torture) broke the secrecy of urban guerrilla organizations and destroyed them, with death tolls in the tens of thousands. The dirty war was a win for repressive military governments and for the US administrations that aided and abetted them. For its idealistic young victims, it was a nightmare.

Chile's dirty war was unleashed after the 1973 overthrow of its socialist president Salvador Allende. Allende had been democratically elected in 1970. Chile's constitutional tradition was the strongest in the region. Allende's government was not Communist, but it certainly was revolutionary. After two tempestuous years in power, Allende's coalition gained strength in the midterm elections. A US-backed military coup soon followed, and the revolutionary president died under attack by his own armed forces. Revolutionary supporters of the Allende government were rounded up and imprisoned, then often tortured and murdered, their deaths denied and their corpses disposed of secretly. The new military government enjoyed strong support from the United States, and it invited economists from the University of Chicago to advise it on how to reestablish a free market economy. The protracted Chilean residency of the Chicago Boys, as the new economic team became known, confirmed the victory of the liberal right over the socialist left in Cold War South America.

Latin America's last spate of Cold War conflicts occurred in 1980s Central America, specifically in Nicaragua, El Salvador, Guatemala, and Honduras. After long years of insurgency, rural guerrillas managed to overthrow Nicaragua's US-supported oligarchy in 1979. The revolutionary Sandinistas took their name from a Nicaraguan nationalist leader who had fought the US marines in the 1920s. They planned a mixed economy and the normal panoply of social-improvement campaigns, but the concerted attack of US proxies kept the Sandinistas absorbed in a defensive war until they were voted out of office in 1989. During the same decade, Salvadoran socialist revolutionaries were defeated by a government closely allied to the United States. The right-wing adversaries of Central American revolutionaries were hailed as freedom fighters by right-wing Republicans in the United States. At one point, these so-called freedom fighters publicly gunned down the archbishop of San Salvador, an outspoken critic of death squads, as he was saying mass. The Christian Democratic government of El Salvador had managed to quell the socialist uprising, but it had abandoned the moral high ground. Shortly after the Nicaraguan revolutionaries laid down their arms, Salvadoran voters elected a socialist president.

Europe saw little violent conflict during the Cold War. The presence of the USSR's army kept Eastern Europe securely in the Russian orbit for forty years after World War Two. Attempts to loosen the Soviet grip got smacked down in Hungary (1956) and Czechoslovakia (1968). Meanwhile, in Western Europe, disgruntled voters were lured away from left-wing temptations by the world's most famous foreign aid program, the Marshal Plan, in which the United States rebuilt the industrial capacity of former World War Two adversaries to shore up the NATO alliance against the USSR.

Cold war confrontations in Europe were dramatic, symbolic, and highly visible. Massed tank battalions faced each other in a Germany divided, as Korea and Vietnam had been, into socialist vs. liberal republics. The so-called Iron Curtain descended across the European continent from north to south, dividing socialist republics from liberal ones. Travel across the dividing line was not frequent. A miniature version of the Iron Curtain, called the Berlin Wall, sliced through the middle of the eponymous German city. East German soldiers shot anyone attempting to cross it. And then, one of the two great adversaries simply collapsed.

During the 1980s, Russian leaders, notably the young Soviet president Mikhail Gorbachev, began a process of political opening (*glasnost*) and restructuring (*perestroika*) that encountered great readiness among the Soviet elite and soon led to the unraveling of the USSR, as its constituent republics severed ties with each other. In 1991, the Union of Soviet Socialist Republics rapidly dissolved. The socialist republics of Eastern Europe, dominated by Russia throughout the Cold War, found themselves without Russian overlords. Poland, Czechoslovakia, Hungary, and East Germany underwent "color revolutions," spontaneous popular uprisings of multitudinous street demonstrators who signaled their unanimity with a particular color or garment. Socialist revolutionaries around the world lost faith in the promise of a revolutionary future. Many laid down their arms. China, too, had lost faith in the promise of revolution. As the USSR crumbled, the Chinese Communist Party maintained control by opening the People's Republic economically to the capitalist world market while maintaining an authoritarian hardline internally.

SOCIALISM HAD NOT DISAPPEARED from the world, but for a moment it almost seemed so. The Cold War was over, and liberalism had won. Or was it capitalism that had won? The official ideology of the United States of America, which regarded itself as the Cold War victor, emphasized liberty, pluralism, individual rights, constitutional government, *and* unfettered consumer capitalism. But it was really consumer abundance—food, clothing, housing, automobiles, electronic devices—that had won the battle for hearts and minds globally. After the Cold War, the world market in consumer goods spread everywhere.

Liberty, pluralism, individual rights, and constitutional government . . . not so much.

CHAPTER FIFTEEN

Redux

The collapse of the USSR in 1991 had been preceded by other sudden and dramatic events, such as mostly peaceful anti-Communist uprisings in Poland and Hungary—also by the spontaneous opening of the Berlin Wall, the most striking visual symbol of the Cold War's end. Given the steady movement toward pragmatic market liberalization in China, the other chief center of the socialist world, Marxism appeared not merely defeated, but also disavowed by its former adherents. With impressive fervor, post-Communist societies cast aside revolutionary symbols and aspired to join an international capitalist consumer culture.

Liberalism had triumphed, and the world's century-long ideological contest had been resolved, or so it seemed, by the decisive defeat of socialism. For a few years, some observers spoke of the "end of history," believing the outcome to be definitively established. Cold War victory leant grand prestige to the United States, long the global champion of liberalism, and now, the one remaining superpower. But it was the military and economic might behind global capitalism that had overwhelmed the USSR. The liberalism that emerged seemingly triumphant was a zealous, fundamentalist variety: *neoliberalism*. Neoliberalism focused almost entirely on promoting free-market economics. Neoliberals believed that the hidden hand of the market could do no wrong. They believed that *anything* the state did, the market could do better, and, given their economic focus, "better" always meant less expensively. Consequently, neoliberals wanted to privatize many functions once reserved to the national state. Priceless values like social justice and equality got lost in the shuffle. Prisons for profit, "privatized" social security systems, mercenary "security contractors" in war zones—these were neoliberal-style innovations. In the neoliberal playbook, economic objectives trumped political ones every time. Unconstrained, consumer-driven capitalism was the neoliberals' universal model, and promoting it was the relentless focus of the one remaining superpower. After the Cold War, during the 1990s, when no significant military rivals remained standing, the United States spent more on its armed forces than the rest of the world combined.

Meanwhile, political liberalism withered away in the post-Cold War world. The attempt to create more inclusive and equitable societies had gone out of style. The Russia that emerged after 1991, its tricolor national flag replacing the red banner of Communism, fervently embraced capitalism but remained deeply authoritarian. China's rapid industrialization for the world market also occurred without significant political liberalization. Nor did equality, democracy, social justice, minority rights, or the rule of law thrive overall in the post-Cold War world. Instead, authoritarianism increased across the board, and divisive ethnic or racial nationalism, globally disgraced since the defeat of Nazism, prominently reemerged in country after country, mostly notably in India, soon to become the world's most populous country. The only liberty that expanded worldwide was that of the market. Chronic, systematic abuse of the poor and powerless majority remained a routine global reality at the dawn of the twenty-first century. What did thrive was consumer-driven capitalism. After the Cold War, the world market expanded and intensified for three decades in a process popularly called globalization.

Globalization

Globalization was a new term but not a new phenomenon. It accelerated and intensified a process that had begun centuries ago, when

Europeans established a world economy. The Industrial Revolution had intensified economic integration in the 1800s and early 1900s, until a tenth of world production was traded internationally. That process had stalled in the 1930s when a global financial crisis severely damaged the international trading system and various empires formed closed trading spheres. Multinational corporations expanded after World War Two, but Cold War rivalries continued to constrain globalization until the 1990s. Then the global triumph of capitalism opened the floodgates. Soon, a quarter of all global trade was international.

The end of the Cold War allowed the profitable exploitation of new resources. Neoliberals held that private ownership and management are more efficient, inherently better, than public ownership and management. This ideology was applied internationally by the World Bank and the International Monetary Fund, two lending organizations that, along with the United Nations, stood at the center of the postwar liberal order. The World Bank and the IMF urged developing countries to privatize state-owned enterprises and minimize government social programs. Often, this was a prerequisite for their loans or aid. Privatization and government austerity (i.e., limiting subsidies and social programs) were guidelines of what was called the Washington Consensus. In post-Communist states, privatizing meant, in practice, auctioning national resources to the highest bidder or, as often happened in practice, to cronies of the auctioneers. The results were normally regrettable. In the former USSR, a new class of ultra-rich oligarchs emerged in close association with the authoritarian state. The world economy benefited, and the World Trade Organization, formed in 1995 (to replace a relatively weak anti-tariff General Agreement on Tariffs and Trade) tried to prevent member states from regulating the free market in any way, anywhere in the world.

Several technological developments also accelerated globalization in the 1990s and afterward. One was the increasing containerization of maritime shipping, which carried the enormous bulk of international trade. Previously, ships' holds had been loaded object by object, crate by crate, barrel by barrel, but now goods moved in huge steel containers precisely fitted to tractor-trailer truck bodies or railroad boxcars, so that they could be transferred by crane from shore to ship, and from ship to shore. The increase in speed and volume, coupled with the reduction of costs at large-scale container ports, became crucial to international trade. Other late twentieth-century technological contributions to globalization were the expansion of commercial air travel, telecommunications, and the internet.

After World War Two, commercial air travel soared. The proliferation of wartime bombers had offered ready frames for postwar passenger airliners. In the 1950s, when trans-Atlantic passengers normally still crossed by sea, average middle-class people seldom traveled abroad for tourism or social reasons. Jet engines, with their greater speed and reliability, made the difference beginning in the 1960s. The creation of a worldwide commercial aviation network was an enormous task, involving much more than reliable aircraft. Most passengers, by far, were people of the global north, but the inexorable growth of the market led to increasing competition and economies of scale that drove down costs for everyone. By the 1980s, people were flying a trillion kilometers a year, and by 2016, seven trillion.

Other changes happened in telecommunications. Pre-World War Two had involved mostly stamps and letters, an occasional telegram—hopefully a radio in the living room, and in the most developed countries, a telephone for local calls. Back then, movie theaters frequently began their showings with a newsreel about international events, a way to be in touch with the wider world. Inexpensive television and easily portable transistor radios appeared in the 1950s and 1960s. Rapidly expanding broadcast media's incessant flow of advertisements contributed noticeably to the power of consumer marketing. In the 1990s, mobile telephones became a new consumer necessity. The cost of erecting transmission towers was low when compared with the expense of stringing and maintaining landlines. For this reason, cellular telephones proliferated in developing countries even faster than in developed ones. What used to be called long distance calling, formerly laborious and costly, became fantastically easier and more affordable. By early 2000s, consumers in developed countries could communicate casual salutations by handheld video phones between, say, a sidewalk cafe in Greece and a beach in Australia.

Finally, there was the creation of the internet and the World Wide Web. Computers and digital technology made them possible, along with fiber optic cables that gradually replaced the copper wiring of an earlier era. Electronic computers appeared in the 1950s, and construction of basic networking in the 1960s, but extensive use of personal computers did not begin until the 1980s. Around 2000, use of the internet became a normal part of life, even a central preoccupation, for people in the most developed countries. Global use was uneven, however—over 60 percent in rapidly developing countries, under 50 percent in much of the global south. Still, the internet contributed greatly to global connectivity, far more than television or the telephone had done.

Goods, capital, and labor all flowed around the world more freely than at any time since the 1920s, and in much greater volume. Social and cultural interconnections were less easily traced but tended to follow the flow of goods, capital, and labor. A global elite with easy access to imported consumer goods and global communications lived an international life. Before then, international lives had been sequential—a childhood in Italy, then an adulthood in the United States, for example, with perhaps one sentimental visit back to the "old country" following retirement. Now international lives were more simultaneous. A few people, a global elite, commuted to work between continents, maintaining homes in several countries, attempting international love affairs via internet. The feeling of global interconnectedness came also from increasing pan-global similarities. Consumer capitalism offered the same choices to the middle classes of Moscow, Mumbai, and Miami. Clothing styles, fast food, commercial architecture, music, and entertainment became noticeably more alike on all continents after 1990. Cultural ideas flowed in various directions, but, overall, the uniformity was based on western models.

Imported consumer goods, frequent air travel, and instantaneous global communications made the interconnected world exciting for many, but not for all—in fact, not even for most. Those who could approximate the lifestyle of middle-class people in the world's most prosperous countries may have been a tenth of the global population. Millions of others—another two tenths, say—could reasonably aspire for themselves or for their children to own a modest car someday, or at least, to shop the interconnected world market, and perhaps take an occasional family vacation. The other seven tenths were out of luck. They were not likely ever to approach the life of consumer bliss that pervasive media imagery dangled before their eyes. By boosting the power of world capitalism, globalization raised some living standards and many high hopes. Nonetheless, most income gains went to those already ahead, especially the millionaires. Successful professional families began to buy second and third houses, while homelessness also increased. In wealthy countries, like the United States, that had long enjoyed a high standard of living, the top 10 percent thrived, but a majority felt comparatively worse off. The impact was more positive in developing countries where previous living standards had been low, especially China, and India. Still, the overall picture worldwide was growing income inequality and disparities of wealth, even in rapidly industrializing China, where hope and optimism still reigned.

Successive international crises undermined the promise of globalization, as well. The international financial crisis of 2007–2008 led to a Great Recession in many countries around the world, which in turn contributed to a multiyear European Debt Crisis. New levels of interconnectedness meant that, whatever country sneezed, the whole world caught cold—or some kind of virus. During the coronavirus pandemic that began in 2019, that was not a metaphor. The first true global pandemic did more than undermine optimism. The physical disruption of trade and international travel, including container shipping and air travel, stopped globalization in its tracks, at least for a while.

Meanwhile, the political climate in many countries became more and more conflictive.

Conflict in the Contemporary World

Political conflict did not abate, and even seemed to intensify after the Cold War. Clearly, a clash of ideologies was not the cause. Instead, age-old ethnic and religious grievances came to the fore as "new" rallying cries. Nationalist ideology was dusted off and wheeled out to lend coherence and respectability to the bloodshed. The revival of religiously coded conflict was somewhat unexpected. Especially in Europe, religion had played a diminishing role in people's lives for a century. Europe's great historical churches were now full of tourists, not worshippers. During the post-World War Two era, social, political, economic, and cultural elites—in both the socialist and liberal blocs—believed that science and humanism would gradually replace ancient religions. How wrong they were!

Meanwhile, despite its supposed Cold War triumph, the liberal ideal of civic problem-solving lost ground, even in the world's most established electoral systems. The validity of elections themselves seemed widely imperiled as stresses mounted on liberal democracies. Ironically, in the so-called information age, the internet—especially social media—facilitated *dis*information, now a much-used political tool. Russian computer hackers showed, beginning in 2016, that they could influence other countries' elections through skillful disinformation. Only a small minority of voters gave probing, evidence-based consideration to *issues* such as health care or tax reform or global warming. Unable to evaluate the truth of such matters, upset and ill-informed people voted impressionistically. Unscrupulous leaders played on their fears and prejudices. As politicians vilified their adversaries, and social media amplified the vilification, common ground vanished. The trend was epitomized by the US Republican party's descent into Trumpism and election denial, but political dysfunction gradually threatened many of the world's strongest liberal democratic states.

Fear and rejection of immigrants became a nationalist motif in the United States and many European countries. The immigration phenomenon responded directly to on-going globalization. Long-distance migration was part of the growing global economic integration, also a predictable response to high hopes, rising inequalities, and climate change. But for beleaguered people in receiving countries, the arrival of many young, ambitious, racially diverse immigrants seemed threatening. In Europe, demagogic hatemongers made immigration anxieties a launching pad for new far-right nationalist parties. In the United States, demagogic hatemongers focused on building border walls and restricting voter access.

During the early twentieth century, nationalism had rallied colonized peoples around the world in confrontations against their colonizers. But the nationalist or religious appeals that proliferated in the early twenty-first century most often issued from the mouths of troubled fanatics and wannabe dictators heedless, in either case, of the consequences. World conflicts of the 1990s increasingly became straightforward, zero-sum contests between competing groups, however defined.

The first great post-Cold War crisis, a slaughter unlike anything seen there during the long imperial standoff between the US and USSR, happened in Europe. Nationalist and religiously oriented rhetoric formed the ideological soundtrack throughout. In 1991, post-Communist Yugoslavia exploded in civil war. Unlike the breakup of the Soviet Union that same year, the breakup of Yugoslavia surprised nobody. Since World War Two, Yugoslavia had been a multiethnic, civic nation defined by its socialist ideology. Communist partisans had won lasting respect by resisting Nazi occupation during World War Two. Afterward, the former partisan leader led a strongly united Yugoslavia. Yugoslavia was socialist, but it refused to join the Soviet bloc. Yugoslavia was also an ethnic and religious jigsaw puzzle. Serbians, who were Orthodox Christians, constituted the dominant group. Croats spoke the same language but were Catholics. Bosnians (who also spoke the same language) tended to be Muslims. Two other Yugoslav ethnicities, Slovenes and Macedonians, had contrasting languages. The country had been founded in 1918 as the Kingdom of Serbia, and ethnic Serbs lived throughout the country. In the late 1980s, as socialism entered its global eclipse, the country's Serbian leadership switched to nationalist rhetoric, and Yugoslavia quickly dissolved. By 1992, Slovenia, Croatia, Macedonia, and Bosnia had all broken away from Serbia, and the former Yugoslavia was replaced on the map by seven would-be mini-nation-states. The new national boundaries, as with the earlier India-Pakistan partition, resulted in bitter conflict along ethnic and religious lines. This is the conflict that put the term *ethnic cleansing* in our contemporary vocabulary as a synonym for mass murder.

Also in 1992, India experienced a violent outbreak of *communitarianism*, the Indian term for religiously coded identity politics. The violence destroyed an ancient mosque in the northern city of Ayodhya, not so far from Delhi, in what had been, a half millennium earlier, the Mughal heartland. The Babri mosque, as it was called, had been ordered built by the first Mughal emperor, Babur, and was named after him. It had very probably replaced an earlier Hindu temple on the same site. The Mughals were imperial conquerors, as we know, and replacing the temples of conquered people was standard imperial procedure. But its Mughal origins and mythical Hindu resonances made the Babri mosque a volatile political symbol. The Ramayana, the great quasi-scriptural Hindu narrative of which the Lord Rama is the protagonist, names Ayodhya as the birthplace of Rama. The Babri mosque was closed after India-Pakistan partition.

Communitarian politics troubled the Republic of India from day one. The conflicts worsened after the Cold War, when the Congress Party, which had governed India since independence (hoping for a civic nation, open to people of any creed) lost power. The clearly rising force in 1992 was Hindu nationalism. Even after partition hived off Pakistan (and Bangladesh), India had more Muslims than any other country, an enormous minority group that became the primary target for the nationalist agitation of the religious Hindutva movement. Hindutva defines India as an essentially Hindu ethnic nation, meaning Muslims cannot fully belong to it, even if their ancestors have lived there for ten generations and speak a language descended from Sanskrit. Local Hindu activists agitated against Muslim neighbors for eating beef and indignantly forbade the conversion of India's despised outcaste Dalits, the former so-called untouchables, to whom Islam offers greater dignity and social opportunity. Hindu nationalists formed the Bharatiya Janata Party, or BJP, and began to compete successfully at the national level. It was the BJP that called the faithful to a rally in Ayodhya that 150,000 attended, and during which, by previous arrangement, the police protecting the dilapidated monument fled for their lives, leaving the enraged multitude to level the centuries-old mud-brick structure in a few hours. The drama worked brilliantly to galvanize national support for the BJP. It also inspired Hindu nationalist copycat violence in many cities with large Muslim populations. In 2020, the BJP president personally laid the cornerstone of a new Hindu temple in Ayodhya.

In 1994, the African state of Rwanda, located in the continent's Great Rift Valley, apparent cradle of all humanity, erupted in mayhem. Tiny Rwanda has a jewel-like landscape, one of the most fertile and most densely populated in Africa. To explain the Rwandan Genocide will require a few words of background. For centuries, a people called Tutsi (whose king claimed the normal celestial connections) had lorded over a people called Hutu. Then Rwanda became part of German East Africa in 1885, and after the German defeat in World War One, Tutsis and Hutus were awarded to Belgium as an imperial prize. Both Germans and Belgians governed Rwanda through Tutsi kings. Everyone recognized, however, that the overwhelming Hutu majority would inevitably dominate a democratic Rwanda. When independence swept through central Africa in 1960, the Hutu declared a republic and overthrew the Tutsi ruling class. Hundreds of thousands of Tutsis fled the country. In exile, they formed an organization with a distinctly socialist sounding name, the Rwandan Patriotic Front. In 1990, the exiled Rwandan Patriotic Front reasserted itself militarily and, within a couple of years, made peace with the Hutu president. Then, "Hutu Power" militants, fearing a violent Tutsi comeback, engineered a sudden ethnic cleansing that slaughtered between a half and one million Tutsi victims.

Also in 1994 Africa, Nelson Mandela, the head of the African National Congress, was elected president of South Africa in the country's first multiracial elections. A life-long socialist revolutionary, Mandela had spent twenty-seven years as a political prisoner before becoming president. Formerly, independent South Africa had been best known for the comprehensive system of racial classification, segregation, and repression called apartheid. The apartheid system resembled a more thoroughgoing version of Jim Crow racial segregation that still existed (when apartheid was created in 1948) in the southern United States. Whereas the guideline "separate but equal" supposedly governed US segregation policies—according to segregationists, anyway—no pretense of equality had animated South African apartheid. Instead, the rationale of apartheid was straightforward white supremacy. Apartheid was how the white tenth of the population hoped to keep the other nine tenths working for them in good colonial style after independence. What kind of decolonization was this? No kind that the world could accept. In Nelson Mandela it recognized the leader of a righteous cause, and United Nations condemnation of apartheid helped speed its destruction even before Mandela's 1994 election, powered by old-style decolonizing nationalism.

Meanwhile, US nationalists were moving the opposite direction, toward a revival of white supremacist motifs. During the 1960s, police dogs and firehoses turned on peaceful black demonstrators had constituted an obvious Cold War embarrassment for a country that wanted to be seen as a beacon of social equality and liberal democracy. An antiracist consensus then ended segregation under the leadership of the US Democratic Party. The assassinated civil rights leader Martin Luther King became a street name and a national holiday. In reaction, the US Republican party began to build a new electoral base among the disgruntled whites who regarded civil rights as a matter of unwelcome government interference. As a result, during the 1970s and 1980s, the US South switched parties, becoming solidly Republican. Racial animus clearly drove this major US political realignment, as politicians increasingly catered to a politics of white grievance, competing to assure long prison sentences that filled US penitentiaries with black convicts. Meanwhile, immigration from Mexico supplied workers for jobs in US agriculture, construction, hotels, and restaurants. Immigrants became targets for scapegoating as demagogues promoted a vision of the United States as a white, Christian nation. By the 2010s, paramilitary militias had begun to espouse the new white nationalist cause and prepare for a race war.

Western Europe was experiencing a similar sort of anti-immigration backlash. It was simultaneously trying to move *beyond* nationalism by building a European Union. By 2002, the EU had its own currency, flag, and governing body. Europeans had begun to travel between countries with unprecedented ease. As everywhere, people migrated in the direction of prosperity. Young migrants traversed Europe from Poland or the former East Germany to the former West Germany or England, for example. Many young Europeans became consummate internationalists. At the same time, some of Europe's oldest consolidated nations, such as Spain and the United Kingdom, were threatened by internal movements for regional autonomy. Interestingly, these challenges came from submerged nationalisms like those of Catalonia and Scotland that now reasserted themselves.

The nationalist genie was stirring even within the European Union. An angry nationalist protest vote forced Britain's exit from the European Union, although so-called Brexit proved excruciating to carry out. Immigrants from outside Europe were a chief catalyst of rising nationalist resentment. As people migrated from Africa to France, from Turkey to Berlin, or from Latin America to Spain, many encountered an angry backlash. German, French, English, and other European cities accumulated large unassimilated immigrant populations. In addition to the normal pushback against immigration, Muslim immigrants encountered particular hostility, fueling Islamist resentment in poor immigrant neighborhoods of European cities.

On September 11, 2001, millions witnessed a world-altering drama live on television. The suicidal attack of Islamist terrorists heralded the new prominence of religiously coded political conflicts. For many in the United States, the attack seemed to come out of nowhere. In retrospect, however, the attack does not seem surprising. The 9/11 terrorist attack on the United States had been prefigured by a high-profile clash with Iran's Islamic Revolution.

Iran, let us remind ourselves, is the modern name of Persia. Iranians constructed the world's first great empire and dominated southwest Asia for more than two thousand years. Iran has not, however, been a world power since the Safavid Empire ended two-and-a-half centuries ago. A second reminder: The Safavids established Shi'a Islam—the Muslim world's scattered and perpetually oppositional minority creed—as their state religion. Unlike the rest of the Muslim world, Iran and next-door Iraq are majority Shi'a. Finally, the crucial backstory. In 1979, the king, or shah, of Iran was overthrown by an Islamic Revolution. The shah had been a Cold War–era US ally and became, to some degree, a creature of the CIA. Now the ayatollahs, religious leaders with black robes and long beards, steeped in scripture, ruled Iran. Their Islamic Revolution took over CIA headquarters in Teheran, held its staff hostage for 444 days, and generally introduced the world to a new political phenomenon. Islamism censored expression, dress, and behavior, forcing conformation to fundamentalist Muslim religious norms.

The advent of the Islamic Revolution frightened neighboring states with large Muslim populations. One was the USSR, which had occupied Afghanistan during the 1980s precisely to contain the spread of

Islamism. Local Islamists, the Afghan mujahedeen, fought a guerrilla war against Soviet occupation. Iraqi dictator Saddam Hussein likewise feared the Islamic Revolution. To prevent Islamist overtures to Iraq's Shi'a population, he attacked Iran. The Iran-Iraq War took a vast toll in blood and dragged on indecisively through the 1980s. The Islamic Revolution survived, and Islamism of one kind or another gained influence throughout the Muslim world.

By the beginning of the twenty-first century, the Muslim world—hugely diverse in culture, language, economy—accounted for roughly a quarter of global population, divided among forty-nine countries. In most Muslim-majority countries, Islam was the official religion. Several, most notably Iran and Saudi Arabia, formally declared themselves Islamic States. Indonesia and Turkey, large majority Muslim countries with officially secular states, experienced rising Islamist pressure. India had the largest Muslim population of any country, although still dwarfed by a multitudinous Hindu majority. Despite this political fragmentation, the community of all Muslim faithful, the ummah (which, significantly, can translate as nation in Arabic) provided a strong shared identity.

Imperial powers of European origin are often regarded as hereditary enemies in the Muslim world. After all, practically the entire Muslim world was once colonized by European powers. Additionally, there is a thousand-year history of conflict between Christians and Muslims (and Jews) still vivid in the thinking of Islamists, who make frequent mention of modern-day "crusaders." Therefore, Muslims across Africa and Asia tend to identify with the plight of stateless Palestinians in Israel and to regard harassment of Muslims anywhere as an attack on the global ummah. Moreover, contemporary globalization has exposed conservative Muslims, the clear majority, to a permissive, individualist consumerism that they regard as morally repugnant and corrosive to their traditions. Islamism finds its religious roots in austere teachings from the upland interior of Saudi Arabia, today commonly termed Salafism. Like Protestant Christian-

ity at its beginning, Salafism began as a back-to-basics religious purification movement. Modern Islamist militants tend to cultivate anger
toward both internal and external adversaries, whom they regard as
God's enemies.

The 9/11 attack on New York's World Trade Center was carried
out by Saudi-born Islamists. They represented a loosely coordinated
group of like-minded militants who made suicide attacks their signature strategy. While they might attack police or military targets,
suicide bombers wearing high-explosive vests frequently targeted
civilian populations in crowded markets or buses. Indiscriminate
slaughter of noncombatant "enemies" (*terrorism*, because it works
to create a climate of terror) had not affected Europe or the United
States very much since World War Two, when entire cities were obliterated in protracted bombing campaigns directed partly at civilian
populations. The 9/11 attack was the work of al Qaeda, a loosely
organized Islamist terror network that eventually had affiliates
throughout the Muslim world. Islamism gained global influence in
the early twenty-first century, thanks partly to encouragement from
Saudi Arabia, because the origins of modern Islamism are closely tied
to the history of Arabia's reigning Saud dynasty.

After 2000, Islamism became a potent political tool in states with
well-established electoral systems. Turkey, a majority Muslim state,
had been defined in strictly secular nationalist terms when, after
World War One, it was founded in the ruins of the Ottoman Empire.
The portrait of its founder, Ataturk, appeared everywhere, a sort of
secular icon. Turkey became a poster child that demonstrated the
transformational power of modern nationalism. Then, beginning in
2002, a highly popular president, with the support of religious Turks
in conservative areas distant from cosmopolitan Istanbul, moved
Turkey steadily toward Islamism. Paradoxically, to Western viewers,
majority rule began to make Turkey *less* liberal.

Meanwhile in Indonesia, which experienced a democratic opening
in 1998 after thirty-two years of military dictatorship, Islamist poli-

tics had a similar constricting impact. Muslims comprised almost 90 percent of the Indonesian population. After Dutch colonizers withdrew from Indonesia, political conflict had remained strictly secular and ideological. The country had been a Cold War flashpoint, long dominated by a pro-US dictator. But now Muslim votes went preferentially to well-organized, Saudi-educated Islamists. Some of them argued that non-Muslim Indonesians should be ineligible to hold political office.

A different sort of religious revival occurred in post-Communist Russia. Vladimir Putin's Leningrad reclaimed its czarist name, Saint Petersburg, as Orthodox churches, used as museums and auditoriums for several generations, filled again with incense. Meanwhile, Putin, a former agent of the KGB secret police, spoke softly, centralized power, kept the lion's share in his own hands, and shrewdly manipulated nationalist impulses. Putin railed against Muslim insurgents in Russian-controlled Chechnya, a part of the old czarist empire. Putin's critics were exiled, imprisoned, or murdered. Like populist strongmen elsewhere, Putin played on popular prejudices, such as anti-homosexuality, which dovetailed with his encouragement of Orthodox Christianity. The revival of Russian Orthodoxy was part of a larger nationalist package that included yearnings for lost greatness—and not merely rhetorical yearnings. Putin's military annexed various parts of the lost Russian Empire long before his full-scale invasion of Ukraine in 2021.

In Latin America, the post-Cold War moment brought a welcome end to ongoing conflicts. Pro-US military rulers went back to the barracks, and free elections produced a crop of US-educated presidents in the 1990s. Globalization was now the only game in town, so to speak, and Latin Americans aimed to play and win. They steered away from confrontation and eagerly surfed the internet. The region's religious energies (and its embrace of global influences) produced a steady growth of Pentecostalism among the poor. Prosperity gospel in Brazil promised worldly abundance in return for donations to prominent US-style televangelists. For a time, the region's major countries all seemed to have neoliberal presidents with MBA degrees.

Overall, the fruits of globalization were disappointing in Latin America, however. The middle classes grew and shopped the international market, but capitalism had never produced general prosperity in Latin America, and it didn't do so now. The largest profits to be made from globalizing the region's economies were always extractive—from mining and timber, for example—or associated with low-wage industries and export agriculture. By the early 2000s, the low-hanging fruit had been harvested, the region's economies struggled, and Latin American voters remembered why they used to prefer nationalists and socialists. So, during the first two decades of the new millennium, the nationalists and socialists returned to office—most notably in Chile, Colombia, and Brazil.

The new Latin American leaders were no longer revolutionaries of the old sort. Their socialist credentials, their past as guerrilla fighters and torture victims, supplied compelling personal narratives but did not limit their dealings with the World Bank, the International Monetary Fund, and the World Trade Organization. Despite many continuities, democratic socialism now clearly upstaged the old revolutionary kind on the Latin American left. Meanwhile, the socialists' adversaries often aped US-style right-wing populism, founded on media-savvy vested interests and religiously derived cultural conservatism.

In sum, the rhetoric surrounding world conflicts altered dramatically in the 1990s and early 2000s. Conflicts were presented more often now, both to spectators and protagonists, as clashes among racially, ethnically, or religiously defined groups. The question of who would prevail—us or them—was now mostly unadorned by consideration of higher principles. Universal ideals (and the earnest intent to apply them) had faded from the international scene, except for the ideal of free-market globalization. Like our great ethical religions, our modern political ideologies had conspicuously failed to build a more inclusive, less conflictive world.

New Challenges

Distressingly, the failure became obvious just as global challenges increased in severity and cried out for global solutions.

One global challenge was the return of China, after a century-plus hiatus, to its millennial status as the world's manufacturing power-house. That story began in the 1970s, even before the Cold War had ended. After Mao, the Chinese people had yearned to forget the ideological puritanism of the Cultural Revolution. Among the revolutionary veterans who still composed the top Communist Party leadership in the 1970s, the pragmatic Deng Xiaoping became the man of the moment. From 1978 to 1989, without ever becoming head of party or state, Deng Xiaoping steered China's internal market liberalization and opening to the world economy, creating a mix of public and private ownership. The model was tested first in "special economic zones," three of them in Guangdong Province. The brand-new city of Shenzhen, one of Deng's special economic zones, zoomed to a population of twenty million. The country's southeastern region, historically its most outward facing, became ground zero of the New China. Shenzhen, Guangzhou, Fujian, Shanghai, and other coastal cities became booming centers of manufacturing exportation to the world economy, most especially to the United States. The country embarked upon a massive construction campaign, pouring oceans of concrete, as the population of China pushed far beyond the billion mark. The vast reservoirs of the Three Gorges hydroelectric dam project were filling by 2006, while the state put finishing touches on a transportation infrastructure to be envied by Europe and the United States, and towering new apartment blocks marched toward the horizon by the hundreds. Meanwhile the full array of consumer delights, especially the new digital ones, were splashed across advertisements in full-throated consumerist style. The Chinese people were invited unabashedly to embrace the profit motive. They did not have to be invited twice.

China's economic opening to the world market was not accompanied by the political opening that Western observers hoped to see. The leadership of the People's Republic had noted how quickly political liberalization and a lack of consumer goods had brought down the USSR. "Socialism with Chinese Characteristics" became the official state ideology—a nationalist emphasis that meant, in practice, whatever worked. Newly pragmatic in economic matters, the Chinese leadership would not brook any direct challenge to the authority of party and state. That's why, when Chinese students erected their version of a Statue of Liberty in Tiananmen Square in 1989, the symbolic heart of the nation, and when the concentration of people in the vast square, one of the world's largest, peaked around a million, the state moved with overwhelming force to crush the demonstration. The world remembers an iconic image, a lone demonstrator standing in front of tanks, but the events in Tiananmen Square were hushed so effectively that few Chinese today share that memory.

In the next generation, proliferating consumer goods kept Chinese hopes up and Chinese noses to the grindstone, while China became—again, as it had often been over two thousand years, always more economically than militarily—a world power. Having quietly abandoned its promise of a future socialist utopia, the government needed a new narrative. It turned to an old-fashioned program of nationalist grievance, resentment, and deliverance, tirelessly reiterating the (basically true) story of its pre-revolutionary subjugation to imperialist powers, and its return with dignity to the global stage under the direction of the Chinese Communist Party. In schools, museums, monuments, movies, music, and many television serials, a new generation of Chinese young people learned a little about class struggle and a lot about imperialist outrages such as the Opium Wars and the Rape of Nanjing. Even Confucianism, certainly the most Chinese of characteristics (but formerly the target of revolutionary ire) returned to official favor. Amid the truly breathtaking material modernization—sparkling cities, family cars, high-speed trains, cell phones, more cell phones—the state has shaped the most patriotic generation of young Chinese ever. With their acquiescence, it has tightened its authoritarian control and developed a comprehensive system of digital surveillance to monitor the daily life of its gargantuan population. A major focus of the new surveillance systems is now on the Muslim population of Xinjiang in China's far west, targets of the country's war on terrorism.

China's dizzying economic rise changed the world and indirectly challenged the United States. China was still very far from equaling the overall influence, resources, or weaponry of the United States, which enjoyed vastly more per capita wealth and still maintained military bases around the world. The main Chinese "threat" was economic, a crushing trade imbalance, like the one created in past centuries by Chinese silks, porcelains, and tea. Once again, consumers in the West wanted to buy more from China than vice versa, a lot more. China was still strongly authoritarian and still a one-part state, ruled steadfastly by its Communist Party, but in practice it was no longer a revolutionary state, very, very far from pursuing the old dream of a global revolution. Nationalism had trumped socialism as Chinese consumers reached for their piece of the global pie. China had never projected military power overseas and had not expanded territorially since the early Qing dynasty. US fear of China focused on unfair trade practices, but it was really about the comparatively diminishing importance of the United States. It was hard to climb down from being the post-Cold War's one remaining superpower.

Then came the coronavirus pandemic, which began in central China during the 2020 lunar New Year holiday. It was not unexpected but, of course, took everyone by surprise. As the first modern pandemic surged, the sudden global work stoppages, quarantines, and lockdowns were like nothing ever seen before. Nationalist demagogues had a field day, and anti-Chinese fears multiplied.

The real challenge we faced—in China, the United States, and the whole world—was the sum of our shared appetites. By 2020, resource-intensive consumerism was laying waste to the planet. The bright vision of a heavily resource-intensive American Way of Life had inspired wide admiration and helped win the Cold War. Afterward, a mutual desire to emulate new consumer lifestyles—automobile-oriented and fossil-fuel dependent, producing mountains of "disposable" waste—became the world's only discernable consensus. It was a forlorn consensus, though, doomed from the start, because a multiplication of US-style consumerism across the globe was not sustainable, even for the minority who could participate.

The globalization of an American Way of Life was having a grim impact on planet Earth. In the 1950s, when this alluring but deceptive vision went on offer, the global population was still under three billion. By the early twenty-first century, with global population at eight billion, dire results included contamination of air and water, rampant extinction of plants and animals, and overuse of practically all the planet's natural resources. Untold megatons of floating disposable plastic clogged oceans, world fisheries collapsed, erosion destroyed topsoil, unbridled water consumption depleted aquifers and sucked rivers dry, acid rain withered forests. Most insidious, because its effects were so gradual, and irreversible, was carbon-driven global warming. Its principal causes, by far, were greenhouse gases such as methane and carbon dioxide (CO_2), the former deriving especially from agribusiness, the later especially from deforestation, as well as from the signature industrial fuel, coal, and the signature consumer fuel, gasoline. Until around the year 2000, global warming was little noticed by people going about their daily business, but as polar ice caps and subarctic permafrost melted, glaciers retreated, sea level rose, coral reefs bleached, and tropical rainforest went up in smoke, the overall picture led to a complete scientific consensus.

Here's the bird's-eye view. Over fifty million years, our planet cooled as atmospheric CO_2 diminished steadily. Glaciation began in Antarctica about thirty-four million years ago, and glaciers covered large parts of the Northern Hemisphere in the ice ages. Atmospheric CO_2 reversed direction and began to increase markedly with the Industrial Revolution. Emissions of CO_2 have since increased steadily decade by decade, owing principally to fossil fuels as well as the waste and exhaust and resource extraction of consumption-oriented modern life. As greenhouse gases accumulated, the planet began heating up at a dangerous rate. By 2020, according to scientific consensus, a multifaceted global catastrophe could be averted only by rapid and significant changes in modern lifestyles. Such changes appeared out of the question, though. Those lifestyles had become a defining goal in people's lives. Rich-country consumers had come to regard the ecologically suicidal abundance of consumables as their birthright. The huge majority of people on planet Earth were still waiting to share that standard of living and wanted nothing more than to achieve it.

Today, only unselfish cooperation on a global scale can save us. Not only is it nowhere in sight. It is something unknown in human experience.

What now?

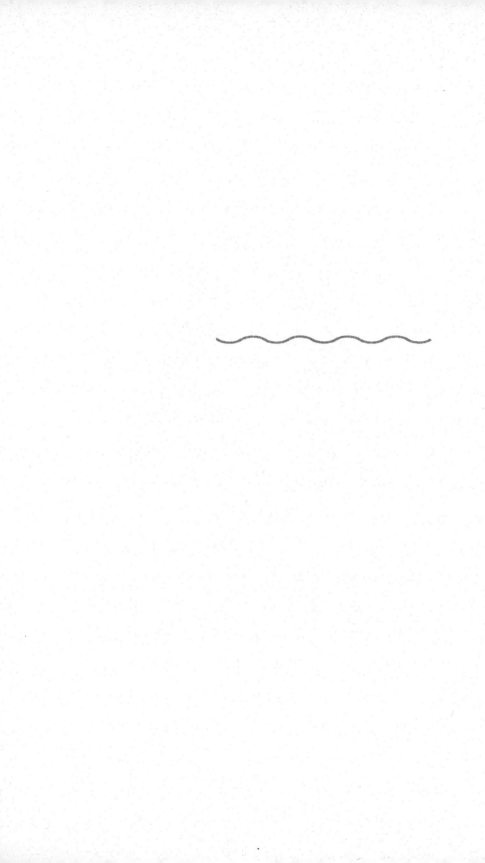

Apocalypse Now?

Consider the 2022 Russian invasion of Ukraine. On one side, an authoritarian state brandishing nationalist motifs to garner internal support for military aggression. On the other side, citizen soldiers resisting attack, trying to forge a nation. Ukrainian nationalism has inspired impressive solidarity in Europe and neo-Europe, and understandably so. We can't lift two fingers as a world community when it comes to saving the planet, it seems, but an international war with tanks and rockets? Now *that* is something we can relate to! But what if it leads to use of nuclear weapons? Our civilization has thousands of years of practice making war—and, increasingly, we make total war that does not spare noncombatants. We have almost *no* practice making global peace, but without it we are doomed. Today's pervasive nationalism is unlikely to help us make global peace. Meanwhile, we face truly existential challenges.

In 2020, atmospheric CO_2 reached levels not seen in the last three million years, and global average temperature has increased by more than one degree centigrade. Another full degree's rise, by sometime in the 2030s, will begin to unleash a cascade of multiplier effects, such as the melting of Antarctica and Northern Hemisphere permafrost, both of which will further accelerate global warming. The challenges that will face humanity by 2050 will make the first pandemic look like child's play.

Only a truly unanimous global effort has any chance to preserve our common home. Good news! The means to end global warming are fully within our grasp. Bad news! If we really want to avoid catastrophic population loss in drought, famine, epidemics, and nuclear war, if we really want to avoid catastrophic destruction of our natural environment on a global scale, we cannot resume our lives in the old, familiar way—even using new power sources. We must stop doing things we started doing very recently, in global terms, only about two hundred years ago. An economy driven by mass consumerism is the crux of the problem. It produces greenhouse gases. It consumes our resources and generally trashes our Earth, not to mention its devastating impact on other living things. We cannot have our planet and trash it, too.

Only intelligent global peace and cooperation can slow climate change. Only a strong sense of global community can preserve our planet's resources and environment for future generations. But we don't have, and have never had, a global community to speak of. The United Nations has been unquestionably our best effort, but it is hardly enough. During all recorded history, human populations have tended to divide into competing groups—clans, castes, classes, tribes, nations, and empires—among whom competition and mutual hostility have been the norm. Nations are our largest effective identity groups, and they are not sufficient to address current global challenges. Only a strong new commitment to our shared humanity, embracing all Earthlings, can motivate the coordinated effort that we require.

Global cooperation to deliver future generations an inhabitable Earth will require large social transformations. Consumer capitalism, the reigning political, social, and economic model worldwide, will have to be radically pruned back to give *Homo sapiens* a much smaller carbon footprint. That change, no matter how urgent and obvious the need, will be enormously disruptive and conflictive. It will require our strongest collective efforts on behalf of each other. It will require willingness to change for the benefit of all. Perhaps we can form more ethical and equitable social relations, design more wholesome and less damaging ways to inhabit our planet. Shaping a new attitude toward each other will be the hardest thing of all. We need more education and art and science, fewer weapons, less marketing and financing, and, above all, better leaders.

But where will our leadership come from, in a world where leaders have specialized in surfing a tsunami of consumer selfishness, a world where demagogues have specialized in setting us at each other's throats? Vested political and economic interests cannot provide the guidance we need to remake our world. We must listen, not to those who lead our current parade of global folly, but to voices from the margins, from people not invested in the current situation and permanently committed to it. We must heed those who dare to stand against conventional wisdom, envision world peace, and speak truth to power. We need new prophets for the third millennium of our Common Era. We must distrust warmongering alpha males and heed voices like that of Greta Thunberg, who, in August 2018, launched her School Strike for Climate in Stockholm at the age of fifteen, triggering a student movement that mobilized millions of young people around the world in a matter of months. Her message was straightforward, honest, urgent, and essential. "I don't want you to feel hopeful," she told the global economic powers-that-be assembled the following year in Davos. "I want you to act as you would in a crisis. I want you to act as if the house was on fire—because it is."

People *can* work together unselfishly for the common good, but unselfish cooperation beyond our close associates is always a challenge for *Homo sapiens*. Selfishness is apparently our default setting. Anyone who has cared for several young children together knows that sharing must be taught, not assumed, and moreover, that teaching it is a challenge. An enormous part of world history is the raw mistreatment of half of humanity by the other half. Obviously, making common cause with the whole world is going to be hard, but we have to try. What if we teach them that all our fates are absolutely intertwined, that no Earthling is an outsider on this blue marble floating in the limitless void, that we do share a common history, and a common destiny, too?

Acknowledgments

THIS BOOK WAS NURTURED AND SHAPED, OVER MORE THAN a decade, by conversations with Norton editor Jon Durbin. Thanks, Jon! I couldn't have done it without you!

Artist Jeremy Hauch was a joy to work with. Even better, he invariably improved on my initial ideas for illustrations. Thanks, Jeremy!

Further Readings

Anderson, Benedict. *Imagined Communities: Reflections of the Origin and Spread of Nationalism*. Verso, 2006.

Anthony, David W. *The Horse, the Wheel, and Language: How Bronze-Age Riders from the Eurasian Steppes Shaped the Modern World*. Princeton University Press, 2007.

Chang, Leslie T. *Factory Girls: From Village to City in a Changing China*. Spiegel and Grau, 2007.

Chatwin, Bruce. *The Songlines*. Franklin Press, 1987

Christian, David. *Maps of Time: An Introduction to Big History*. University of California Press, 2004.

Courtwright, David T. *Forces of Habit: Drugs and the Making of the Modern World*. Harvard University Press, 2001.

Dalrymple, William. *Nine Lives: Encounters with the Holy in Modern India*. Bloomsbury, 2009.

Graeber, David, and David Wengrow. *The Dawn of Everything: A New History of Humanity*. Farrar, Straus and Giroux, 2021.

Harari, Yuval Noah. *Sapiens: A Brief History of Humankind*. Vintage Books, 2015.

Hessler, Peter. *Country Driving: A Chinese Road Trip*. Harper, 2011.

Karamustafa, Ahmet T. *God's Unruly Friends: Dervish Groups in the Islamic Later Middle Period, 1200–1550*. One World Publications, 2006.

Lieberman, Daniel E. *The Story of the Human Body: Evolution, Health, and Disease*. Pantheon, 2013.

Mann, Charles C. *1491: New Revelations of the Americas before Columbus*. Alfred A. Knopf, 2005.

McNeill, William H. *A World History*. Oxford University Press, 1998.

Raleigh, Donald J. *Soviet Baby Boomers: An Oral History of Russia's Cold War Generation*. Oxford University Press, 2012.

Scott, James C. *Seeing Like a State: How Certain Schemes to Improve the Human Condition Have Failed*. Yale University Press, 1999.

Weatherford, Jack. *Genghis Khan and the Making of the Modern World*. Three Rivers Press, 2004.

Art Credits

Drawings done by Jeremy Hauch from the following sources.

An Epiphany: Capitol Steps
On January 6, 2021, rioting followers of the defeated outgoing US
president tried to stop the peaceful transfer of power to his successor.
© *David Wallace—USA TODAY NETWORK*

In the Beginning: Big Bang
Big Bang theory is the current scientific consensus about how the universe
probably began.
Jeremy Hauch, artist's conception

Eden: The Cave of Hands
Hand stencils have been found in cave paintings around the world. These
are from the *Cuevas de las Manos*, near the town of Perito Moreno in
Santa Cruz Province, Argentina.

Dominion: The Ice Man
Archeologists have reconstructed the appearance of a Neolithic hunter
whose mummified body was found in the Alps.
Melotzi

Babylon: The Dancing Girl
This small bronze sculpture, called the dancing girl by archeologists, was
found in the ruins of the early Indus Valley civilization.
Alfred Nawrath

Alexander: Fragmentary Mosaic
The most famous portrait of the famous conqueror was found by
archeologists on a mosaic floor in the ruins of Pompeii.

Classical World: Wang Zhaojun
A legendary heroine of ancient China, she volunteered to create a
marriage alliance with warlike nomads on the frigid steppe, where she
lived for the rest of her life.
Jeremy Hauch, artist's conception

World of Faith: The Kaaba
Located in Mecca, Saudi Arabia, the Kaaba has been the destination
of annual global pilgrimages by observant Muslims for more than a
thousand years.

World of Woe: Joan of Arc
The first known image of Joan of Arc was sketched in the margin of an
official report in 1429.
Clément de Fauquembergue

Worlds Apart: Tezcatlipoca
Tezcatlipoca was an important deity in Mesoamerica before invading
Europeans imposed their own religion and culture after 1492.

New World: Indonesian Ship
The early seagoing traditions of Southeast Asia are represented by this
double outrigger sculpted at the Borobudur Buddhist monument in
Central Java around 800 CE.
Radha Kumud Mukhopadhyay

Colonized World: A Slave Ship's Human Cargo
This famous diagram of the so-called *Brooks* slave ship was pictured in a
British abolitionist report of 1788.
*Plymouth Chapter of the Society for Effecting the Abolition of the
Slave Trade*

Modern World: Cotton Mill Worker
This young worker appeared in a documentary photograph of an early twentieth-century South Carolina cotton mill.
National Child Labor Committee Photographs taken by Lewis Hine

Liberty: Delacroix Painting
The drawing details Delacroix's famous painting entitled "Liberty Leading the People," which now hangs in the Louvre.
Eugene Delacroix, Oil on Canvas, 1830

Nations: Gandhi Spinning
As a form of boycott against British cloth, Gandhi spun thread on his spinning wheel to make his own clothing.
Estate of Margaret Bourke-White, Life Collection/Shutterstock

Revolution: Che Guevara
Ernesto "Che" Guevara was a young physician whose face became an international icon of revolution in the 1960s.
Alberto Korda photograph

Redux: Tank Man
One man stands alone in front of a line of tanks headed toward Beijing's Tiananmen Square to clear it of demonstrators in 1989.
Photograph by Jeff Widener

Apocalypse Now?: Greta Thunberg
The young climate activist Greta Thunberg holds a sign that translates to "school strike for climate" in August 2018.
Photograph by Anders Heilberg

Index

[TK]